For the
Sad Sads,
or really anytime.
I love you dude!
Yeah, yeah, Yeah!

♡ your
co-worker
and
accomplice

HOWLAND-
BOLTON

Unfortunate
Situations,

Flawed coping
mechanisms,

Mayhem,

and other Things

That Happened

Hyperbole

and a Half

Allie Brosh

A Touchstone book
Published by Simon & Schuster
New York   London   Toronto   Sydney   New Delhi

Touchstone
A Division of Simon & Schuster, Inc.
1230 Avenue of the Americas
New York, NY 10020

Portions of this book have been previously published on the author's blog.

First Touchstone hardcover edition November 2013

TOUCHSTONE and colophon are registered trademarks of Simon & Schuster, Inc.

For information about special discounts for bulk purchases,
please contact Simon & Schuster Special Sales at
1-866-506-1949 or business@simonandschuster.com.

The Simon & Schuster Speakers Bureau can bring authors to your live event.
For more information or to book an event, contact the
Simon & Schuster Speakers Bureau at 866-248-3049 or
visit our website at www.simonspeakers.com.

Interior design by Ruth Lee-Mui

Manufactured in the United States of America

3 4 5 6 7 8 9 10

Library of Congress Cataloging-in-Publication data is available.

ISBN 978-1-4767-6459-7
ISBN 978-1-4516-6617-5 (pbk)
ISBN 978-1-4516-6618-2 (ebook)

Copyright strictly enforced by
the copyright monster.

For Scott.
What now, fucker?

Also for Mom, Dad, Kaiti, Laurie,
Duncan, Sarah, Joey, and Lee.
You're all great.

Contents

Introduction

It seems like there should be some sort of introduction to this. Here is a re-creation of a drawing I did when I was five:

It's a guy with one normal arm and one absurdly fucking squiggly arm. If you look really closely, you can see the normal arm under the squiggly one. What you can't see is that in the original, the squiggly arm continues for the entire length of a roll of butcher paper. It started on one end and then just kept going until I ran out of paper.

I remember drawing it and thinking, *This is insane. . . I can't even believe how long this guy's arm is.* If I had not run out of paper, who knows what would have happened.

In its entirety, the arm takes up more paper than this book.

Theoretically, I could have cut the roll of butcher paper into squares, stapled them together, and created *Squiggly Arm Book*.

I didn't, though.

I considered that possibility, but, in the end, I decided I couldn't realistically expect to get away with it.

Warning Signs

When I was ten years old, I wrote a letter to my future self and buried it in my backyard. Seventeen years later, I remembered that I was supposed to remember to dig it up two years earlier.

I looked forward to getting a nostalgic glimpse into my childhood—perhaps I would marvel at my own innocence or see the first glimmer of my current aspirations. As it turns out, it just made me feel real weird about myself.

The letter was scrawled in green crayon on the back of a utility bill. My ten-year-old self had obviously not spent much time planning out the presentation of it. Most likely, I had simply been walking through the kitchen and suddenly realized that it was entirely possible to write a letter to my future self.

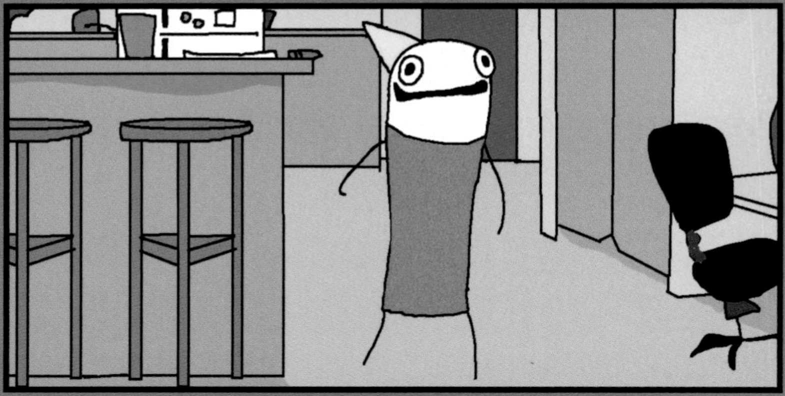

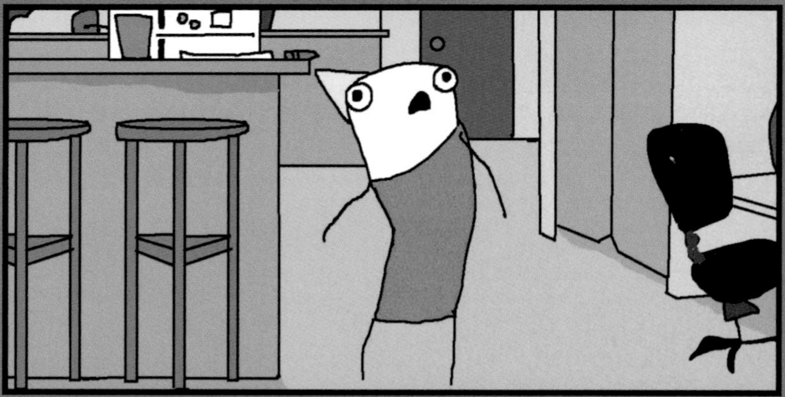

The overwhelming excitement of this realization probably caused me to panic and short-circuit, making me unable to locate proper writing implements. There was no time for that kind of thing.

I did, however, manage to fight through the haze of chaos and impulse long enough to find a crayon stub and a paper surface to mash it against.

The letter begins thusly:

Dear 25 year old [note: not "Dear 25-year-old me" or "Dear 25-year-old self," just "Dear 25 year old"],

*Do you still like dogs? What is your favarite dog? Do you have
a job tranning dogs? Is Murphy still alive? What is youre favarite
food?? Are mom and dad still alive?*

I feel it's important to note the order of those questions. Obviously, dog-related subjects were my chief concern (Murphy was my family's dog), followed closely by the need to know my future favorite food (I feel that the double question marks speak to how important I thought that question was). Only then did I pause to wonder whether my parents had survived.

Priorities:
- Dogs
- Dogs
- Dogs
- specific dog
- Food
- Lifespan of Parents

The letter continues with a section titled "About me":

*My name is Allie and I am ten years old. I have blound hair and
blue eyes. My favarite dog is a german shepard. My second
favarite dog is a husky. My third favarite dog is a Dobberman
Pincher.*

This is troubling for a number of reasons, the first of which is that I apparently thought my future self wouldn't be aware of my name or eye color.

woh. what if...
- in the future -
I'm Not even me anymore
I WON'T KNOW WHAT I AM

The second thing is the fact that I just tacked on my favorite dog breeds at the end there, like it was every bit as important to my identity as the other things. As if my past self had imagined my future self standing in the yard above the upturned earth, clutching my letter and screaming, "*BUT WHAT DOGS DID I LIKE??? HOW AM I SUPPOSED TO UNDERSTAND MY IDENTITY WITHOUT KNOWING WHAT DOGS I LIKED WHEN I WAS TEN???*"

I took a break from writing at that point to draw several pictures of what appear to be German shepherds.

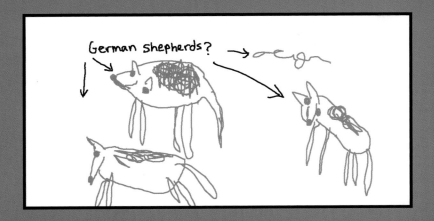

Below the German shepherds, I wrote the three most disturbing words in the entire letter—three words that revealed more about my tenuous grasp on reality than anything else I have uncovered about my childhood. There, at the bottom of the letter, I had taken my crayon stub and used it to craft the following sentence:

Please write back.

Judging by the thick, purposeful lines in each letter, I was applying a truly impressive amount of pressure to the crayon. The sincerity of the request is unmistakable. When I asked my future self what my favorite dog is or whether my mom and dad were still alive, I actually expected to get answers. And, apparently, I still expected to be ten years old when I got those answers.

Please write back. I imagine myself patiently standing in the yard, day after day, thinking, *Any time now ... It's going to happen soon, I just know it ...*

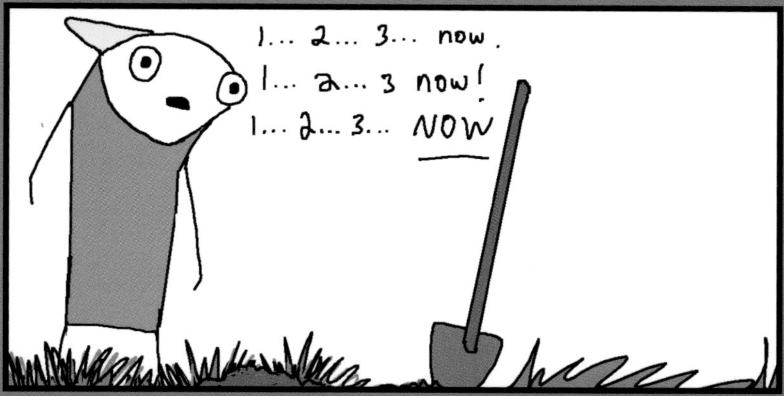
1... 2... 3... now.
1... 2... 3 now!
1... 2... 3... NOW

Time travel is a complex subject that I don't expect a ten-year-old to fully understand, but this is more than just a basic misunderstanding of time travel.

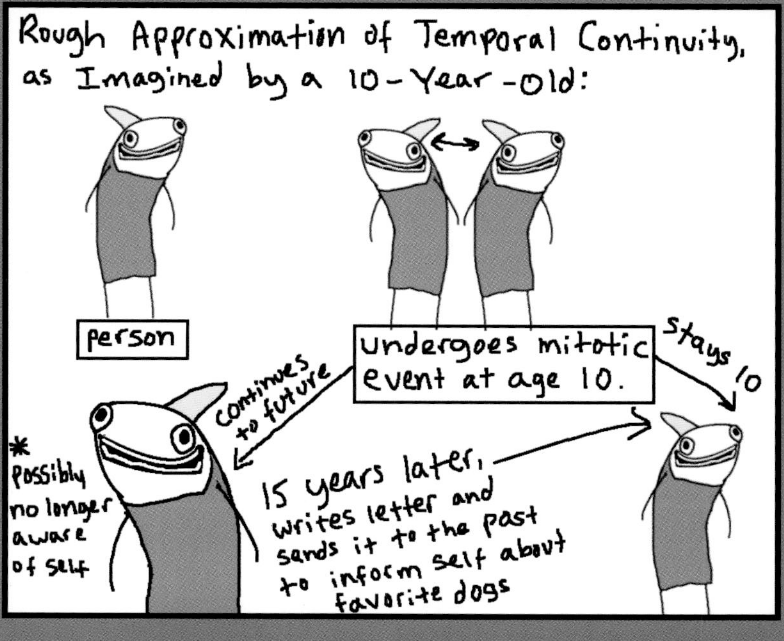
Rough Approximation of Temporal Continuity, as Imagined by a 10-Year-Old:
person
Undergoes mitotic event at age 10.
continues to future
Stays 10
* possibly no longer aware of self
15 years later, writes letter and sends it to the past to inform self about favorite dogs

I'm almost definitely not a time traveler, but in case I am, I decided to write back. In fact, I decided to write letters to several iterations of my past self, because I felt there were important things I could explain to myself or things I could warn myself about.

Allow me to begin with a letter to my two-year-old self:

Dear two-year-old,

Face cream is not edible—no matter how much it looks like frosting, no matter how many times you try—it's always going to be face cream and it's never going to be frosting.

I promise I wouldn't lie to you about this. It's honestly never going to be frosting.

For the love of fuck, please stop. I need those organs you're ruining.

Dear four-year-old,

Allow me to preface this by saying that I don't know why you started eating salt in the first place, but regardless of the precipitating circumstances, there you are.

As soon as you became aware that eating huge amounts of salt is really, really, uncomfortably salty, you should have stopped eating salt. That's the solution. The solution is not to begin eating pepper to cancel out the salt.

You've found yourself in this predicament several times now, and every time you get trapped in this totally preventable cycle. You've done more than enough experimenting to come to the conclusion that pepper is not the opposite of salt all by yourself, but somehow you seem to remain stubbornly unaware of this fact.

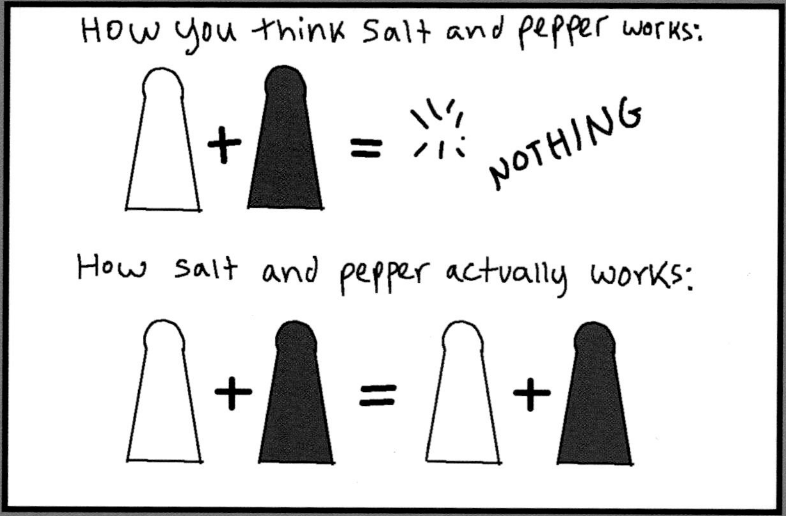
How you think salt and pepper works:
+
=
NOTHING
How salt and pepper actually works:
+
=
+

To reiterate, no matter how much pepper you eat, it won't undo the ludicrous amount of salt you ate before it. The only thing you are accomplishing by eating pepper is making your mouth taste like pepper AND salt.

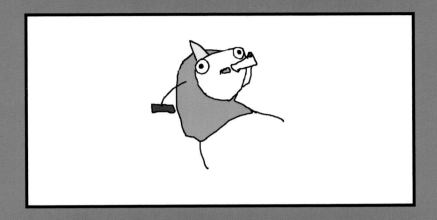

Similarly, switching back to salt again won't cancel out the burning from the pepper you ate to cancel out the original salt. How is this so difficult to understand? You can stop whenever you want to.

As a side note, you really need to start learning from your mistakes. Believe me, I know what happens when you discover electric fences next year, and you could do without that seventh jolt of electricity.

Dear five-year-old,

What the fuck is wrong with you? Normal children don't have dead imaginary friends. Normal children don't pick open every single one of their chicken pox scabs and then stand naked and bleeding in the darkened doorway to their bedroom until someone walks past and asks what they are doing. Furthermore, normal children don't respond by saying, "I wanted to know what all my blood would look like." Normal children also don't watch their parents sleep from the corner of the room. Mom was really scarred by *The Exorcist* when she was younger, and she doesn't know how to cope with your increasingly creepy behavior. Please stop. Please, please stop.

Dear six-year-old,

You're having an absurdly difficult time learning the letter R. You practice all the time, and you have mastered every other letter in the alphabet—both uppercase and lowercase—but for reasons beyond my comprehension, R just *destroys* you.

Look at this:

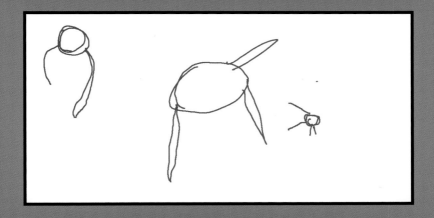

How does that happen?? How do you mess something up *that* badly?

The first one is understandable, but what's going on with that middle one? How did that extra protrusion get there? And look at the tiny one on the right—that one has *four protrusions*. I'm not an expert on protrusions, but that's way too many.

I think if you took some time to relax and really *look* at the letter R, you'd see that it's not nearly as complicated as you're making it.

Dear seven-year-old,

Look at the other children around you. Do you see how they're wearing clothing? That's because they're seven years old and they've all realized that it is no longer appropriate to take their clothes off in public. But you haven't realized that, have you. People have tried to explain it to you. Your teachers have tried, your parents have tried, even the other students have expressed discomfort with your persistent and inexplicable nakedness. But you just don't stop.

Why do you want to be naked so badly? Do you even know why? Are you overtaken by forces beyond your control that make you do this?

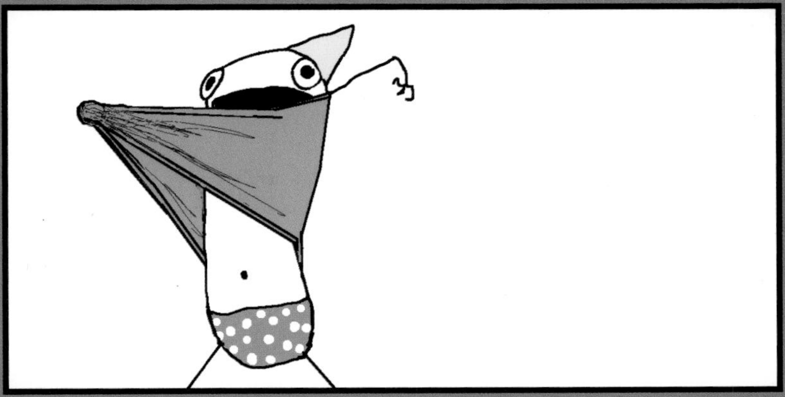

Regardless, clothing is a reality that you need to accept. There are no loopholes to this. You can't take your clothes off and hide in the corner hoping no one notices. You can't trick the teachers into letting you be naked by burying yourself in the sandbox—your clothes are in a pile next to you. They know.

Dear ten-year-old,

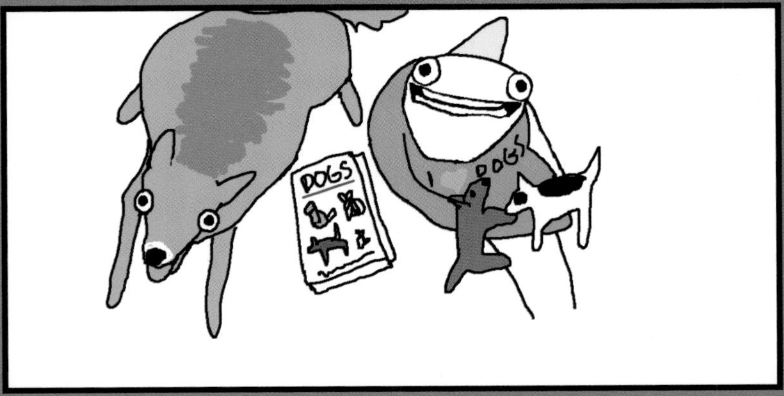
DOGS
DOGS

Wow, you really like dogs. In fact, you like dogs so much that I'm not even sure it's emotionally healthy. It might be normal to love dogs a lot, or to be really interested in dogs, but you go way, way past that. Normal children don't walk around pretending to be a dog nearly as much as you do, for example. You're ten. It makes people wonder about your developmental progress when you growl and bark at them.

An even more concerning issue is the obstacle course. Fine, you want to train your dog to run through an obstacle course. That's pretty normal. What isn't normal is making your mother time *you* as you crawl through the course on all fours, over and over and over again. You're making Mom think that she did something wrong to make you this way.

Now that we've gotten that out of the way, allow me to answer your questions:

Do you still like dogs? Yes, but not as much as you do. I've developed a healthy relationship with dogs.

What is your favarite dog? I don't know. This may come as a surprise to you, but knowing exactly where each dog breed ranks on my list of favorites isn't the pressing issue that it used to be.

Do you have a job tranning dogs? No. I can't even train my own dogs, let alone the dogs of other people.

Is Murphy still alive? Of course not. I don't know whether you're being optimistic or you actually don't understand that dogs usually won't live to be twenty-five, but you really set yourself up for a lot of disappointment there.

What is youre favarite food? Nachos. Which is fortunate, because in the future, you're dysfunctional and you don't take care of yourself, so you end up eating a whole lot of nachos.

Are mom and dad still alive? Actually, you turned out to be Batman, so we had to have them put down for story-line purposes.

Dear thirteen-year-old,

I think everyone was relieved when you started to grow out of your unhealthy obsession with dogs. Unfortunately, now you think you are a wizard. I know this because I found your collection of spells.

Tell me, how does mixing Dijon mustard with sand and then eating it make someone love you?

First of all, I thought your extensive early experiences with ingesting non-food substances would put you off of attempting something like this. Secondly, no one is going to love you until you stop doing things like trying to make them love you by eating mustard–sand.

Dear other iterations of my past self,

Thank you for not being so goddamn weird that I felt I had to address you personally in a letter from the future. I commend you.

The Simple Dog

A lingering fear of mine was confirmed last night: my dog might be slightly retarded.

I've wondered about her intelligence ever since I adopted her and subsequently discovered that she was unable to figure out how stairs worked.

I blamed her ineptitude on the fact that she'd spent most of her life confined to a small kennel because her previous owners couldn't control her. I figured that maybe she just hadn't been exposed to stairs yet. Accepting the noble responsibility of educating this poor, underprivileged creature, I spent hours tenderly guiding her up and down the staircase—placing biscuits on each step to lure her and celebrating any sign of progress. When she still couldn't successfully navigate the stairs at the end of her first week with me, I blamed it on her extreme lack of motor control. This dog is uncoordinated in a way that would suggest her canine lineage is tainted with traces of a species with a different number of legs—like maybe a starfish or a snake.

The next clue came when I started trying to train her. I thought, *How difficult can training a dog be? It seems easy enough.*

I was wrong. Not only is training my dog outlandishly difficult, it is also heartbreaking. She wants so badly to please me. Every fiber of her being quivers with the desire to do a good job.

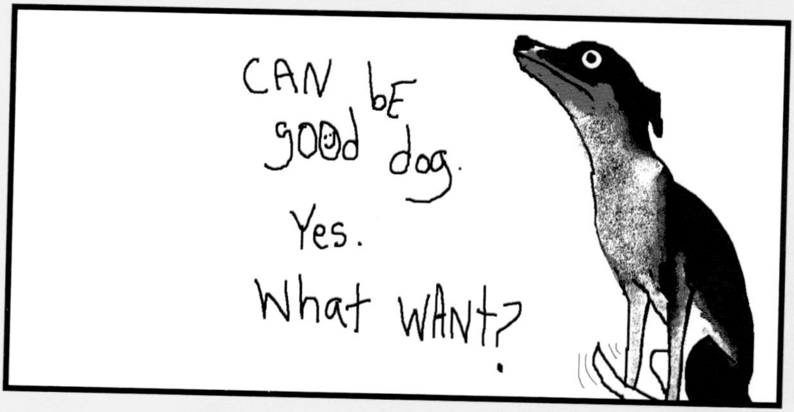
CAN bE good dog.
Yes.
What WANT?!

She tries really hard.

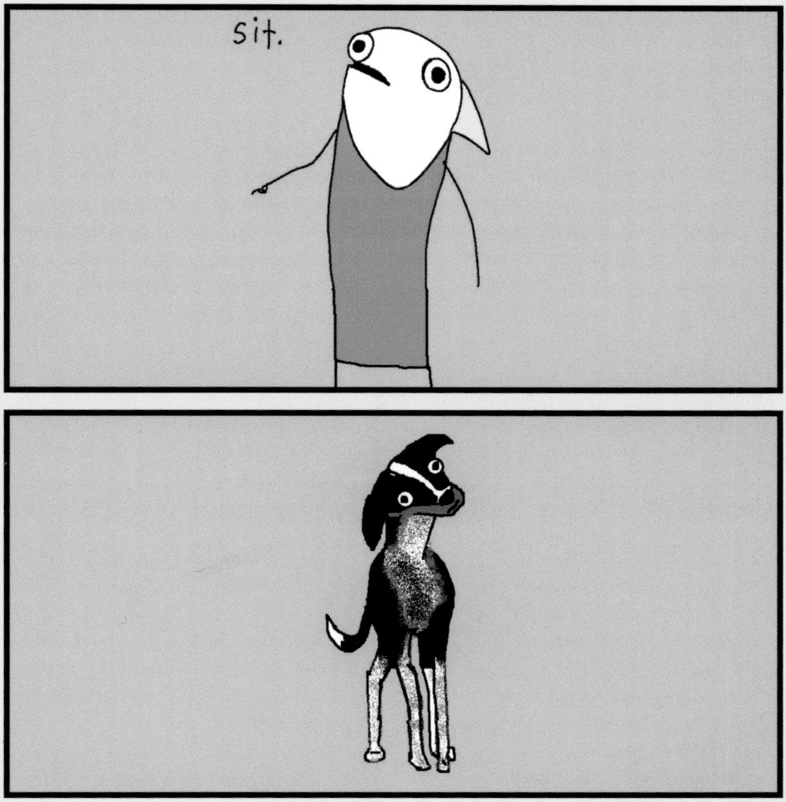
sit.

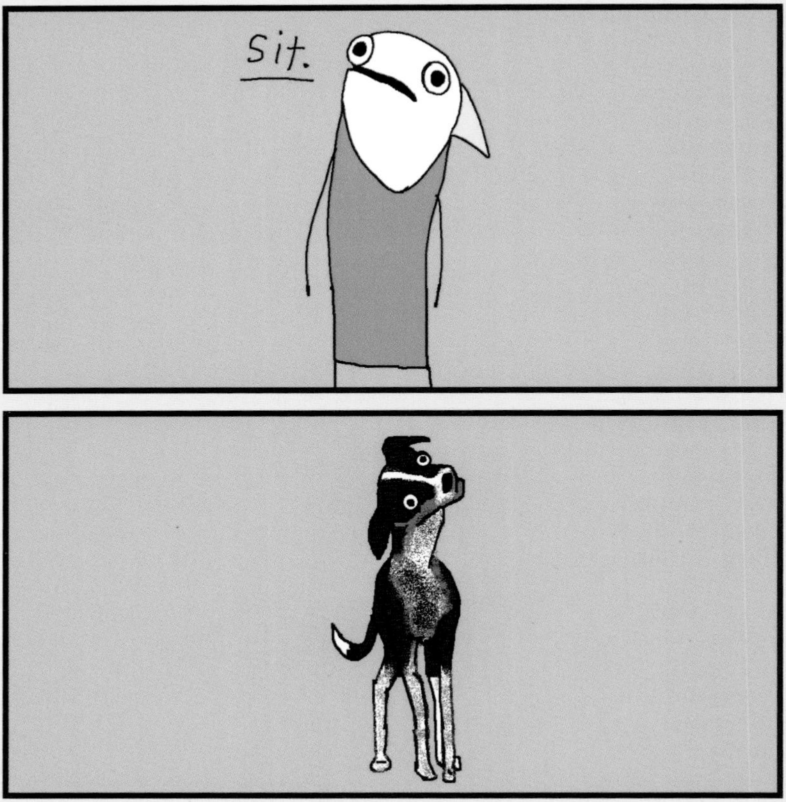
sit.

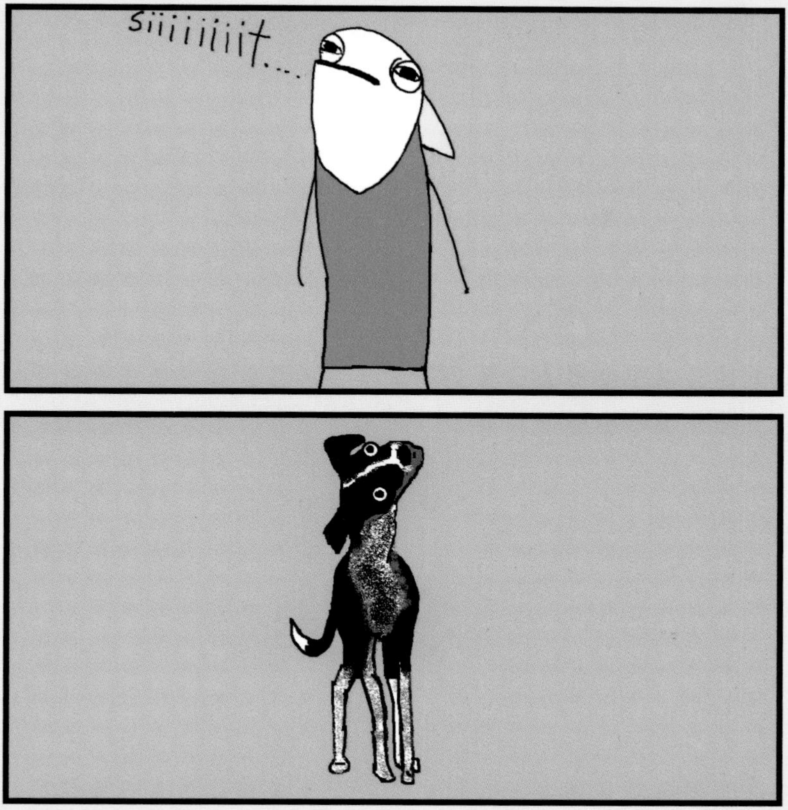
siiiiiiiit....

But when turning her head at an extreme angle fails to produce a life-altering epiphany, she usually just short-circuits and rolls onto her back.

Over the past two months, she's made some progress, but it's been painfully slow and is easily forgotten. Still, I was living under the assumption that maybe my dog just had a hidden capacity for intelligence—that all I had to do was work hard enough and maybe she'd wake up one day and be smart and capable like a normal dog.

But one night I was sitting on my couch mindlessly surfing the Internet when I looked up and noticed my dog licking the floor. Just licking and licking. At first I thought maybe I'd spilled something there, but her licking did not appear to be localized to one spot. Rather, she was walking around the room licking seemingly at random. She lay down on her side and kept licking out of the side of her mouth while staring directly at me.

At that moment I realized that I needed to know for sure whether my dog was retarded or not.

I Googled "how to tell if your dog is retarded" and after a bit of research, I found a dog IQ test that looked fairly legitimate. It involved testing your dog's ability to solve a few very basic problems, like figuring out how to get out from underneath a blanket.

I gathered the necessary supplies and began testing.

The first test asked me to call my dog using a variety of words that were not her name to gauge whether she could tell the difference. I called out "refrigerator!" and was pleased to see that my dog did not respond. She also failed to respond to "movie," "dishwasher," and "banana." I was beginning to feel very proud of her. Then came the crucial step: I called her name. Nothing. I called it a few more times to be sure. Still nothing.

The words hung like a neon sign broadcasting my dog's failure. *It's okay*, I thought. *She'll do better on the next one.*

In the second test, I had to put a blanket over my dog and time her to see how long it took her to escape. I threw the blanket over her and started my stopwatch. She made some cursory attempts at freeing herself, but as the seconds ticked by, it became clear that she was not going to pass.

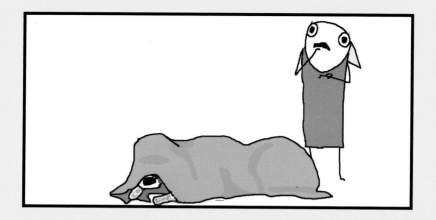

Still, I gave her the benefit of the doubt and assumed that she just enjoyed being under there and could get out if she wanted to. I added an extra couple points to her tally for faith's sake.

After flagrantly failing three more tests, it came down to the final trial. If she could score five out of five possible points on this section of the test, she could bump herself out of the bottom category into "below average."

First, I had to make her sit, which was a test in and of itself. Then I was supposed to show her a biscuit, let her sniff it, then—after making sure she was watching—place the biscuit on the ground and put a plastic cup over it. If she knocked over the cup to get the biscuit within a certain amount of time, she'd pass the test.

I put the biscuit under the cup and started the timer.

My dog ran over to the cup and sniffed it. She walked around it once and then looked up at me like I was some sort of wizard. I pointed to the cup. I knew it was cheating, but I wanted to help my dog pass her test.

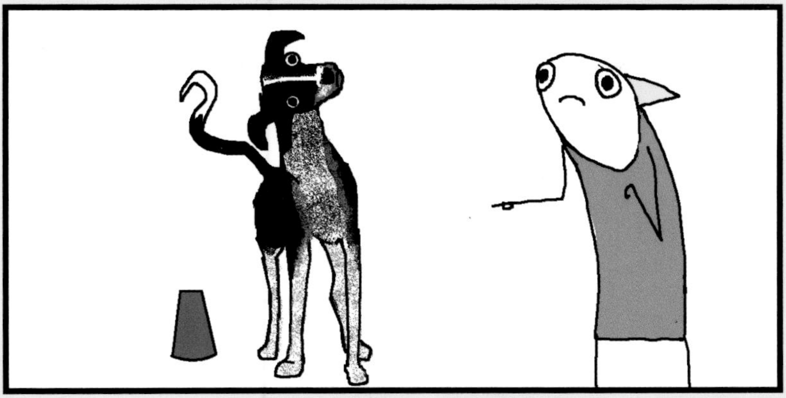

She didn't understand, but she knew she was supposed to do *something,* so she just started frantically doing things because maybe—just maybe—one of those things would be the right thing and the magical wizard cup would let her know where the treat went.

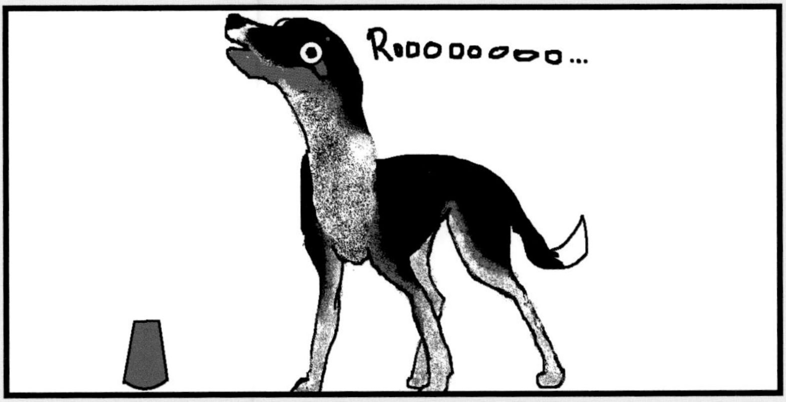
Rooooooooo...

After five minutes of watching my dog aimlessly tear around the house, I finally accepted that she was not going to pass any part of the test and yes, she was most likely mentally challenged. But damn it, I was not going to let my poor, retarded dog feel like she had failed.

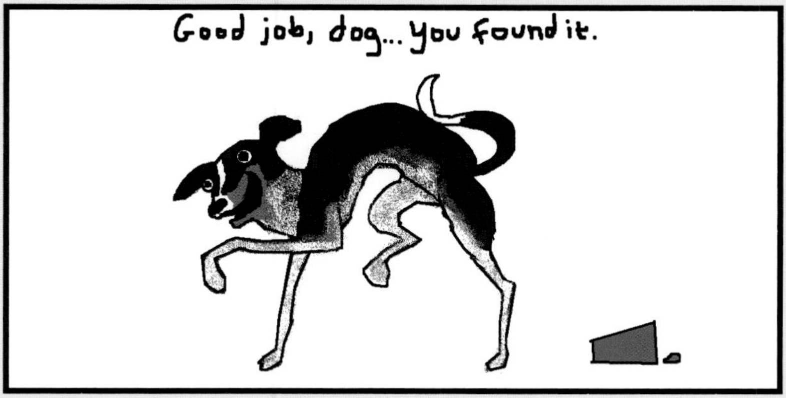
Good job, dog... you found it.

Motivation

One of the most terrifying things that has ever happened to me was watching myself decide over and over again—thirty-five days in a row—to not return a movie I had rented. Every day, I saw it sitting there on the arm of my couch. And every day, I thought, *I should really do something about that . . .* and then I just *didn't.*

After a week, I started to worry that it wasn't going to happen, but I thought, *Surely I have more control over my life than this. Surely I wouldn't allow myself to NEVER return the movie.*

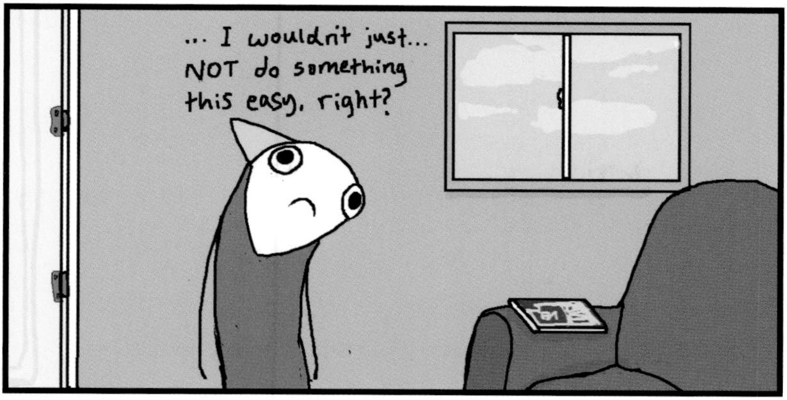
... I wouldn't just... NOT do something this easy, right?

But that's exactly what happened. After thirty-five days, I decided to just never go back to Blockbuster again.

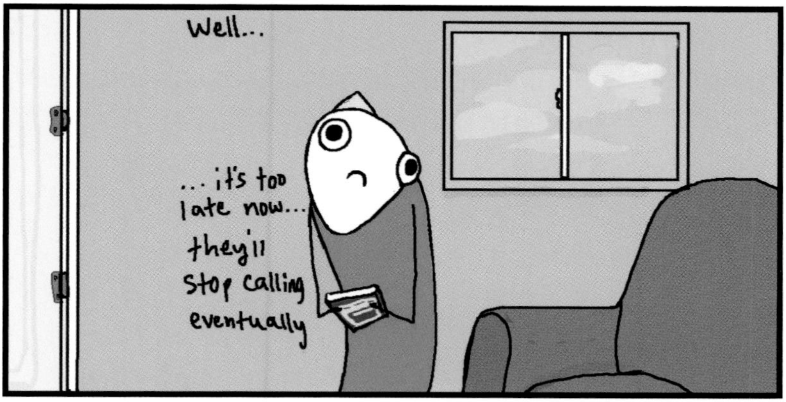
Well...
... it's too late now... they'll stop calling eventually

Most people can motivate themselves to do things simply by knowing that those things need to be done. But not me. For me, motivation is this horrible, scary game where I try to make myself do something while I actively avoid doing it. If I win, I have to do something I don't want to do. If I lose, I'm one step closer to ruining my entire life. And I never know whether I'm going to win or lose until the last second.

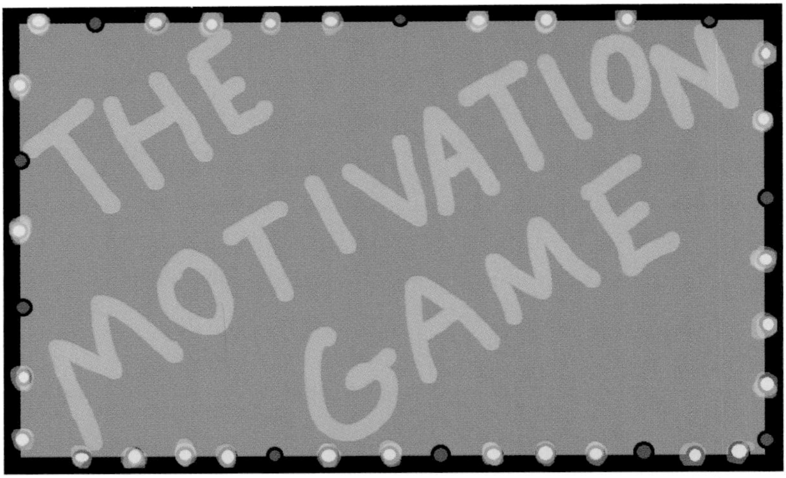
THE MOTIVATION GAME

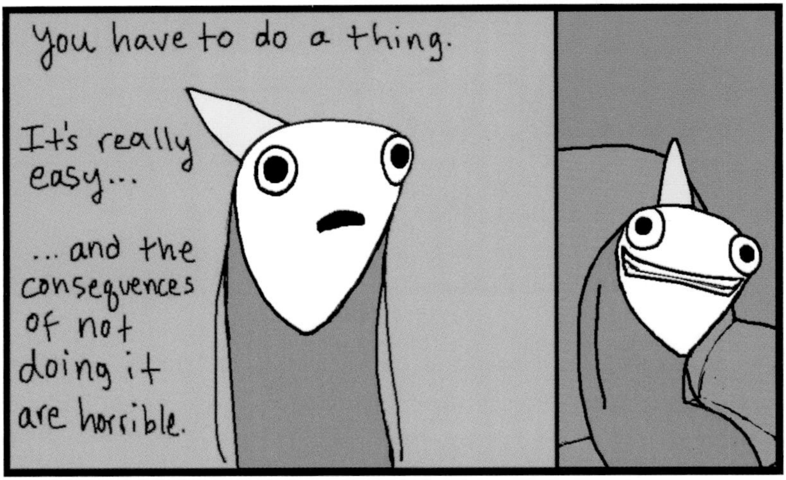
you have to do a thing.
It's really easy...
...and the consequences of not doing it are horrible.

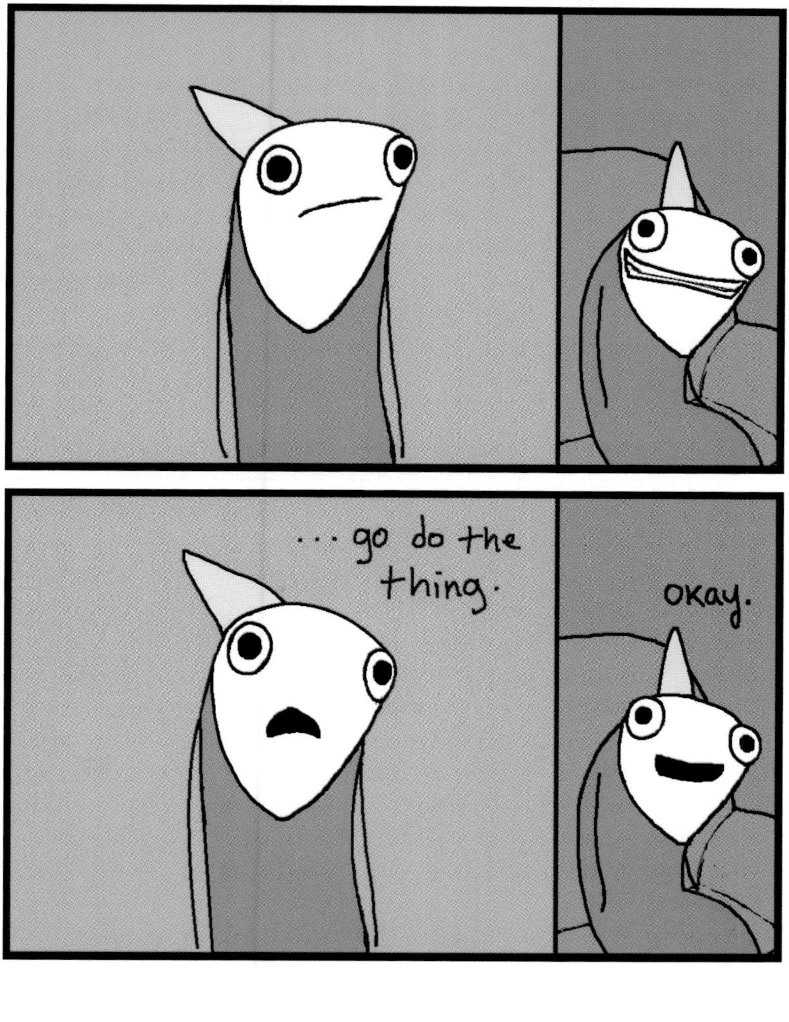
...go do the thing.
okay.

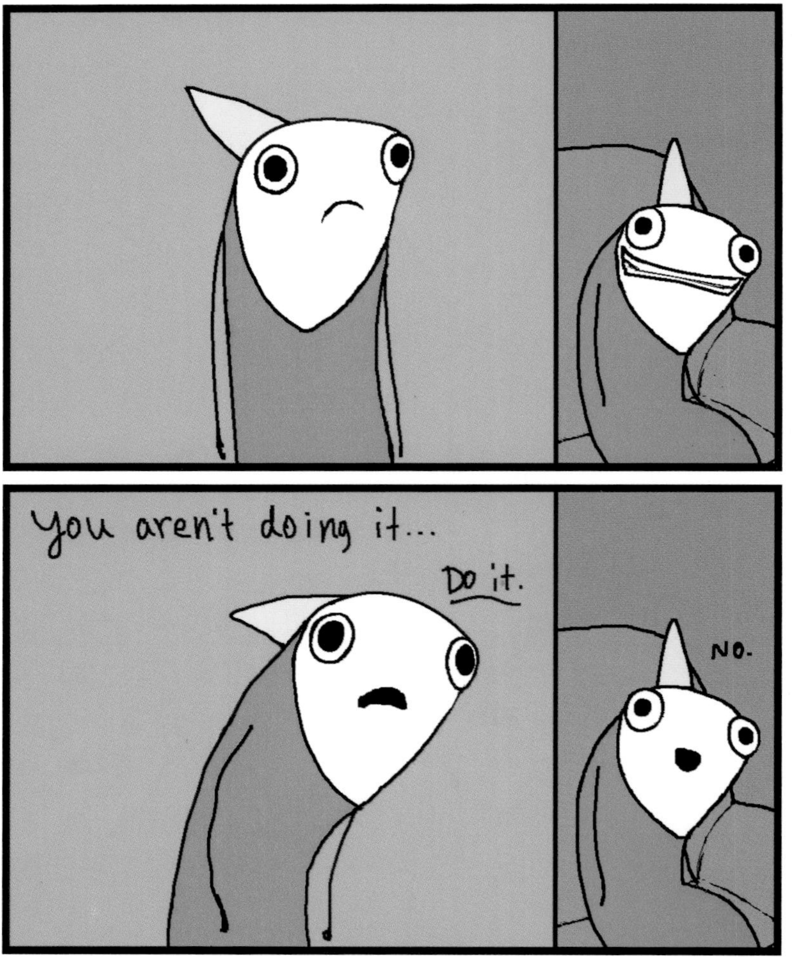
You aren't doing it...
Do it.
NO.

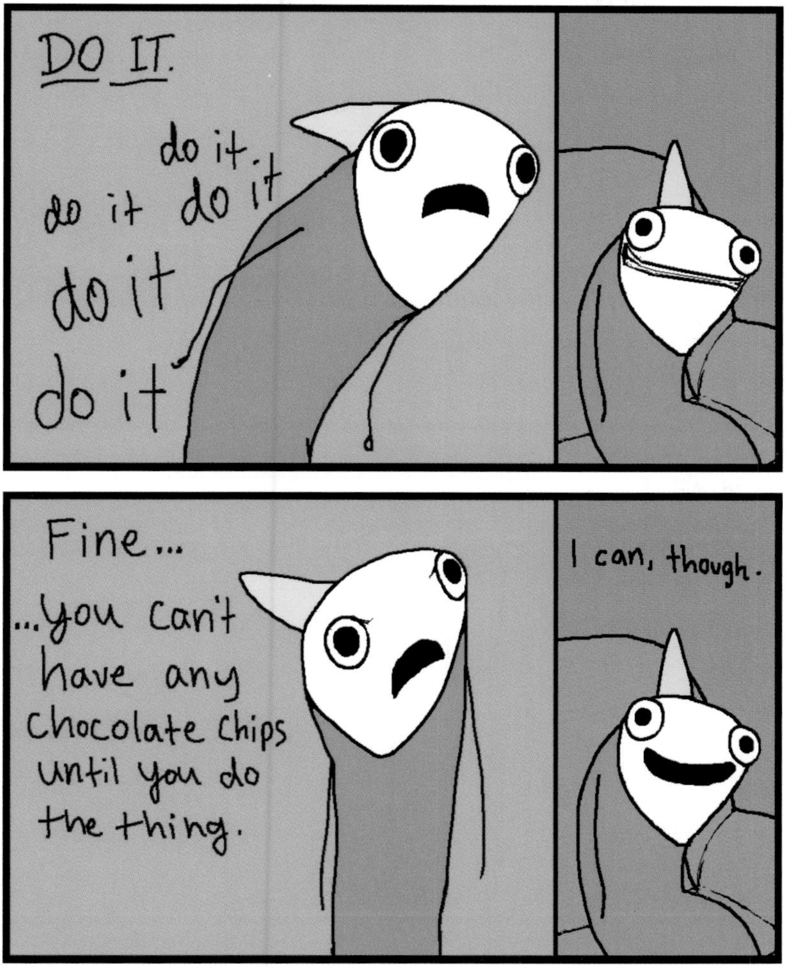
DO IT.
do it.
do it do it
do it
do it
Fine...
...you can't have any chocolate chips until you do the thing.
I can, though.

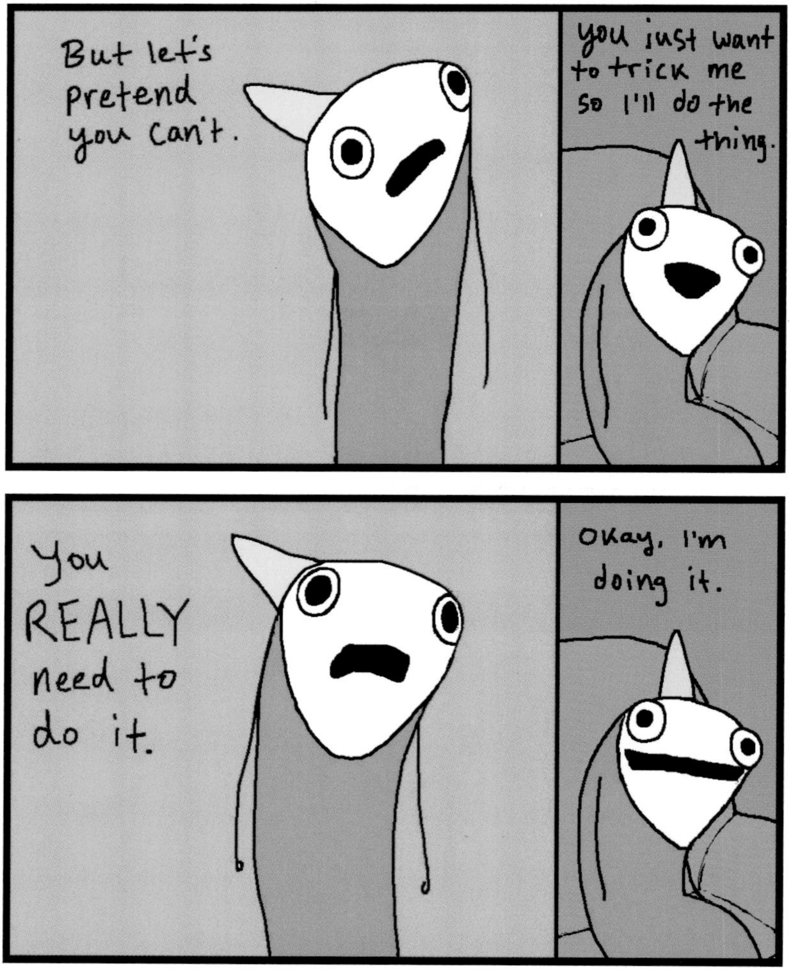
But let's pretend you can't.
You just want to trick me so I'll do the thing.
You REALLY need to do it.
Okay, I'm doing it.

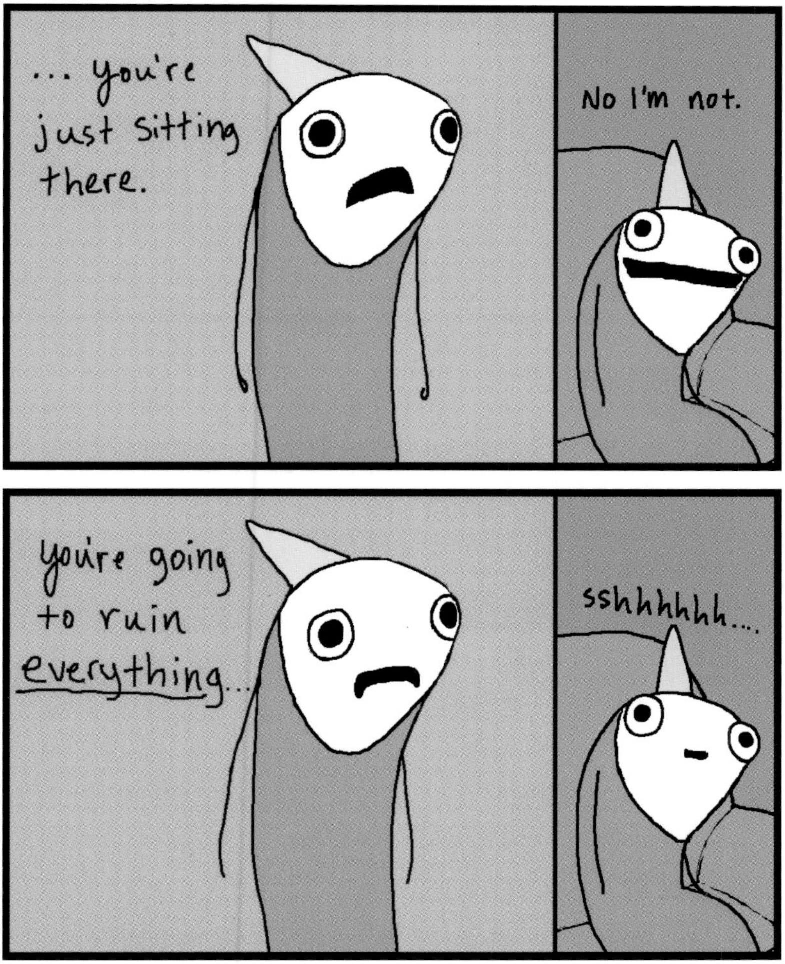
... you're
just sitting
there.
No I'm not.
you're going
to ruin
everything...
sshhhhhh....

I'm always surprised when I lose.

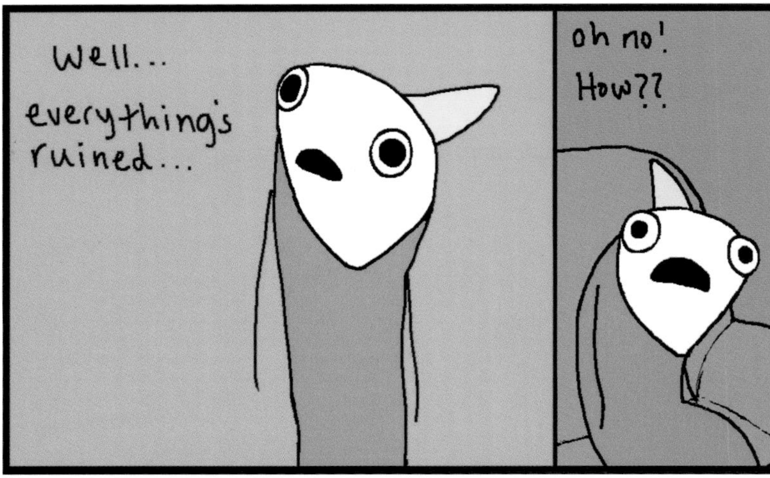
Well...
everything's ruined...
oh no!
How??

But I keep allowing it to happen because, to me, the future doesn't seem real. It's just this magical place where I can put my responsibilities so that I don't have to be scared while hurtling toward failure at eight hundred miles per hour.

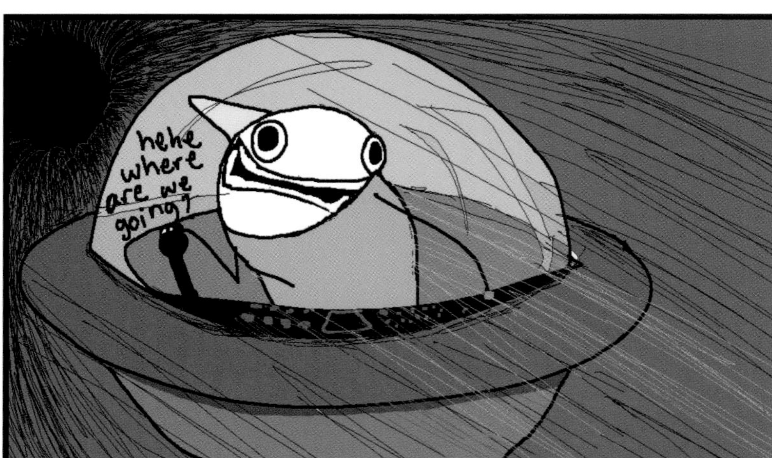
hehe where are we going?

Or at least that's how it used to be. I've experienced enough failure at this point to become suspicious of where I'm going and what's going to happen when I get there. And for the last helpless moments of the journey, I'm fully aware and terrified.

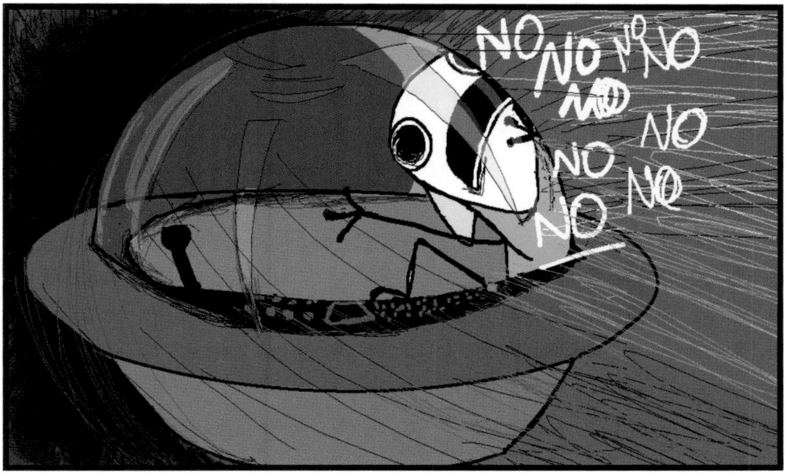
NO NO NO NO
NO
NO NO
NO NO

Fortunately, it turns out that being scared of yourself is a somewhat effective motivational technique.

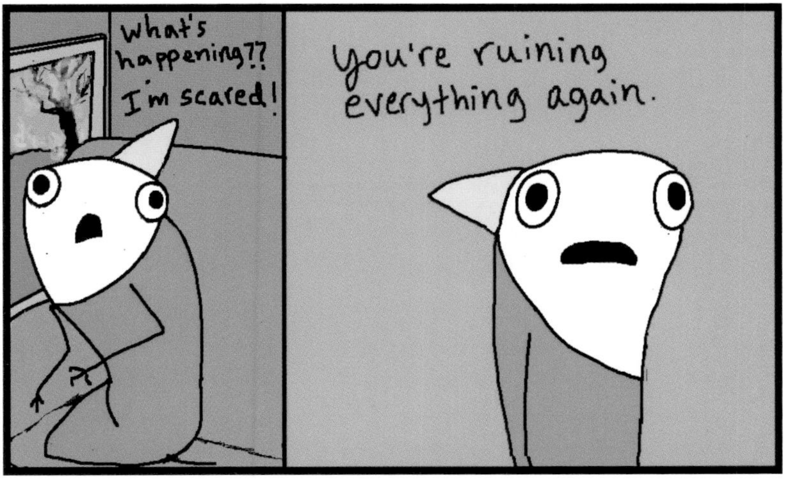
what's happening?? I'm scared!
you're ruining everything again.

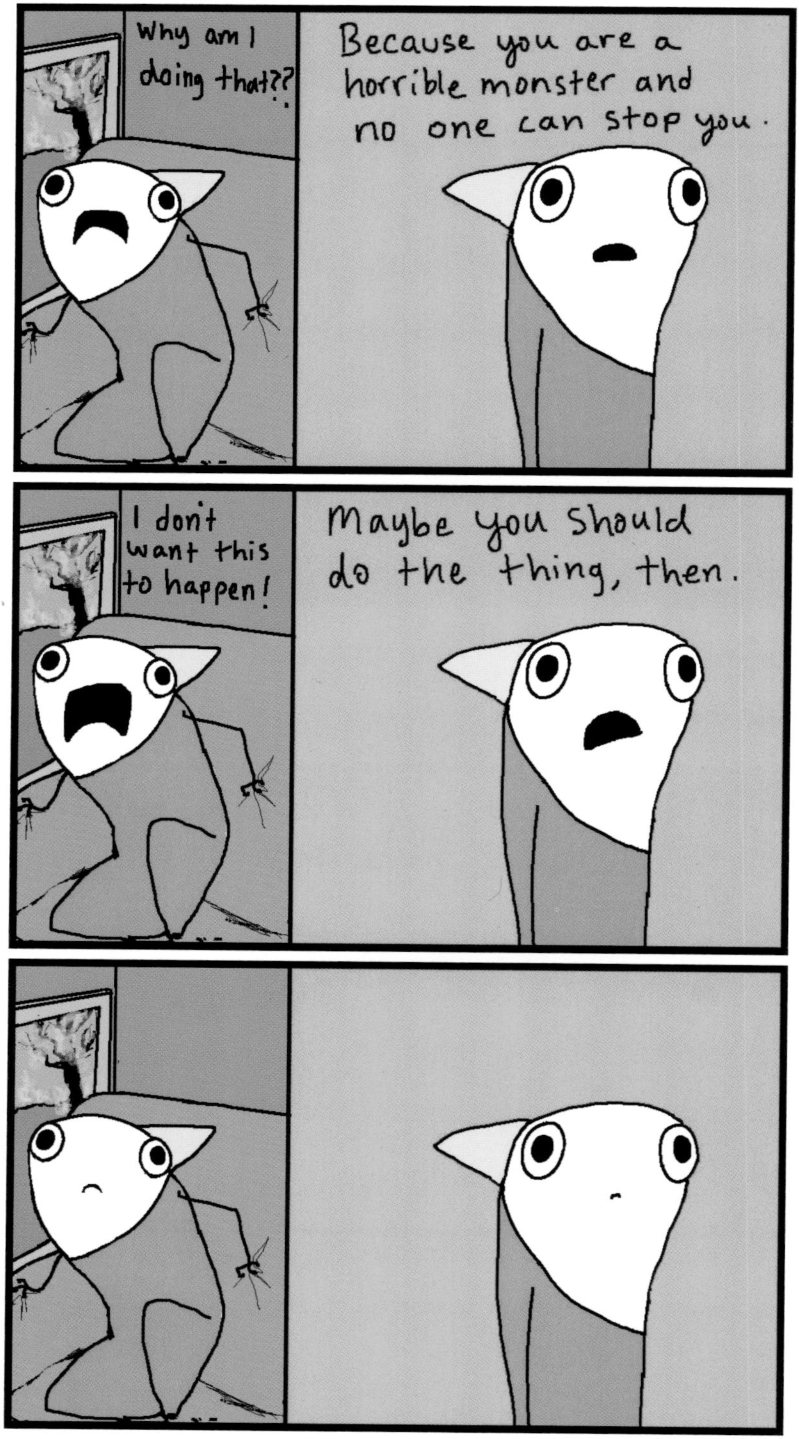

Why am I doing that??
Because you are a horrible monster and no one can stop you.
I don't want this to happen!
Maybe you should do the thing, then.

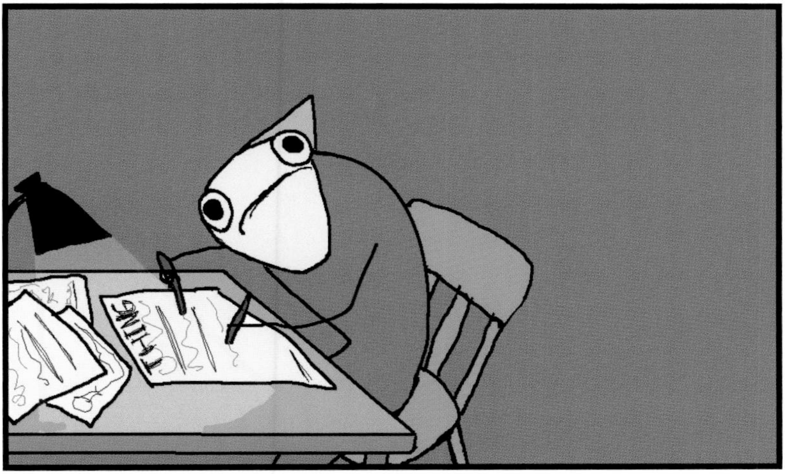
THING

It's *so* somewhat effective that I now rely on it almost exclusively when I need to get myself to do something important.

Of course, it isn't without its flaws—the biggest flaw being that I still have to get very close to failure before I recognize some of the landmarks and panic.

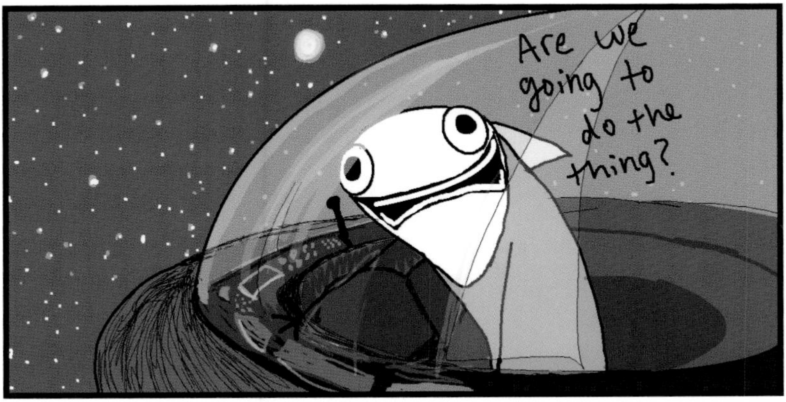
Are we going to do the thing?

But as long as I figure out what's going to happen before it actually happens—or hell, even *while* it's happening—all the struggling and flailing might propel me away from it in time.

Procrastination has become its own solution—a tool I can use to push myself so close to disaster that I become terrified and flee toward success.

A more troubling matter is the day-to-day activities that don't have massive consequences when I neglect to do them. I haven't figured out how to solve the problem in a normal way, but I *did* learn how to make myself feel so ashamed that I'm willing to take action.

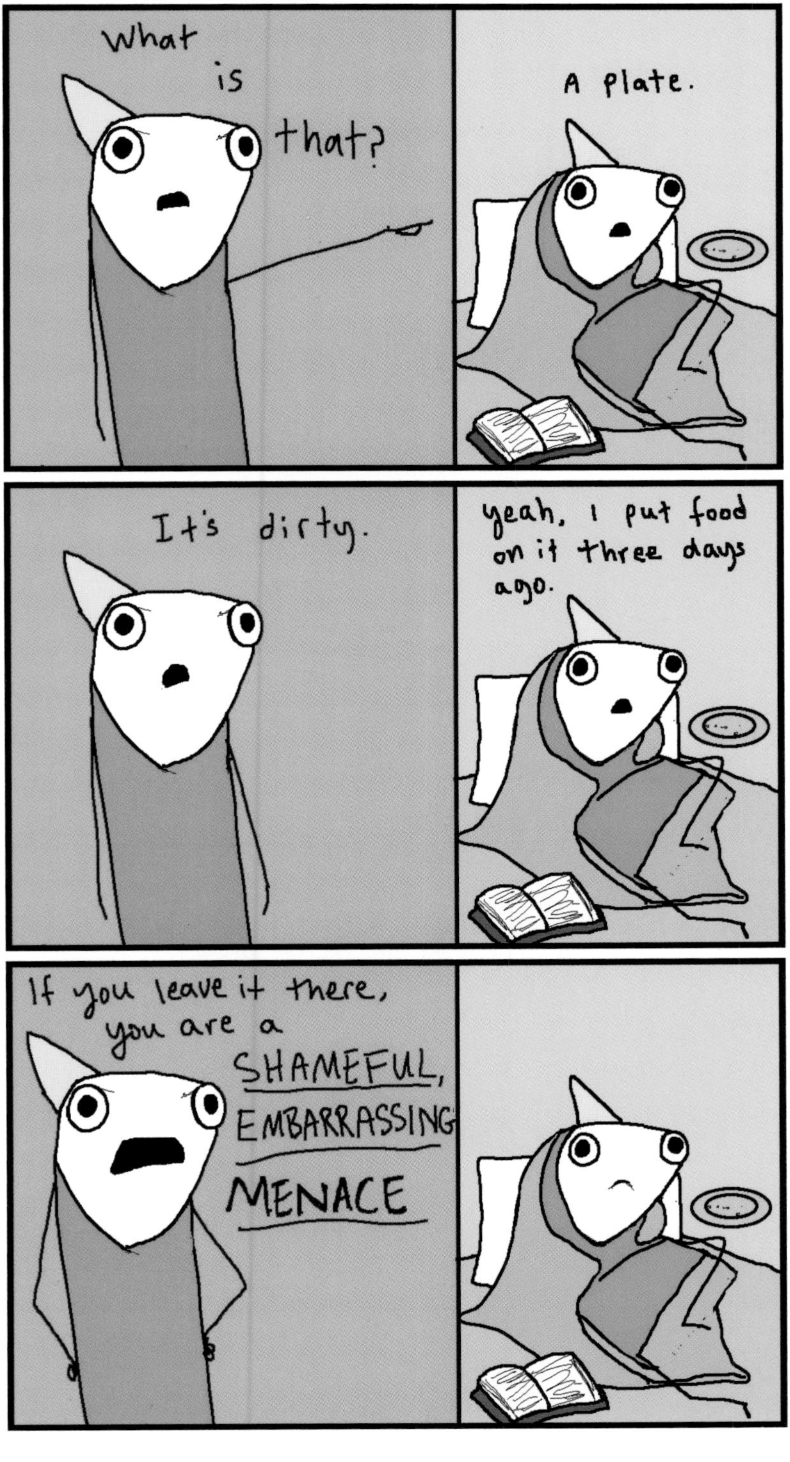
What is that?
A plate.
It's dirty.
yeah, I put food on it three days ago.
If you leave it there, you are a SHAMEFUL, EMBARRASSING MENACE

It usually doesn't work right away.

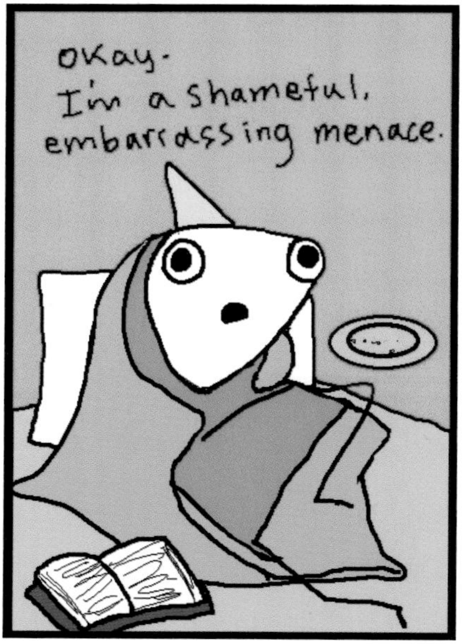
okay.
I'm a shameful, embarrassing menace.

Sometimes it doesn't work for days.

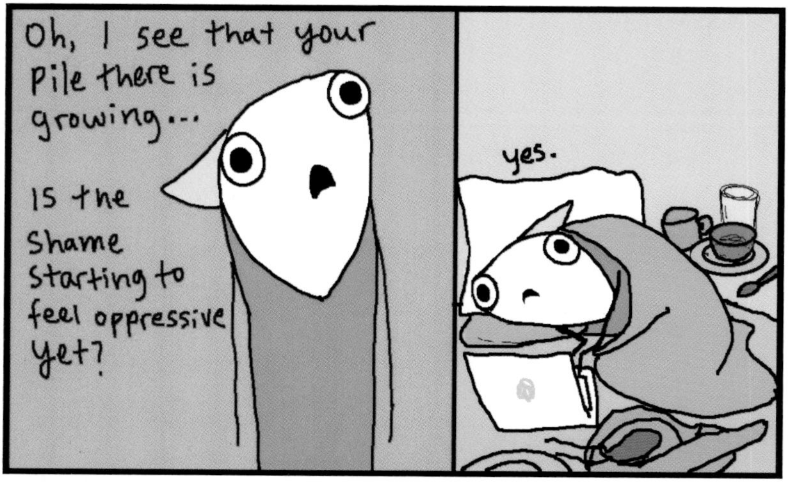
Oh, I see that your pile there is growing...
Is the shame starting to feel oppressive yet?
yes.

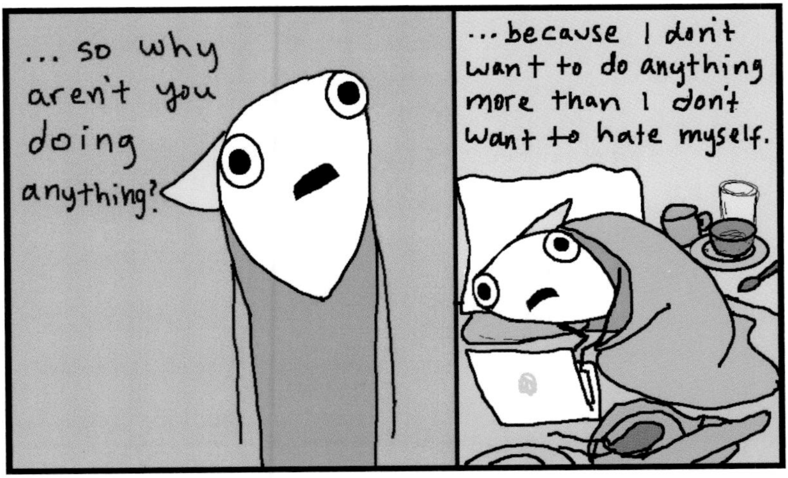
... so why aren't you doing anything?
...because I don't want to do anything more than I don't want to hate myself.

But it always gets to me eventually.

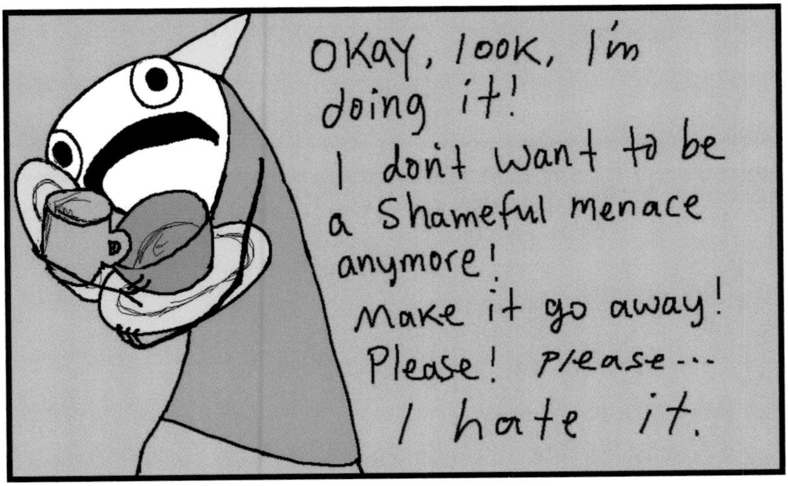
OKAY, look, I'm doing it!
I don't want to be a Shameful menace anymore!
Make it go away!
Please! please...
I hate it.

I've gotten pretty good at making myself feel ashamed. I can even use shame in a theoretical sense to make myself do the right thing BEFORE I do the wrong thing. This skill could be described as "morality," but I prefer to call it "How Horrible Can I Be Before I Experience a Prohibitive Amount of Shame?"

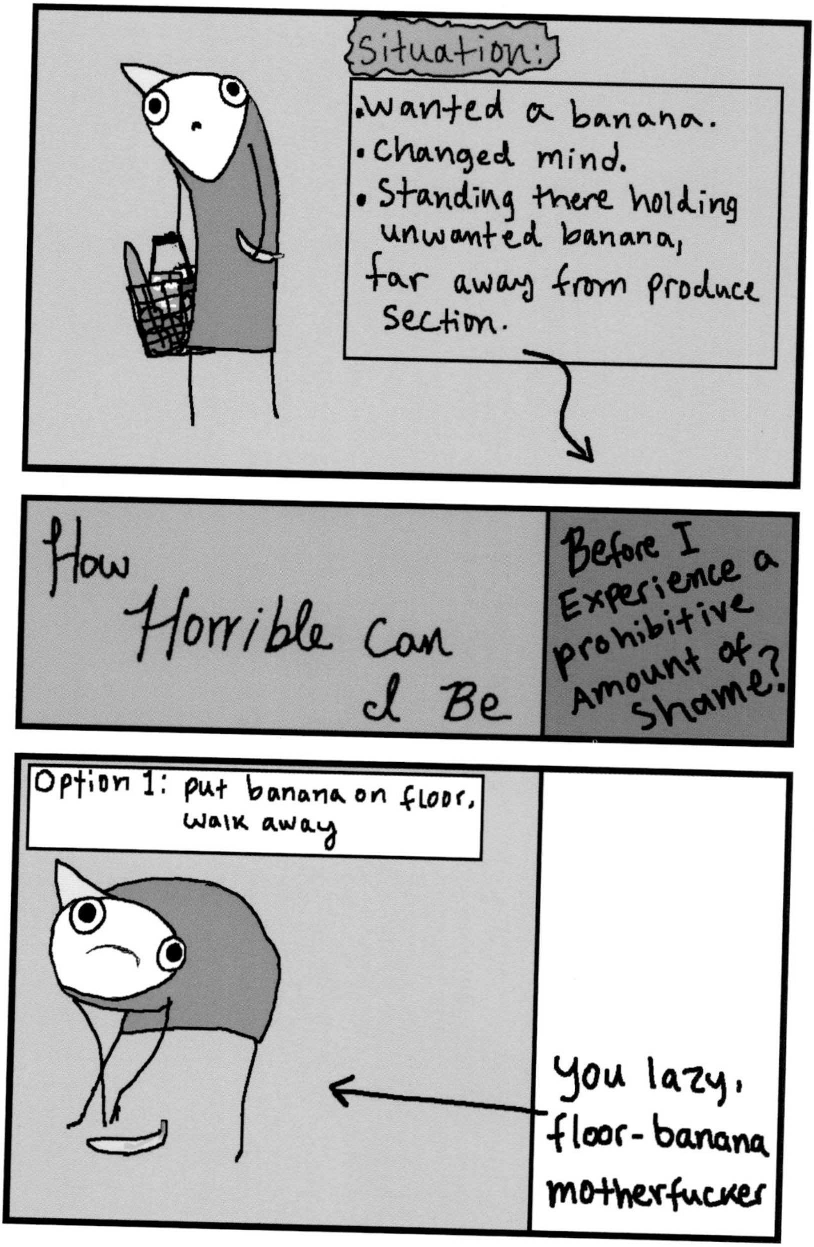
Situation:
•Wanted a banana.
•Changed mind.
•Standing there holding unwanted banana, far away from produce section.
How Horrible Can I Be
Before I Experience a prohibitive Amount of Shame?
Option 1: put banana on floor, walk away
You lazy, floor-banana motherfucker

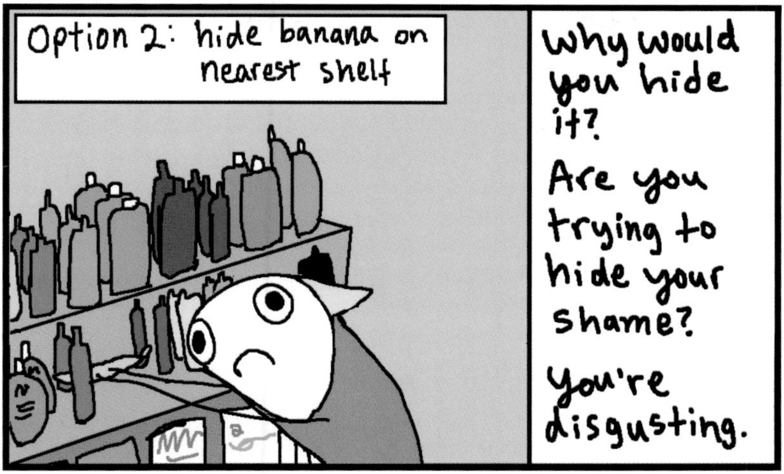
Option 2: hide banana on nearest shelf
Why would you hide it?
Are you trying to hide your shame?
You're disgusting.

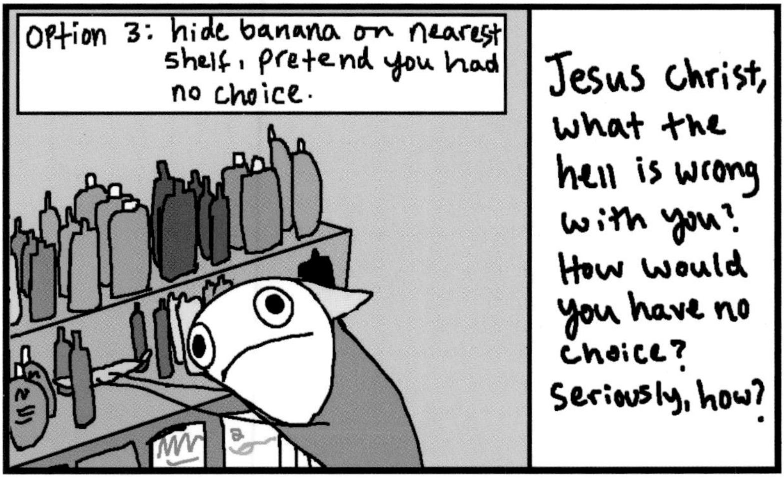
Option 3: hide banana on nearest shelf, pretend you had no choice.
Jesus Christ, what the hell is wrong with you? How would you have no choice? Seriously, how?

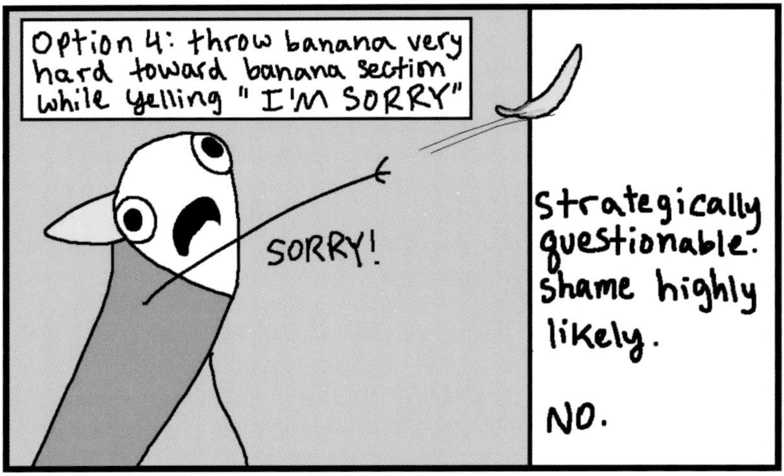
Option 4: throw banana very hard toward banana section while yelling "I'M SORRY"
SORRY!
Strategically questionable. shame highly likely.
NO.

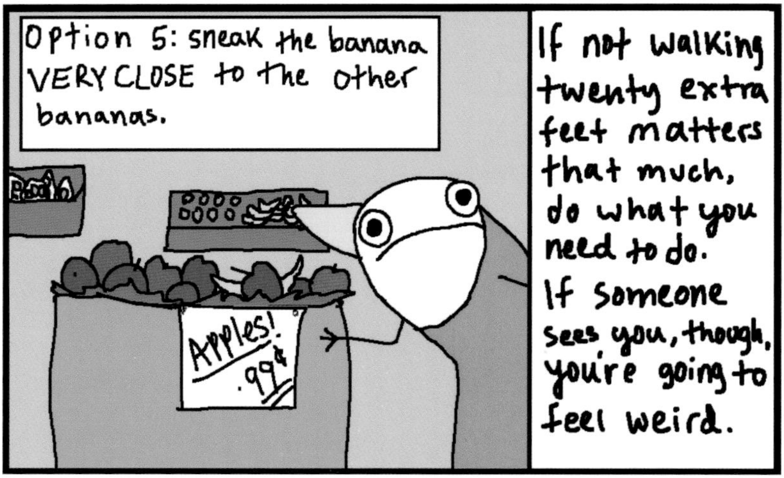
Option 5: sneak the banana VERY CLOSE to the other bananas.
Apples! .99¢
If not walking twenty extra feet matters that much, do what you need to do.
If someone sees you, though, you're going to feel weird.

Fear and shame are the backbone of my self-control. They are my source of inspiration, my insurance against becoming entirely unacceptable. They help me do the right thing. And I am terrified of what I would be without them. Because I suspect that, left to my own devices, I would completely lose control of my life.

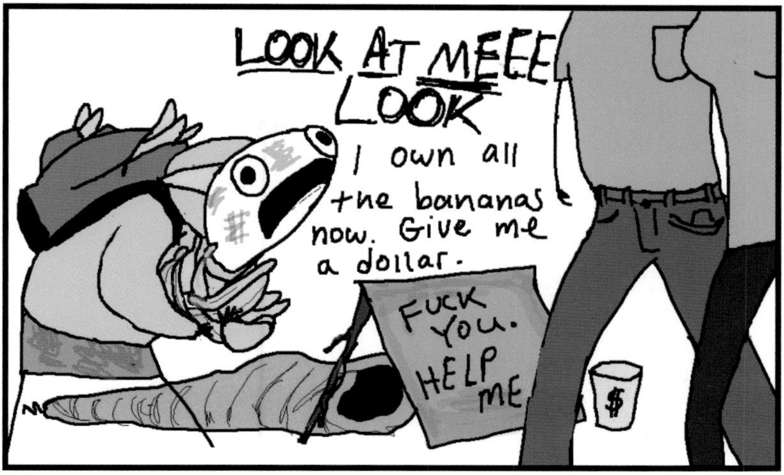
LOOK AT MEEEE
LOOK
I own all the bananas now. Give me a dollar.
FUCK YOU. HELP ME
$

I'm still hoping that perhaps someday I'll learn how to use willpower like a real person, but until that very unlikely day, I will confidently battle toward adequacy, wielding my crude skill set of fear and shame.

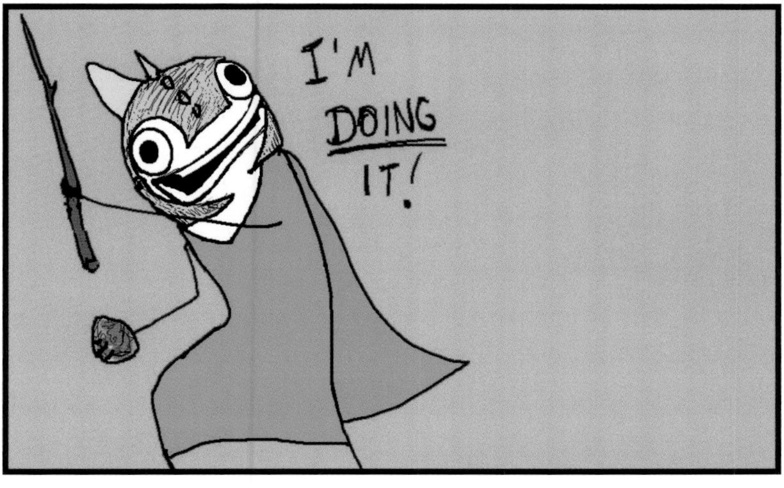
I'M DOING IT!

The God of Cake

My mom baked the most fantastic cake for my grandfather's seventy-third birthday party. The cake was slathered in impossibly thick frosting and topped with an assortment of delightful creatures that my mom crafted out of mini-marshmallows and toothpicks. To a four-year-old child, it was a thing of wonder—half toy, half cake, and all glorious possibility.

But my mom knew that it was extremely important to keep the cake away from me because she knew that if I was allowed even a tiny amount of sugar, not only would I become intensely hyperactive, but the entire scope of my existence would funnel down to the singular goal of obtaining and ingesting more sugar. My need for sugar would become so massive that it would collapse in upon itself and create a vacuum into which even more sugar would be drawn until all the world had been stripped of sweetness.

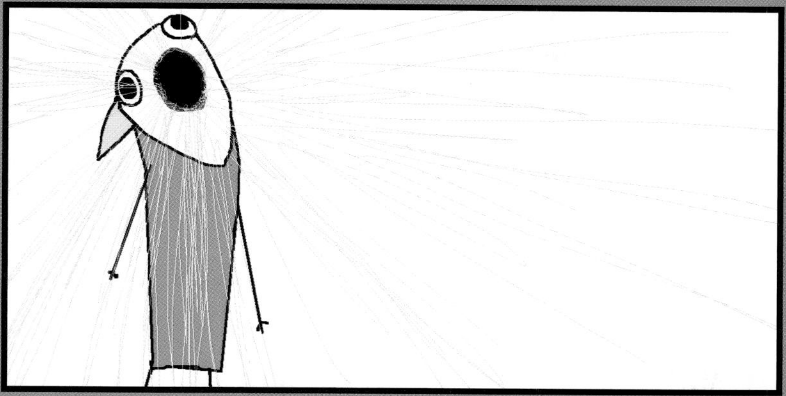

So when I managed to climb onto the counter and grab a handful of cake while my mom's back was turned, an irreversible chain reaction was set into motion.

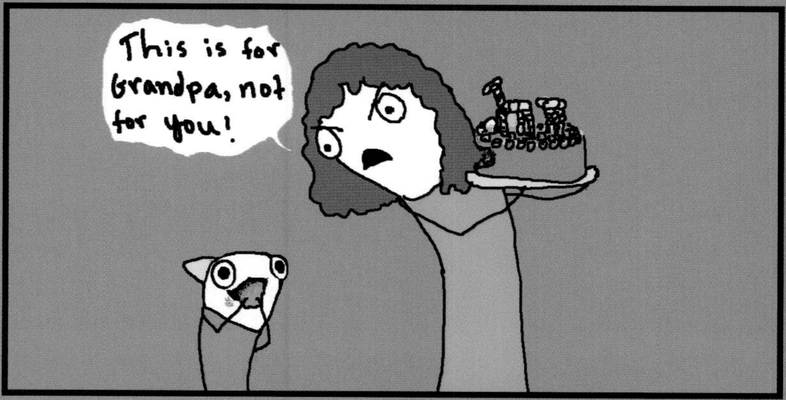
This is for Grandpa, not for you!

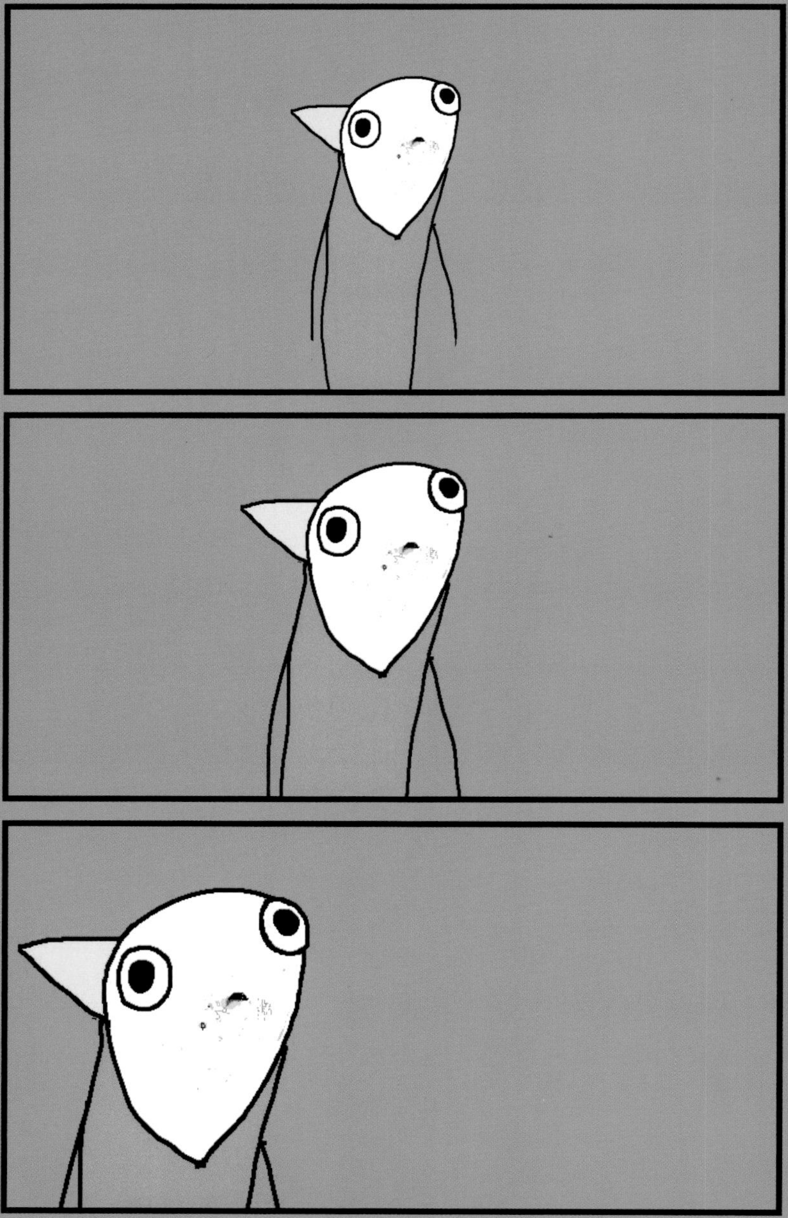

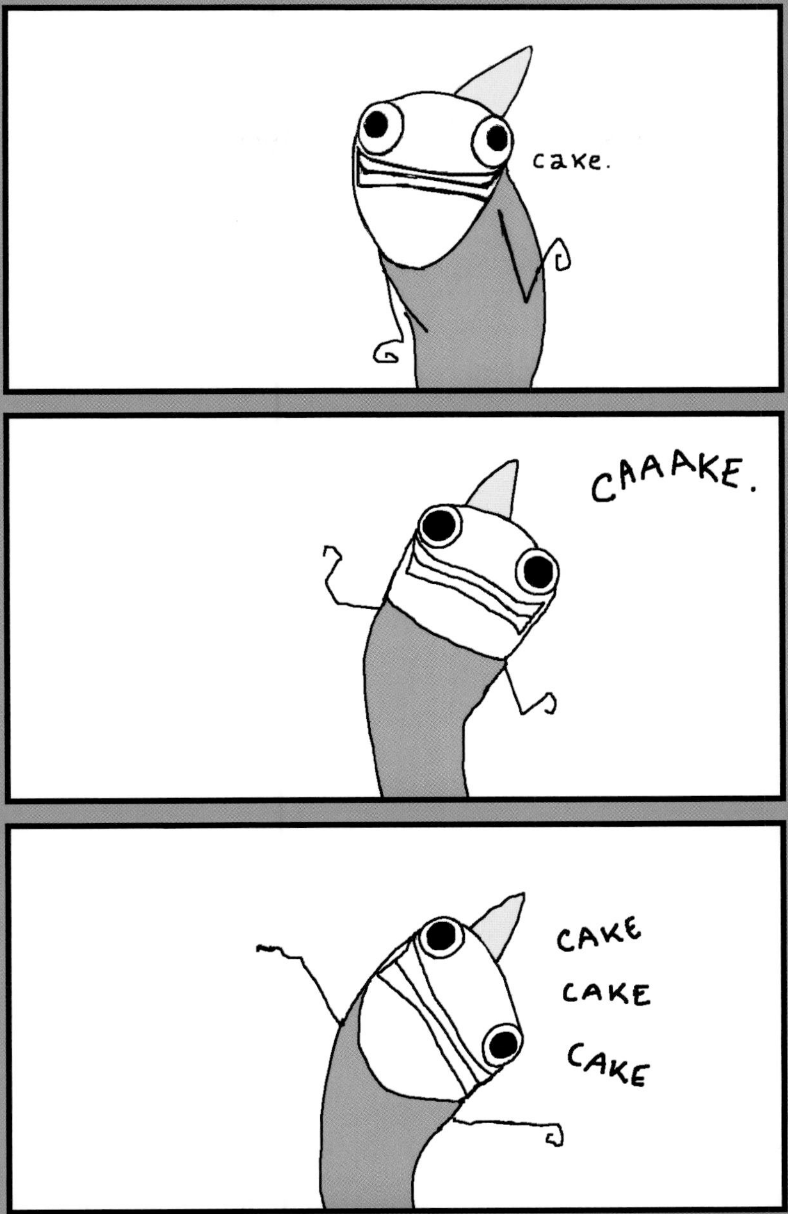
cake.
CAAAKE.
CAKE
CAKE
CAKE

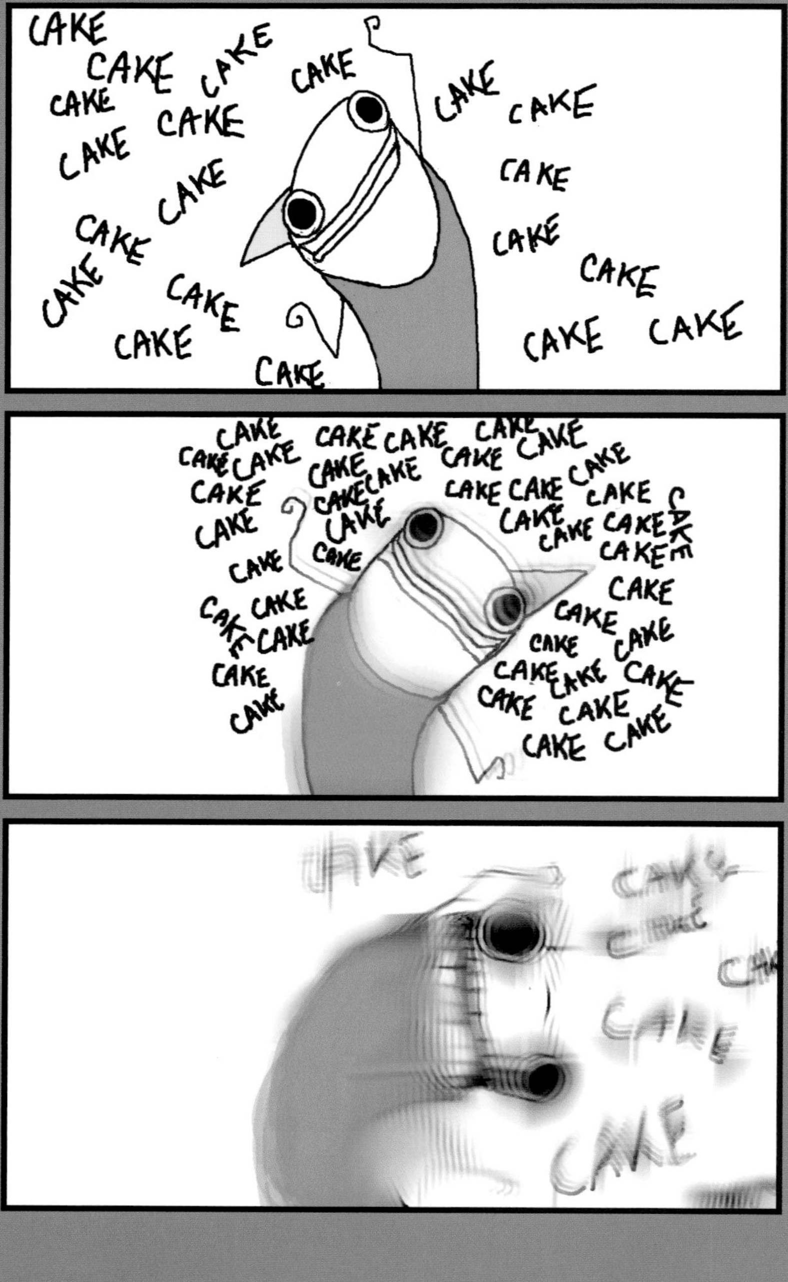
CAKE
CAKE
CAKE
CAKE
CAKE
CAKE
CAKE
CAKE
CAKE
CAKE
CAKE
CAKE
CAKE
CAKE
CAKE
CAKE
CAKE
CAKE
CAKE
CAKE
CAKE
CAKE
CAKE
CAKE
CAKE
CAKE
CAKE
CAKE
CAKE
CAKE
CAKE
CAKE
CAKE
CAKE
CAKE
CAKE
CAKE
CAKE
CAKE
CAKE
CAKE
CAKE
CAKE
CAKE
CAKE
CAKE
CAKE
CAKE
CAKE
CAKE
CAKE
CAKE
CAKE
CAKE
CAKE

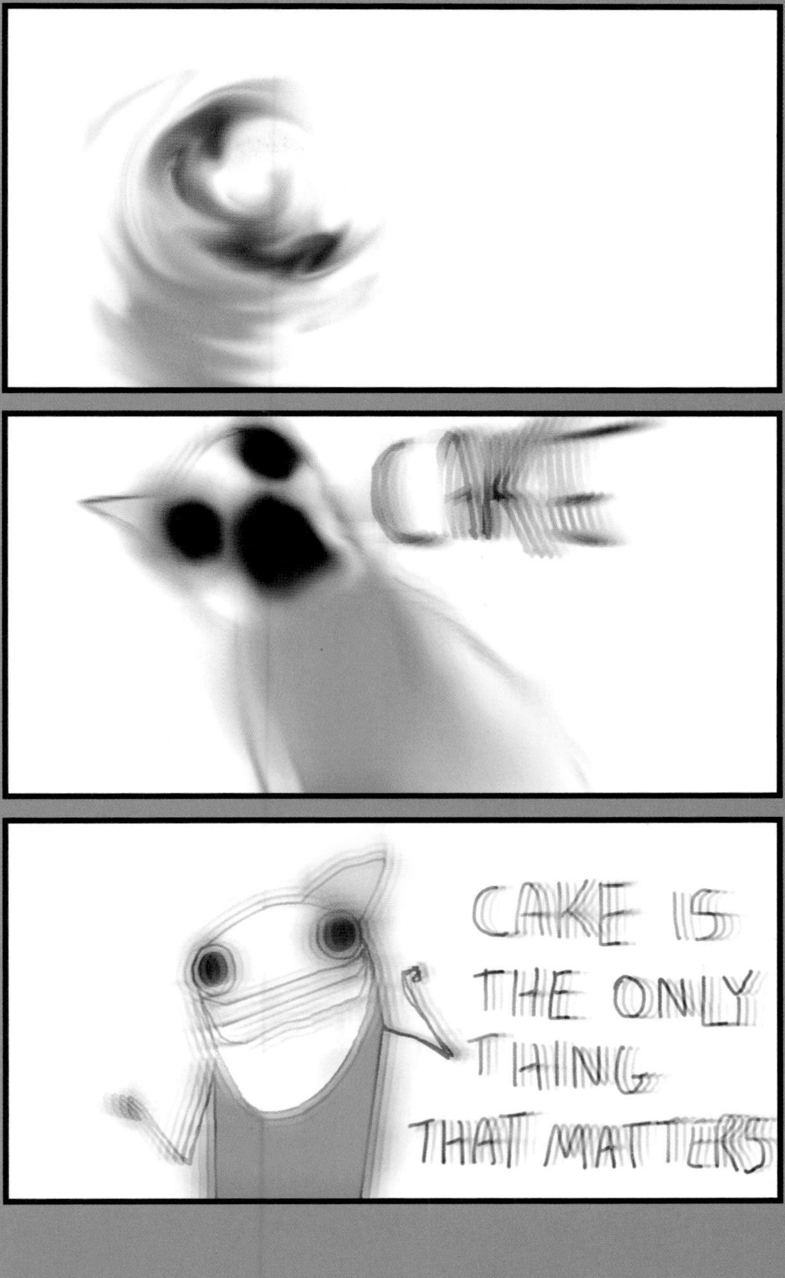
CAKE
CAKE IS THE ONLY THING THAT MATTERS

I had tasted cake and there was no going back. My tiny body had morphed into a writhing mass of pure tenacity encased in a layer of desperation. *I would eat all of the cake or I would evaporate from the sheer power of my desire to eat it.*

My mom had prepared the cake early in the day to get the task out of the way. She thought she was being efficient, but really she had only ensured that she would be forced to spend the whole day protecting the cake from my all-encompassing need to eat it. I followed her around doggedly, hoping that she would set the cake down—just for a moment.

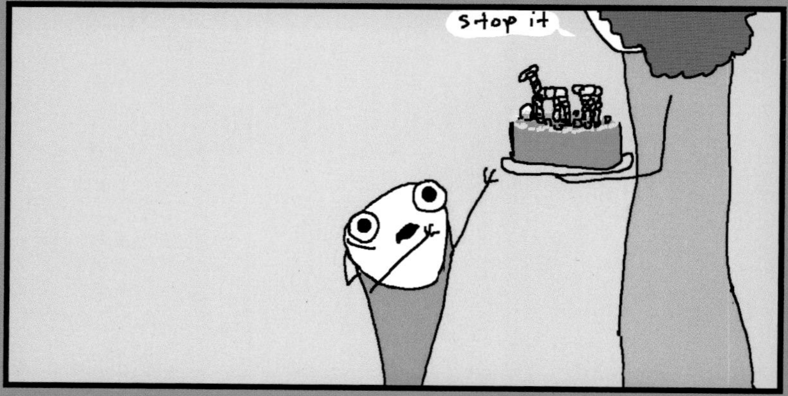
stop it

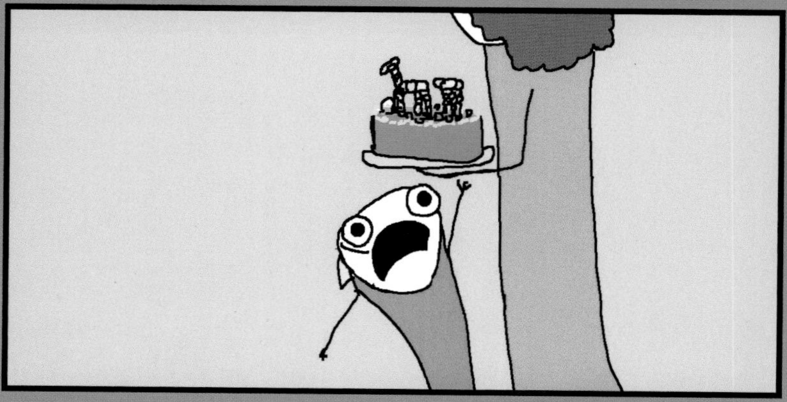

My mom quickly tired of having to hold the cake out of my reach. She tried to hide the cake, but I found it almost immediately. She tried putting the cake on top of the refrigerator, but my freakish climbing abilities soon proved it to be an unsatisfactory solution.

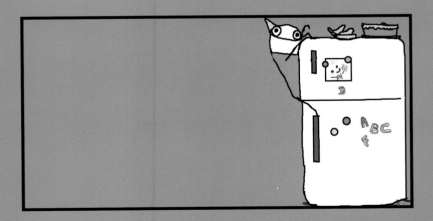

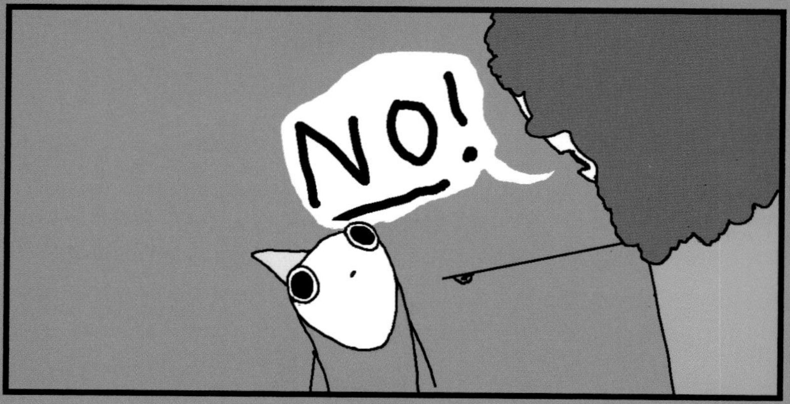
NO!

Her next attempt at cake security involved putting the cake in the refrigerator and then placing a very heavy box in front of the refrigerator's door.

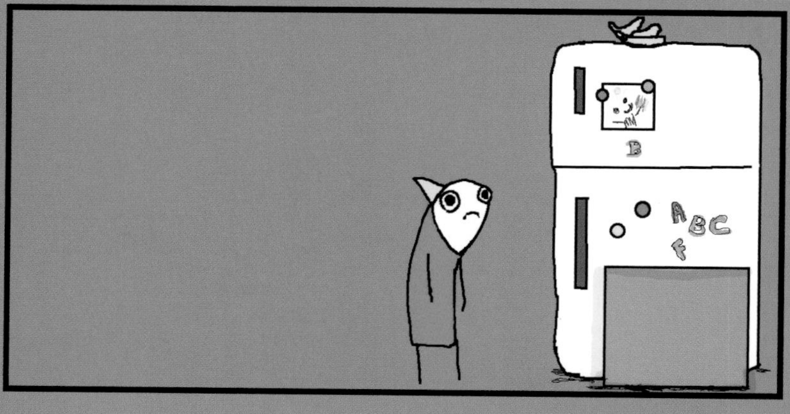
B
ABC
F

The box was far too heavy for me to move. When I discovered that I couldn't move the box, I decided that the next-best strategy would be to dramatically throw my body against it until my mom was forced to move it or allow me to destroy myself.

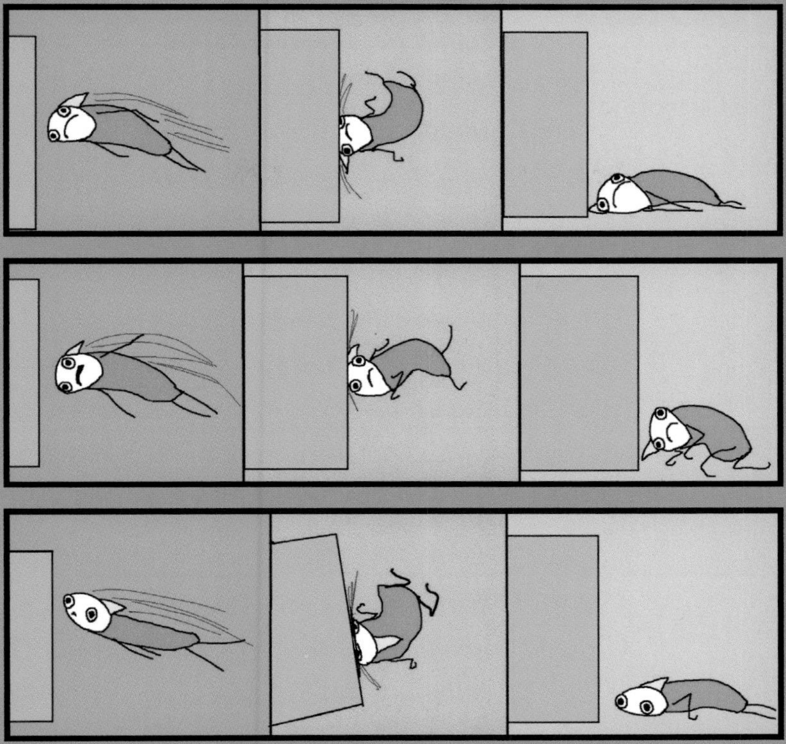

Surprisingly, this tactic did not garner much sympathy.

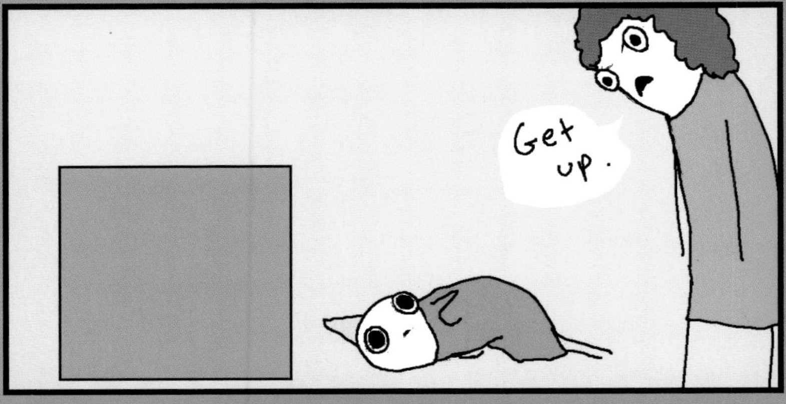
Get up.

I went and played with my toys, but I did not enjoy it.

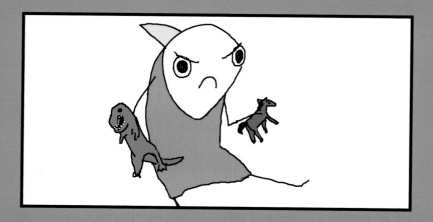

I had to stay focused.

I played vengefully for the rest of the afternoon. All of my toys died horrible deaths at least once. But I never lost sight of my goal.

My mom finally came to get me. She handed me a dress and told me to put it on because we were leaving for the party soon. I put the dress on backward just to make her life slightly more difficult.

I was herded into the car and strapped securely into my car seat. As if to taunt me, my mom placed the cake in the passenger seat, just out of my reach.

We arrived at my grandparents' house and I was immediately accosted by my doting grandmother while my mom walked away holding the cake.

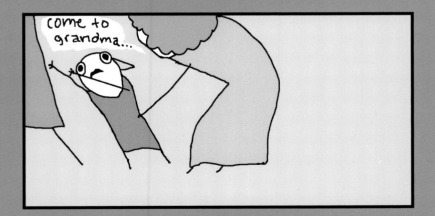

I could see my mom and the cake disappearing into the hallway as I watched helplessly. I struggled against my grandmother's loving embrace, but my efforts were futile. I heard the sound of a door shutting and then a lock sliding into place. My mom had locked the cake in the back bedroom. How was I going to get to it *now*? I hadn't yet learned the art of lock-picking and I wasn't nearly strong enough to kick the door in. It felt as though all my life's aspirations were slipping away from me in a landslide of tragedy. How could they do this to me? How could they just sit there placidly as my reason for living slowly faded from my grasp? I couldn't take it. My little mind began to crumble.

And then, right there in my grandmother's arms, I lapsed into a full-scale psychological meltdown. My collective frustrations burst forth from my tiny body like bees from a nest that had just been pelted with a rock.

It was unanimously decided that I would need to go play outside until I was able to regain my composure and stop yelling and punching. I was banished to the patio, where I stood peering dolefully through the sliding glass door, trying to look as pitiful as possible.

I knew the cake was locked securely in the bedroom, but if I could just get them to let me inside . . . maybe. Maybe I could find a way to get to it. After all, desperation breeds ingenuity. I could possibly build an explosive device or some sort of pulley system. I had to try. But at that point, my only real option was to manipulate their emotions so they'd pity me and willfully allow me to get closer to the cake.

When my theatrics failed to produce the desired results, I resorted to crying very loudly, right up against the glass.

I carried on in that fashion until my mom poked her head outside and, instead of taking pity on me and warmly inviting me back inside as I had hoped, told me to go play in the side yard because I was fogging up the glass and my inconsolable sobbing was upsetting my grandmother.

I trudged around to the side of the house, glaring reproachfully over my shoulder and thinking about how sorry my mom would be if I were to die out there. She'd wish she would have listened. She'd wish she had given me a piece of cake. But it would be too late.

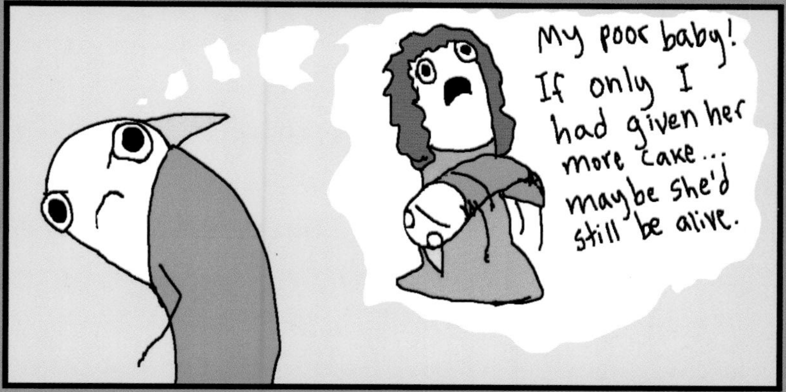
My poor baby! If only I had given her more cake... maybe she'd still be alive.

But as I rounded the corner, the personal tragedy I was constructing in my imagination was interrupted by a sliver of hope.

Just above my head, there was a window. On the other side of that particular window was the room in which my mom had locked the cake. The window was open.

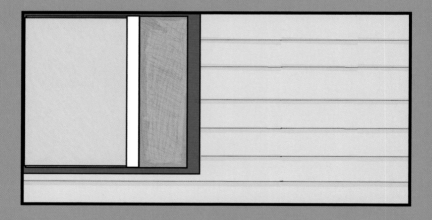

The window was covered by a screen, but my dad had shown me how to remove a screen as a preemptive safety measure in case I was trapped in a fire and he couldn't get to me and I turned out to be too stupid to figure out how to kick in a screen to escape death by burning.

I clambered up the side of the house and pushed the screen with all my strength.

It gave way, and suddenly there I was—mere feet from the cake, unimpeded by even a single obstacle.

I couldn't fully believe what had just occurred. I crept toward the cake, my body quivering with anticipation. It was mine. All mine.

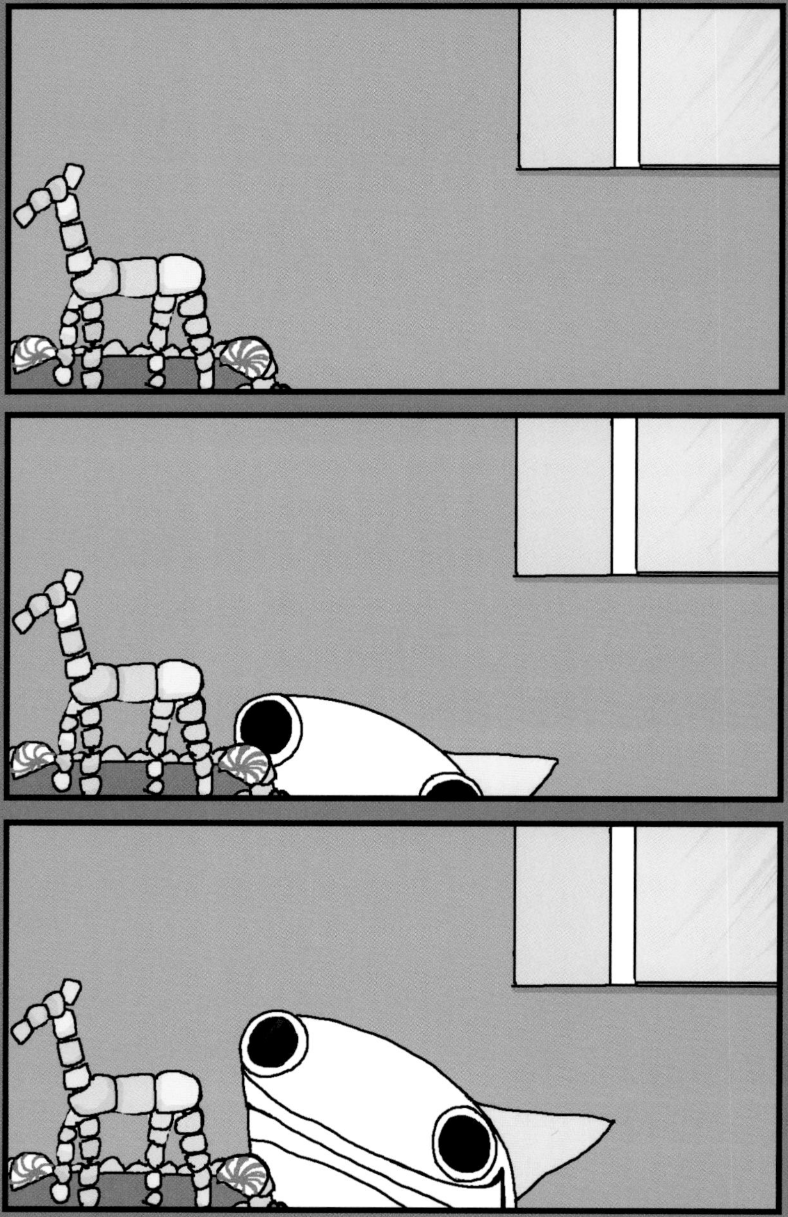

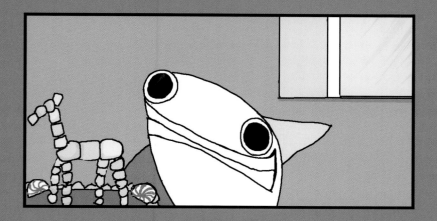

I ate the entire cake. At one point, I remember becoming aware of the oppressive fullness building inside of me, but I kept eating out of a combination of spite and stubbornness. No one could tell me not to eat an entire cake—not my mom, not Santa, not God—no one. It was my cake and everyone else could go fuck themselves.

Meanwhile, in the kitchen, my mother suddenly noticed that she hadn't heard my tortured sobbing in a while.

She became concerned because it was unusual for my tantrums to stop on their own like that, so she went looking for me.

When she couldn't find me anywhere, she finally thought to unlock the bedroom door and peek inside.

And there I was.

I spent the rest of the evening in a hyperglycemic fit, alternately running around like a maniac and regurgitating the multicolored remains of my conquest all over my grandparents' carpet. I was so miserable, but my suffering was small compared to the satisfaction I felt every time my horrible, conniving mother had to watch me retch up another rainbow of sweet, semidigested success: *This is for you, Mom. This is what happens when you try to get between me and cake.* I silently challenged her to try again to prevent me from obtaining something I wanted. Just once. Just to see what would happen. It didn't matter how violently ill I felt; in that moment, I was a god—the god of cake—and I was unstoppable.

The Helper Dog Is an Asshole

A few months after we adopted the simple dog, we decided that we didn't have enough dog-related challenges in our lives, so we set out to find a friend for the simple dog.

This is pretty difficult already...
Why not adopt the worst dog we can find and make it *impossible?*

yeah! Let's see what happens!

When we arrived at the shelter, they were like, "Hello, we've got all sorts of wonderful animals here!" and we said, "No thanks. Just go back there and bring us the most hopeless, psychologically destroyed dog-monster you can find."

One of the shelter workers led us to a kennel in the very back corner. It contained a mangy German shepherd mix that had been there for months because nobody else wanted it.

The shelter worker said, "This one hates everything and she doesn't know anything, and I hope you aren't planning on taking her outside ever because she's more like a bear than a dog, really, and unfortunately, she can scale a seven-foot-tall fence like the fucking Spider-Man."

And we were like, "Sure, why not."

We were feeling pretty optimistic because, on some level, we both felt like maybe we were dog whisperers and we could use our magical powers to convince this new dog to not be any of the things the shelter worker had just said.

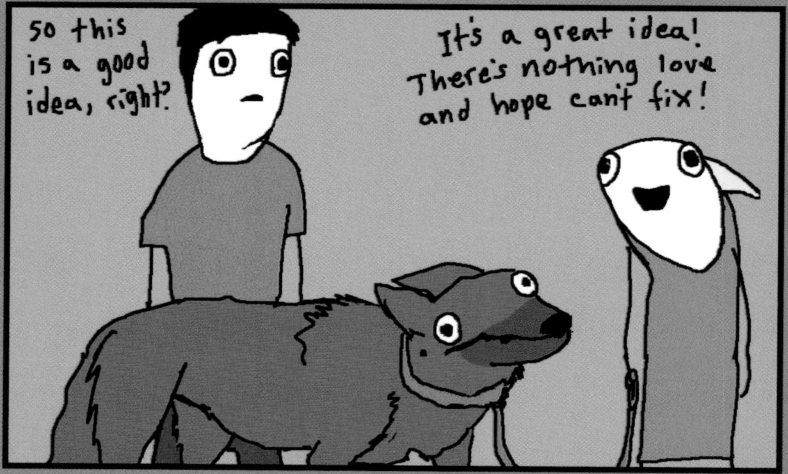
So this
is a good
idea, right?
It's a great idea!
There's nothing love
and hope can't fix!

As it turns out, we are not dog whisperers. We should have known this because of our struggles with the simple dog, but we thought *maybe the simple dog doesn't understand dog whispering. There are lots of things the simple dog doesn't understand.*

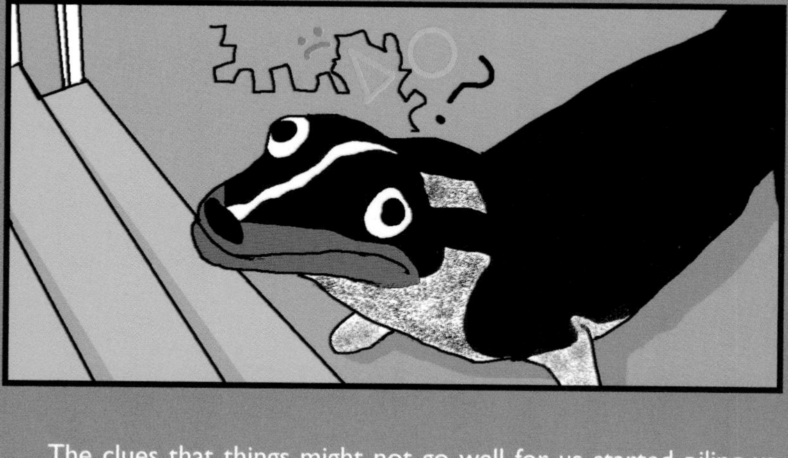

The clues that things might not go well for us started piling up almost immediately.

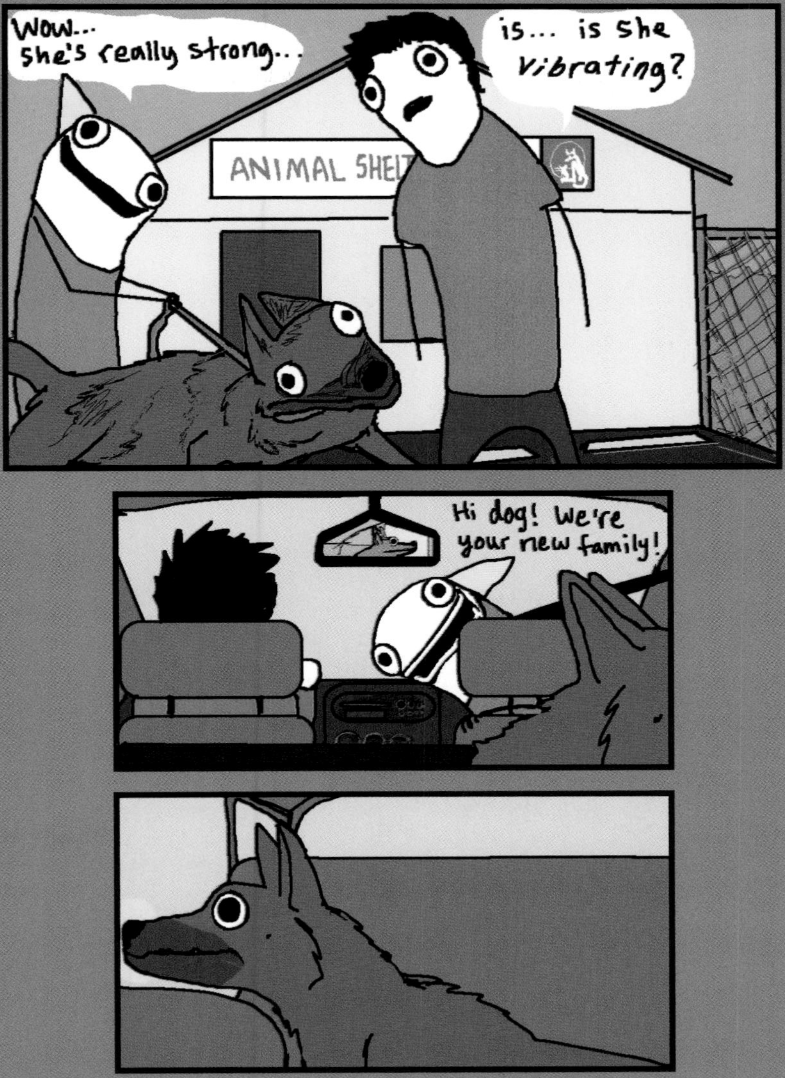

Wow...
she's really strong...
is... is she
vibrating?
ANIMAL SHEL
Hi dog! We're
your new family!

The helper dog—who earned that title on the car ride home while we were gleefully entertaining the notion that this new dog could act as a service animal for the simple dog—did not appear overly interested in interacting with us.

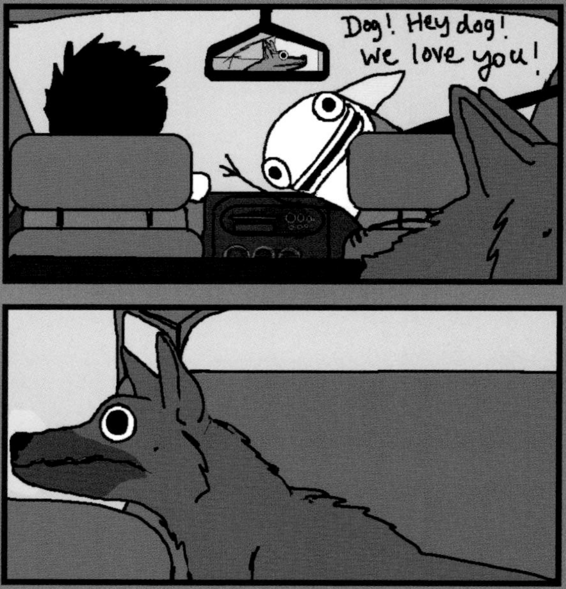
Dog! Hey dog! we love you!

She was very focused on *something,* though. We didn't know what it was yet, but this dog clearly had a plan—a plan that shelter imprisonment had prevented her from working on. And now that she'd been freed, this plan—whatever it was—was the only thing that mattered. We were simply a means to an end.

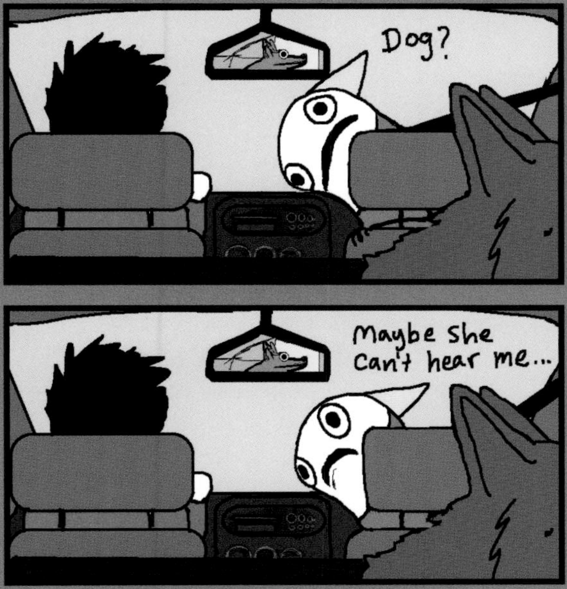
Dog?
Maybe she can't hear me...

It was sort of like being the taxi-driver character in a Bruce Willis movie. You try to make small talk with Bruce Willis on his ride home from prison, where he spent the last nine years becoming hardened and vengeful, but he is finally free to pursue his plan and he doesn't give a *shit* about small talk. He doesn't have time. There are important things to focus on, and the taxi driver is not one of them.

We uncovered a major clue about the helper dog's plan when we tried to introduce her to the simple dog.

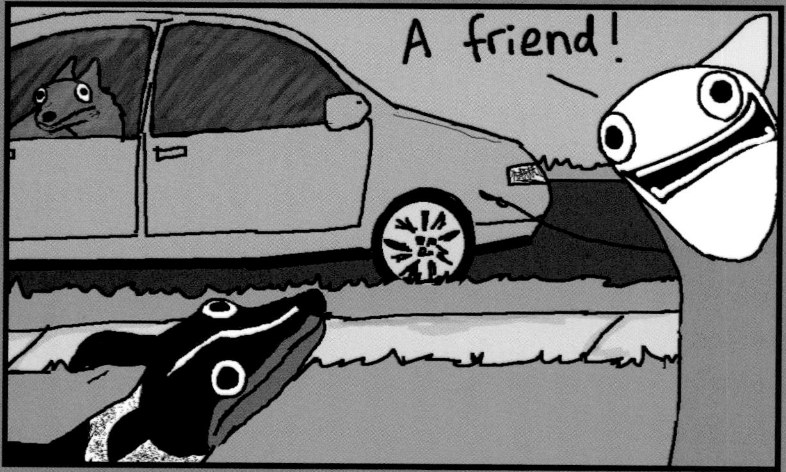
A friend!

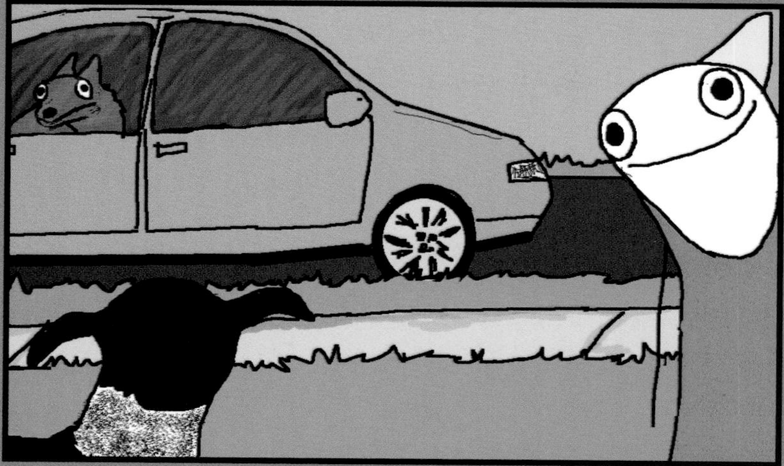

The simple dog has a lot of weird qualities that make her seem un-dog-like. She's more like a sea cucumber with legs. Which is for-tunate, because otherwise, the helper dog may have never agreed to tolerate her.

From what we can tell, the helper dog holds a firm belief that other dogs should not exist. The fact that they do fills her with uncontrollable, psychotic rage. Even the slightest hint of another dog's existence will throw her into a hysterical fit of scream-barking.

But she can't do anything to prevent the world from containing other dogs, so instead, she is determined to make sure that no other dogs can *enjoy* existing. If she senses that another dog is enjoying itself nearby, she will do everything within her power to ruin that dog's day.

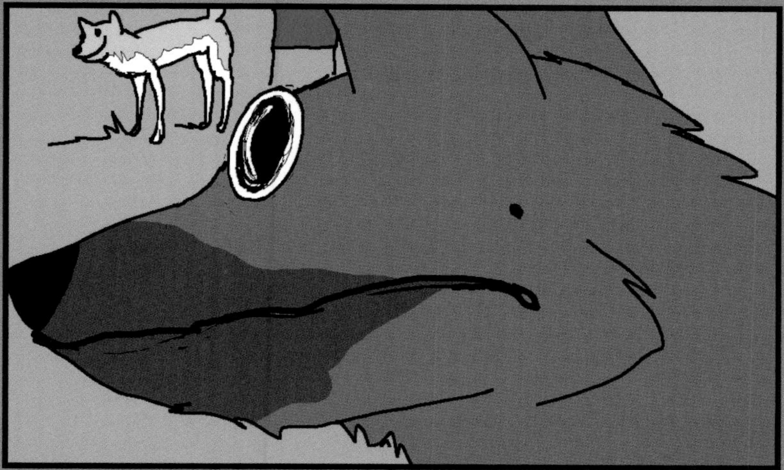

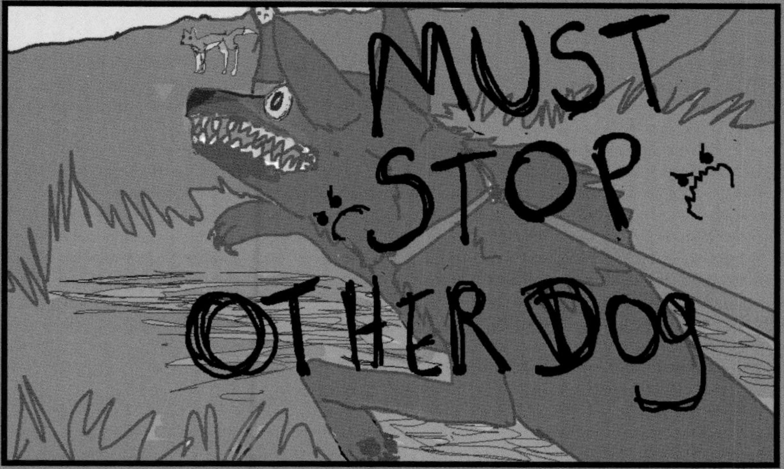

MUST
STOP
OTHER DOG

And when she does this, other people glare at us like, "What horrible people they must be to have such an angry animal. MY dog would never do that. People like that should be in *jail.*"

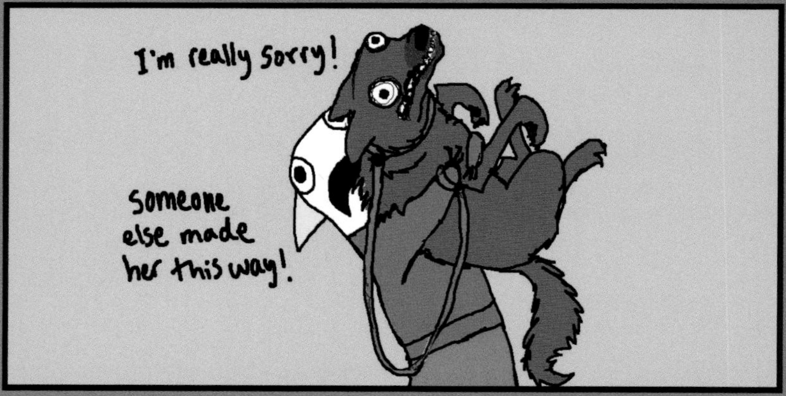
I'm really sorry!
someone else made her this way!

Still, we thought, *Okay, this is horribly stressful and embarrassing. But we can teach her.*

Everyone told us, "*Oh, it's easy to train dogs! You just give them a treat when they do something you like!*" We asked, "But what if they never do anything you like?" And everybody said, "*Oh, then just wait until the dog stops doing what you don't like, give it a treat, and presto! It's really, really, really, really, really, really, really, absurdly, unbelievably easy! It has a 100 percent success rate on every dog ever. There is literally nobody in the entire world who has been unsuccessful with this method.*"

This is what was supposed to happen:

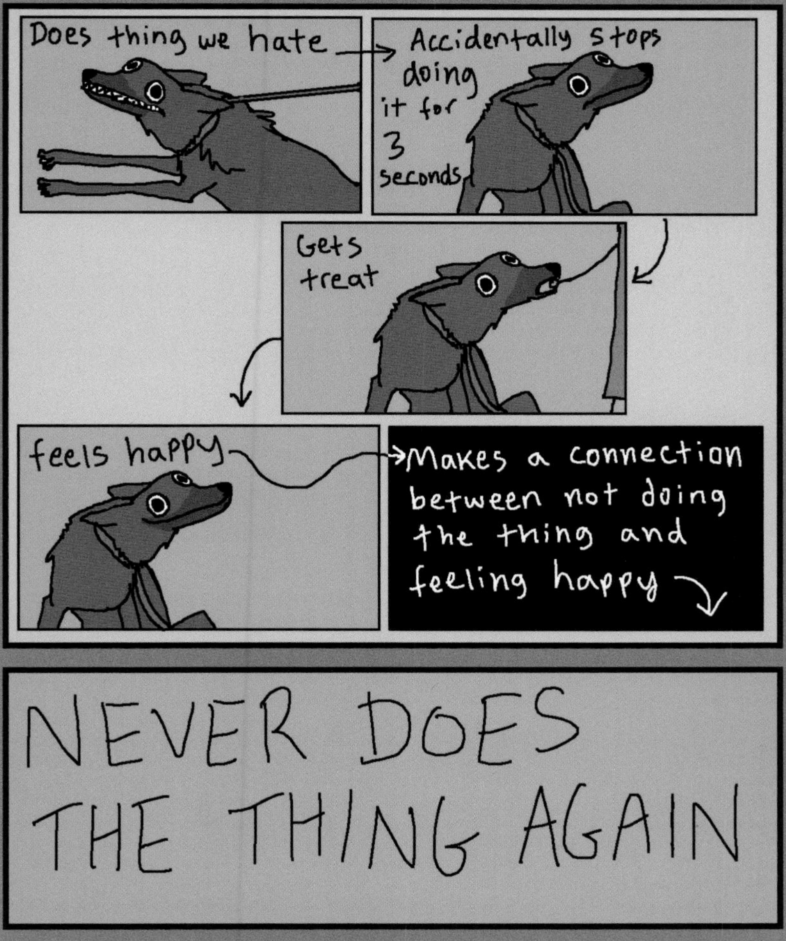
Does thing we hate
Accidentally stops doing it for 3 seconds
Gets treat
feels happy
Makes a connection between not doing the thing and feeling happy
NEVER DOES THE THING AGAIN

But the only thing we managed to accomplish was to teach the helper dog that if she starts doing something we hate, and then stops doing that thing very briefly, she can get a treat. And then she can go back to doing the thing we hate.

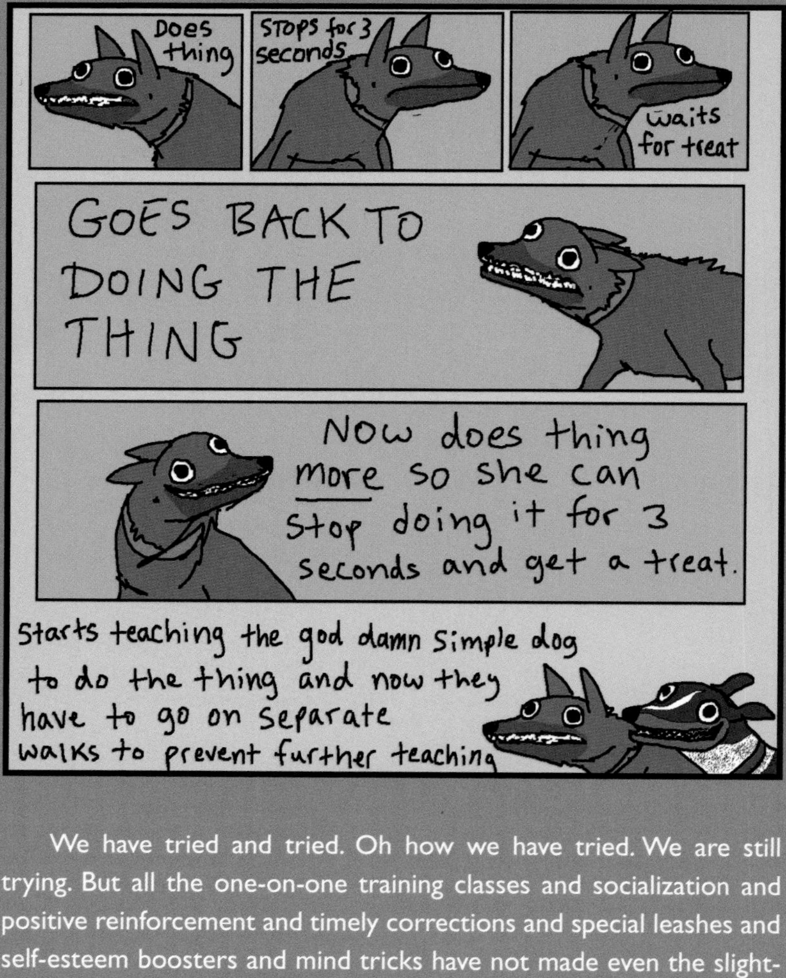
Does thing
STOPS for 3 seconds
waits for treat
GOES BACK TO DOING THE THING
Now does thing more so she can stop doing it for 3 seconds and get a treat.
Starts teaching the god damn simple dog to do the thing and now they have to go on separate walks to prevent further teaching

We have tried and tried. Oh how we have tried. We are still trying. But all the one-on-one training classes and socialization and positive reinforcement and timely corrections and special leashes and self-esteem boosters and mind tricks have not made even the slightest dent in her hatred of other dogs. Nor have they solved any of the other problems she has. And she has HEAPS of other problems. If you could stack the helper dog's problems one on top of the other, they would reach all the way to the moon. And then they would shove the moon out of the way aggressively and continue in a completely straight line for an infinite distance.

You might be thinking, *How many problems can a dog actually have? There are only, like, eight things dogs can do.* And that's what I thought too. I also thought there would be spaces in between the problems— happy little spaces where I could bask in the love and appreciation that would surely reward my efforts. Or at least times where the helper dog would be asleep.

But she doesn't sleep.

She doesn't even relax.

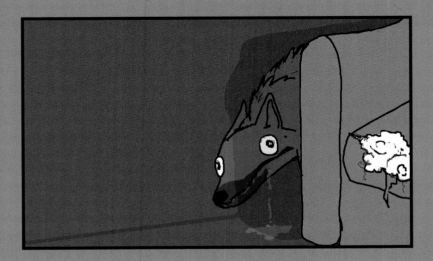

At night, she crouches in the corner of the room, as rigid as a block of wood, and just stares at us.

The staring was a bit unsettling, but that wasn't what forced us to move the helper dog's bed into the hallway. What did that was the neighbor's dog.

The problem with the neighbor's dog is that it exists. It especially exists at five o'clock in the morning. We know this because whenever the helper dog senses its presence, she scream-growls and runs into the sliding glass door with a tremendous amount of force.

And then she paces and makes whining and gurgling sounds for the next three hours because *that dog was out there and surely it's still somewhere.*

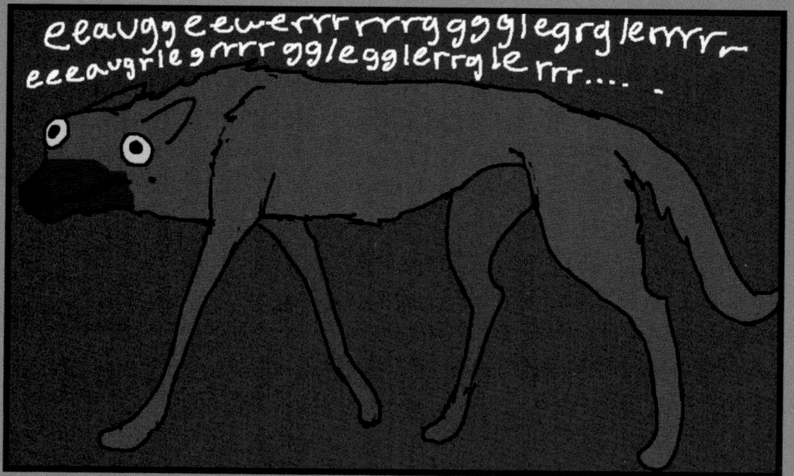
eeauggeewerrrrrrrggggglegrglerrrrr
eeeaugrlegrrrrggleggglerrglerrr....

Three nights of this in a row was enough for the helper dog to be transplanted to the hallway, where she would have no view of the neighbor's yard and no view of the neighbor's dog. I thought that this would fix the problem. But she didn't stay in the hallway like I thought she would. She went downstairs and lurked next to the back door all night long, just waiting for the neighbor's dog to emerge. At which point, she scream-growled and ran into the glass as usual.

So it wasn't an issue of being circumstantially exposed to the neighbor's dog and overreacting. It was more that the helper dog is a psychotic, creepy dog-bear-beast and she *wants* to see the neighbor dog and feel all the feelings that it makes her feel.

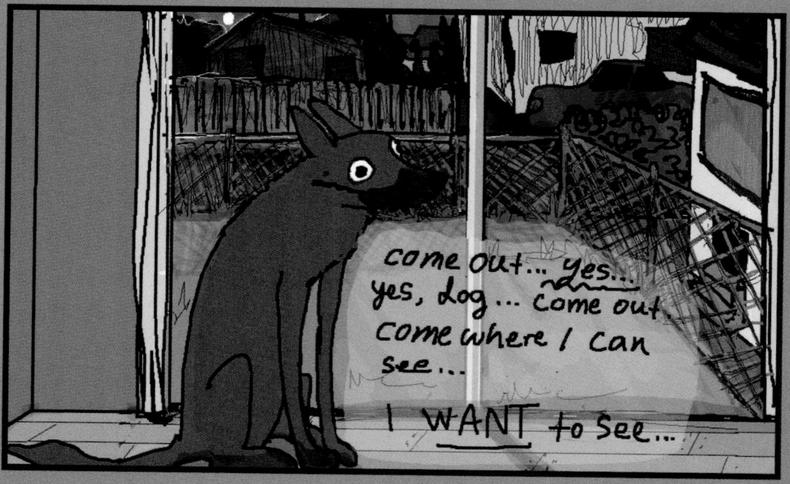
come out... yes... yes, dog... come out. come where I can see...
I WANT to see...

The next day, we bought a baby gate, which we put at the top of the stairs to keep the helper dog in the upstairs hallway. Where she could not, in any way, see the neighbor's dog.

We were awakened at five o'clock the next morning by the sound of the baby gate falling down the stairs, and then, five seconds later, the sound of the helper dog slamming herself into the back door repeatedly, biting the glass and roaring.

We set the vacuum cleaner in front of it. The helper dog hates the vacuum cleaner. But apparently she doesn't hate it as much as she hates the neighbor's dog, because we were awakened at the stroke of five by both the baby gate AND the vacuum cleaner AND the helper dog crashing down the stairs.

We secured the baby gate with rope so that she couldn't knock it over. She lurked in the shadows until five o'clock, then leapt over it, tumbled down the stairs, and proceeded as usual.

We bought a box fan. *Maybe she can hear the neighbor's dog and that's how she knows it's out there,* we thought.

But she doesn't need to see or hear the neighbor's dog. She can *sense* it. And even when there is no possible way for her to get downstairs because we've piled everything we own into an eight-foot-tall stair-blocking super-barrier, she can slam herself against our bedroom door until we lock her in the bathroom and reconsider all our decisions.

Yet somehow . . .

. . . even though the helper dog hates everything and doesn't know anything . . .

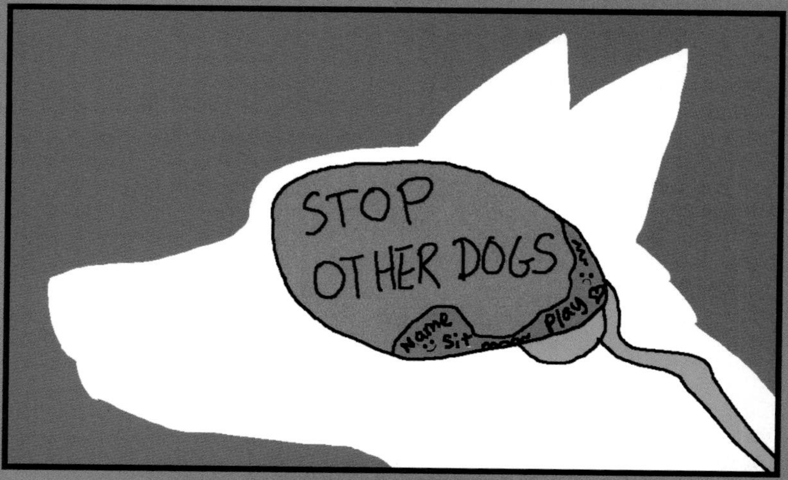
STOP
OTHER DOGS
Name
Sit
Play

. . . and even though I'm pretty certain all the hate inside her crowds out her ability to feel love . . .

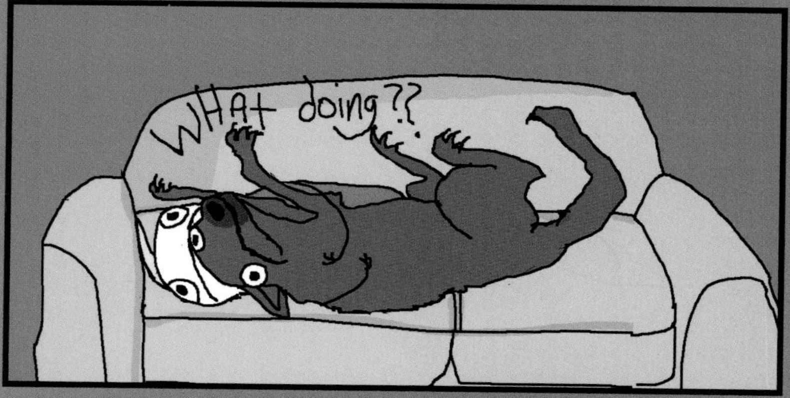
WHAt doing??

…and even though she has pretty much every single problem that it is possible for a dog to have…

Barking
Chewing
Escaping
Digging
Jumping all over
Scaring children
Scaring other dogs
Pulling on leash hard enough to
win the motherfucking Iditarod,
which would be cool if we were
competing in the Iditarod, but
we aren't. We're walking to Safeway

whining in the car,
stealing food while
no one is looking,
peeing on the floor,
Eating socks,
Growling

…plus some new problems that she invented all by herself…

Doesn't sleep
Licks own body for five
hours in a row while
staring at guests and
making them uncomfortable
Makes creaking/groaning
sounds when understimulated
Possibly made out of boards
Hates hugs
Hates birds

…she is our dog. And because she is our dog, we can pick out the tiny, almost imperceptible good qualities from the ocean of terrible qualities, and we can cling to them. Because we want to love our dog.

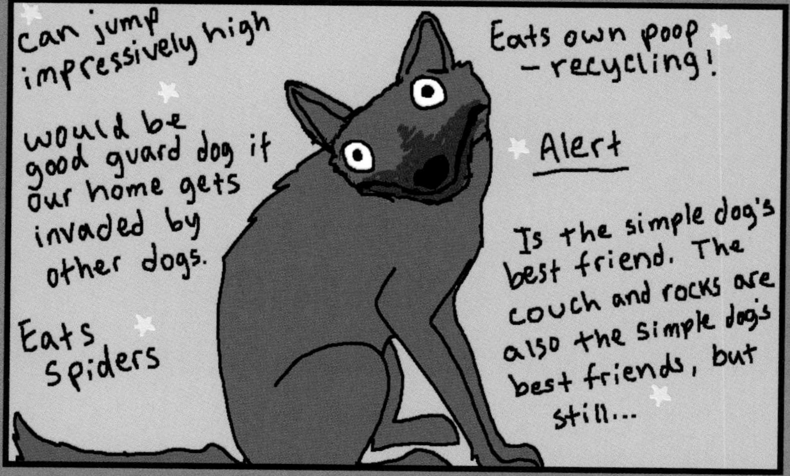
can jump impressively high
would be good guard dog if our home gets invaded by other dogs.
Eats spiders
Eats own poop - recycling!
Alert
Is the simple dog's best friend. The couch and rocks are also the simple dog's best friends, but still...

Also, we accidentally discovered that she can't sense the neighbor dog from the bathroom.

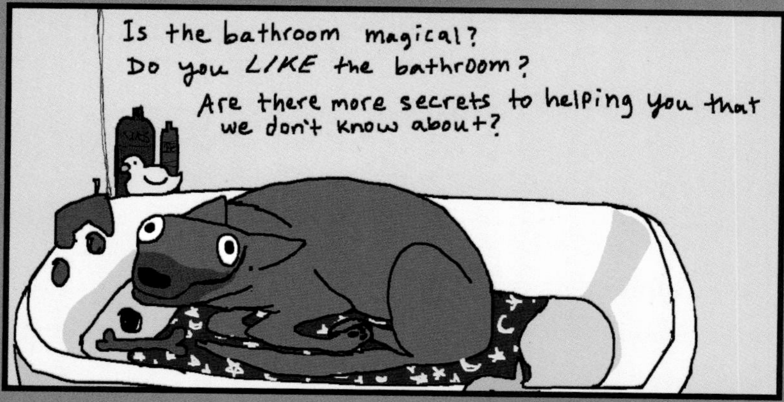
Is the bathroom magical?
Do you LIKE the bathroom?
Are there more secrets to helping you that we don't know about?

Depression Part One

Some people have a legitimate reason to feel depressed, but not me. I just woke up one day feeling arbitrarily sad and helpless.

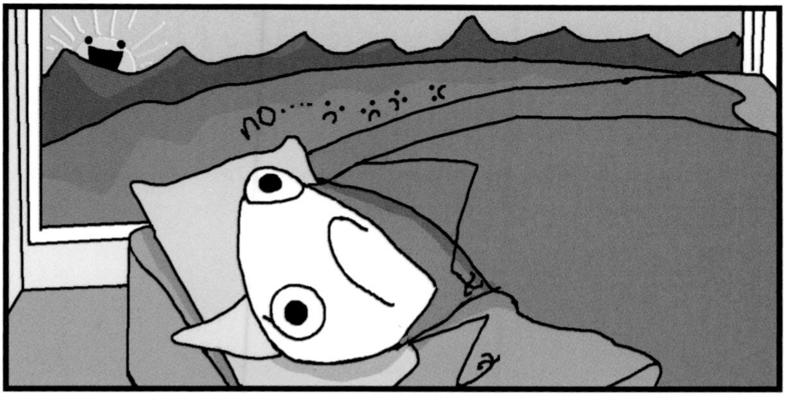
no.... :' :' :' :(

It's disappointing to feel sad for no reason. Sadness can be almost pleasantly indulgent when you have a way to justify it. You can listen to sad music and imagine yourself as the protagonist in a dramatic movie. You can gaze out the window while you're crying and think, *This is so sad. I can't even believe how sad this whole situation is. I bet even a reenactment of my sadness could bring an entire theater audience to tears.*

But my sadness didn't have a purpose. Listening to sad music and imagining that my life was a movie just made me feel kind of weird because I couldn't really get behind the idea of a movie where the character is sad for no reason.

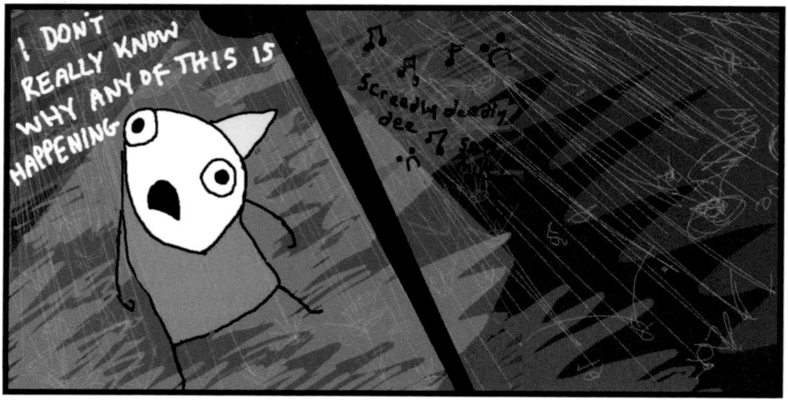
I DON'T REALLY KNOW WHY ANY OF THIS IS HAPPENING
Screedly deedly dee

Essentially, I was being robbed of my right to feel self-pity, which is the only redeeming part of sadness.

And for a little bit, that was a good enough reason to pity myself.

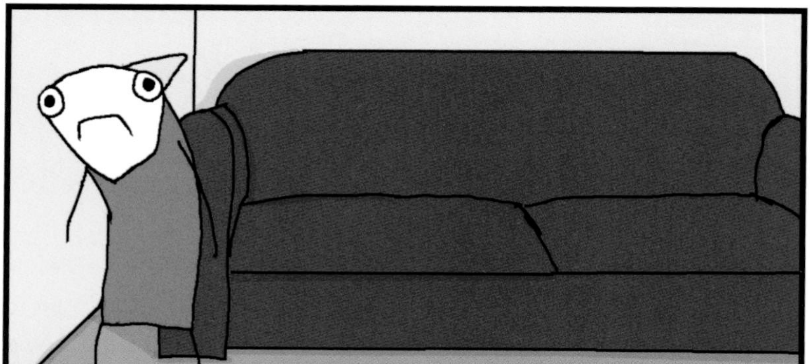

Standing around feeling sorry for myself was momentarily exhilarating, but I grew tired of it quickly. *That will do,* I thought. *I've had my fun, let's move on to something else now.* But the sadness didn't go away.

I tried to force myself to not be sad.

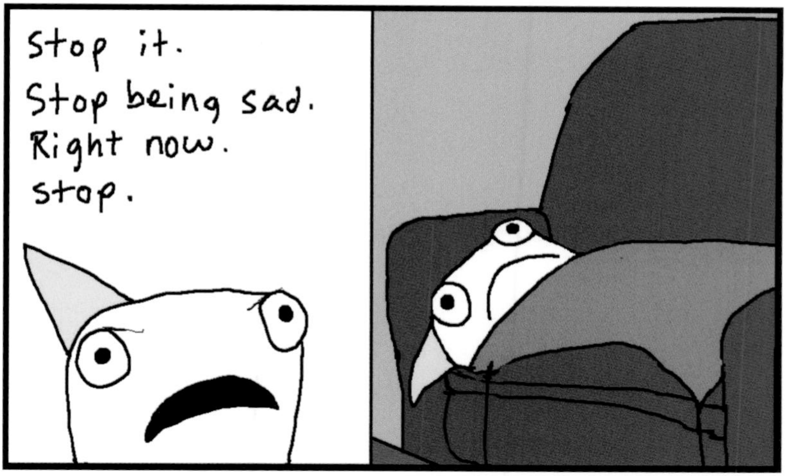
Stop it.
Stop being sad.
Right now.
Stop.

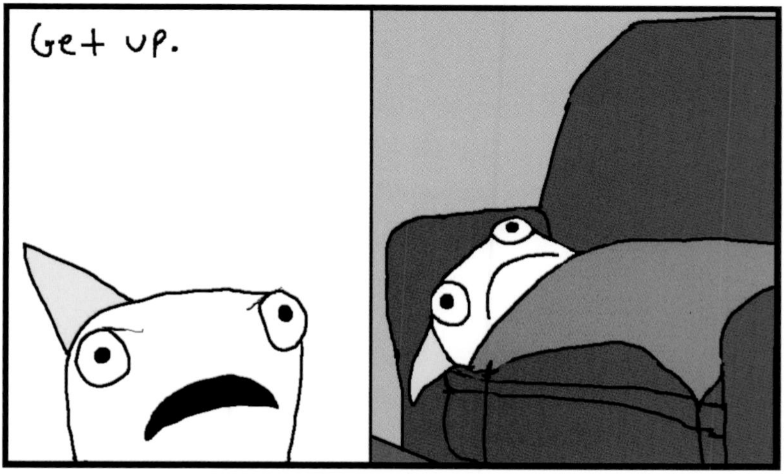
Get up.

But trying to use willpower to overcome the apathetic sort of sadness that accompanies depression is like a person with no arms trying to punch themselves until their hands grow back. A fundamental component of the plan is missing and it isn't going to work.

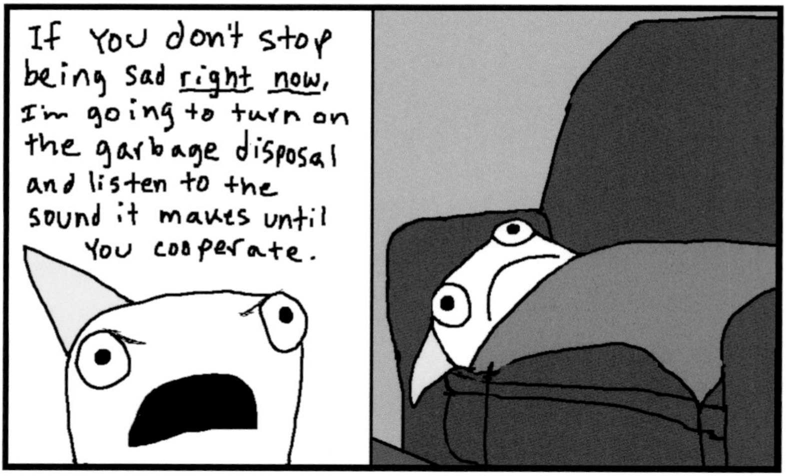
If you don't stop being sad right now, I'm going to turn on the garbage disposal and listen to the sound it makes until you cooperate.

When I couldn't will myself to not be sad, I became frustrated and angry. In a final, desperate attempt to regain power over myself, I turned to shame as a sort of motivational tool.

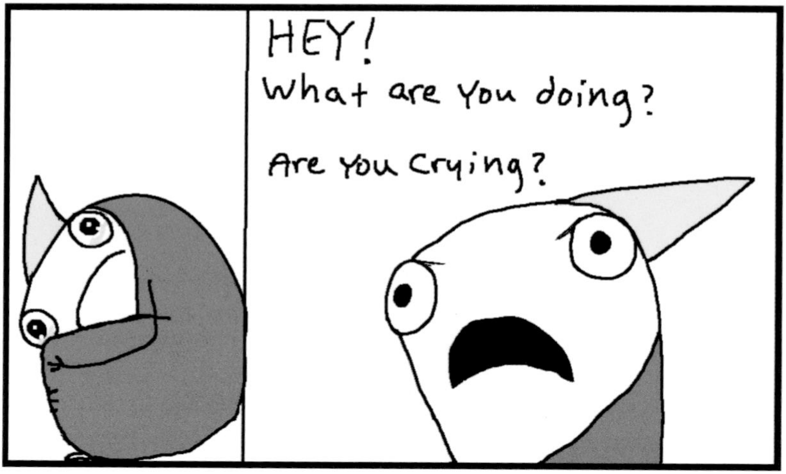
HEY!
What are you doing?
Are you crying?

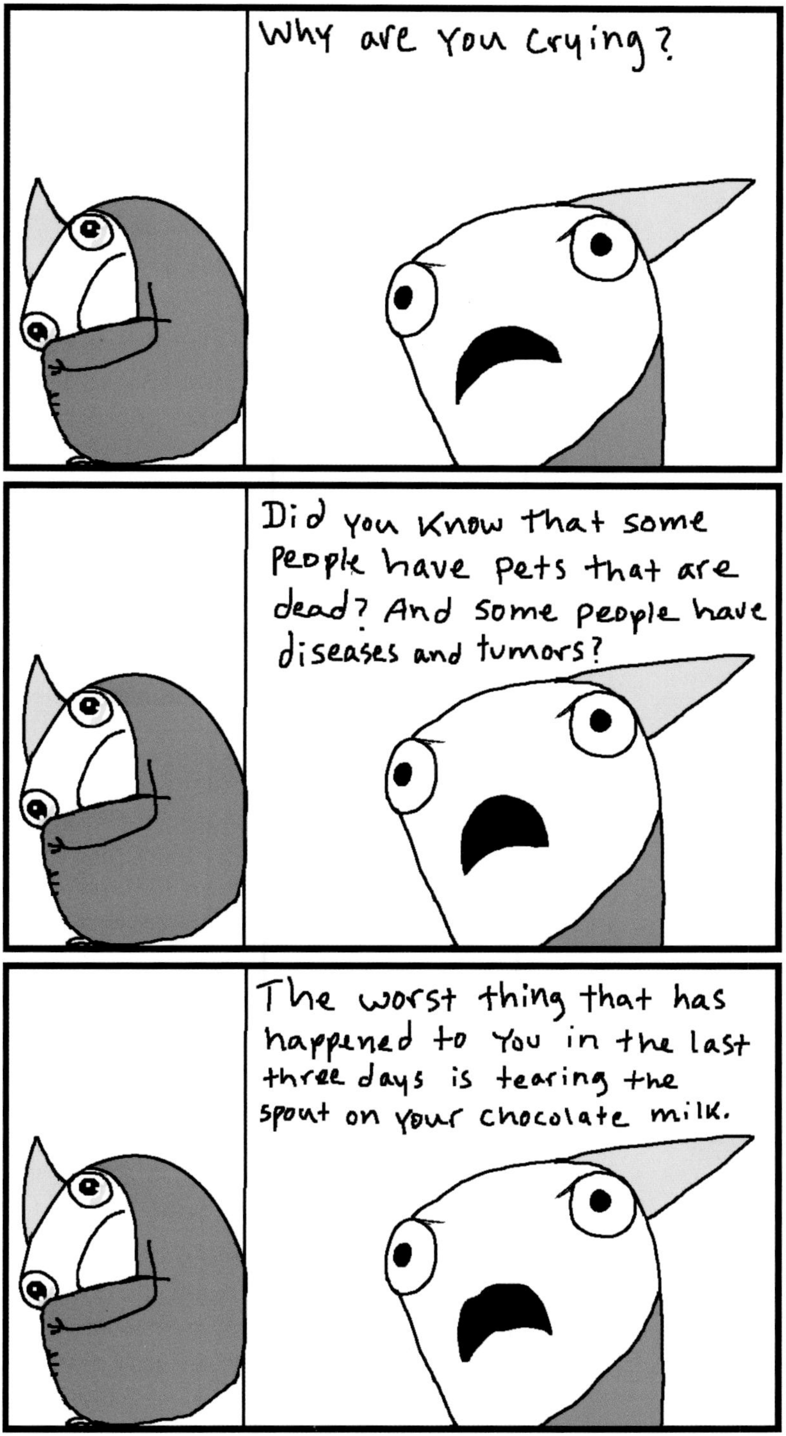
Why are you crying?
Did you know that some people have pets that are dead? And some people have diseases and tumors?
The worst thing that has happened to you in the last three days is tearing the spout on your chocolate milk.

But, since I was depressed, this tactic was less inspirational and more just a way to oppress myself with hatred.

maybe I'll go outside today.

Nope.
I hate myself too much.

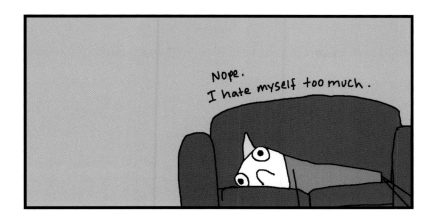

Which made me more sad.

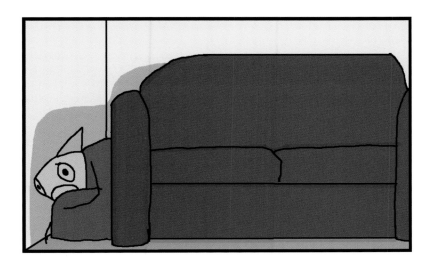

Which then made me more frustrated and abusive.

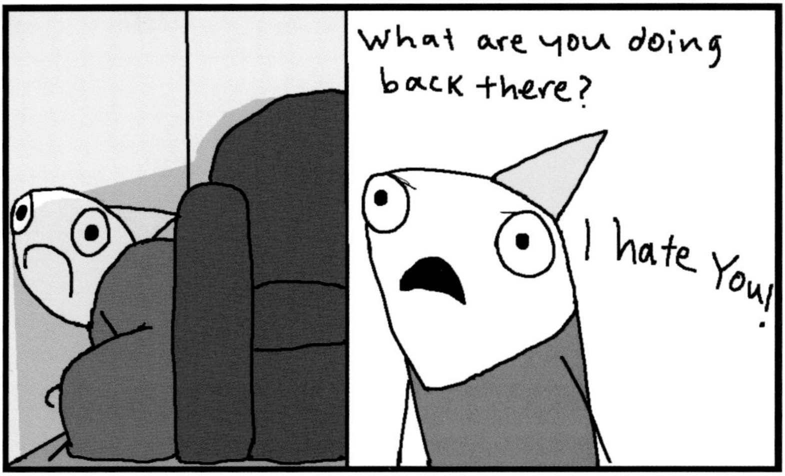
What are you doing back there?
I hate You!

And that made me *even more sad,* and so on and so forth until the only way to adequately express my sadness was to crawl very slowly across the floor.

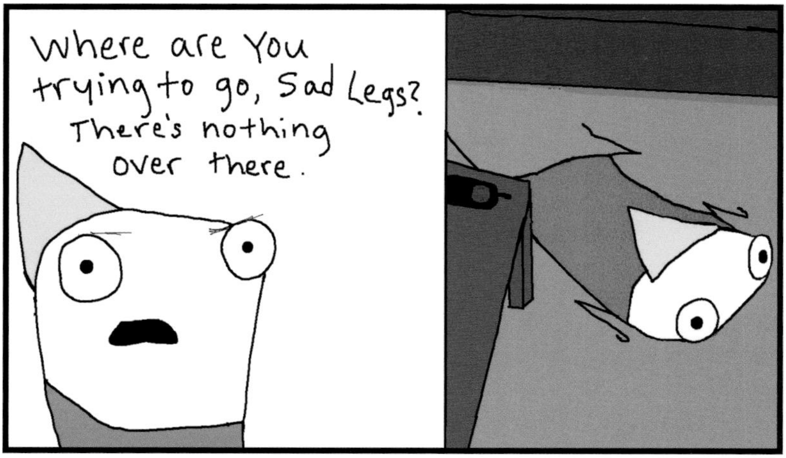
Where are You trying to go, Sad Legs? There's nothing over there.

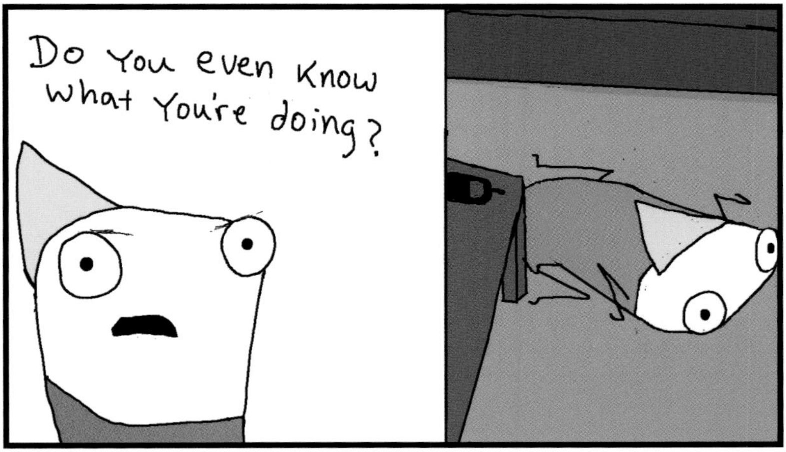
Do You even Know what You're doing?

The self-loathing and shame had ceased to be even slightly productive, but it was too late to go back at that point, so I just kept going. I followed myself around like a bully, narrating my thoughts and actions with a constant stream of abuse.

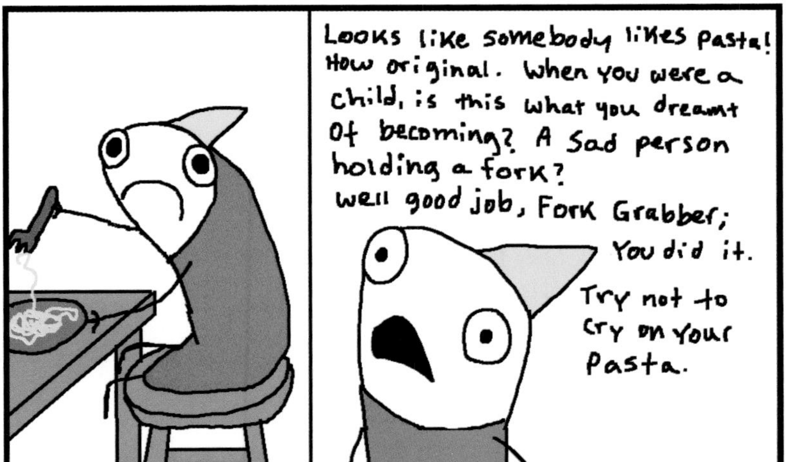
Looks like somebody likes pasta! How original. When you were a child, is this what you dreamt of becoming? A sad person holding a fork?
well good job, Fork Grabber; You did it.
Try not to cry on your pasta.

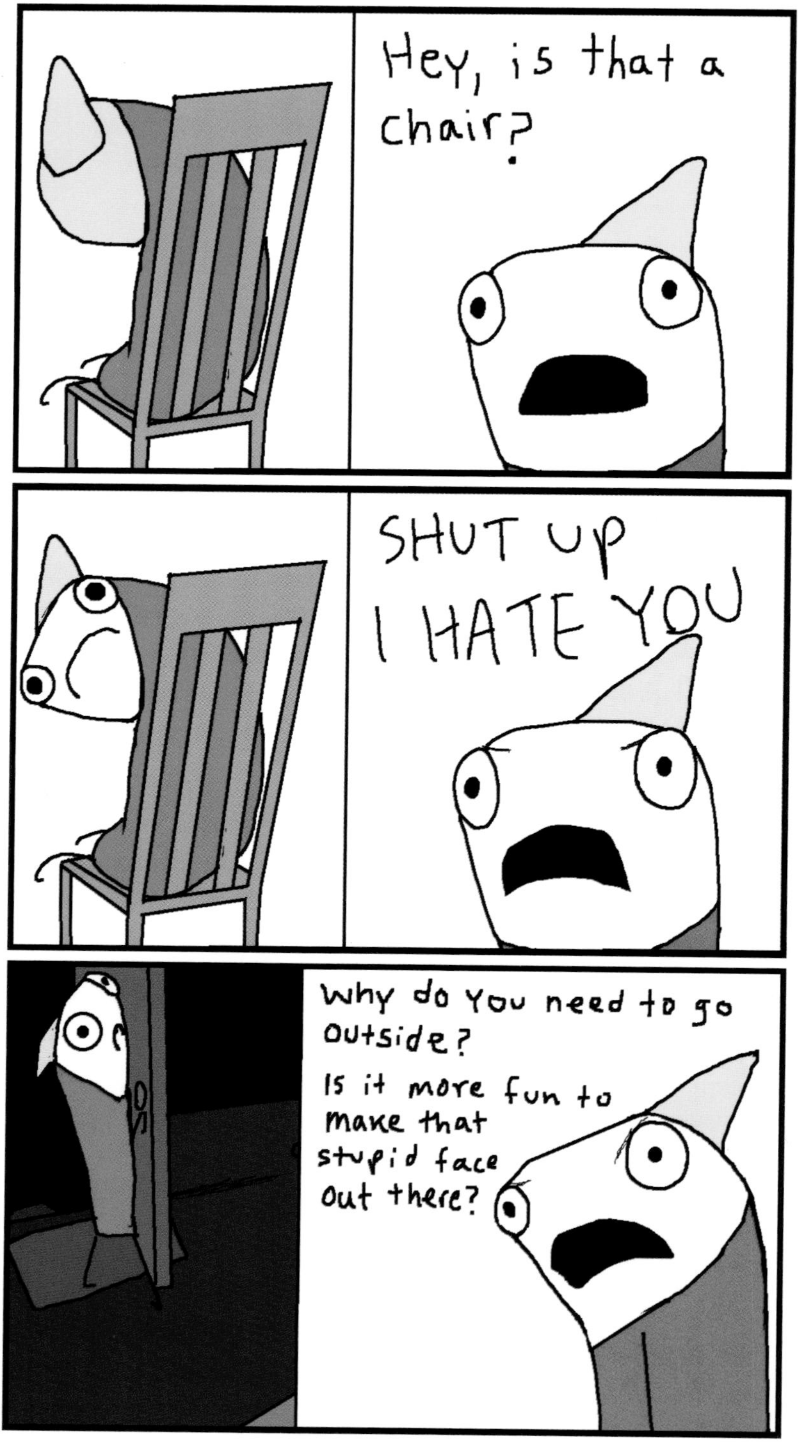
Hey, is that a chair?
SHUT UP
I HATE YOU
Why do You need to go outside?
Is it more fun to make that stupid face out there?

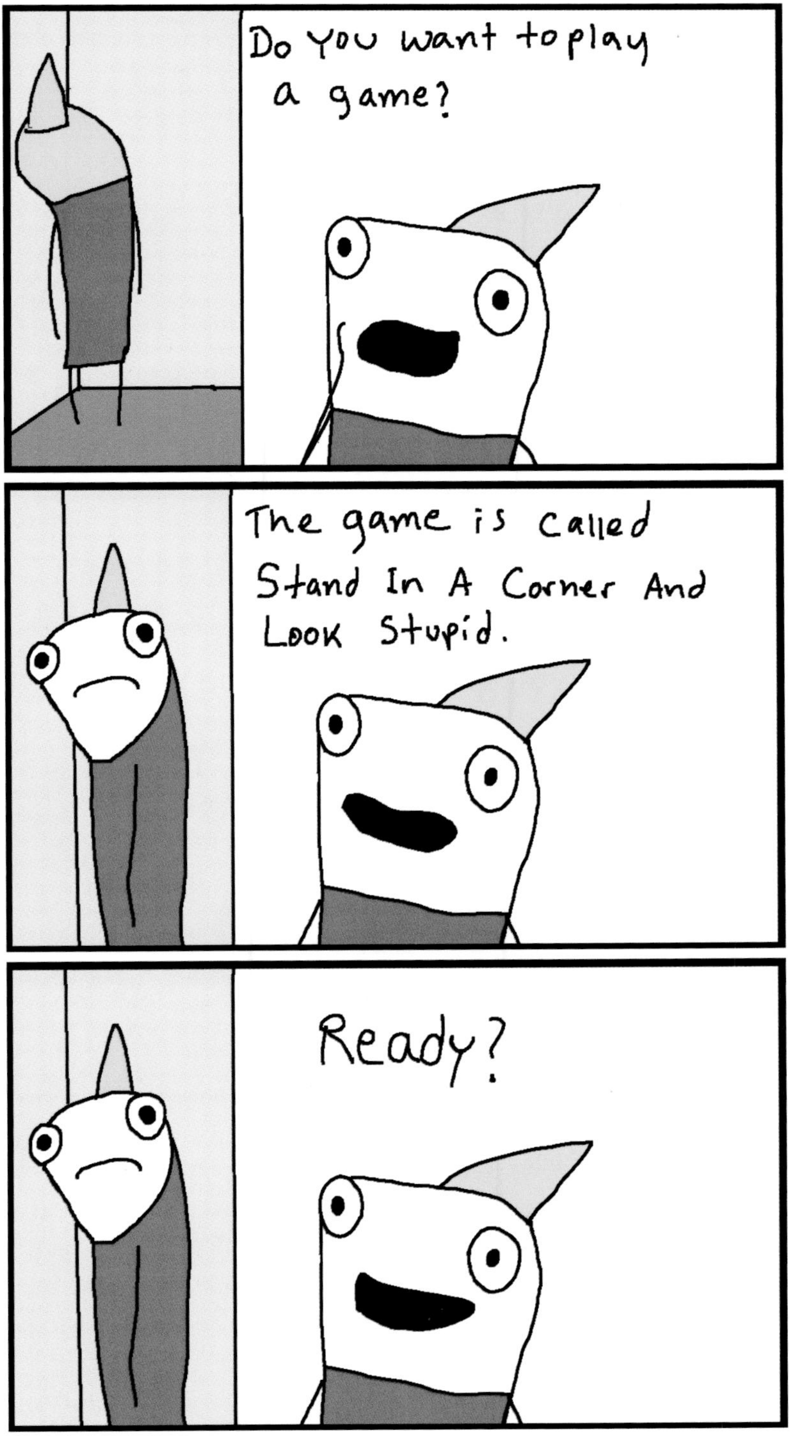
Do you want to play a game?
The game is called Stand In A Corner And Look Stupid.
Ready?

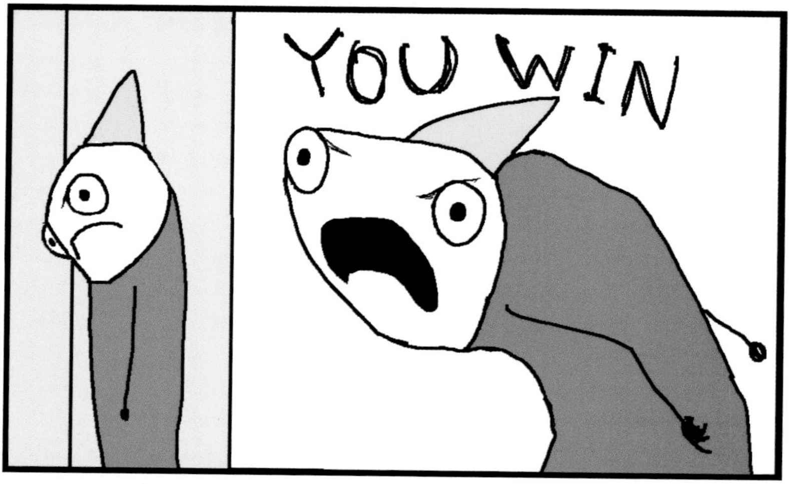
YOU WIN

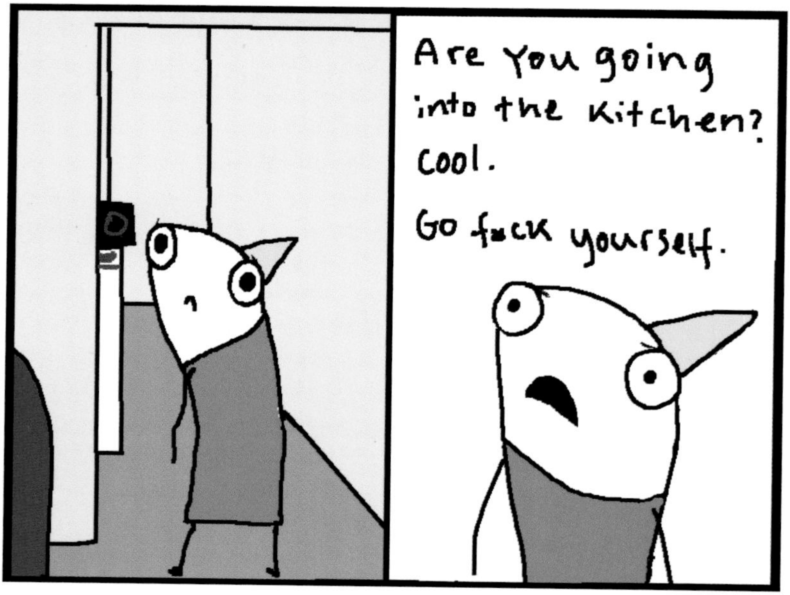
Are you going
into the kitchen?
cool.
Go f*ck yourself.

I spent months shut in my house, surfing the Internet on top of a pile of my own dirty laundry, which I set on the couch for "just a second" because I experienced a sudden moment of apathy on my way to the washer and couldn't continue. And then, two weeks later, I still hadn't completed that journey. But who cares—it wasn't like

I had been showering regularly, and sitting on a pile of clothes isn't necessarily uncomfortable. But even if it was, I couldn't feel anything through the self-hatred anyway, so it didn't matter. *JUST LIKE EVERYTHING ELSE.*

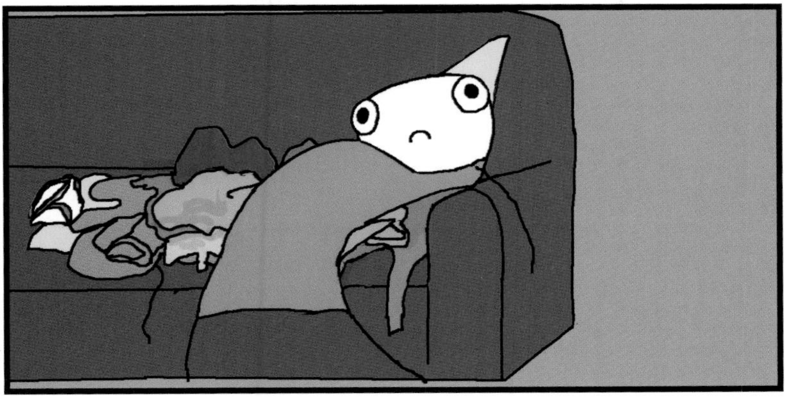

Slowly, my feelings started to shrivel up. The few that managed to survive the constant beatings staggered around like wounded baby deer, just biding their time until they could die and join all the other carcasses strewn across the wasteland of my soul.

I couldn't even muster the enthusiasm to hate myself anymore.

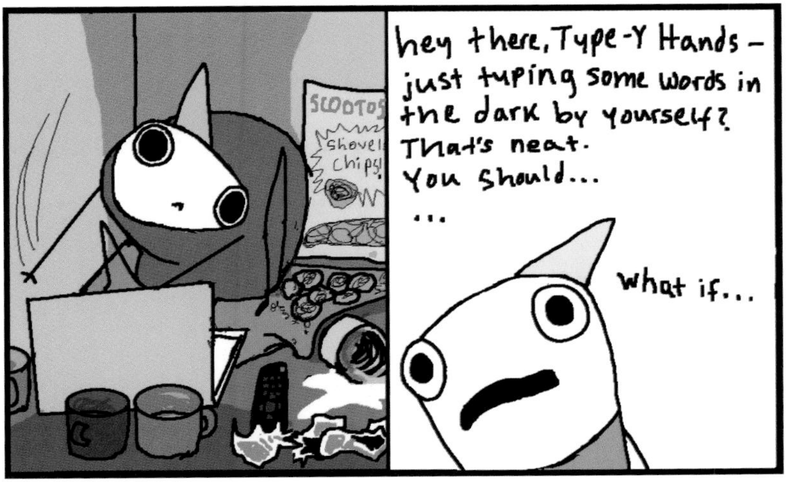
SCOOTOS
Shovel Chips!
hey there, Type-Y Hands – just tuping some words in the dark by yourself? That's neat. You should...
...
what if...

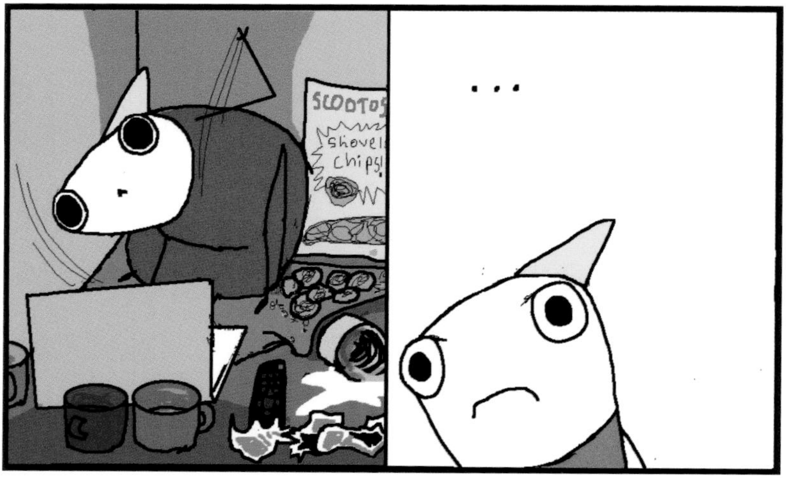

SCOOTOS
shovels chips!
...

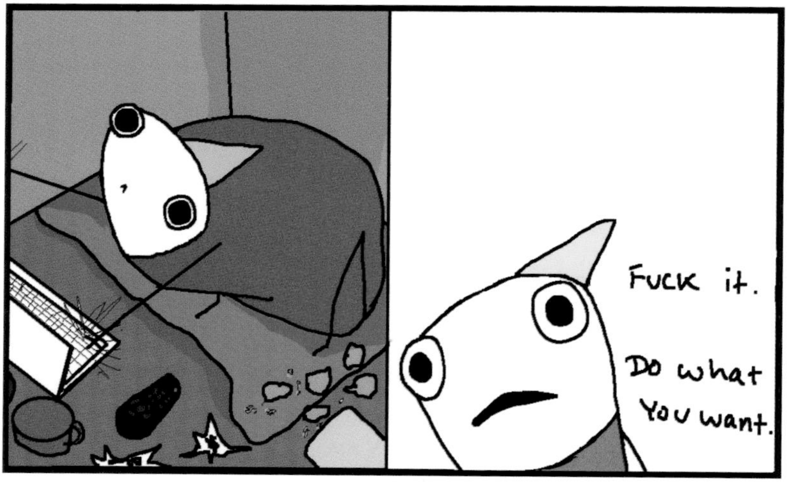

Fuck it.
Do what You want.

I just drifted around, completely unsure of what I was feeling or whether I could actually feel anything at all.

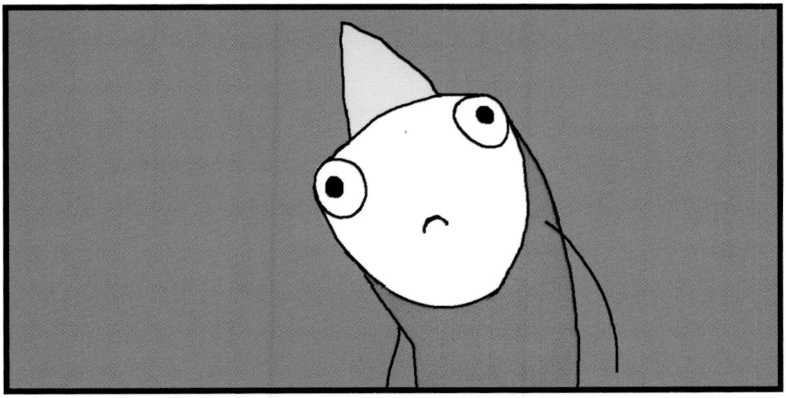

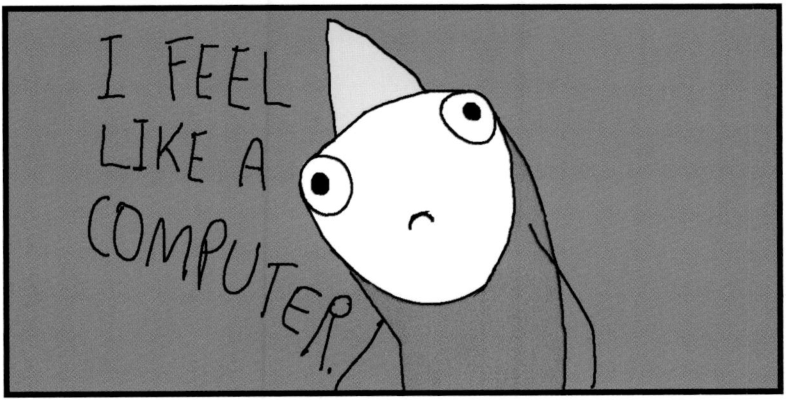
I FEEL LIKE A COMPUTER.

If my life was a movie, the turning point of my depression would have been inspirational and meaningful. It would have involved wisdom-filled epiphanies about discovering my true self and I would conquer my demons and go on to live out the rest of my life in happiness.

Instead, my turning point mostly hinged upon the fact that I had rented some movies and then I didn't return them for too long.

The late fees had reached the point where the injustice of paying any more than I already owed outweighed my apathy. I considered just keeping the movies and never going to the video store again, but then I remembered that I still wanted to rewatch *Jumanji*.

I put on some clothes, put the movies in my backpack, and biked to the video store. It was the slowest, most resentful bike ride ever.

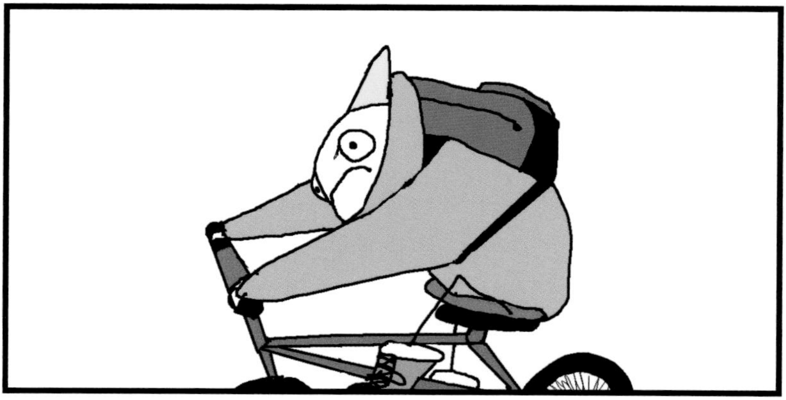

And when I arrived, I found out that they didn't even have *Jumanji* in.

Just as I was debating whether I should settle on a movie that wasn't *Jumanji* or go home and stare in abject silence, I noticed a woman looking at me weirdly from a couple rows over.

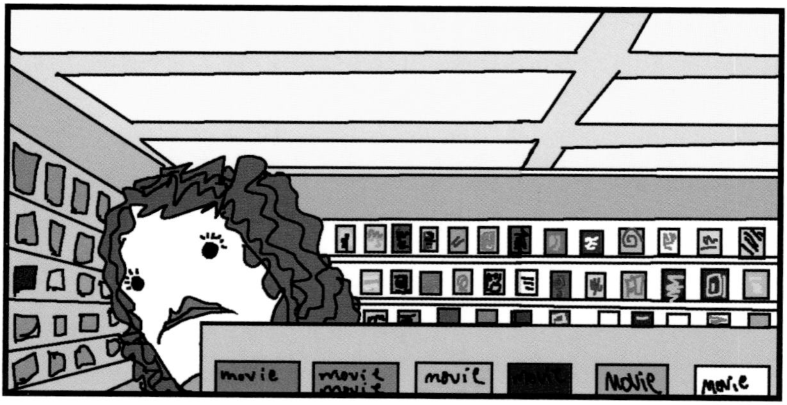
movie
movie
Movie
movie

She was probably looking at me that way because I looked really, really depressed and I was dressed like an Eskimo vagrant.

Normally, I would have felt an instant, crushing sense of self-consciousness, but instead, I felt nothing.

I've always wanted to not give a fuck. While crying helplessly into my pillow for no good reason, I would often fantasize that maybe someday I could be one of those stoic badasses whose emotions are mostly comprised of rock music and not being afraid of things. And finally—*finally*—after a lifetime of feelings and anxiety and more feelings, I didn't have any feelings left. I had spent my last feeling being disappointed that I couldn't rent *Jumanji*.

I felt invincible.

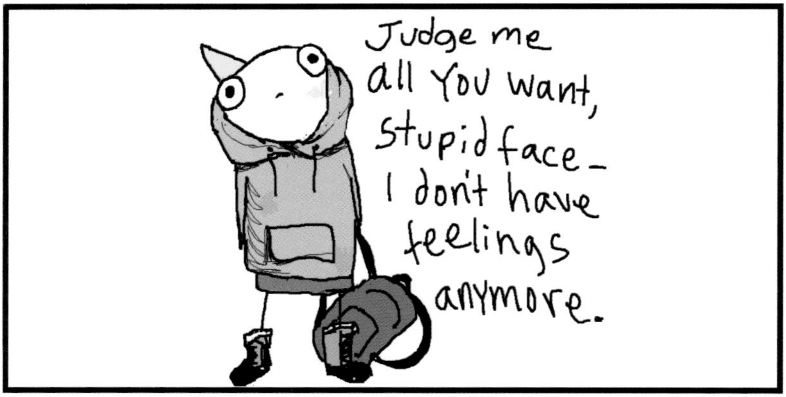
Judge me
all You want,
stupid face–
I don't have
feelings
anymore.

And thus began a tiny rebellion.

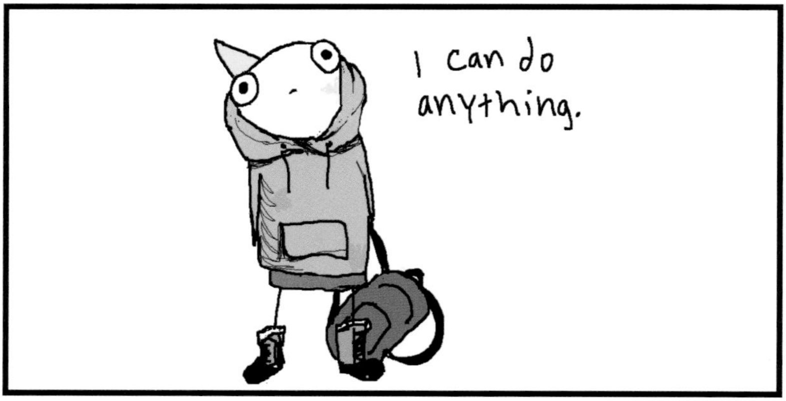
I can do
anything.

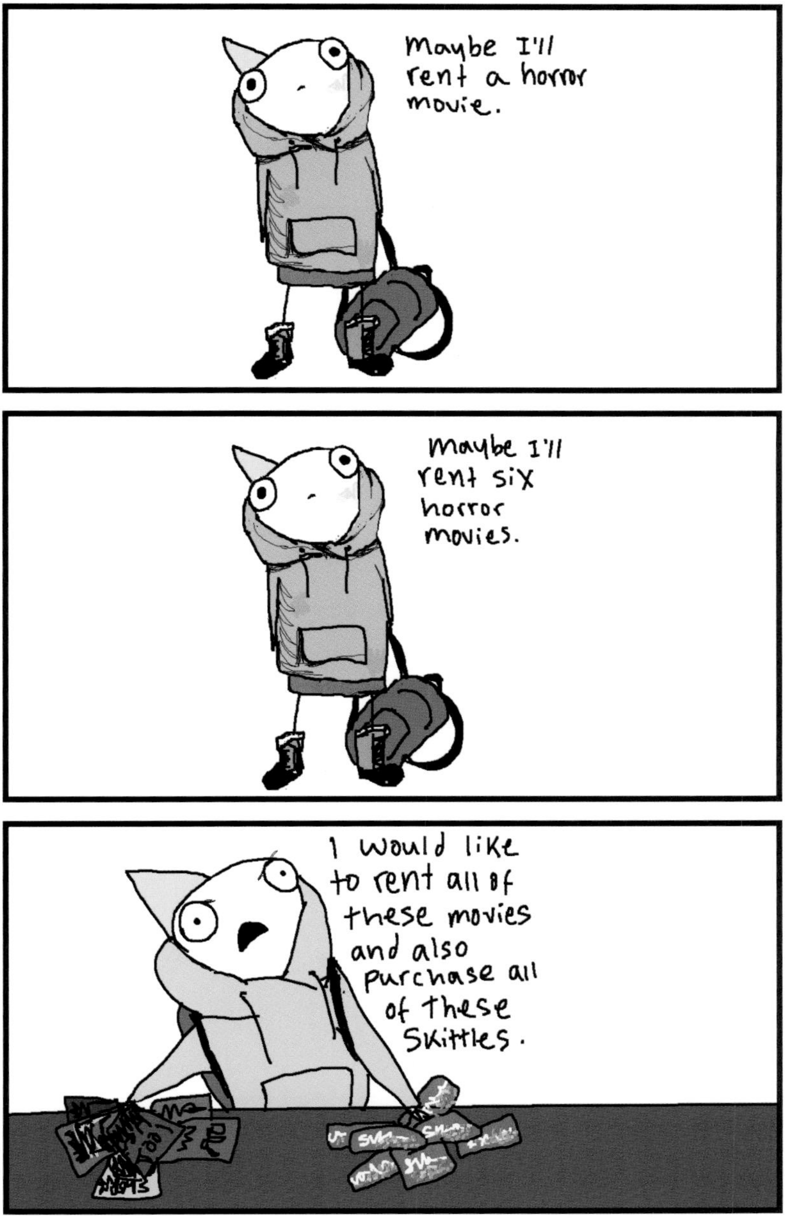
Maybe I'll rent a horror movie.
Maybe I'll rent six horror movies.
I would like to rent all of these movies and also purchase all of these Skittles.

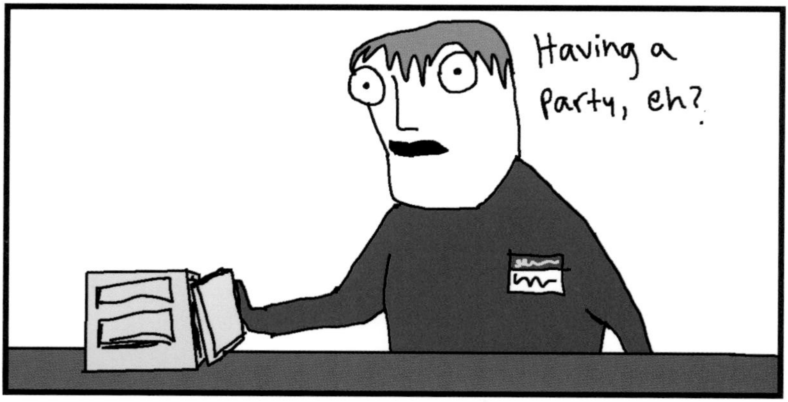
Having a party, eh?

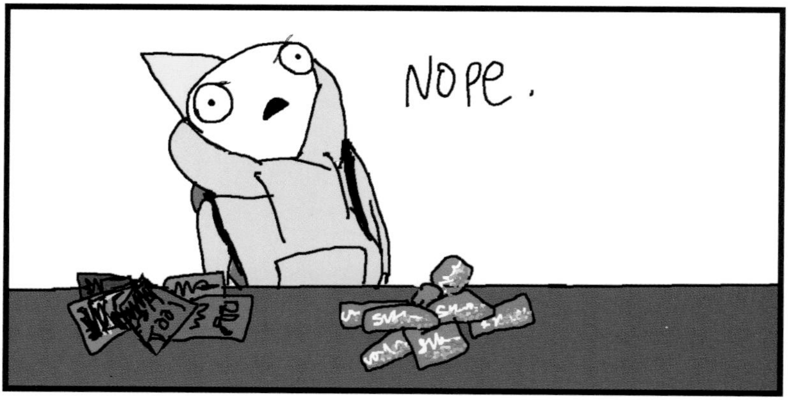
NOPE.

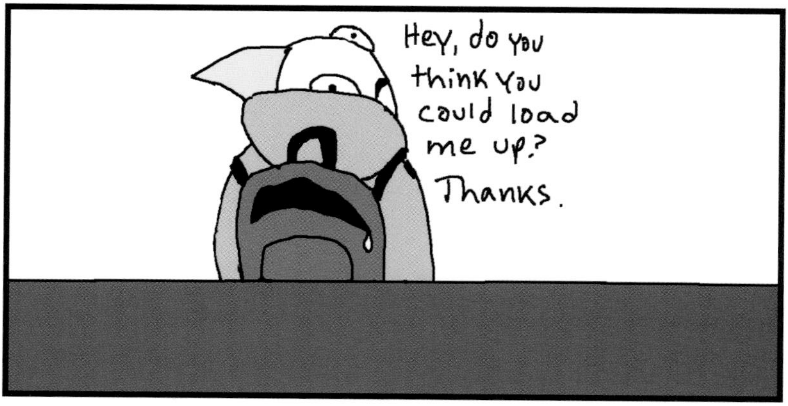
Hey, do you think you could load me up? Thanks.

Then I swooped out of there like the Batman and biked home in a blaze of defiant glory.

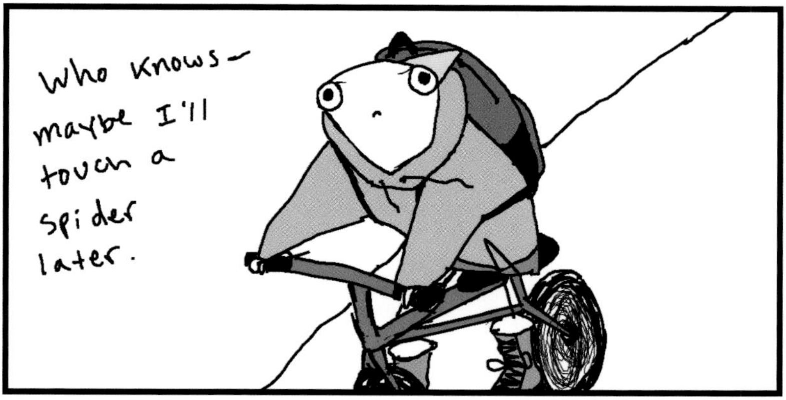
Who knows—
maybe I'll
touch a
spider
later.

And that's how my depression got so horrible that it actually broke through to the other side and became a sort of fear-proof exoskeleton.

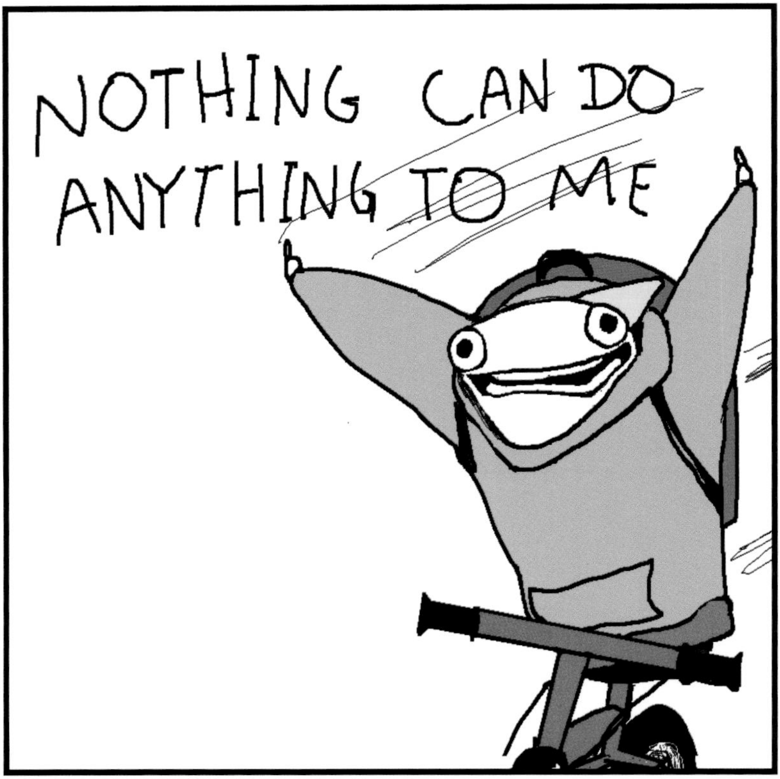
NOTHING CAN DO ANYTHING TO ME

Depression Part Two

I remember being endlessly entertained by the adventures of my toys. Some days they died repeated, violent deaths; other days they traveled to space or discussed my swim lessons and how I absolutely should be allowed in the deep end of the pool, especially since I was such a talented doggy-paddler.

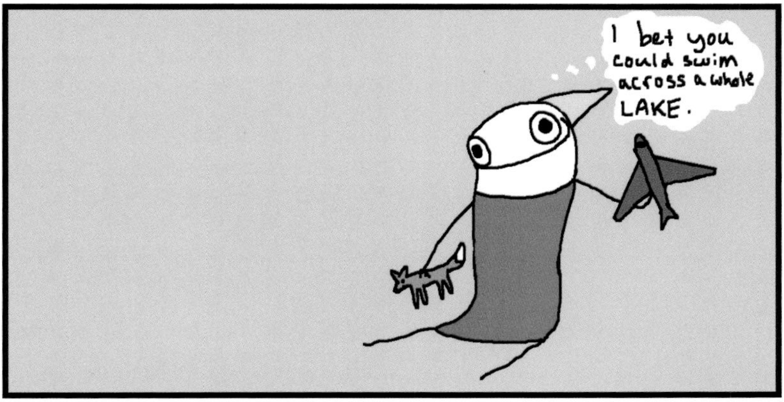
I bet you could swim across a whole LAKE.

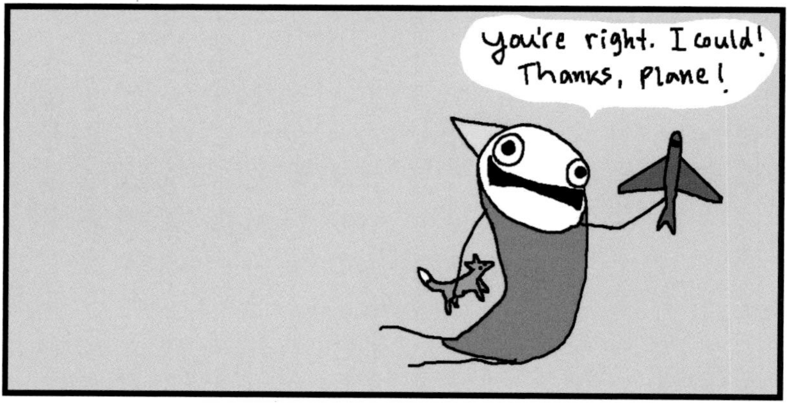
You're right. I could! Thanks, Plane!

I didn't understand why it was fun for me, it just was.

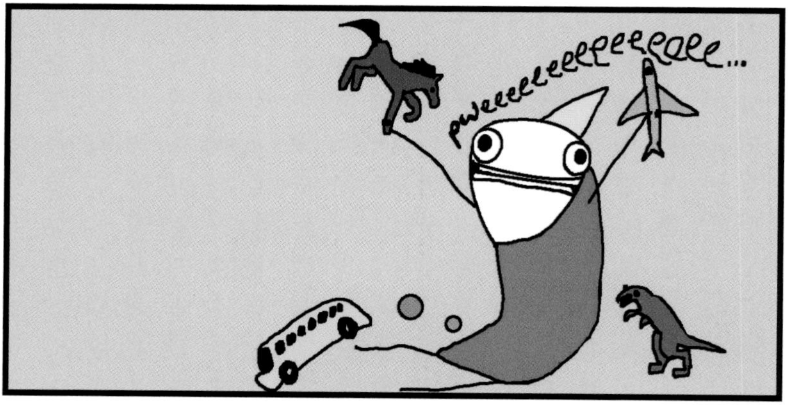
pweeeeeeeeeeeeeeee...

But as I grew older, it became harder and harder to access that expansive imaginary space that made my toys fun. I remember looking at them and feeling sort of frustrated and confused that things weren't the same.

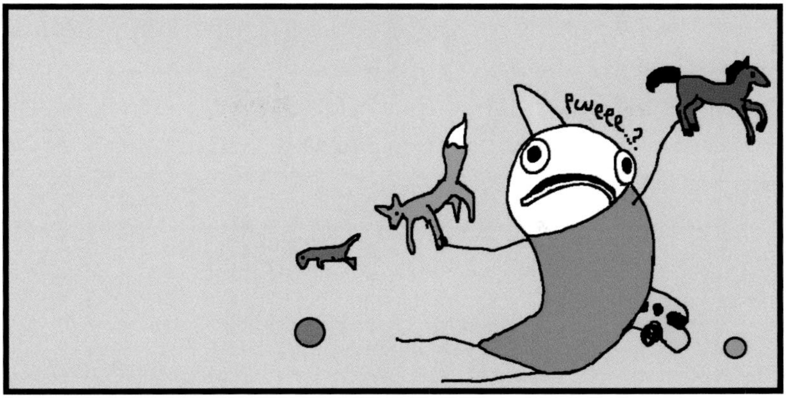
Pweee..?

I played out all the same story lines that had been fun before, but the meaning had disappeared. Horse's Big Space Adventure transformed into holding a plastic horse in the air, hoping it would somehow be enjoyable for me. Prehistoric Crazy-Bus Death Ride was just smashing a toy bus full of dinosaurs into the wall while feeling sort of bored and unfulfilled. I could no longer connect to my toys in a way that allowed me to participate in the experience.

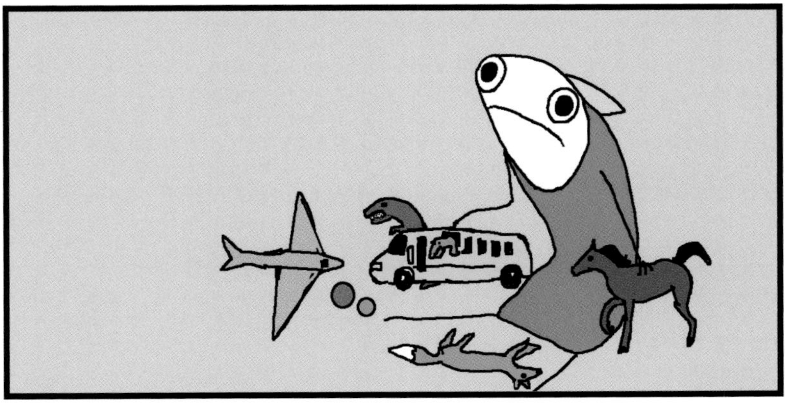

The second half of my depression felt almost exactly like that, except about everything.

At first, though, the invulnerability that accompanied the detachment was exhilarating. At least as exhilarating as something can be without involving real emotions.

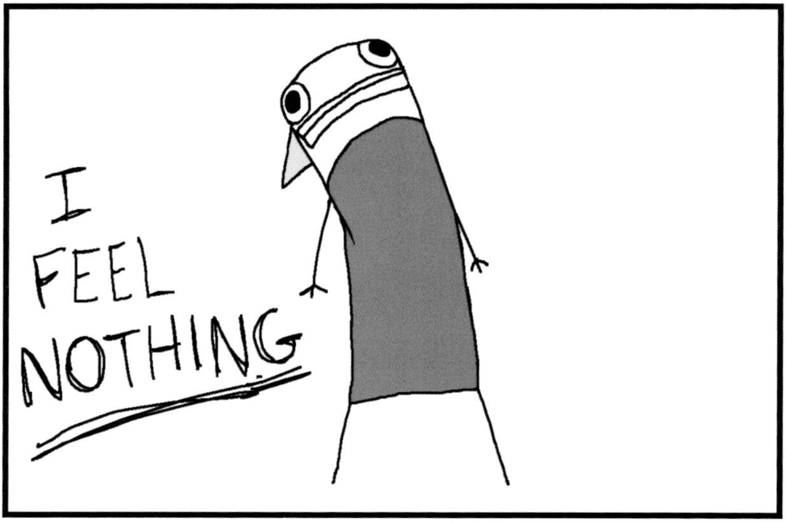
I FEEL NOTHING

The beginning of my depression had been nothing *but* feelings, so the emotional deadening that followed was a welcome relief. I had always viewed feelings as a weakness—annoying obstacles on my quest for total power over myself. And I finally didn't have to feel them anymore.

But my experiences slowly flattened and blended together until it became obvious that there's a huge difference between not giving a fuck and not being *able* to give a fuck. Cognitively, you might know that different things are happening to you, but they don't feel very different.

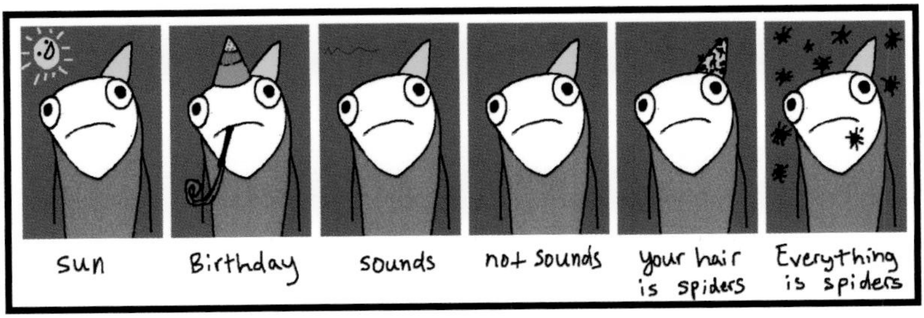
sun
Birthday
sounds
not sounds
your hair is spiders
Everything is spiders

Which leads to horrible, soul-decaying boredom.

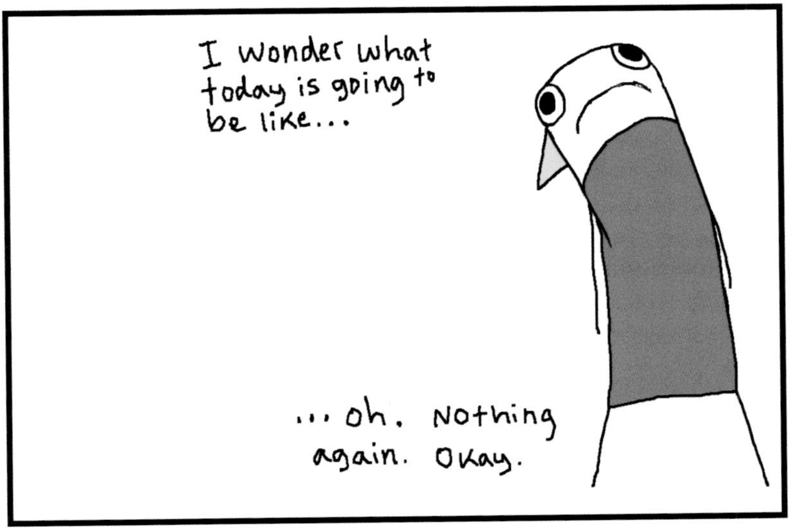
I wonder what today is going to be like...
...oh. Nothing again. Okay.

I tried to get out more, but most fun activities just left me existentially confused or frustrated with my inability to enjoy them.

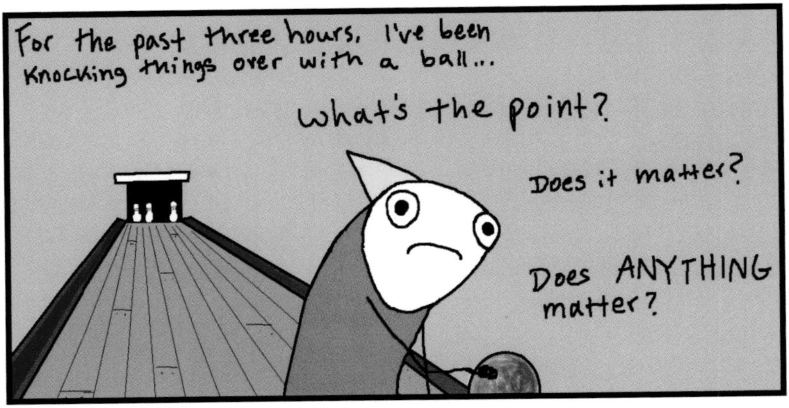
For the past three hours, I've been knocking things over with a ball...
What's the point?
Does it matter?
Does ANYTHING matter?

Months oozed by, and I gradually came to accept that maybe enjoyment was not a thing I got to feel anymore. I didn't want anyone to know, though. I was still sort of uncomfortable about how bored and detached I felt around other people, and I was still holding out hope that the whole thing would spontaneously work itself out. As long as I could manage to not alienate anyone, everything might be okay!

However, I could no longer rely on genuine emotion to generate facial expressions, and when you have to spend every social interaction consciously manipulating your face into shapes that are only approximately the right ones, alienating people is inevitable.

So I did that triathlon...
how do you make the face for "yay"?
Am I doing it?
I hope I'm doing it.
Yeah, some guy had a heart attack and drowned!
uh oh... SAD FACE
SAD FACE

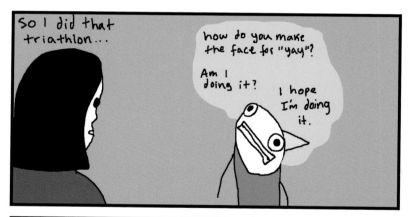

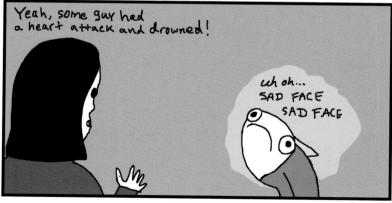

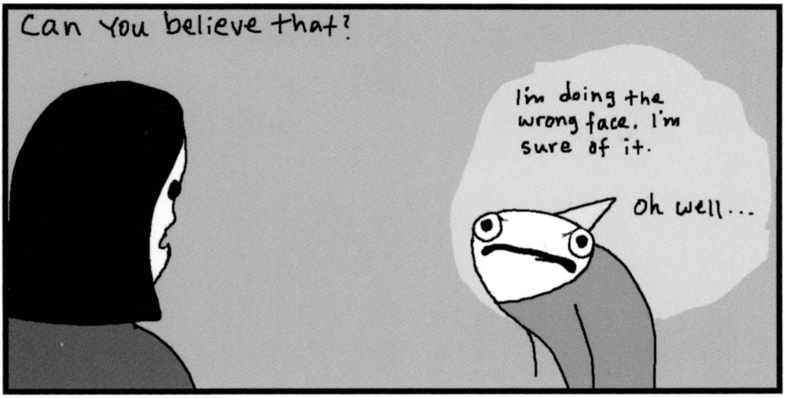
Can you believe that?
I'm doing the wrong face. I'm sure of it.
Oh well...

Everyone noticed.

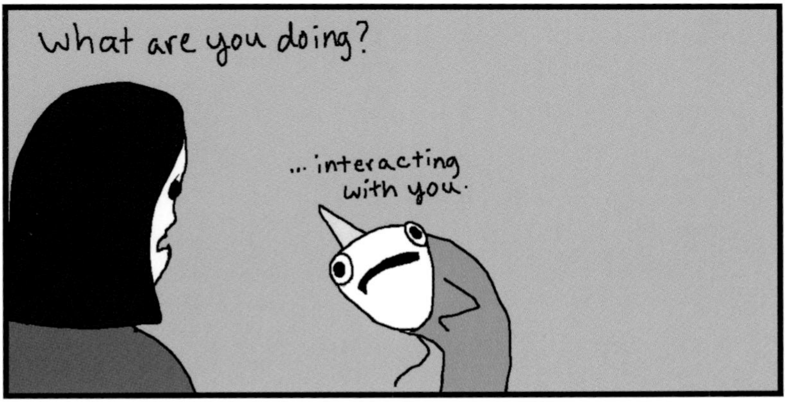
What are you doing?
... interacting with you.

It's weird for people who still have feelings to be around depressed people. They try to help you have feelings again so things can go back to normal, and it's frustrating for them when that doesn't happen. From their perspective, it seems like there has *got* to be some untapped source of happiness within you that you've simply lost track of, and if you could just see how beautiful things are . . .

you should do yoga while watching the sunrise. It's literally impossible to feel negative and sad while appreciating the wonder of the universe.

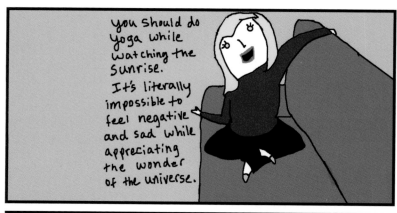

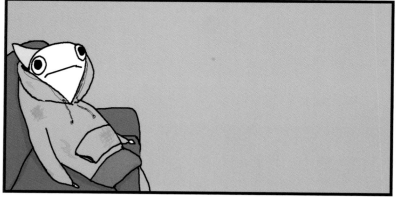

At first, I'd try to explain that it's not really negativity or sadness anymore, it's more just this detached, meaningless fog where you can't feel anything about anything—even the things you love, even fun things—and you're horribly bored and lonely, but since you've lost your ability to connect with any of the things that would normally make you feel less bored and lonely, you're stuck in the boring, lonely, meaningless void without anything to distract you from how boring, lonely, and meaningless it is.

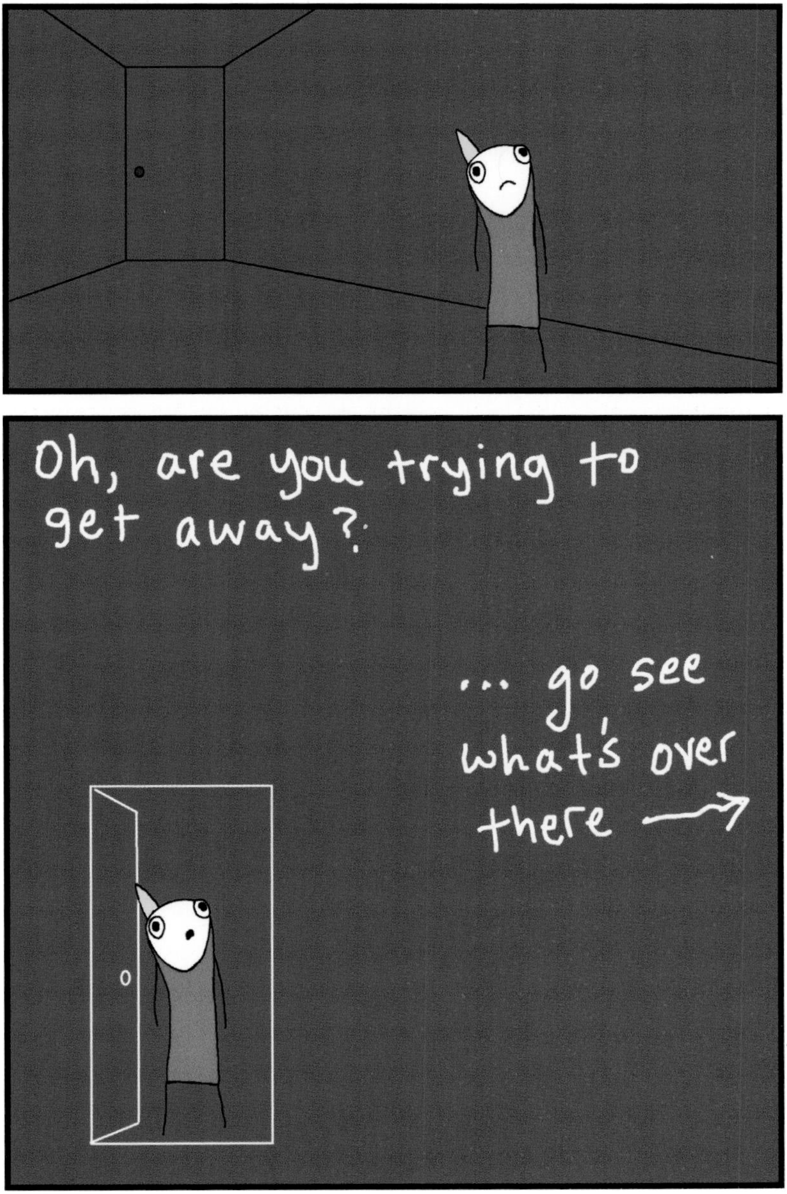
Oh, are you trying to get away?
... go see what's over there

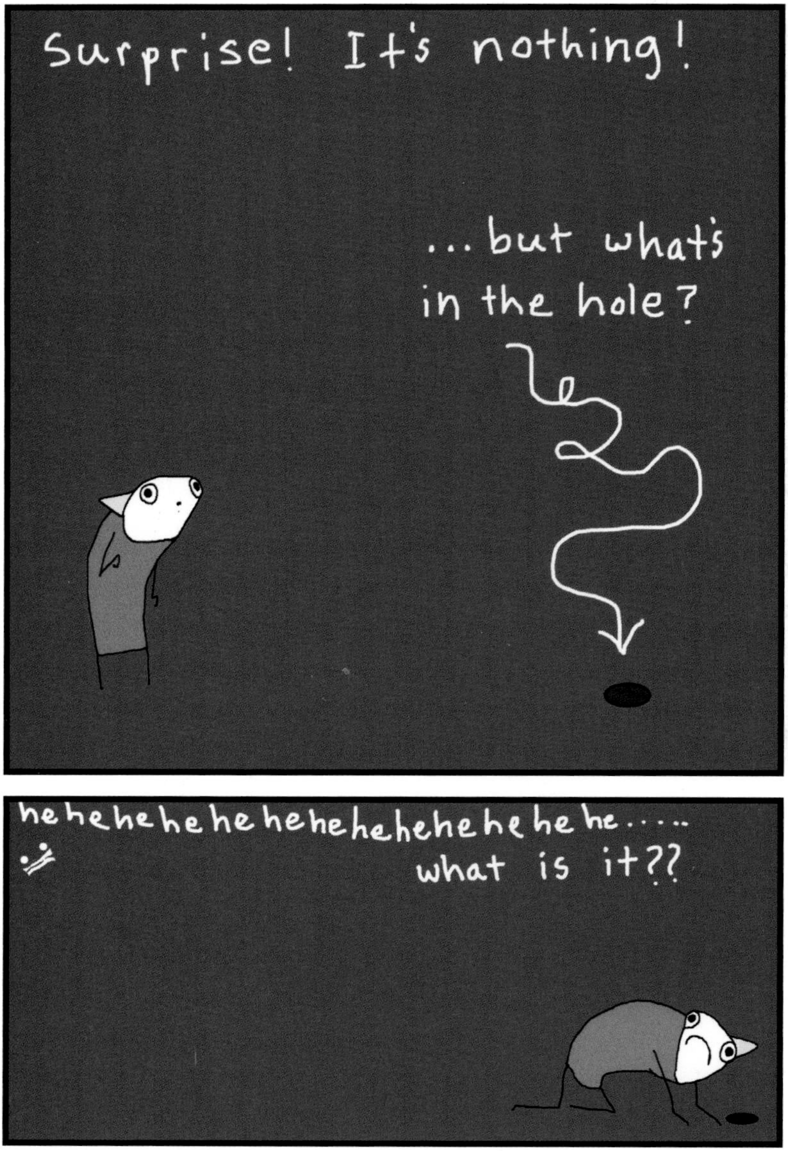
Surprise! It's nothing!
...but what's in the hole?
hehehehehehehehehehehehehehehe.....
what is it??

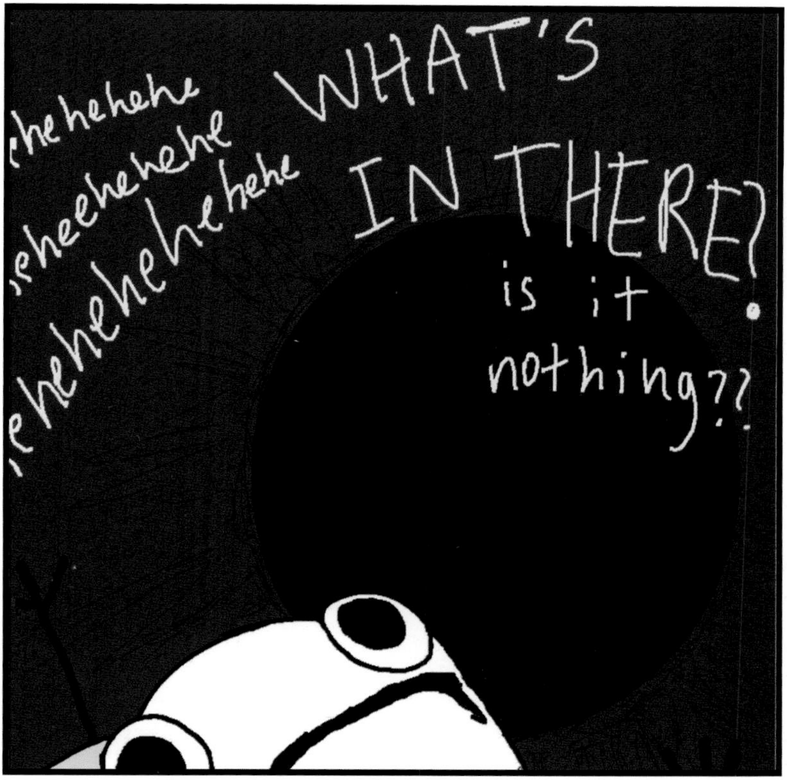
hehehehe
hehehehehe
hehehehehehehe
hehehe
WHAT'S IN THERE?
is it nothing??

But people want to help. So they try harder to make you feel hopeful and positive about the situation. You explain it again, hoping they'll try a less hope-centric approach, but re-explaining your total inability to experience joy inevitably sounds kind of negative, like maybe you WANT to be depressed. So the positivity starts coming out in a spray—a giant, desperate happiness sprinkler pointed directly at your face. And it keeps going like that until you're having this weird argument where you're trying to convince the person that you are far too hopeless for hope so that they'll give up on their optimism crusade and let you go back to feeling bored and lonely by yourself.

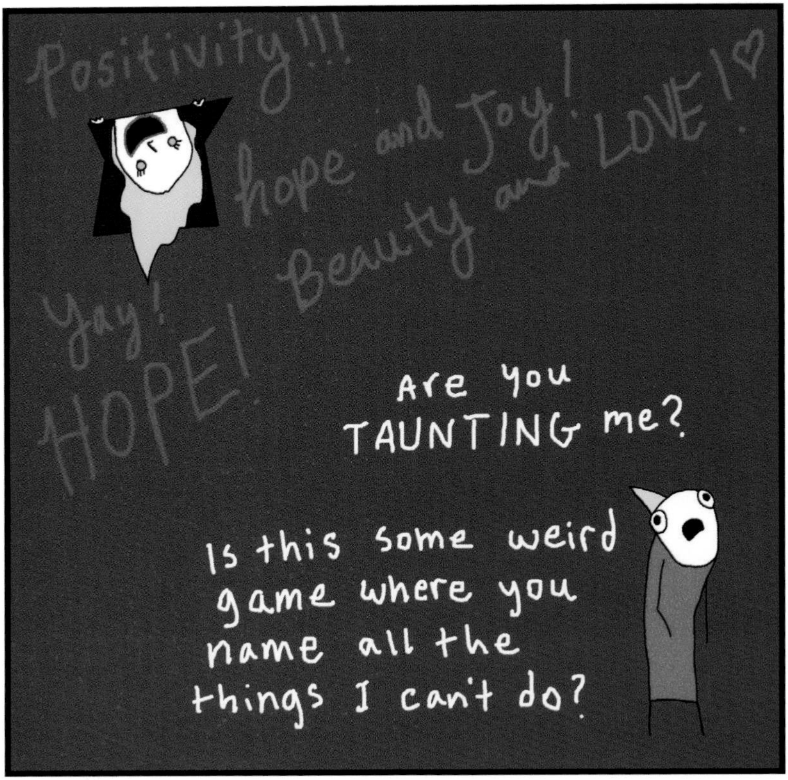
Positivity!!!
hope and Joy!
Beauty and LOVE!
Yay!
HOPE!
Are you TAUNTING me?
Is this some weird game where you name all the things I can't do?

And that's the most frustrating thing about depression. It isn't always something you can fight back against with hope. It isn't even something—it's nothing. And you can't combat nothing. You can't fill it up. You can't cover it. It's just there, pulling the meaning out of everything. That being the case, all the hopeful, proactive solutions start to sound completely insane in contrast to the scope of the problem.

It would be like having a bunch of dead fish, but no one around you will acknowledge that the fish are dead. Instead, they offer to help you look for the fish or try to help you figure out why they disappeared.

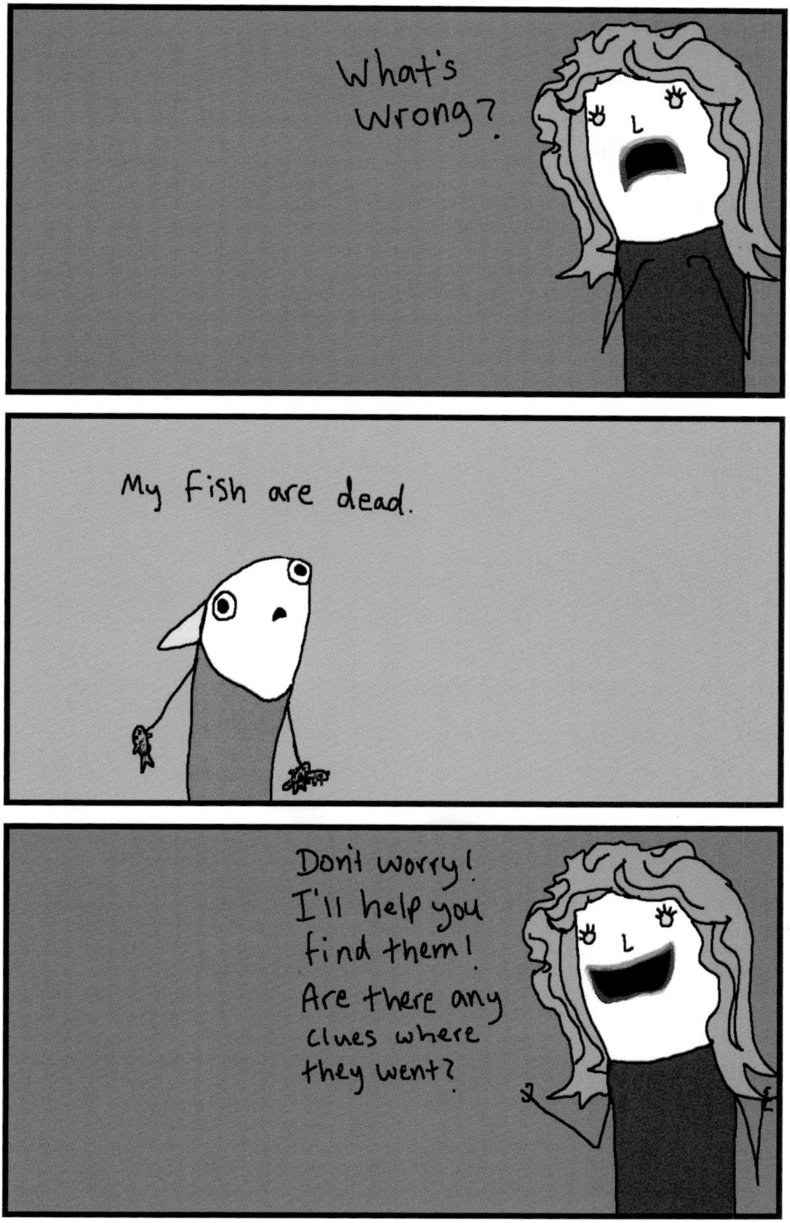
What's wrong?
My fish are dead.
Don't worry! I'll help you find them! Are there any clues where they went?

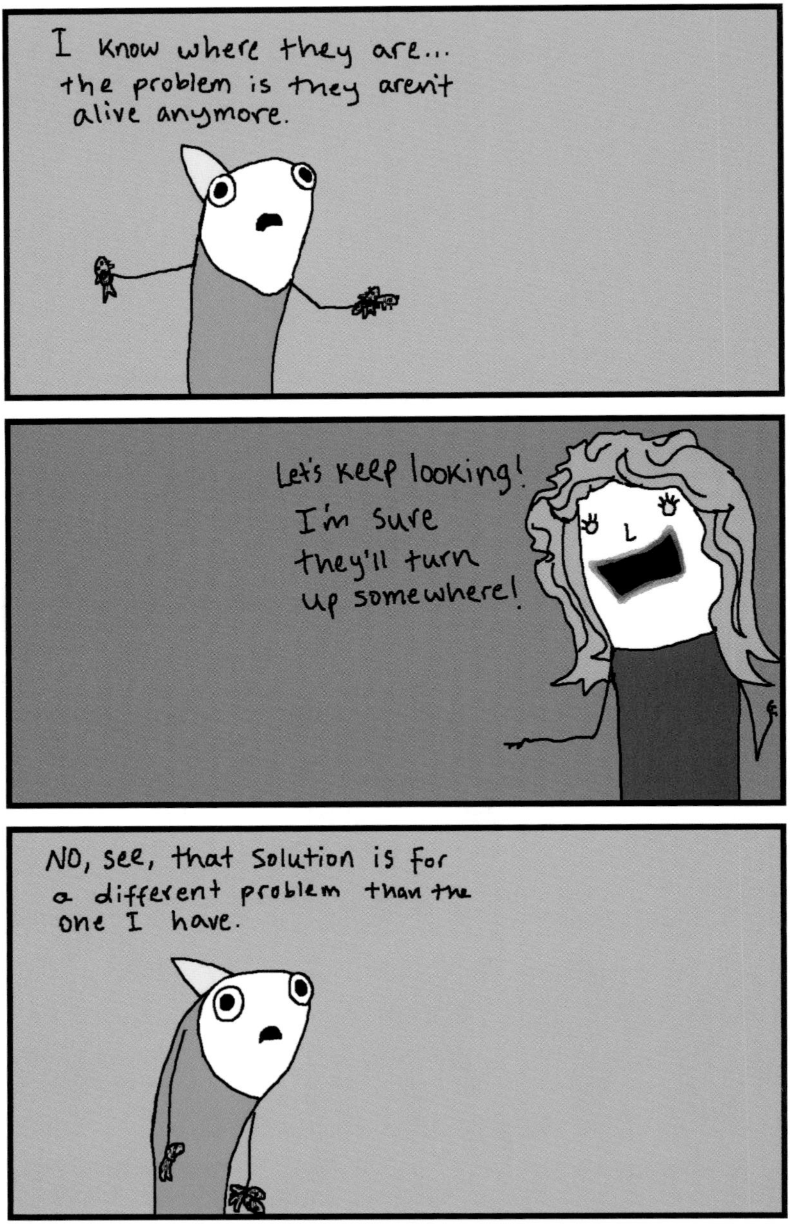
I know where they are...
the problem is they aren't
alive anymore.
Let's keep looking!
I'm sure
they'll turn
up somewhere!
NO, see, that solution is for
a different problem than the
one I have.

The problem might not even *have* a solution. But you aren't necessarily looking for solutions. You're maybe just looking for someone to say "Sorry about how dead your fish are," or "Wow, those are super dead. I still like you, though."

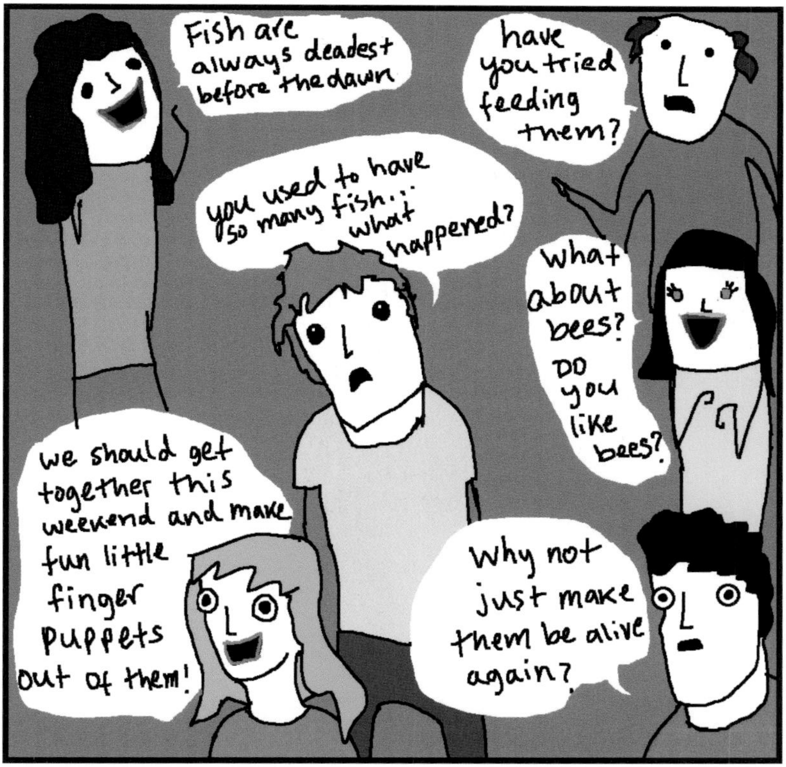
Fish are always deadest before the dawn
have you tried feeding them?
you used to have so many fish... what happened?
what about bees? DO you like bees?
we should get together this weekend and make fun little finger puppets out of them!
Why not just make them be alive again?

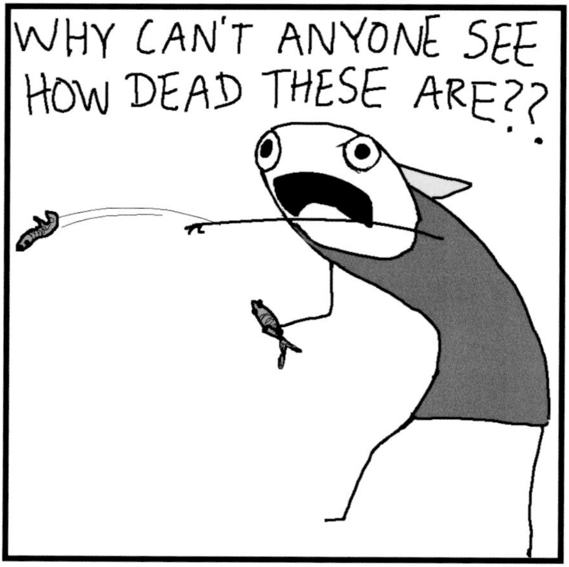
WHY CAN'T ANYONE SEE HOW DEAD THESE ARE??

I started spending more time alone.

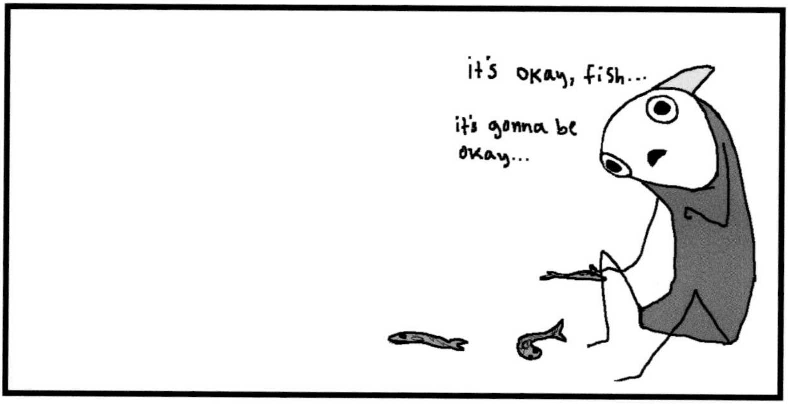
it's okay, fish...
it's gonna be okay...

Perhaps it was because I lacked the emotional depth necessary to panic, or maybe my predicament didn't feel dramatic enough to make me suspicious, but I somehow managed to convince myself that everything was still under my control right up until I noticed myself wishing that nothing loved me so I wouldn't feel obligated to keep existing.

YOU R SO bRUETiFUL... how R U SO BRUTEFUL and good?

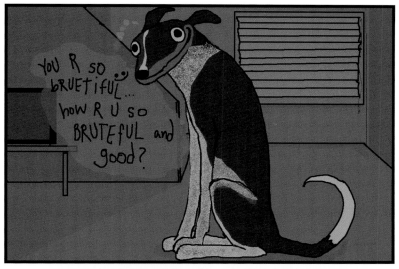

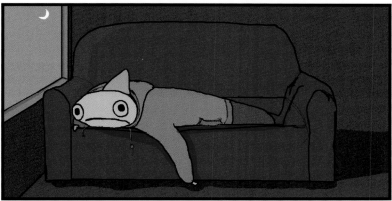

It's a strange moment when you realize that you don't want to be alive anymore. If I had feelings, I'm sure I would have felt surprised. I have spent the vast majority of my life actively attempting to survive. Ever since my most distant single-celled ancestor squiggled into existence, there has been an unbroken chain of things that wanted to stick around.

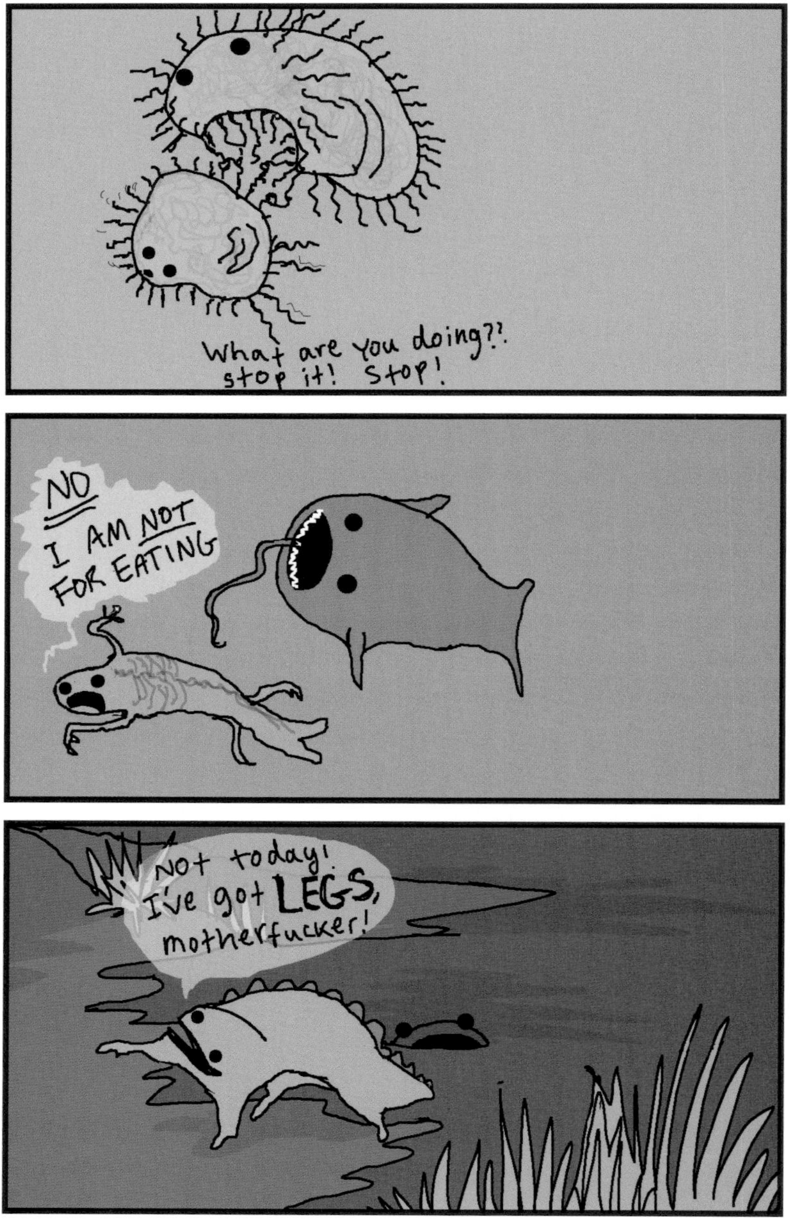
What are you doing??.
stop it! Stop!
NO
I AM NOT FOR EATING
Not today! I've got LEGS, motherfucker!

Yet there I was, casually wishing that I could stop existing in the same way you'd want to leave an empty room or mute an unbearably repetitive noise.

That wasn't the worst part, though. The worst part was deciding to keep going.

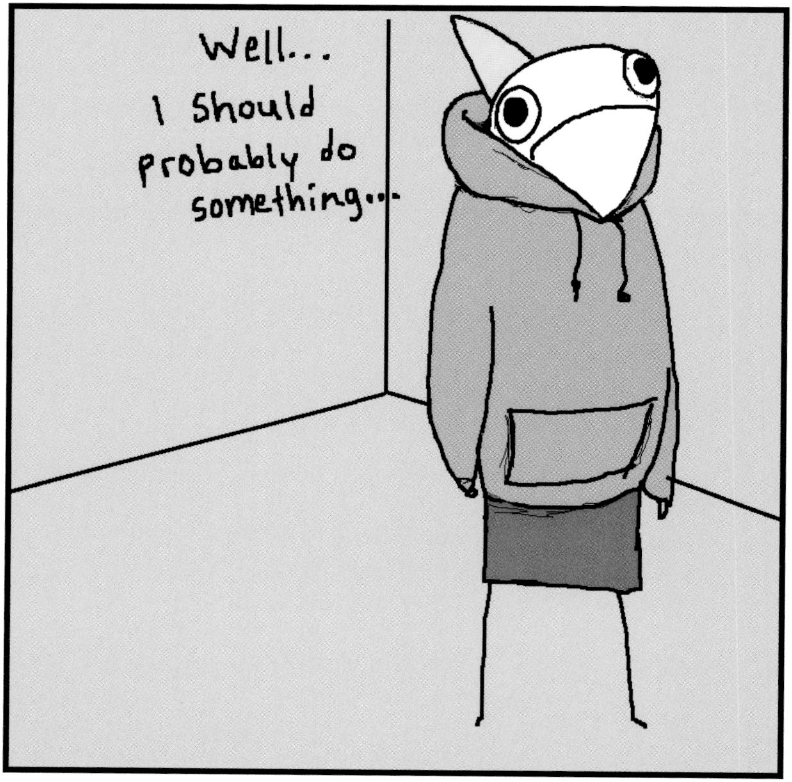
Well...
I should
probably do
something...

When I say that deciding to not kill myself was the worst part, I should clarify that I don't mean it in a retrospective sense. From where I am now, it seems like a solid enough decision. But at the time, it felt like I had been dragging myself through the most miserable, endless wasteland, and—far in the distance—I had seen the promising glimmer of a slightly less miserable wasteland. And for just a moment, I thought maybe I'd be able to stop and rest. But as soon as I arrived at the border of the less miserable wasteland, I found out that I'd have to turn around and walk back the other way.

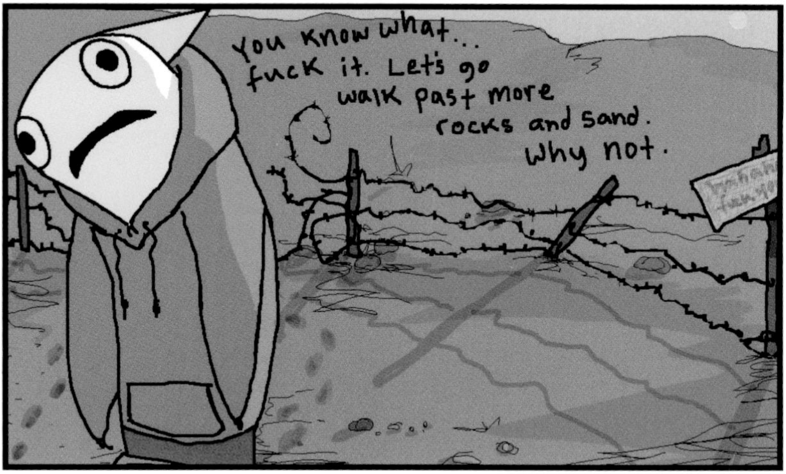
you know what... fuck it. Let's go walk past more rocks and sand. Why not.

Soon afterward, I discovered that there's no tactful or comfortable way to inform other people that you might be suicidal. And there's definitely no way to ask for help casually.

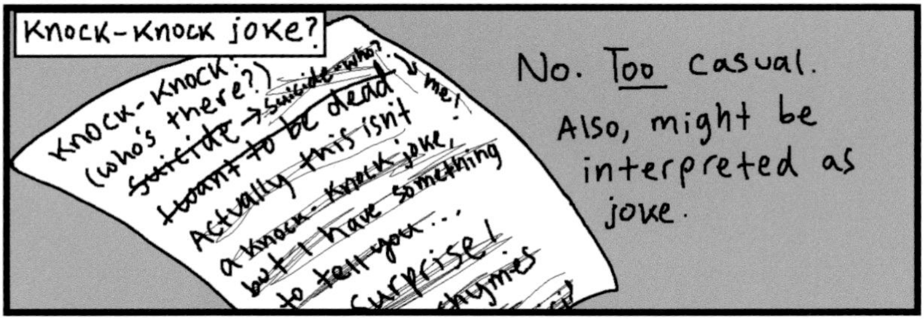
Knock-Knock joke?
Knock-Knock!
(who's there?)
~~Suicide~~ → ~~Suicide who?~~ → me!
~~I want to be dead~~
~~Actually this isn't a Knock-Knock joke, but I have something to tell you...~~
~~surprise!~~
~~rhymes~~
No. Too casual.
Also, might be interpreted as joke.

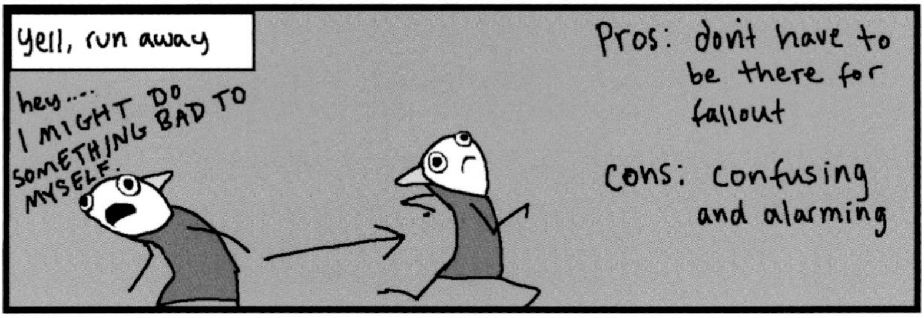
yell, run away
hey.... I MIGHT DO SOMETHING BAD TO MYSELF.
Pros: don't have to be there for fallout
Cons: confusing and alarming

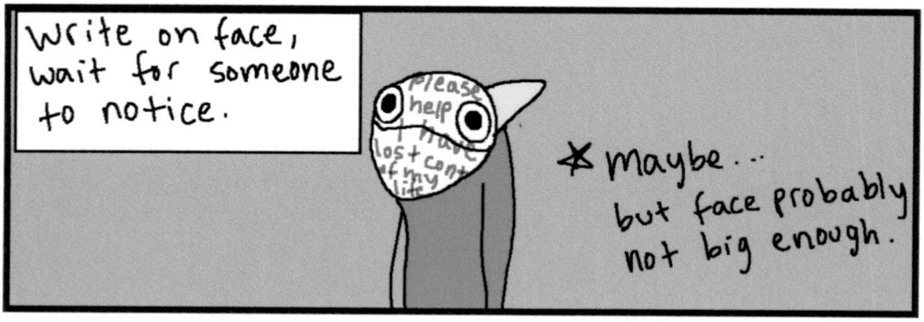
Write on face, wait for someone to notice.
please help
*maybe... but face probably not big enough.

I didn't want it to be a big deal. However, it's an alarming subject. Trying to be nonchalant about it just makes it weird for everyone.

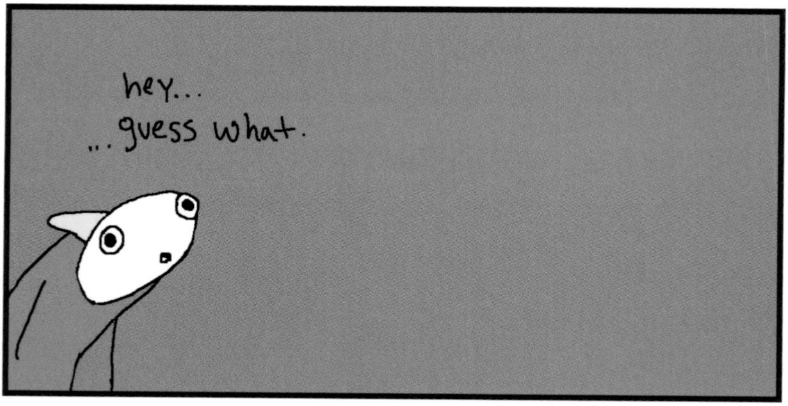
hey...
...guess what.

I was also extremely ill-prepared for the position of comforting people. The things that seemed reassuring to me at the time weren't necessarily comforting for others.

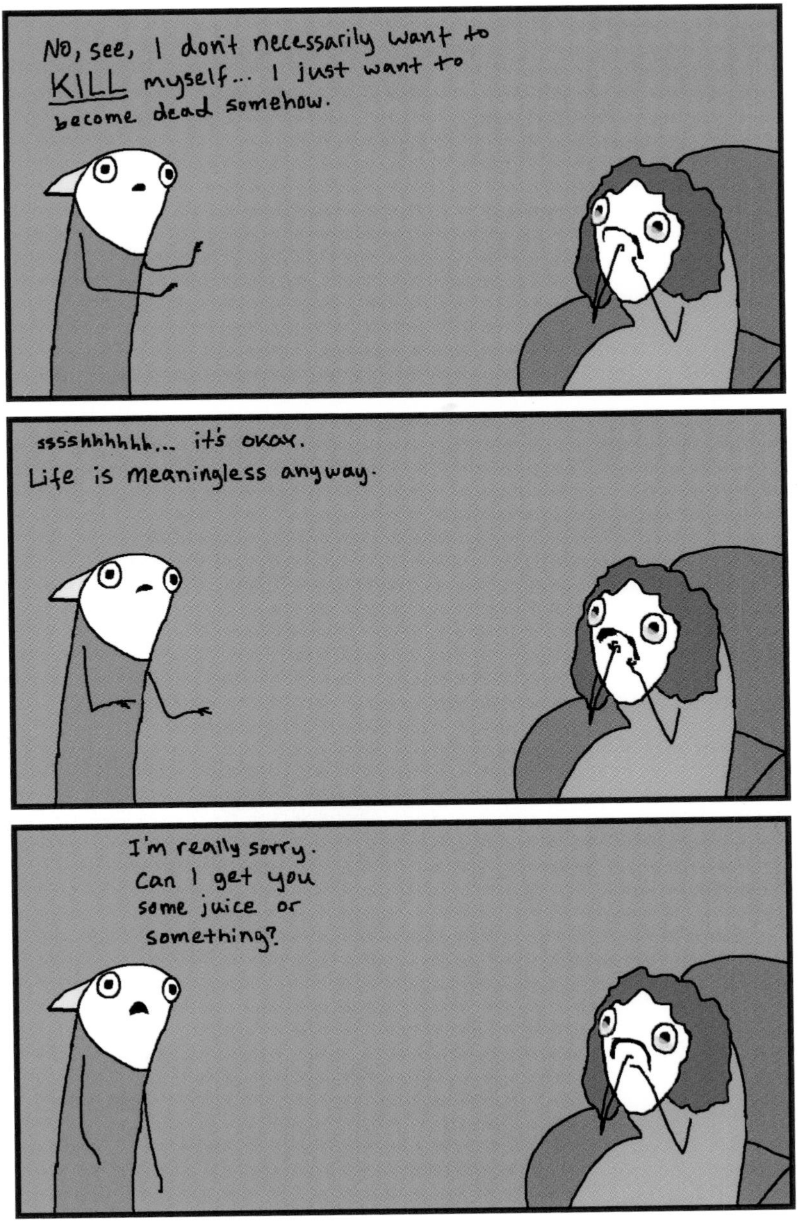
No, see, I don't necessarily want to KILL myself... I just want to become dead somehow.
sssshhhhhh... it's okay. Life is meaningless anyway.
I'm really sorry. Can I get you some juice or something?

I had so very few feelings, and everyone else had so many, and it felt like they were having all of them in front of me at once. I didn't really know what to do, so I agreed to see a doctor so that everyone would stop having all of their feelings at me.

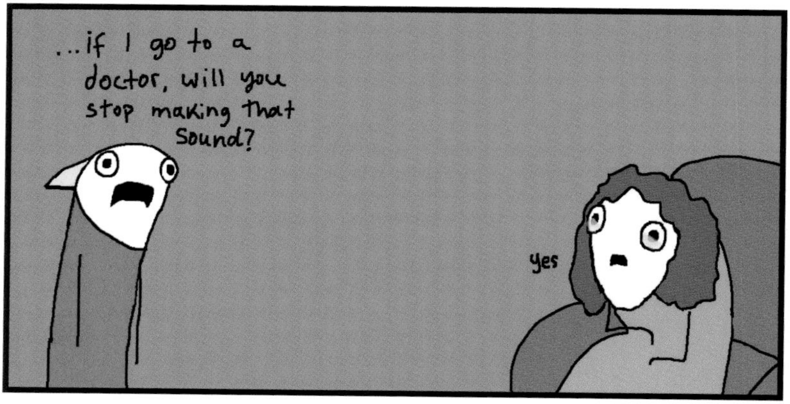
...if I go to a doctor, will you stop making that sound?
yes

The next few weeks were a haze of talking to relentlessly hopeful people about my feelings that didn't exist so I could be prescribed medication that might help me have them again.

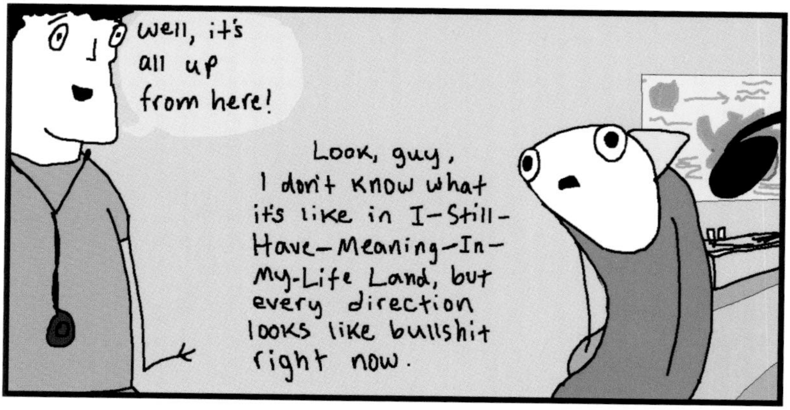
well, it's all up from here!
Look, guy, I don't know what it's like in I-Still-Have-Meaning-In-My-Life Land, but every direction looks like bullshit right now.

And every direction WAS bullshit for a really long time, especially up. The absurdity of working so hard to continue doing something you don't like can be overwhelming. And the longer it takes to feel different, the more it starts to seem like everything might *actually* be hopeless bullshit.

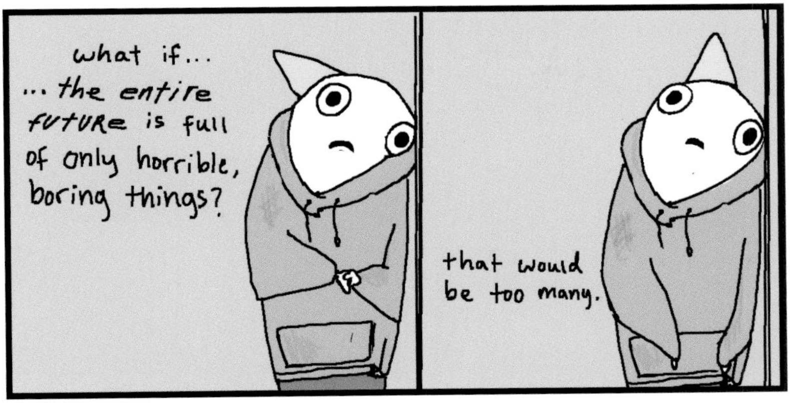
what if...
... the entire FUTURE is full of only horrible, boring things?
that would be too many.

My feelings did start to return eventually. But not all of them came back, and they didn't arrive symmetrically.

I had not been able to care for a very long time, and when I finally started being able to care about things again, I HATED them. But hatred is technically a feeling, and my brain latched on to it like a child learning a new word.

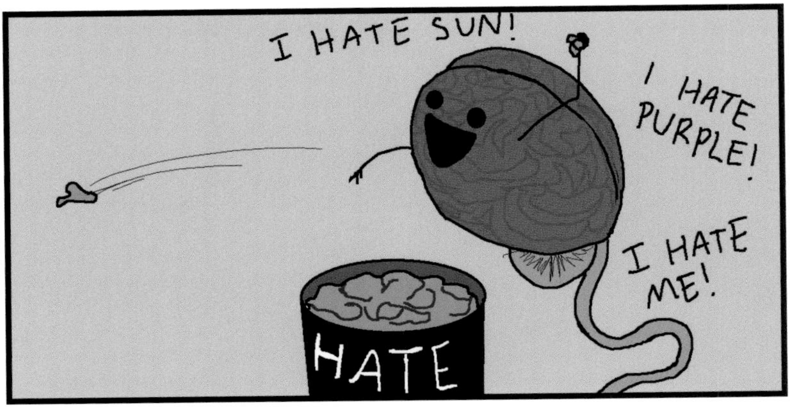
I HATE SUN!
I HATE PURPLE!
I HATE ME!
HATE

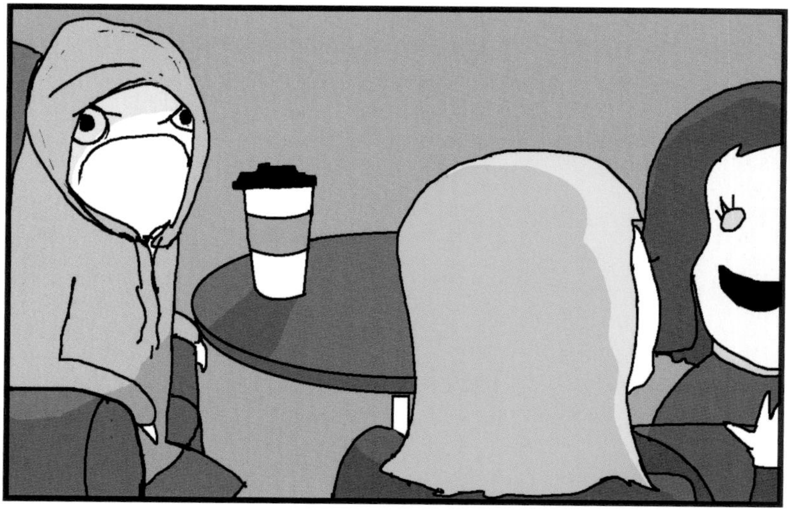

Hating everything made all the positivity and hope feel even more unpalatable. The syrupy, oversimplified optimism started to feel almost offensive.

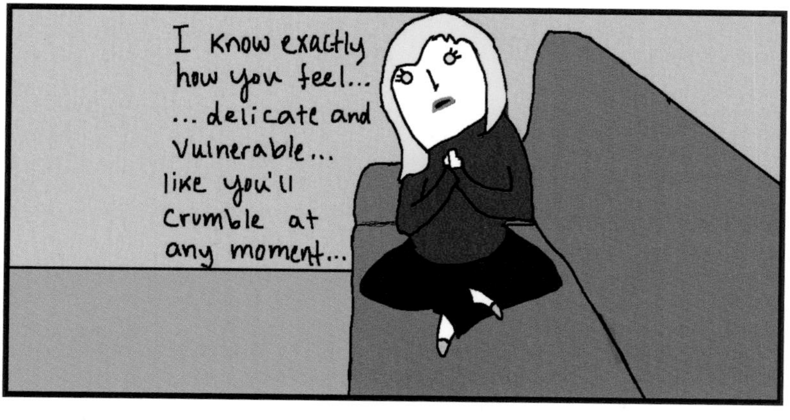
I know exactly how you feel...
... delicate and vulnerable...
like you'll crumble at any moment...

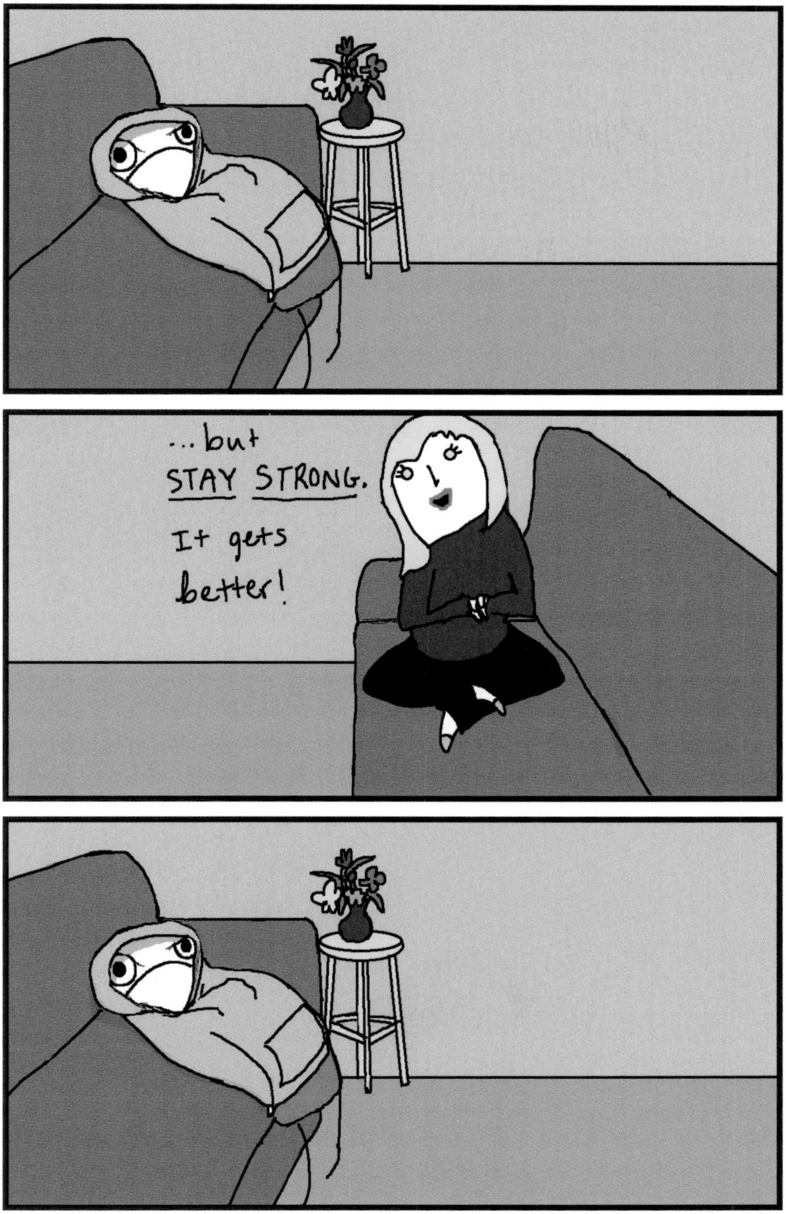
...but STAY STRONG.
It gets better!

Thankfully, I rediscovered crying just before I got sick of hating things. I call this emotion "crying" and not "sadness" because that's all it really was. Just crying for the sake of crying. My brain had partially learned how to be sad again, but it took the feeling out for a joyride before it had learned how to use the brakes or steer.

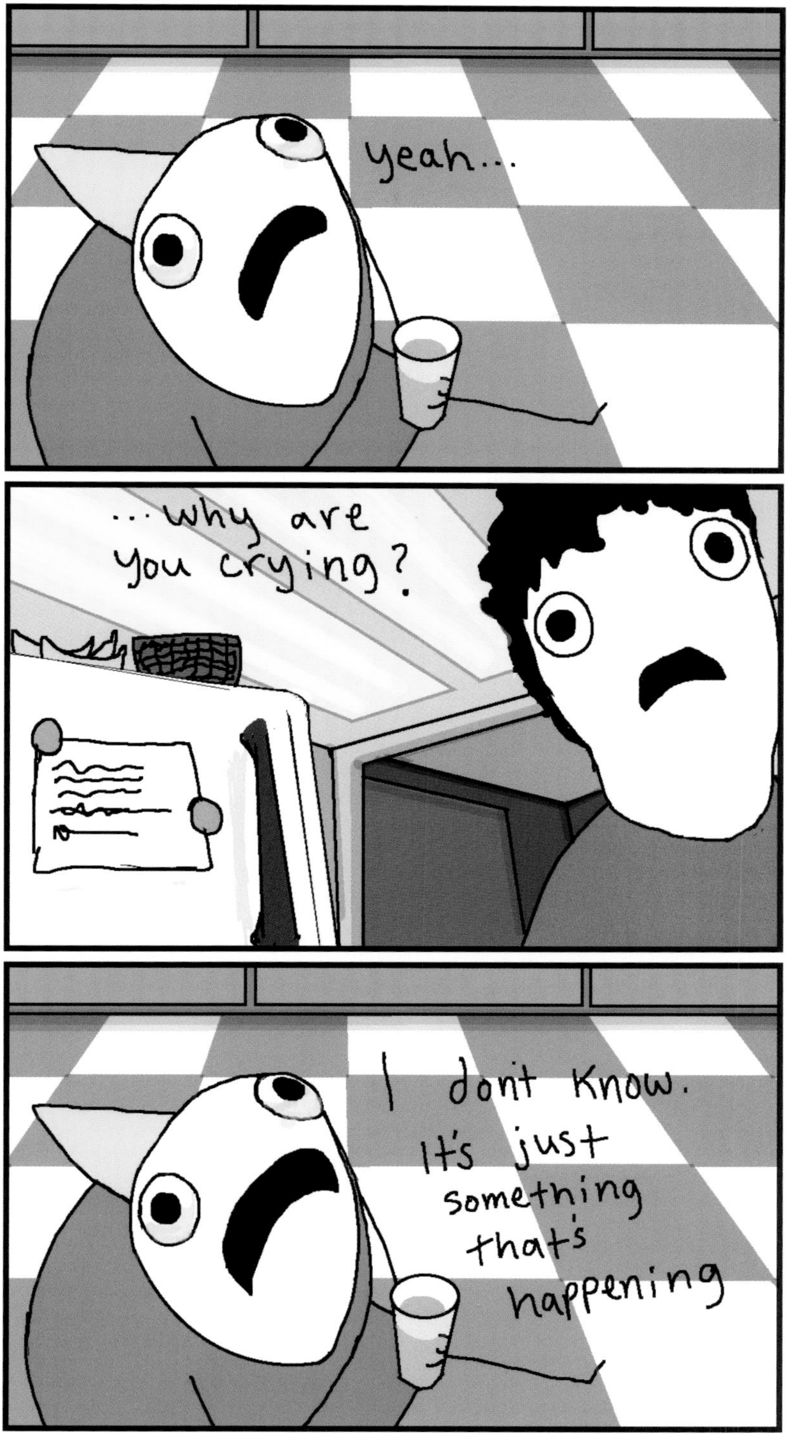
yeah...
...why are you crying?
I don't know. It's just something that's happening

At some point during this phase, I was crying pointlessly on the kitchen floor. As was common practice during bouts of floor-crying, I was staring straight ahead at nothing in particular and feeling sort of weird about myself. Then, through the film of tears and nothingness, I spotted a tiny, shriveled piece of corn under the refrigerator.

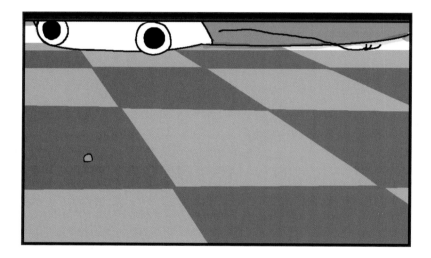

I don't claim to know why this happened, but when I saw the piece of corn, something snapped inside me, and then that thing twisted through a few permutations of logic that I don't understand, and produced the most confusing bout of uncontrollable, debilitating laughter that I have ever experienced.

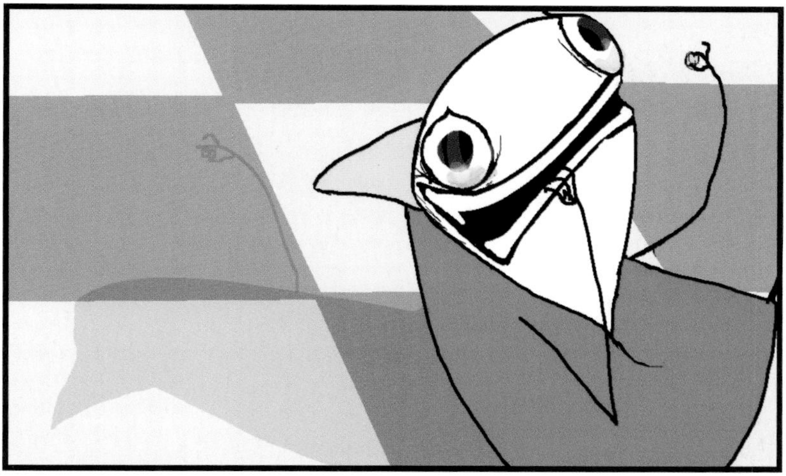

I had absolutely no idea what was going on.

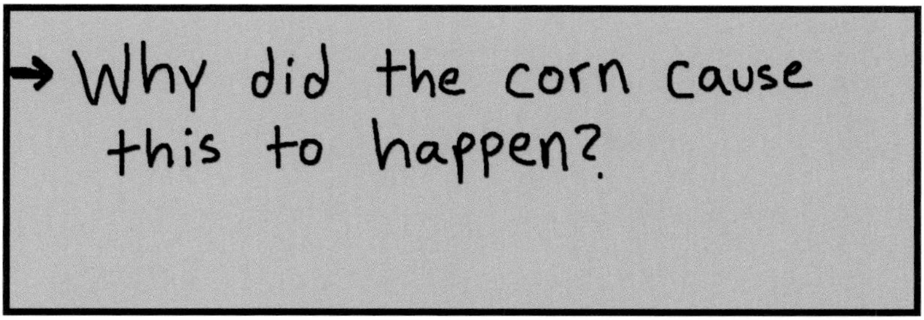
→ Why did the corn cause this to happen?

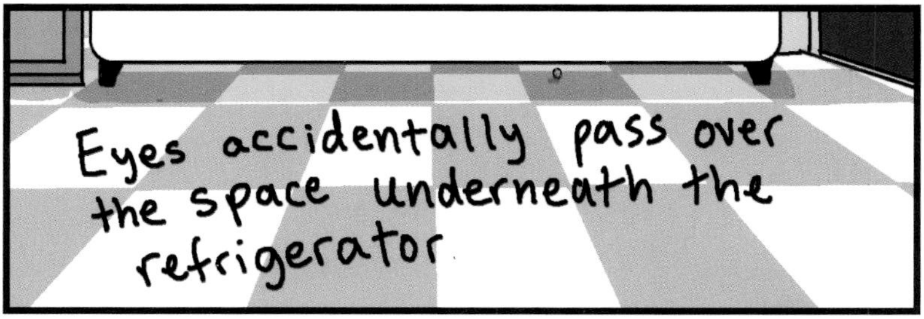
Eyes accidentally pass over the space underneath the refrigerator.

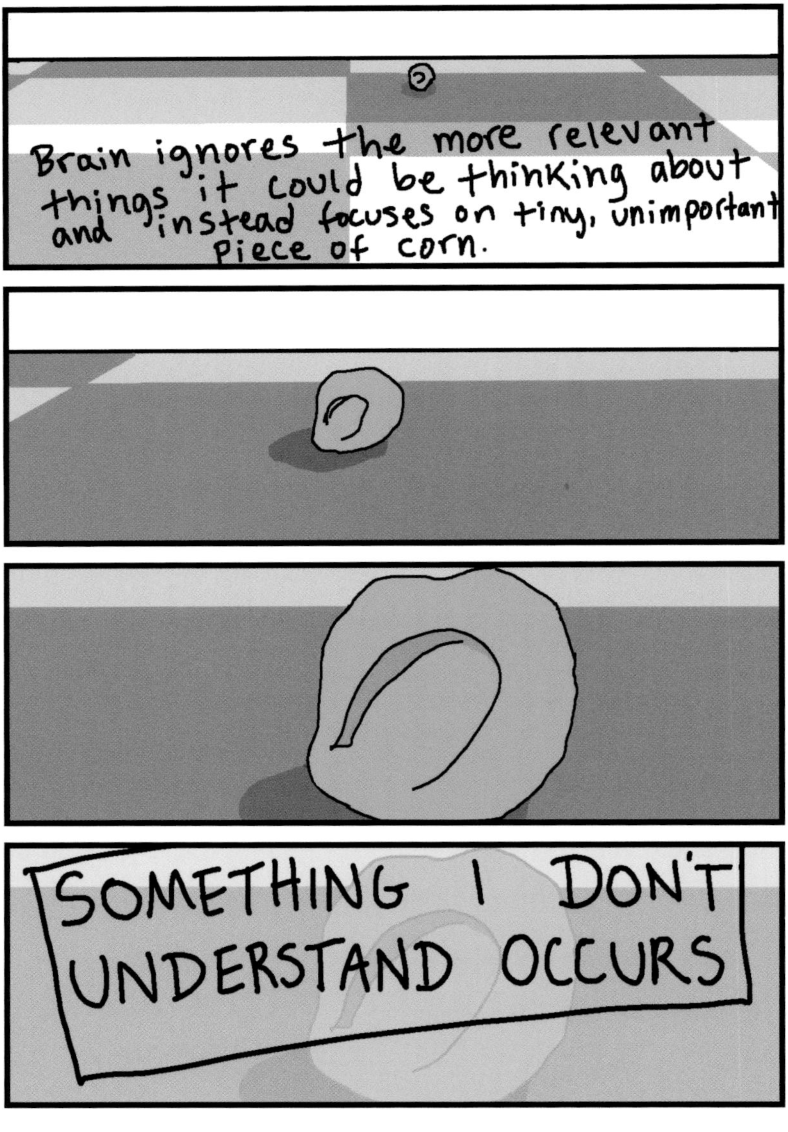
Brain ignores the more relevant things it could be thinking about and instead focuses on tiny, unimportant piece of corn.
SOMETHING I DON'T UNDERSTAND OCCURS

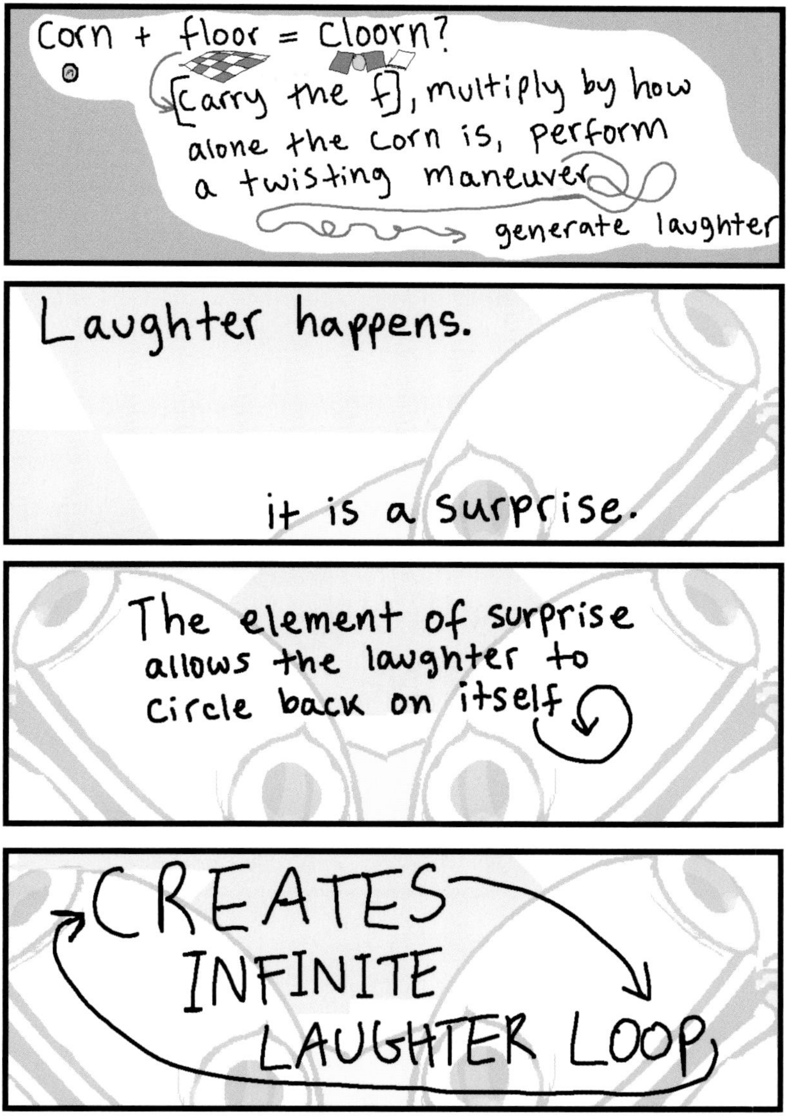
Corn + floor = Cloorn?
[carry the f], multiply by how alone the corn is, perform a twisting maneuver
generate laughter
Laughter happens.
it is a surprise.
The element of surprise allows the laughter to circle back on itself
CREATES
INFINITE
LAUGHTER LOOP

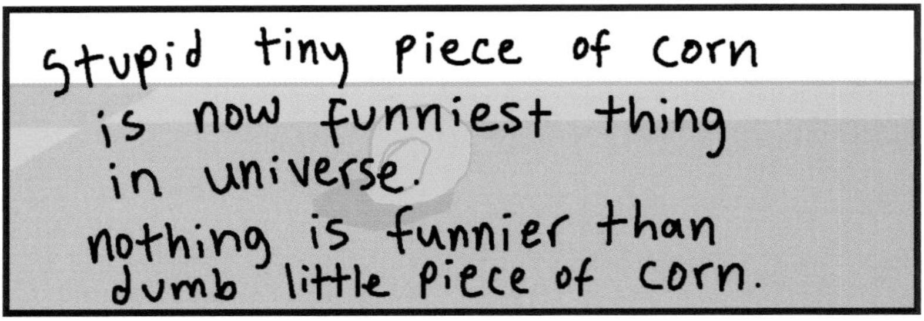
stupid tiny piece of corn is now funniest thing in universe.
nothing is funnier than dumb little piece of corn.

My brain had apparently been storing every unfelt scrap of happiness from the last nineteen months, and it had impulsively decided to unleash all of it at once in what would appear to be an act of vengeance.

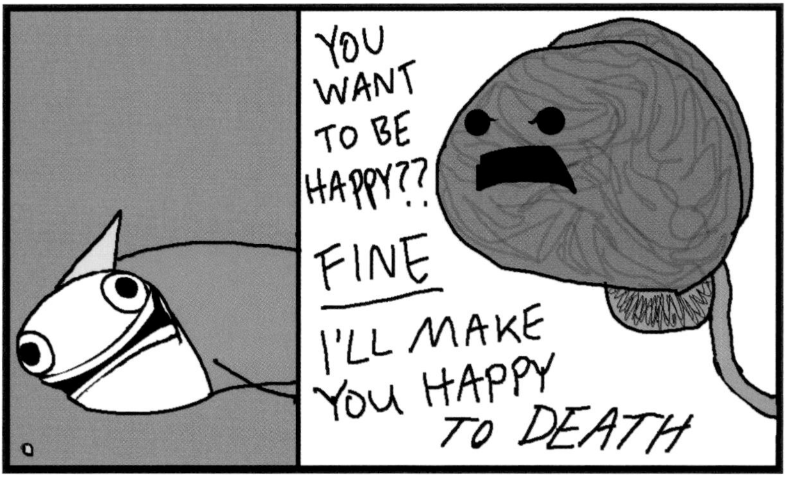
YOU WANT TO BE HAPPY??
FINE
I'LL MAKE YOU HAPPY TO DEATH

That piece of corn is the funniest thing I have ever seen, and I cannot explain to anyone why it's funny. *I* don't even know why. If someone ever asks me "What was the exact moment where things started to feel slightly less shitty?" instead of telling a nice, heartwarming story about the support of the people who loved and believed in me, I'm going to have to tell them about the piece of corn. And then I'm going to have to try to explain that no, really, it was funny. Because, see, the way the corn was sitting on the floor . . . it was so alone . . . and it was just *sitting* there! And no matter how I explain it, I'll get the same confused look. So maybe I'll try to show them the piece of corn—to see if they get it. They won't. Things will get even weirder.

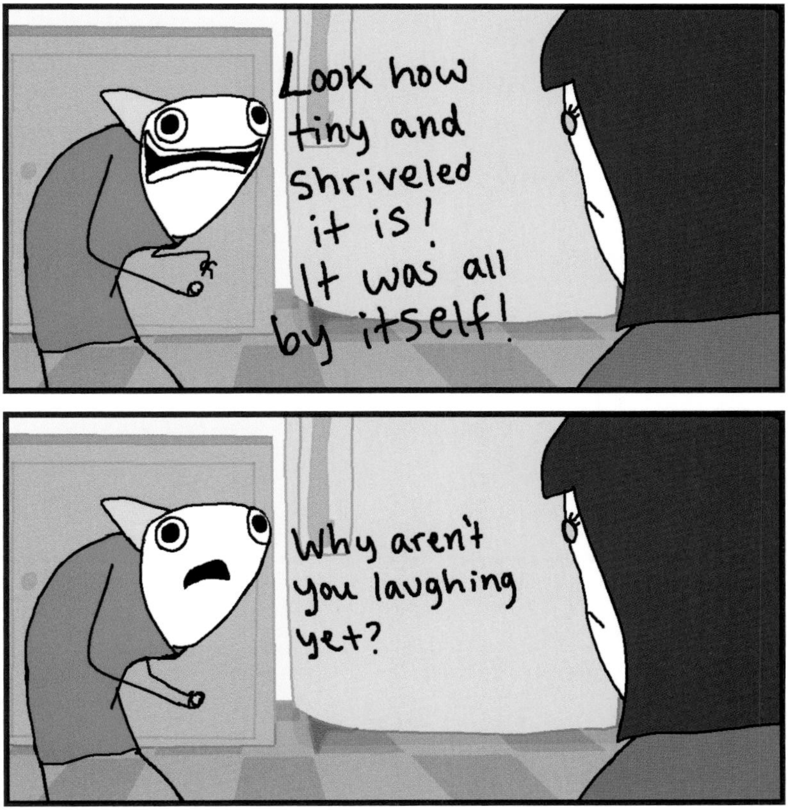
Look how tiny and shriveled it is! It was all by itself!
Why aren't you laughing yet?

Anyway, I wanted to end this on a hopeful, positive note, but seeing as how my sense of hope and positivity is still shrouded in a thick layer of feeling like hope and positivity are bullshit, I'll just say this: Nobody can guarantee that it's going to be okay, but—and I don't know if this will be comforting to anyone else—the possibility exists that there's a piece of corn on a floor somewhere that will make you just as confused about why you are laughing as you have ever been about why you are depressed. And even if everything still seems like hopeless bullshit, maybe it's just *pointless* bullshit or *weird* bullshit or possibly not even bullshit.

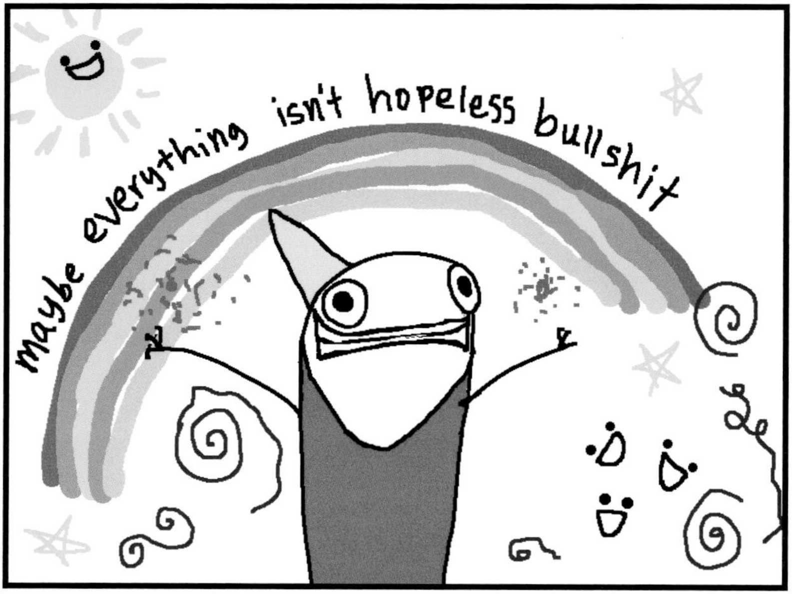
maybe everything isn't hopeless bullshit

I don't know.

But when you're concerned that the miserable, boring wasteland in front of you might stretch all the way into forever, not knowing feels strangely hope-like.

Lost in the Woods

One morning, shortly after my family relocated to the mountains of northern Idaho, my sister and I woke up to find our mother lurking impatiently in our bedroom doorway. She was dressed like a woodsman.

Apparently, sometime during the night, she had awakened to the urgent realization that she lived near an area of wilderness, and, coincidentally, she had learned a few wilderness-related things from a short stint in the Girl Scouts, therefore she needed to take her children into the wilderness so that she could teach them the ways of the forest.

It was a noble goal.

We set out shortly after sunrise on a path that twisted down a hill and eventually led to a fence, beyond which lay thousands of acres of wilderness. Our dog—a fat, disobedient Labrador mix named Murphy—trotted along next to us.

Once we crossed the fence, we had to cut our own trail through the underbrush, ducking under branches and stepping over fallen logs. Our mom tried to teach us things while we ran around like maniacs, kicking trees, throwing sticks at birds, and uprooting random plants simply because we were children and they were plants.

That plant you're holding can be used to make ointment!

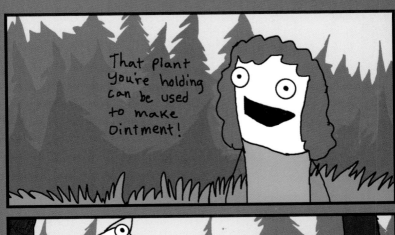

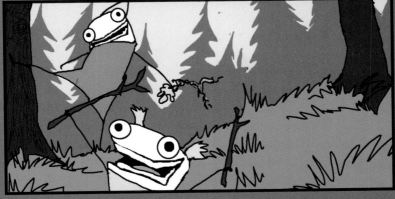

By late afternoon, we had worn ourselves out.

And Murphy, who had spent all day dragging huge logs around for no reason, was looking a little weary as well.

Our mother attempted to lead us back the way we came, but unfortunately, her natural sense of direction was no match for the sheer amount of directions there are, and she became disoriented.

She tried to be confident and follow her instincts, but after an hour of trudging through unfamiliar, waist-high plants, she accepted that she had no idea where she was going. She was lost in the forest with two young children and she was completely terrified.

She didn't want to alarm us, so she tried to play it off like it was her choice to still be in the woods—like she was having so much fun that she couldn't stand the idea of going home yet. But, you know, if she *wanted* to go home, she totally could.

When my sister asked where we were, our mother whirled around with a grin plastered across her face. "We're in this little swampy area! Isn't it fun?!" she said.

We weren't able to muster the same amount of enthusiasm about the little swampy area.

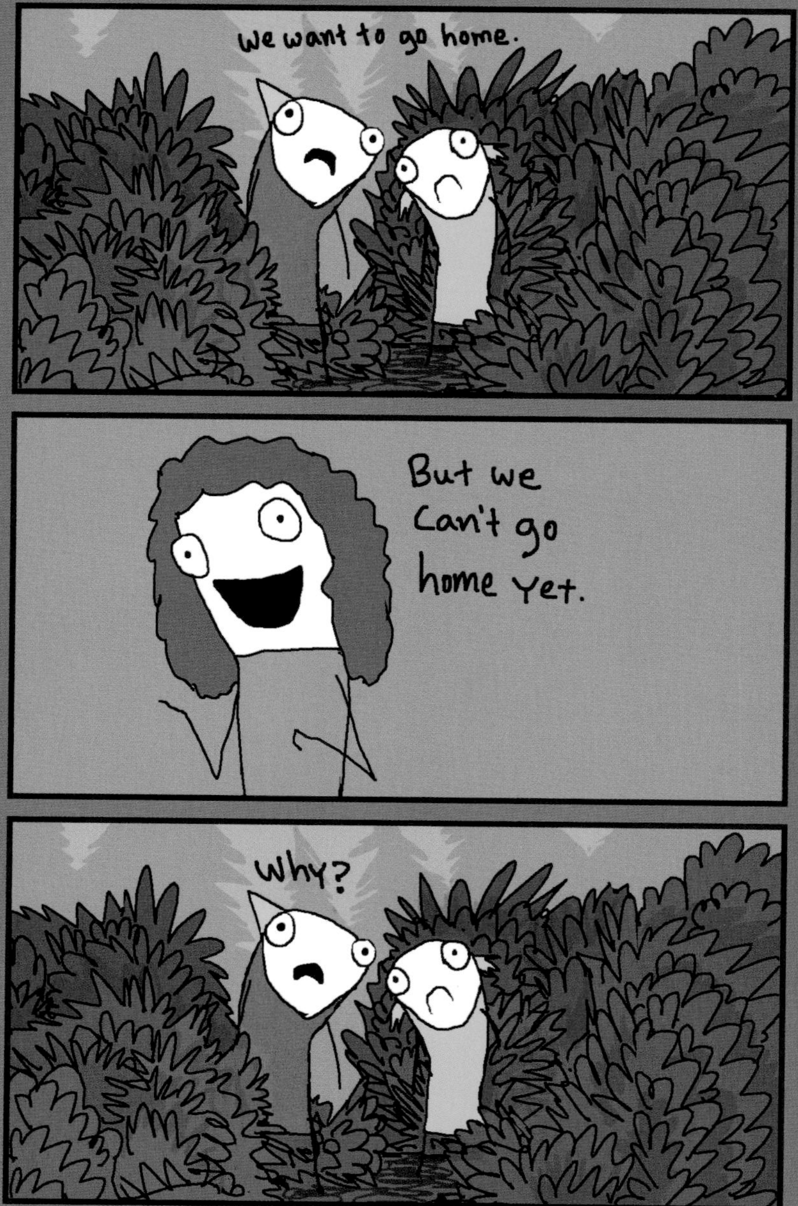
We want to go home.
But we can't go home yet.
Why?

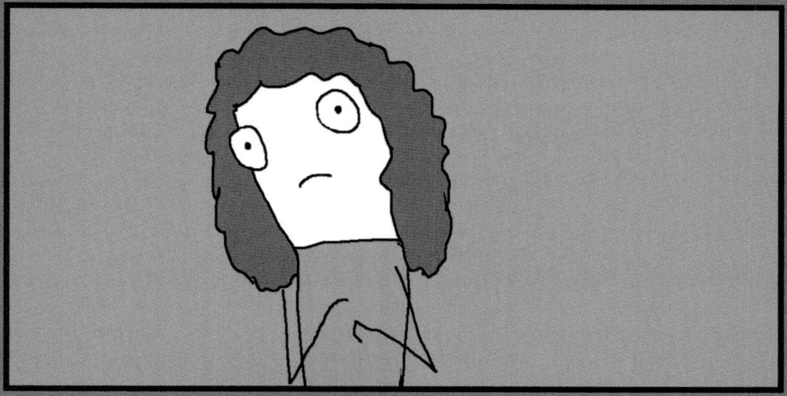

She had to think fast if she wanted to maintain the illusion that we were still hanging out in the forest on purpose.

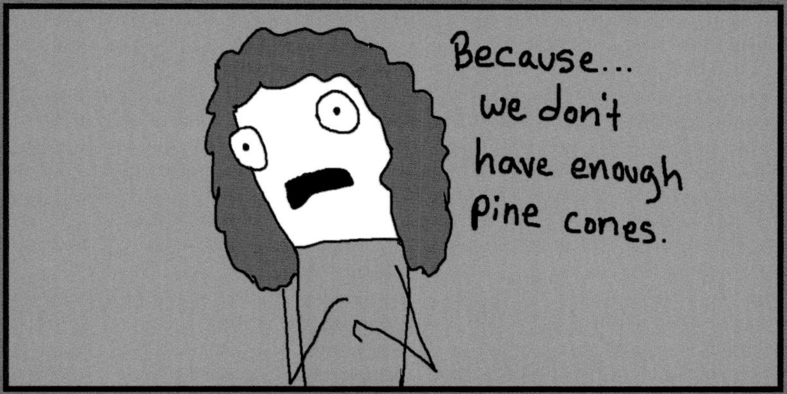
Because... we don't have enough pine cones.

We didn't want to find pine cones. We wanted to go home. But we didn't really have a choice. Our leader wanted us to collect pine cones, so we obeyed, hoping that we could placate her as quickly as possible and move on.

We had severely underestimated how difficult the task was going to be.

We'd gather a bunch of pine cones, then trot over to our mother and ask her if we had found enough to be able to go home. "No. But maybe there are more on the other side of that hill," she'd say. So we'd march over the hill to look for more. When we were on the other side of the hill, she'd say, "See where Murphy is on the far side of that meadow? I bet there are bigger pine cones over there. Let's go find out!" Then she wanted browner pine cones. Then heavier pine cones.

Several hours later, we had come no closer to meeting our mother's ludicrous standards. We were beginning to lose hope.

mom, these are poking us and our arms are bleeding.
And they smell bad and sometimes there are spiders.

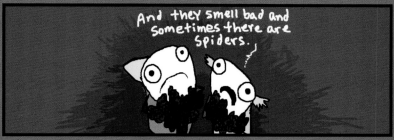

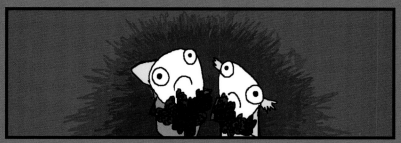

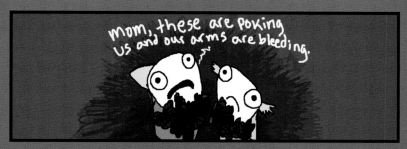

She was going to have to change her strategy.

We're going to play a different game now. It's called "who can yell 'help' the loudest and the most."

But what about our pine cones?

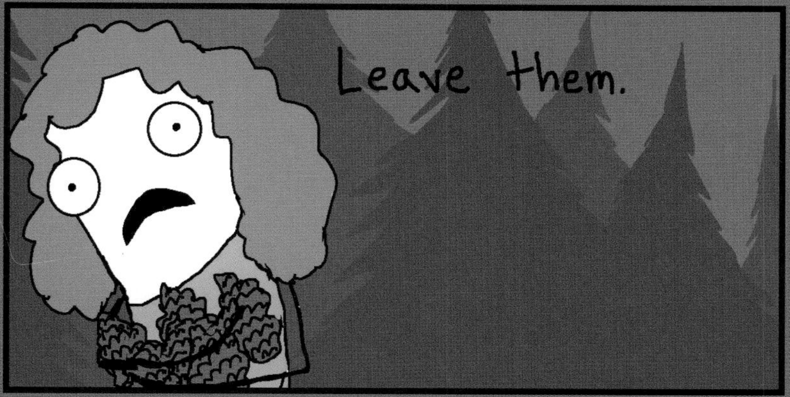
Leave them.

We had spent hours combing the forest for the biggest, brownest, heaviest, cleanest pine cones it could offer, hoping that maybe, just maybe, if we found exactly the right ones, our mother would let us go home. We had bled for them. And now she was telling us that we had to abandon them.

We were confused and more than a little demoralized, but we dutifully piled our pine cones near some bushes while our mom started playing "who can yell 'help' the loudest and the most" by herself.

It was a pretty anticlimactic game and we lost interest quickly.

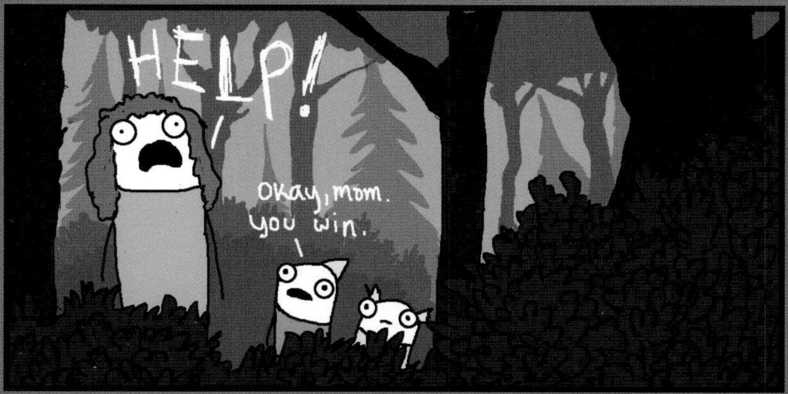
HELP!
okay, mom.
you win.

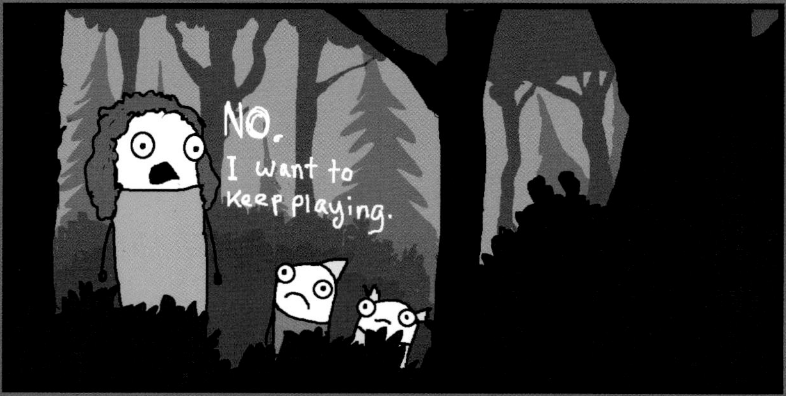
NO.
I want to
Keep playing.

We didn't understand why she had suddenly become so intensely interested in playing these stupid games. Did she not realize it was getting dark?

"Please, Mom. Please, please, please let us go home. Please," we pleaded. She just looked at us and said, "We haven't even played 'walk over that hill and see what's on the other side' yet."

We tried to reason with her. "Mom, aren't you hungry? And what about Dad? Don't you miss Dad?"

Still, she refused to go home.

Our mother was clearly insane, so, as the eldest child, it fell upon me to step up and take charge of the situation. But without knowing how to find my way home, my options were pretty limited.

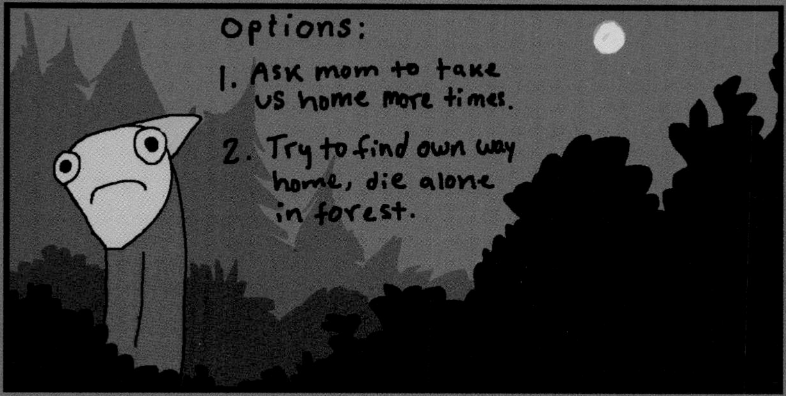
Options:
1. Ask mom to take us home more times.
2. Try to find own way home, die alone in forest.

I silently assessed our predicament before deciding to implement the only real plan I could come up with. It was a risky plan—a plan that could easily backfire. But it was my only option.

I was going to have to scare my mother out of the forest.

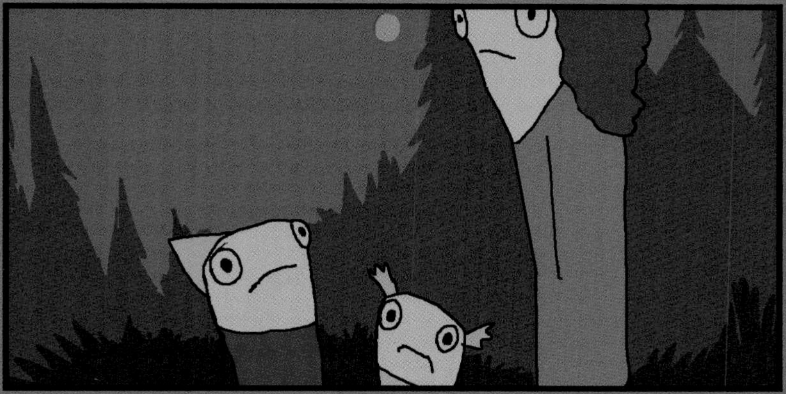

Normally, I wouldn't have been able to think of anything frightening enough to breach her grown-up resistance to scary kid stories. But a few nights earlier, she had watched *The Texas Chainsaw Massacre* while she thought I was asleep.

Unfortunately, I wasn't asleep. I was hiding behind the couch.

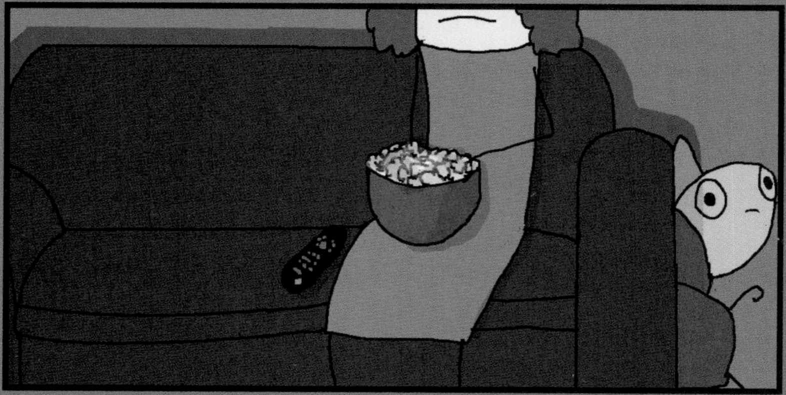

And I had imprinted everything I'd seen that night.

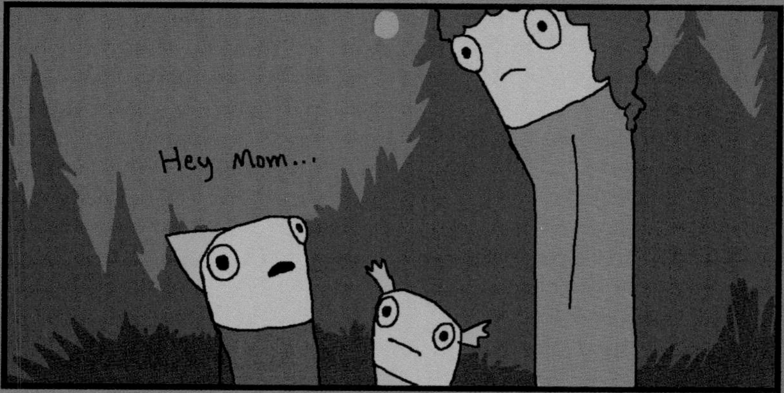
Hey Mom...

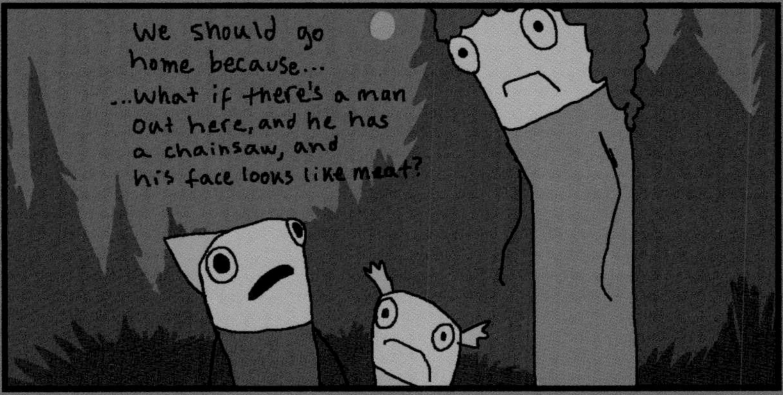
We should go home because...
...what if there's a man out here, and he has a chainsaw, and his face looks like meat?

I imagine it would be pretty terrifying to be wandering through the forest at night when, out of nowhere, your eight-year-old child begins describing the plot from the horror film you watched the other night, which, as far as you know, she hadn't seen. But my mother maintained her composure very well—until a twig snapped, at which point she whirled around shrieking, "WE HAVE A DOG!" As if Murphy's presence were enough to deter a homicidal psychopath with a chainsaw.

It was too much. All the helplessness and frustration that she had been trying so hard to hide from us came rushing to the surface.

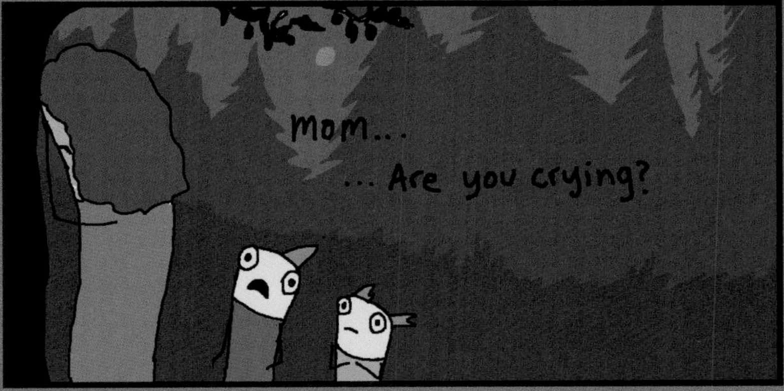
mom...
... Are you crying?

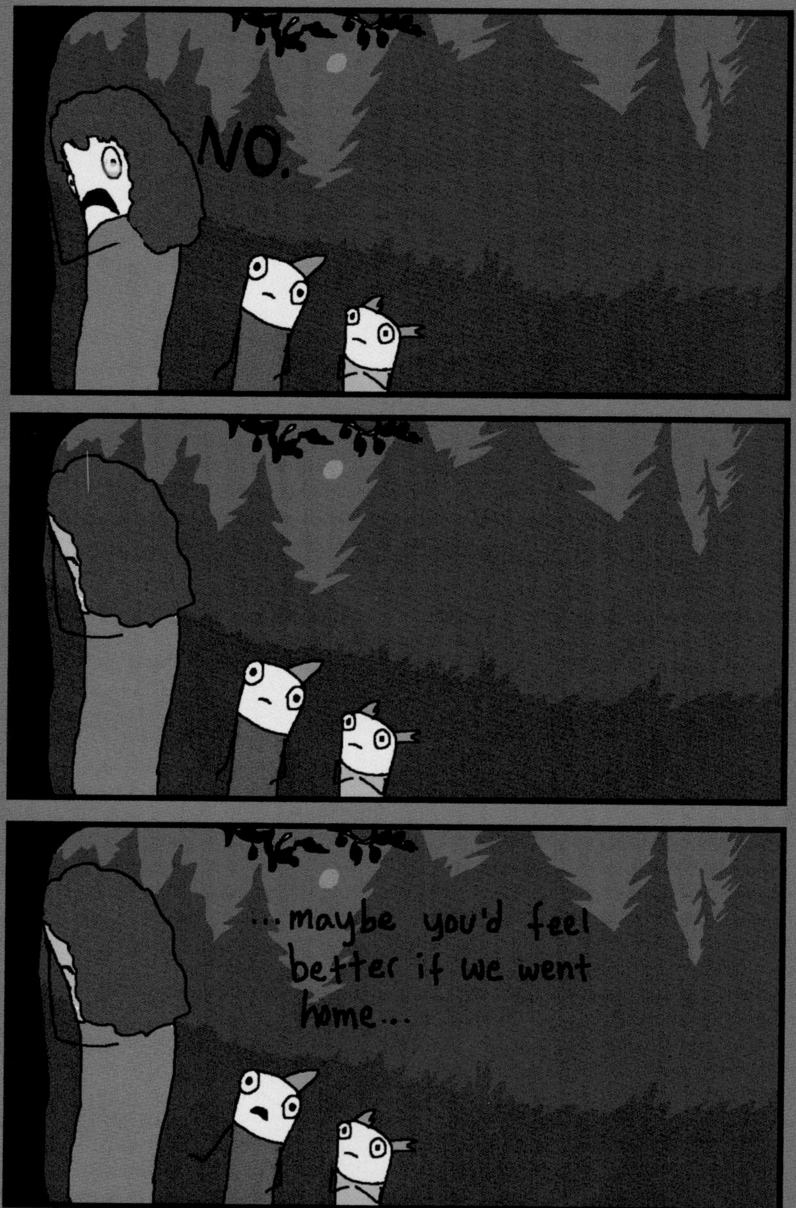
NO.
...maybe you'd feel better if we went home...

She couldn't keep up the illusion forever. At some point we were going to figure out that the last seven hours of our adventure had not been on purpose. And then we were going to panic as we realized that—contrary to our prior assumptions—we did not have the option of going home.

She pulled herself together and broke the news as gently as possible.

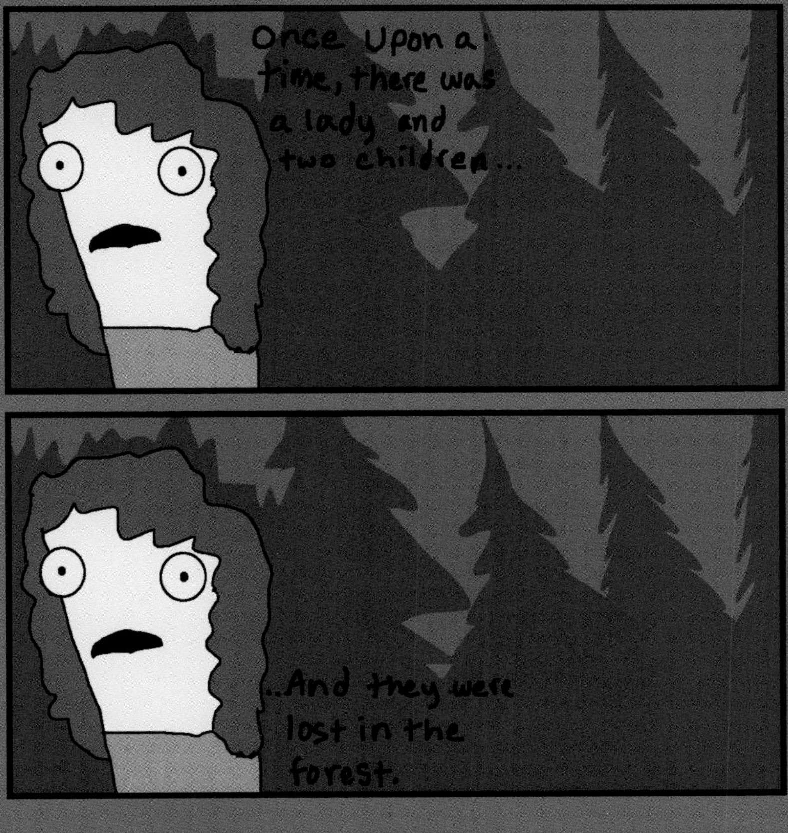
Once upon a time, there was a lady and two children...
...And they were lost in the forest.

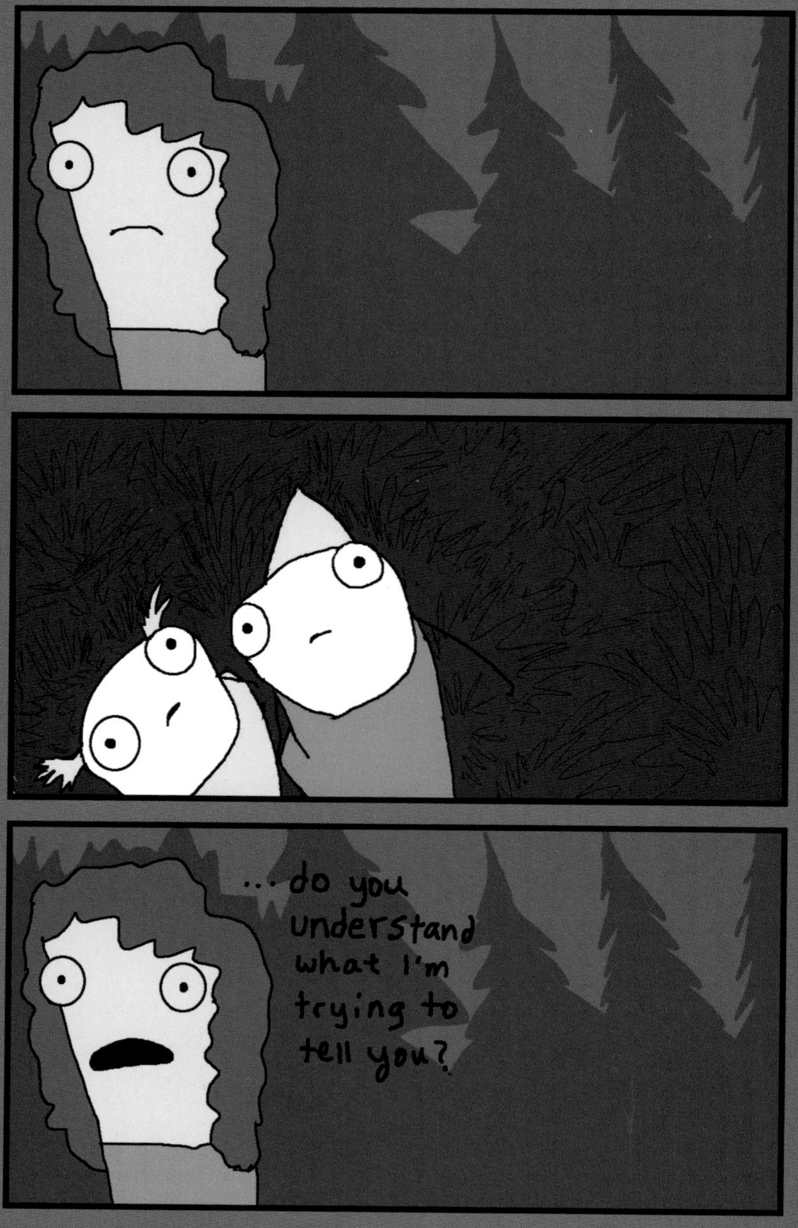
...do you understand what I'm trying to tell you?

It must have been difficult for her to watch our innocent, hopeful little faces go blank in confusion, and then slowly contort in horror as our sense of security shattered.

And it must have been especially horrible when my sister panicked and started scream-crying uncontrollably.

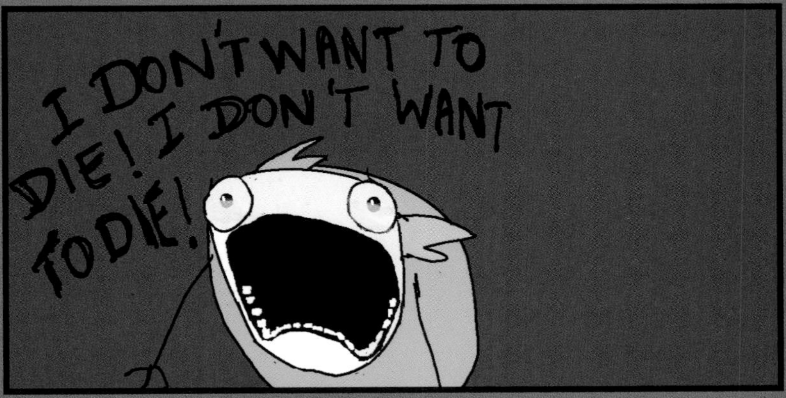
I DON'T WANT TO DIE! I DON'T WANT TO DIE!

Sensing that there was something amiss, Murphy picked up the largest stick she could find and ran loops around the meadow.

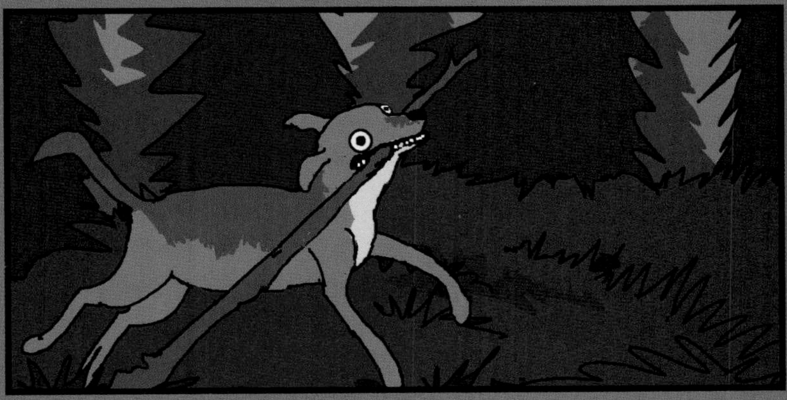

Our mother stared at Murphy in silence for a long time. Finally, she spoke.

"Maybe Murphy knows the way." She reasoned that, because Murphy was a dog, she would have an innate homing instinct.

She spoke to Murphy in a slow, deliberate voice. "Murphy … home? Murphy go home? Home? Home, Murphy. *Hoooome*."

We waited for Murphy to seize the heroic opportunity that was upon her.

But Murphy wasn't like the dogs you see in movies like *Homeward Bound*. Her chief concern seemed to be treating sticks as violently as possible.

However, she was our only hope.

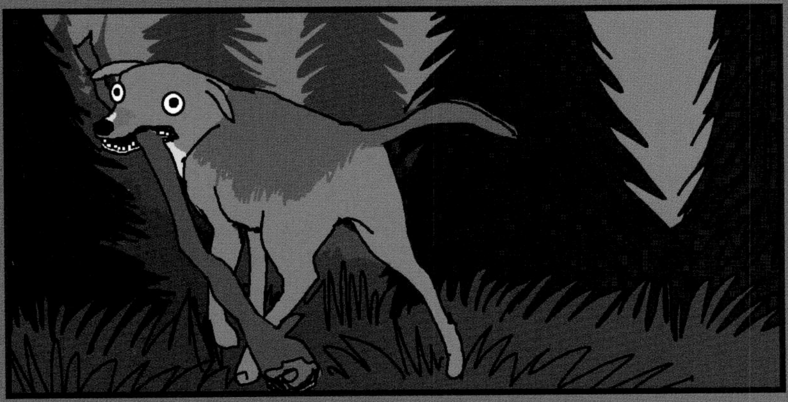

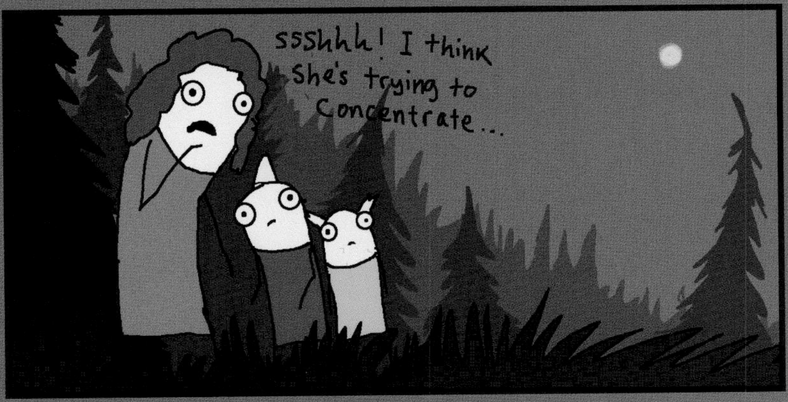
ssshhh! I think she's trying to concentrate...

Murphy's actions over the next few hours didn't seem particularly purposeful. But at some point during one of her stick-thrashing sprees, she took off into the woods—presumably to see what it would feel like to run into a lot of objects while holding a small tree trunk in her mouth—and her path of travel happened to intersect with an old logging road. We followed the logging road to a clearing, and on a hill in the distance we could see a house with its lights on.

The house belonged to an elderly couple who were quite alarmed when our mother banged on their front door so late at night, but kindly offered to let her use their phone to call our dad.

And finally, we got to go home.

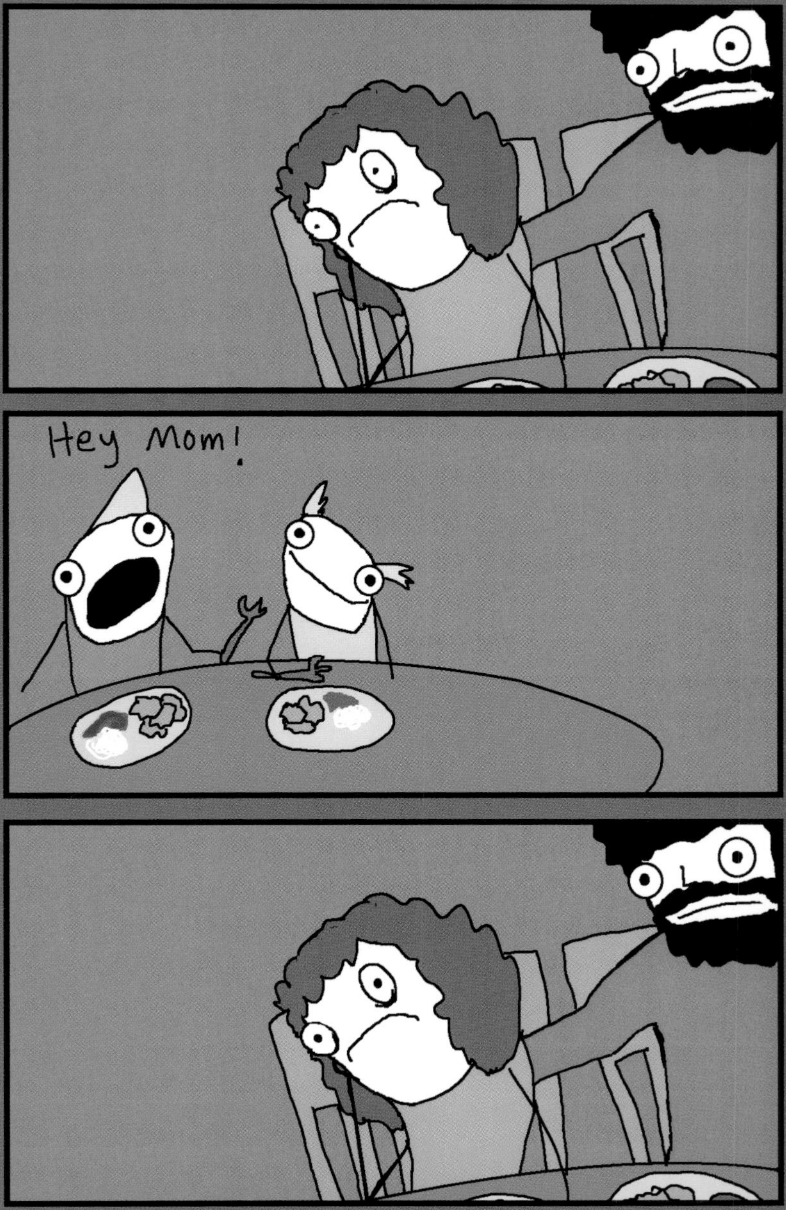
Hey Mom!

We need to go back for the pine cones!

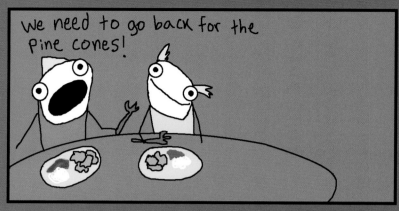

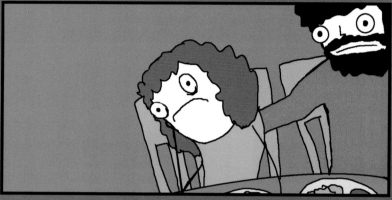

We never did go back for the pine cones.

Dogs Don't Understand Basic Concepts Like Moving

Packing all of your belongings into a U-Haul and then transporting them across several states is nearly as stressful and futile as trying to run away from lava in swim fins.

I know this because Duncan and I moved from Montana to Oregon several years ago. But as harrowing as the move was for us, it was nothing compared to the confusion and insecurity our two dogs had to endure.

When we started packing, the helper dog knew immediately that something was going on. I could tell that she knew because she becomes extremely melodramatic when faced with even a trivial amount of uncertainty. She started following me everywhere, pausing every so often to flop to the ground in an exaggeratedly morose fashion—because maybe that would make me realize how selfish I was being by continuing to pack despite her obvious emotional discomfort.

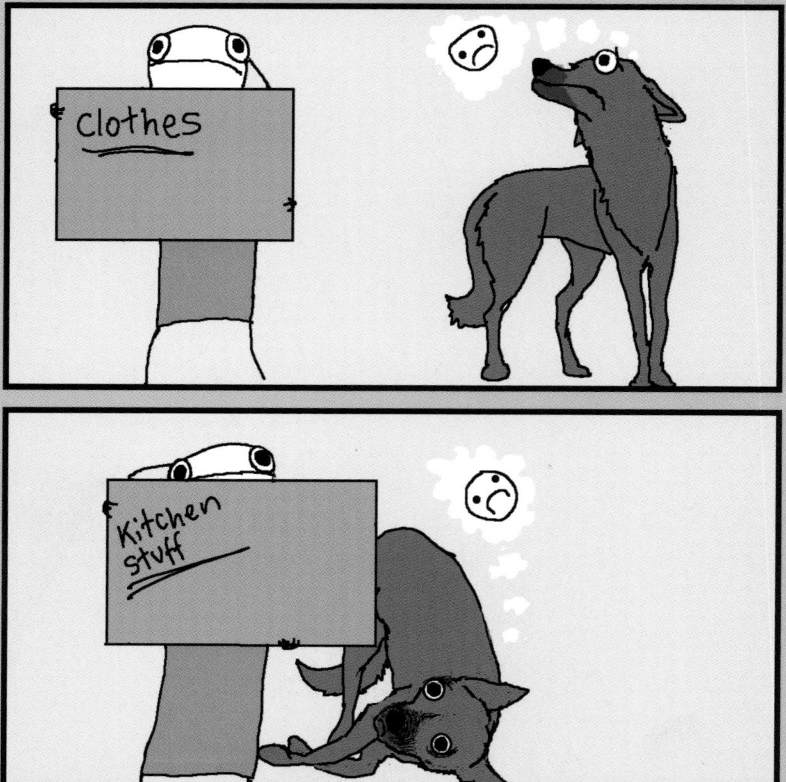
Clothes
Kitchen stuff

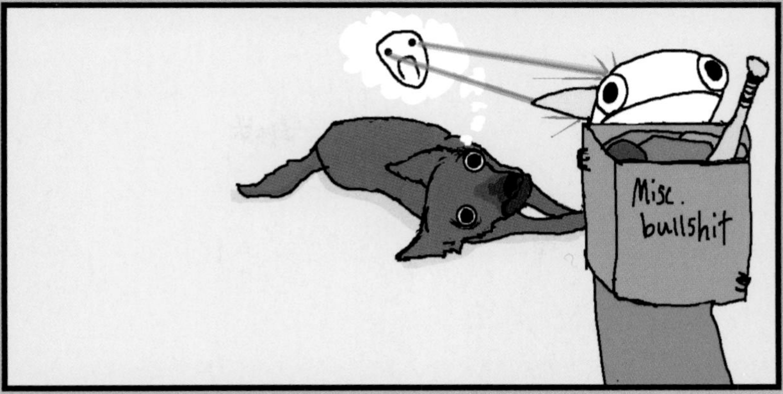
Misc.
bullshit

When the soul-penetrating pathos she was beaming at me failed to prevent me from continuing to put things in boxes, the helper dog became increasingly alarmed. Over the ensuing few days, she slowly descended into psychological chaos. The simple dog remained unfazed.

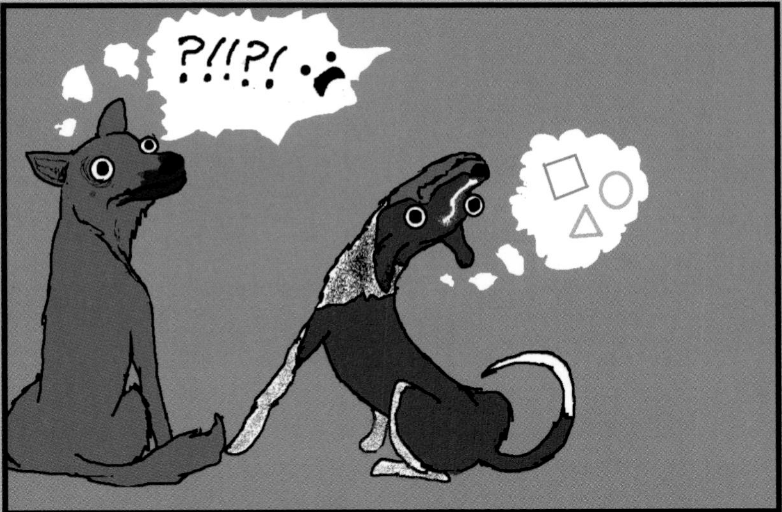
?!!?!

Unfortunately for the helper dog, it took us nearly a week to get everything packed up. By the time we were ready to begin the first part of our two-day journey to Oregon, she seemed almost entirely convinced that she was going to die at any moment. She spent the entire car ride drooling and shaking uncontrollably.

But the simple dog seemed to enjoy the trip.

Even though she threw up seven times.

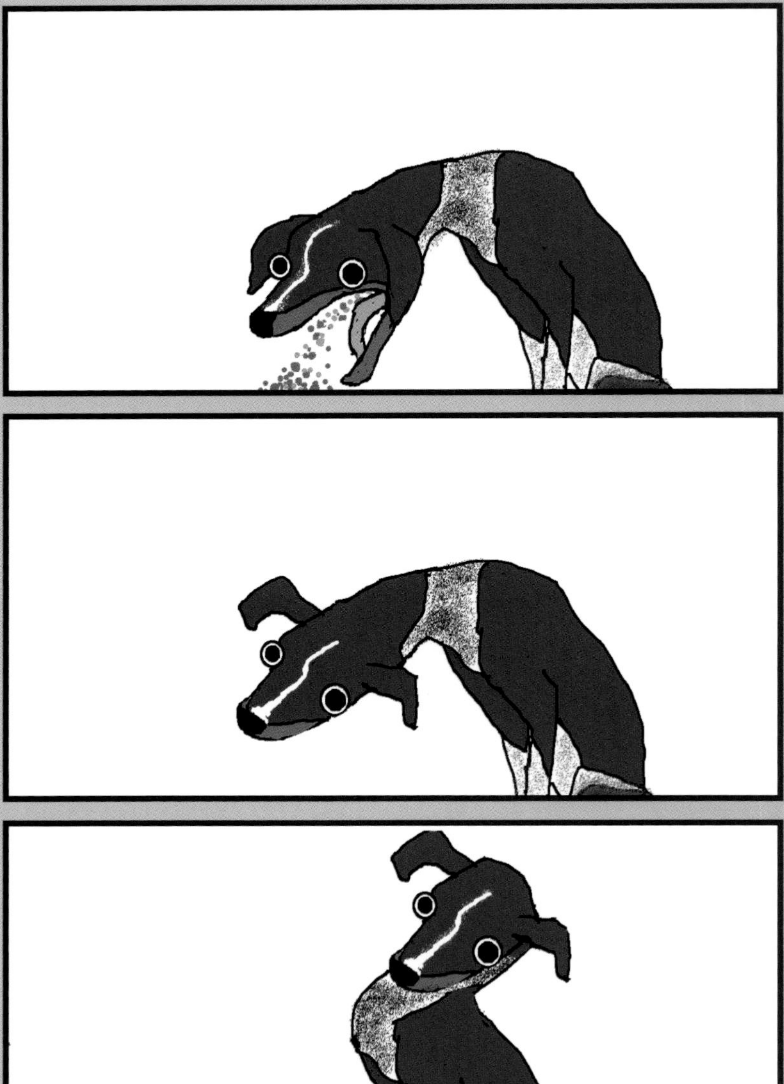

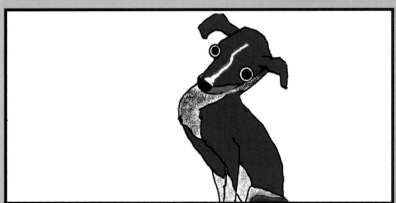

She actually seemed to like throwing up. To the simple dog, throwing up was like some magical power that she never knew she possessed—the ability to create infinite food. I was less excited about the discovery because it turned my dog into a horrible, vomit-making perpetual-motion machine. Whenever I heard her retch in the backseat, I had to pull over as quickly as possible to prevent her from reloading her stomach and starting the whole cycle over again.

But as far as the simple dog was concerned, it was the best, most exciting day of her life.

It wasn't until we stopped for the night that the simple dog became aware that there was any reason for her to feel anxious. But at around two o'clock in the morning, the simple dog finally realized that something was different and maybe she should be alarmed.

This particular dog is not anywhere near the gifted spectrum when it comes to solving problems. In fact, she has only one discernible method of problem solving and it isn't even really a method.

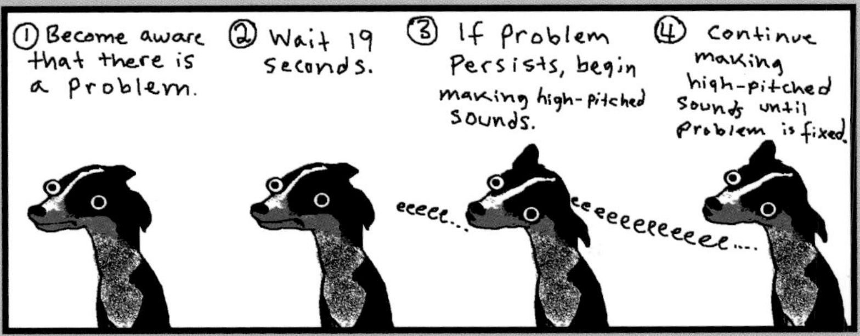
① Become aware that there is a problem.
② Wait 19 seconds.
③ If problem persists, begin making high-pitched sounds.
④ Continue making high-pitched sounds until problem is fixed.
eeeee...
eeeeeeeeeeeeee....

But making high-pitched noises won't solve your problem if your problem is a complete inability to cope with change. Unfortunately for everyone involved, the simple dog did not understand this concept and she went right ahead and made an interminable amount of noise that was just invasive enough to make sleeping impossible.

After an hour of failed attempts at comforting the simple dog, her constant, high-pitched emergency-distress-signal became a huge problem.

I tried to communicate my displeasure to the simple dog, but communicating with the simple dog usually goes like this:

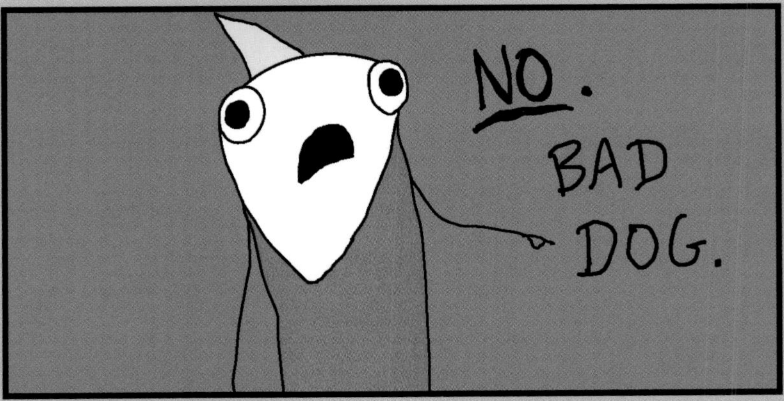
NO.
BAD
DOG.

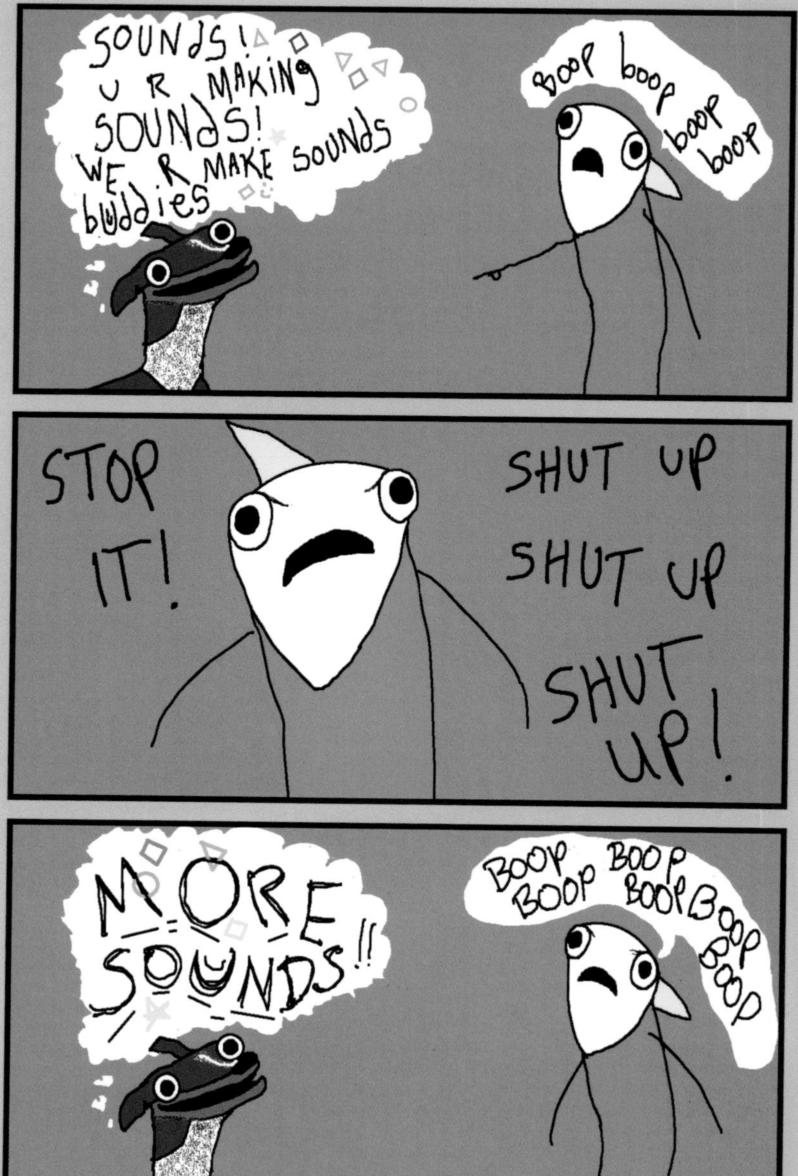
SOUNDS! U R MAKING SOUNDS! WE R MAKE SOUNDS buddies
boop boop boop boop
STOP IT!
SHUT UP SHUT UP SHUT UP!
MORE SOUNDS!!
BOOP BOOP BOOP BOOP BOOP BOOP

You're making everyone miserable...
BOOOOOOOOOOOOP!
boop boop boop

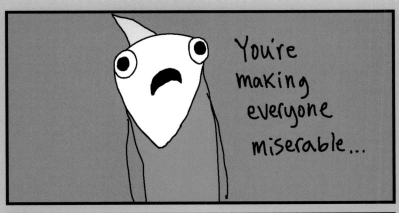

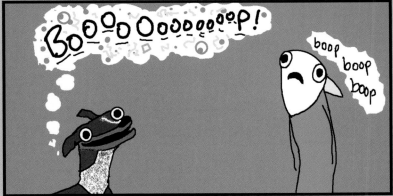

She was going to make that sound forever if she felt it was necessary. We tried everything from spooning her to locking her in the bathroom, but none of it was even the slightest bit effective.

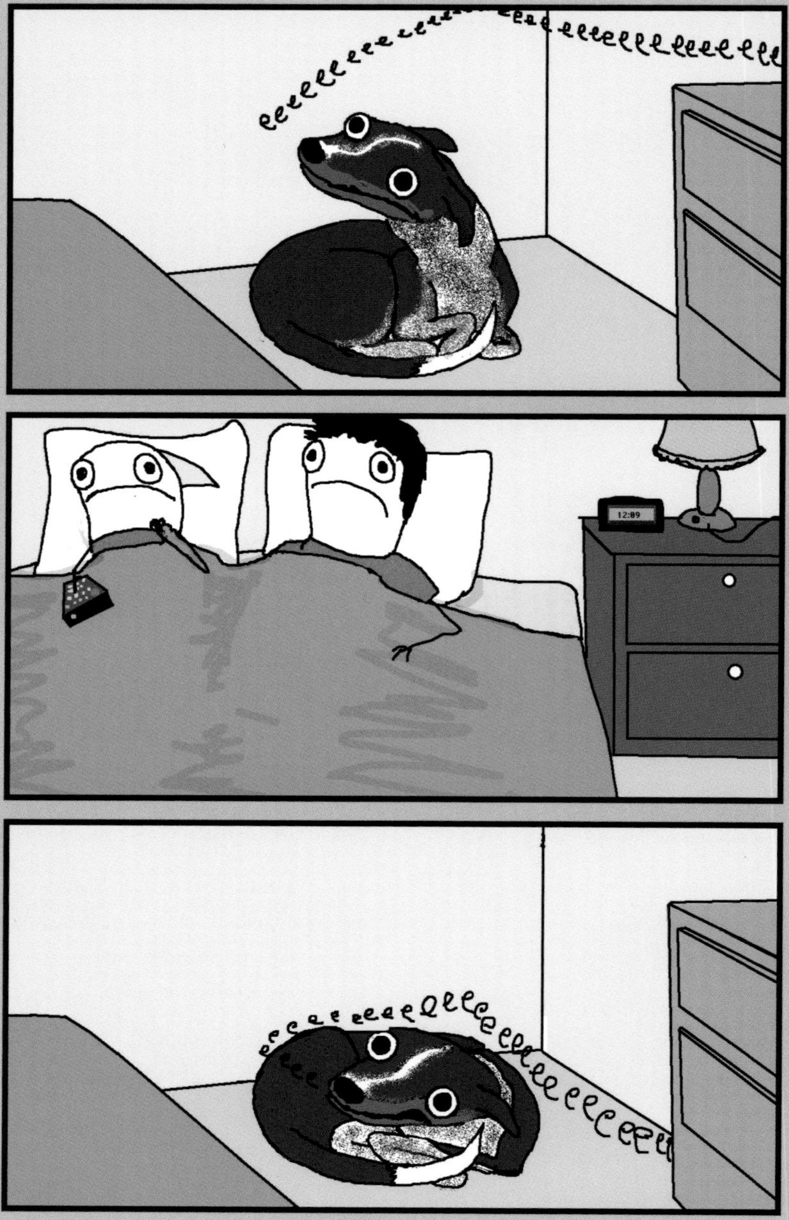

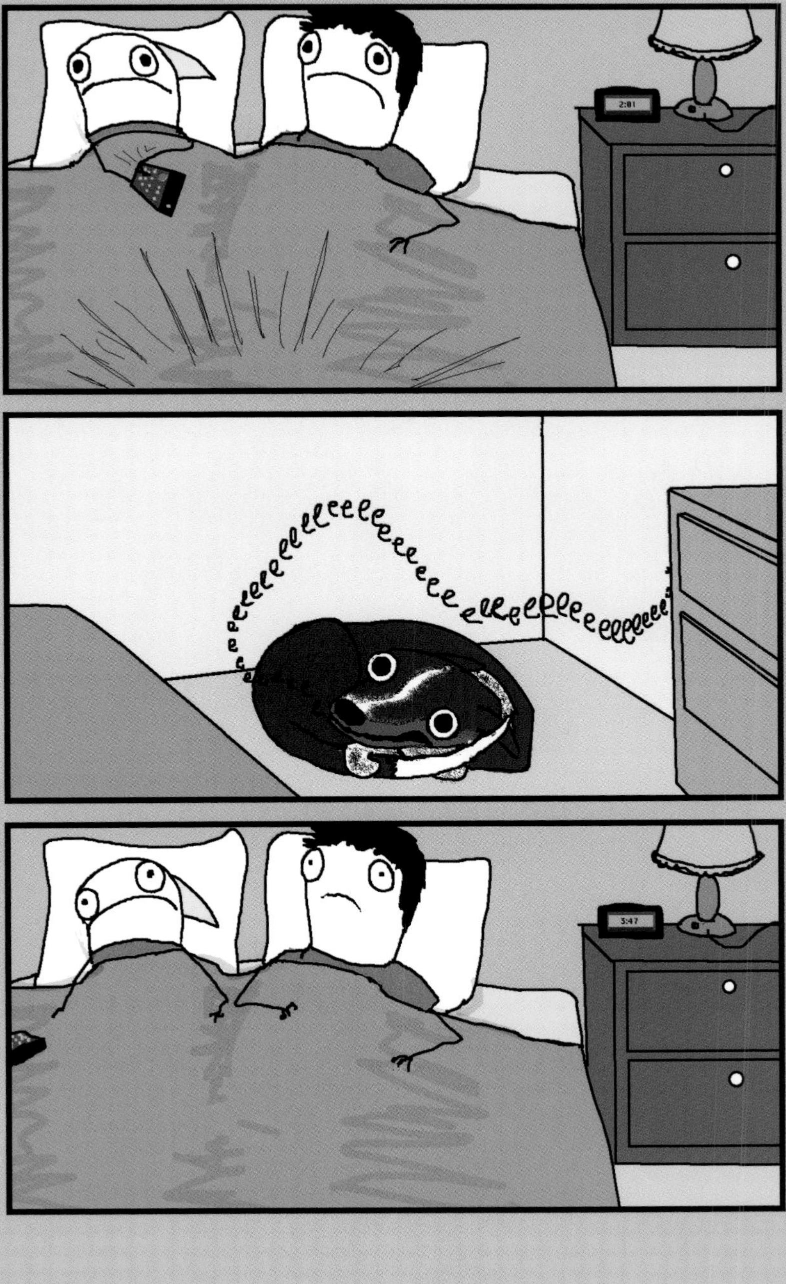
2:01
3:47

The simple dog made the noise all through the night and was still going strong the next morning. When we were loading the dogs into the car, the constant, high-pitched sound emanating from the simple dog finally broke the helper dog. The helper dog wailed in anguish, which alarmed the simple dog. In her surprise, the simple dog let out a yelp, which further upset the helper dog. And so it continued in a wretched positive-feedback loop of completely unnecessary noise.

AOUEOA
AOU AOU
AEE EEE
AOU
AOU
AOU
AOUAOUA
AOU
AO
ROOOOOOOOOOOOO

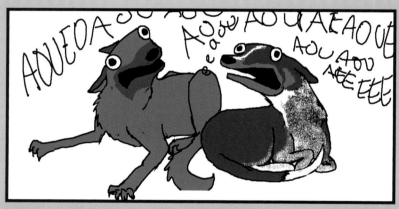

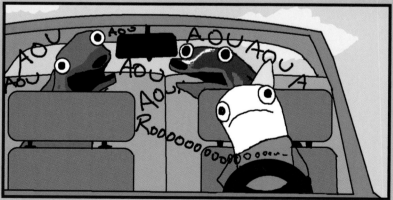

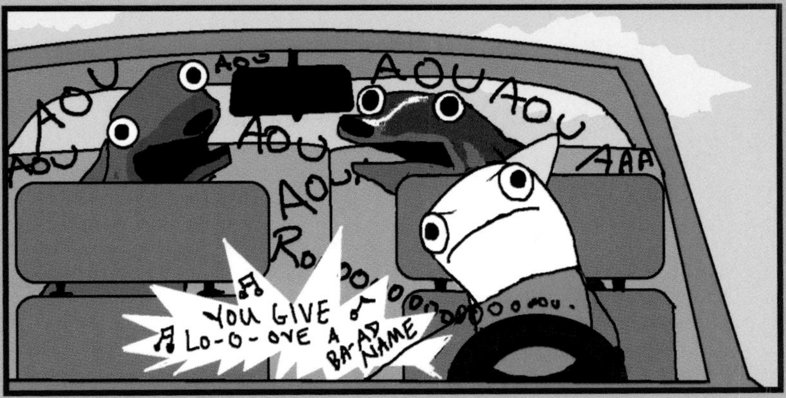
AOU
AOU
AOU
AOU
AOUAOU
AOU
AAA
AOU
RoOOOOOOOOOOAOU.
YOU GIVE LO-O-OVE A BA-AD NAME

When we finally arrived at our new house, the dogs had calmed down considerably. However, it had snowed the night before and there was still snow on our front lawn, and that was enough to catapult both dogs back into hysteria.

The simple dog had either never experienced snow or she'd forgotten that she knew what it was, because when we let her out of the car, she walked around normally for about seven seconds, then she noticed the snow and her feeble little mind short-circuited.

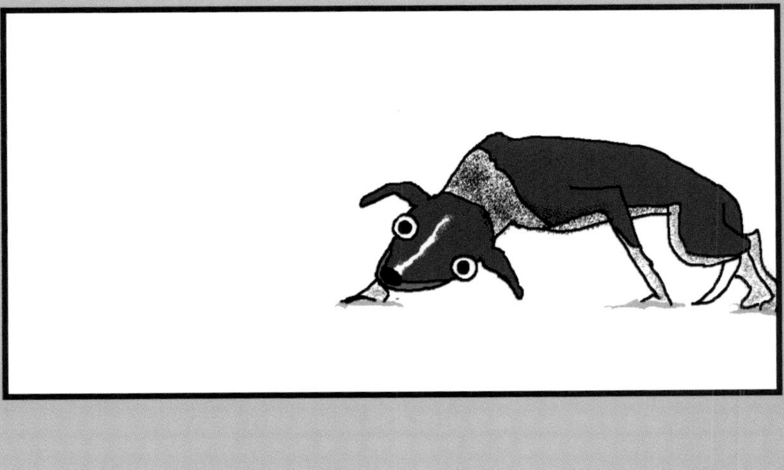

At first, the simple dog was excited about the snow. She started prancing around the yard like she was the star of a one-dog parade—her recent personal crisis overshadowed by a haze of enthusiasm.

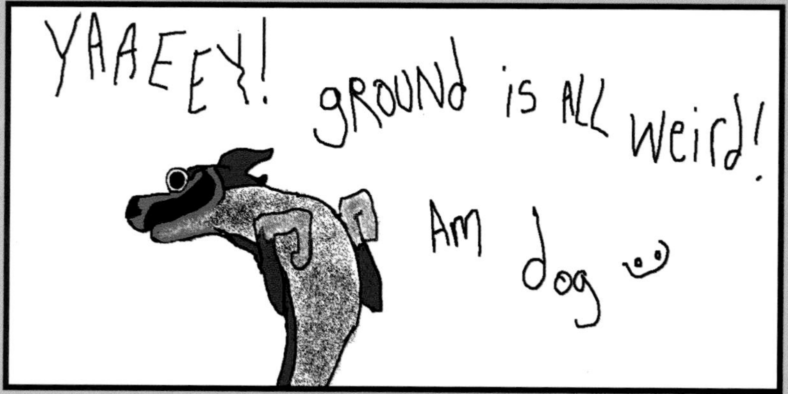
YAAEEY!
ground is ALL weird!
Am dog

The prancing turned to leaping and the leaping turned to running chaotically in stupid little circles. Then she just stopped and stared at the ground. There was a visible shift in her demeanor as she realized that she didn't understand snow and it was everywhere and she should probably be scared of it.

She started making the noise again.

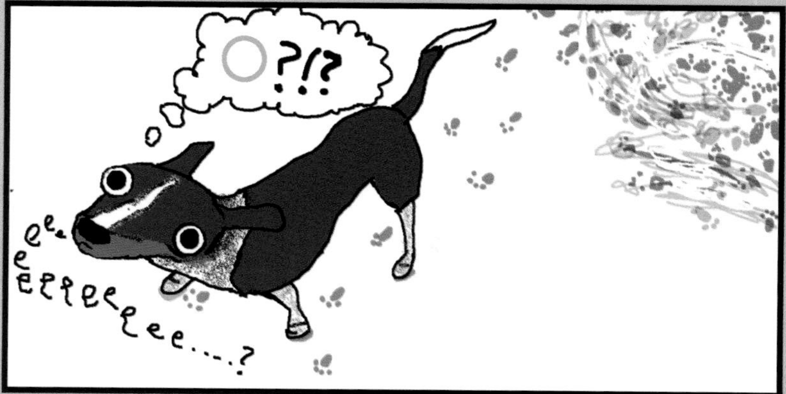
?!?
eeeeeeeeeeeeee....?

Not surprisingly, the helper dog interpreted the snow as a sign of her imminent demise. But she was so exhausted from worrying about all of the other signs of her demise that she just gave up and accepted her death. She peered up at us, half-buried in the snow. Her eyes were filled with pain and helplessness, as if she thought we had summoned the snow for the sole purpose of making her sad.

We decided that it would probably be best to bring the dogs inside.

As a condition for allowing us to have dogs in our rental house, our landlady made us promise that we wouldn't let the dogs scratch the wood floors. We didn't anticipate it being a problem because it hadn't been in the past, but as soon as our dogs set foot in the house, they morphed into perfectly engineered floor-destroying machines. They started sprinting as fast as they could for absolutely no reason, skittering around in circles to avoid running into the walls.

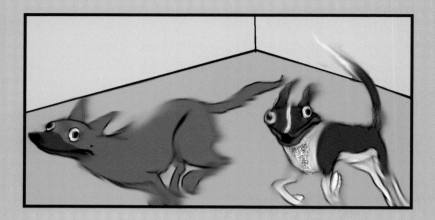

We finally corralled them in the bedroom and shut the door to give ourselves a little time to regroup and come up with a plan. Until we could get some rugs or convince the dogs that it was unnecessary to sprint around chaotically, we would need to find some way to prevent them from scratching the floors. What we ended up doing was going to the pet store and buying two sets of sled-dog booties. It was the only way.

It is easy to imagine that a dog who has recently experienced a dramatic upheaval of its formerly safe and predictable life might not react well to suddenly having strange objects attached to all four of its feet. This was most definitely the case with the booties.

The helper dog panicked and started trying to rip the booties off with her teeth.

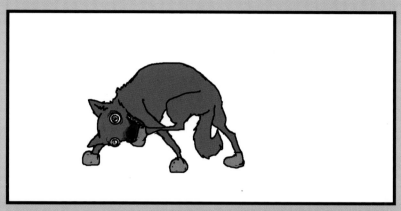

I scolded her and she reacted as if I'd ruined her entire life.

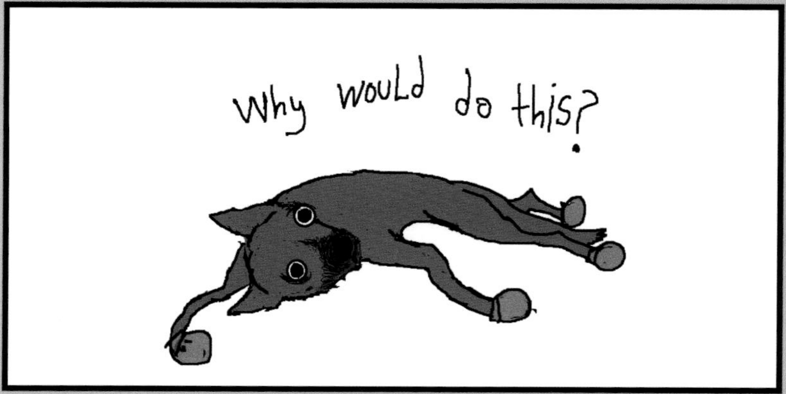
why would do this?

But at least her immobilizing self-pity kept her from chewing the booties off.

The simple dog just stood there and looked at me in a way that would suggest she didn't realize her legs still worked.

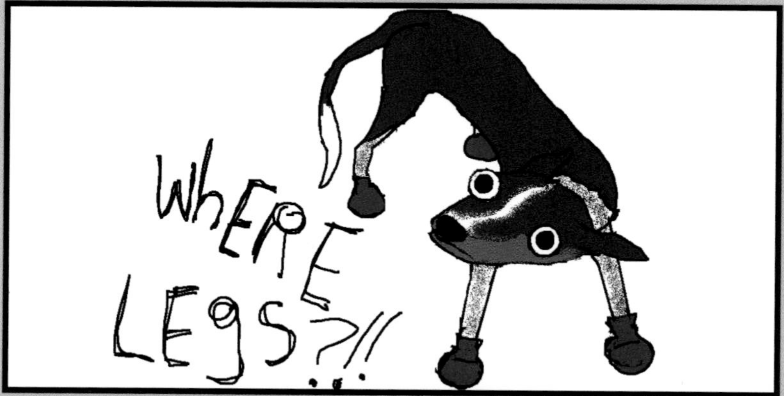
WhERE LEgS?!!

They had to wear the booties for two days. Those two days were filled with the most concentrated display of overemotional suffering I have ever witnessed. The simple dog spent most of her time standing in the middle of the room looking bewildered and hurt, and the helper dog refused to walk, instead opting to flop her way around the house like a dying fish.

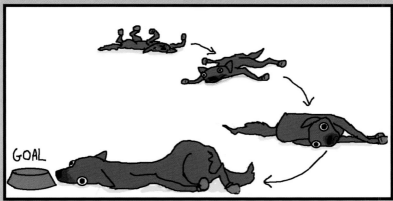

The entire ordeal was punctuated by the simple dog's high-pitched confusion alarm.

We were beginning to think that our dogs were permanently broken. Nothing we did helped at all to convince the dogs that we had only changed houses and our new house was not, in fact, some sort of death camp and we weren't actually planning on killing them to fulfill an organ-harvest ritual. Despite our best efforts, they continued to drift around in a sea of confusion and terror, pausing only to look pitiful.

But while we were unpacking, we found a squeaky toy that had been given to us as a gift shortly before we moved. We offered the toy to the dogs. This may have been a mistake.

Upon discovering that the toy squeaked when it was compressed forcefully, the simple dog immediately forgot that she'd ever experienced doubt or anxiety ever in her life. She pounced on the toy with way more force than necessary, over and over and over. The logic behind her sudden change in outlook was unclear.

Things that will cause the simple dog to suddenly understand and be at peace with changes in her life:

- Reassurance and support — ✗ NO
- The fact that there was nothing wrong in the first place. — ✗ NO
- Time has passed and nothing bad has happened. — ✗ NO
- Logic — ✗ NO
- There is a toy that makes noises when it is squeezed. — ✓ YES

But at least she was happy again.

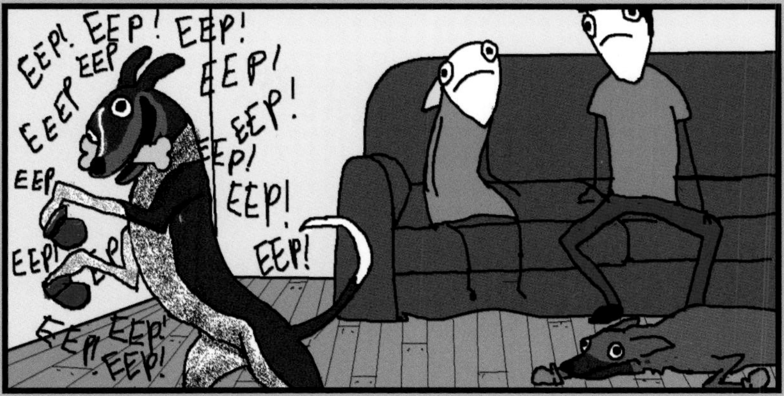
EEP! EEP! EEP!
EEEP EEP
EEP!
EEEP
EEP!
EEP
EEP!
EEP!
EEP!
EEP
EEP!
EEP! EEP!
EEP!

The Hot Sauce Debacle

At some important point during my formative years, I accidentally demonstrated a mildly surprising fortitude against spicy food.

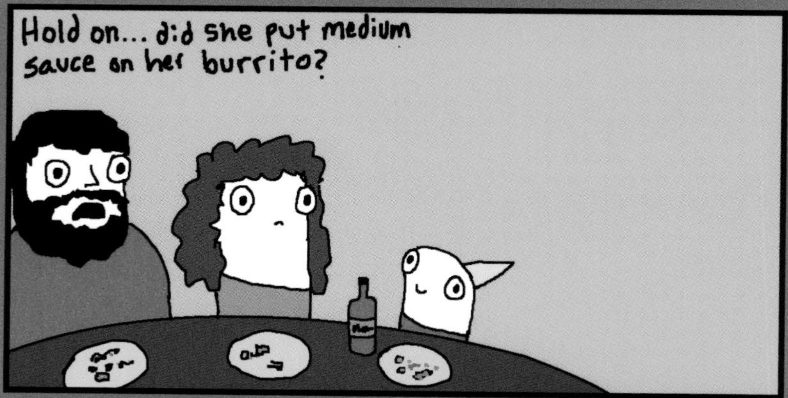
Hold on... did she put medium sauce on her burrito?

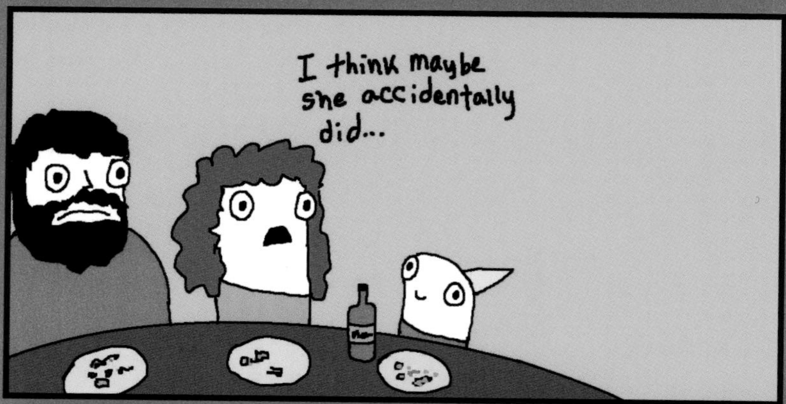
I think maybe she accidentally did...

It wasn't anything objectively amazing—more something to be quietly admired for a moment and then forgotten about forever. But it was the first time I had displayed any sort of discernible talent, so the incident was completely blown out of proportion.

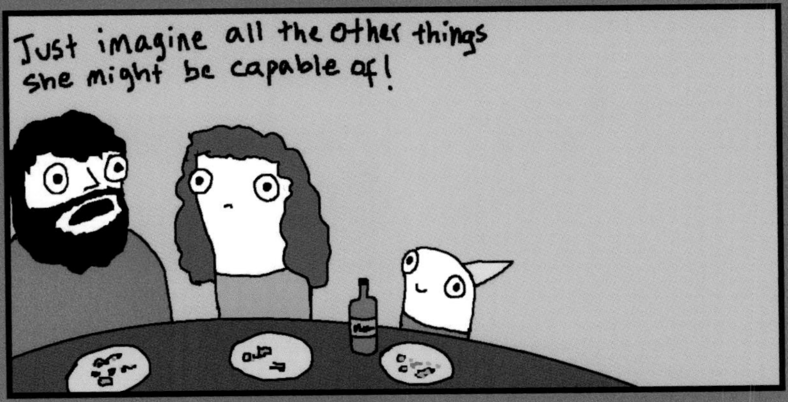
Just imagine all the other things she might be capable of!

The next day at work, my father exaggerated the story slightly.

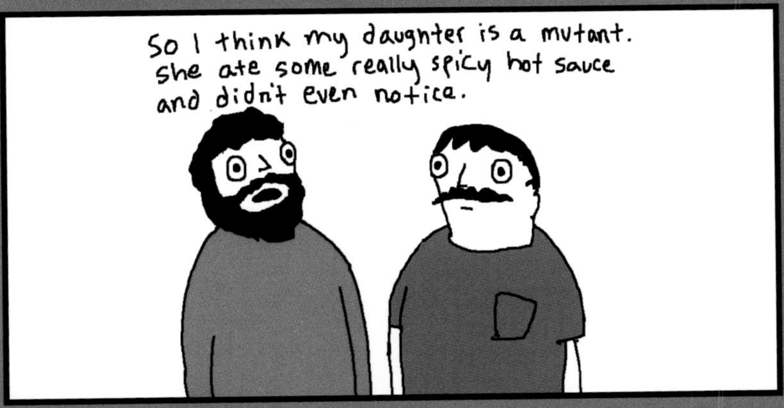
So I think my daughter is a mutant. She ate some really spicy hot sauce and didn't even notice.

Unfortunately, one of my dad's coworkers, Mike, had built part of his identity around his ability to withstand spicy food. Not wanting to be outdone by a child, he attempted to one-up my father's claims.

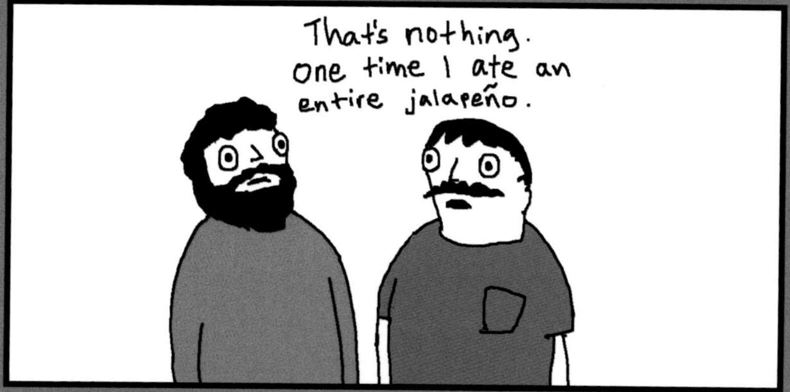
That's nothing. One time I ate an entire jalapeño.

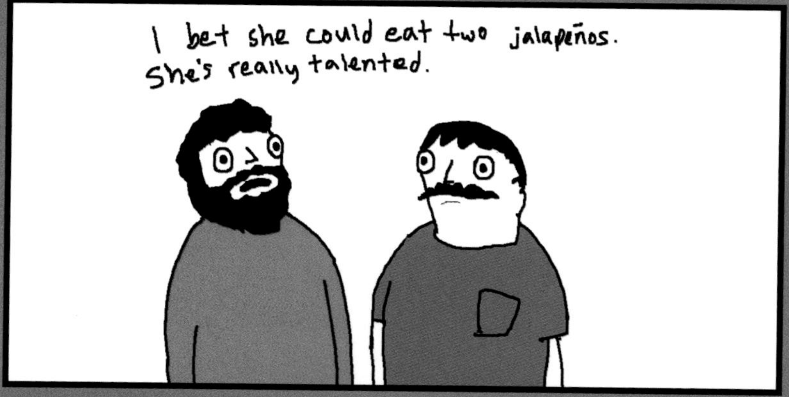
I bet she could eat two jalapeños. She's really talented.

Things escalated quickly, and before the end of the day, my dad had inadvertently volunteered his eight-year-old to face off against a forty-five-year-old man in a hot-sauce-eating challenge.

I think my mom wanted to be against the idea. She made some cursory attempts to oppose it, but . . .

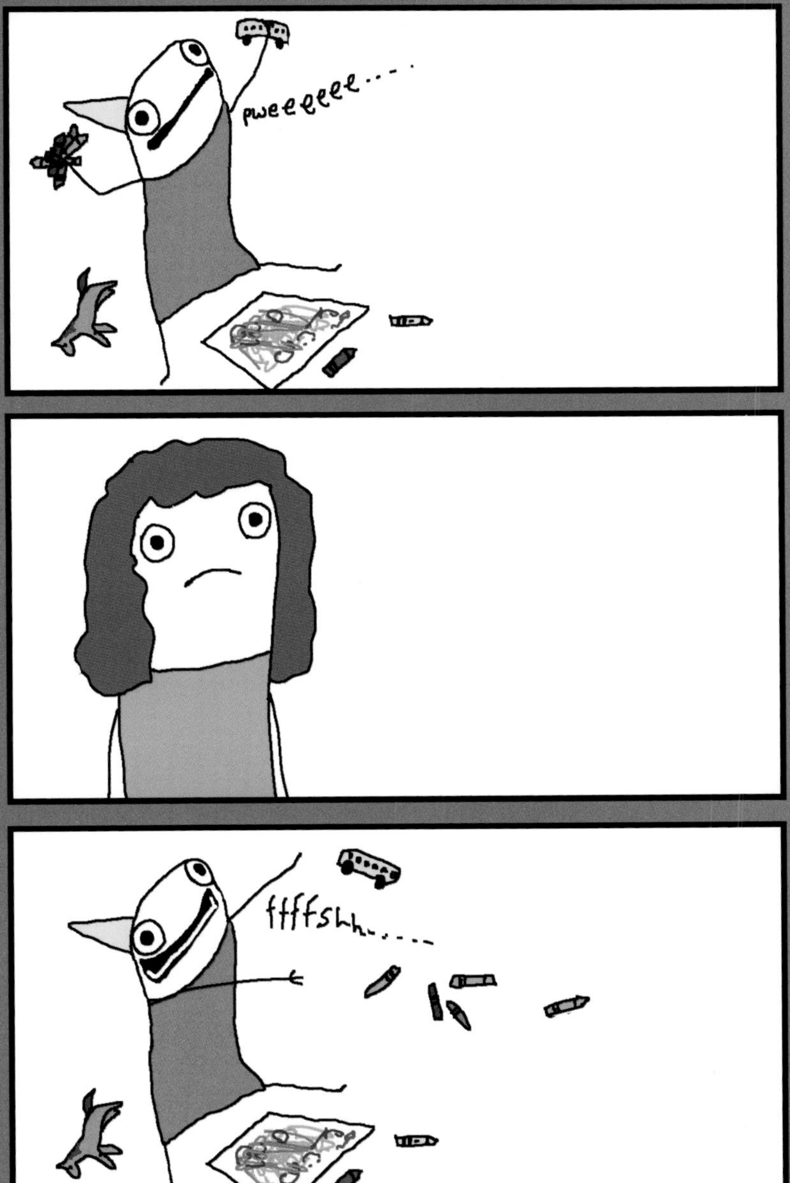
pweeeeee....
ffffshh.....

...maybe it would be good for my self-esteem.
They decided to approach me about it.

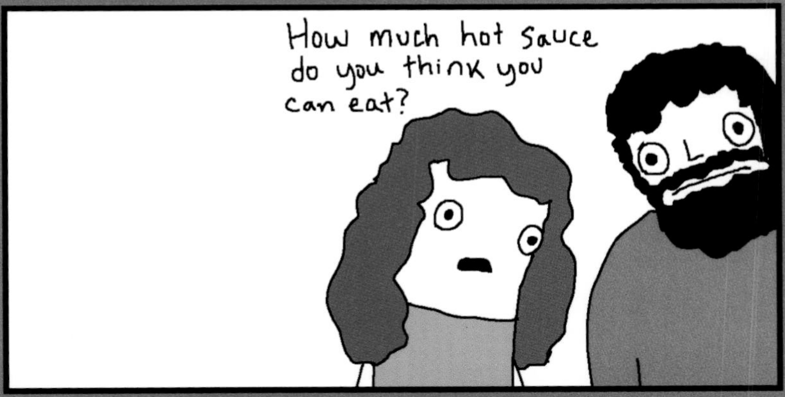
How much hot sauce do you think you can eat?

I considered the question carefully.

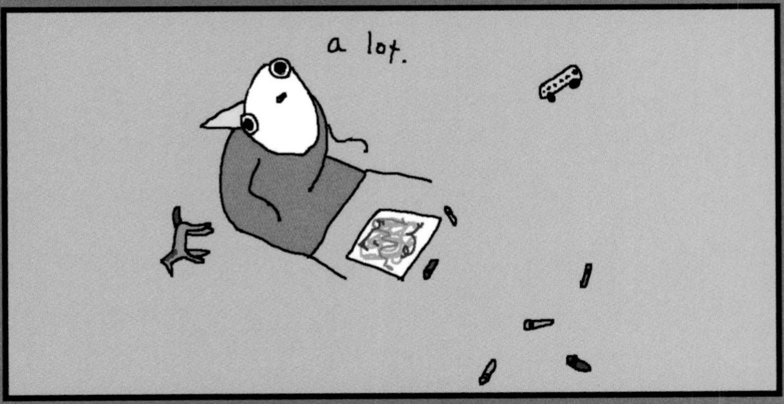
a lot.

Do you think you can eat more than Dad's friend Mike?

My competitive drive hadn't fully developed yet, but, like most children, I yearned for attention and approval, and I couldn't exactly afford to be picky about how I earned it.

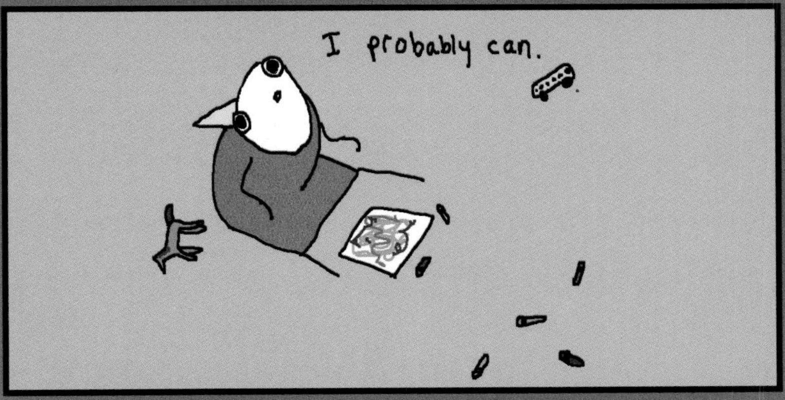
I probably can.

The competition was scheduled for the following Friday. Mike arrived with his weapon of choice—a habanero pepper sauce. We agreed that we would eat increasingly large amounts of the sauce until one of us couldn't take the pain anymore.

I remember being really surprised at how badly the sauce burned. But it was the first time I had ever really had the chance to win anything, and I wanted my parents to be proud of me. I'd rather allow the insides of my mouth to be liquefied than face the shame of defeat, so I carried on as if I didn't even notice the fiery agony engulfing my face.

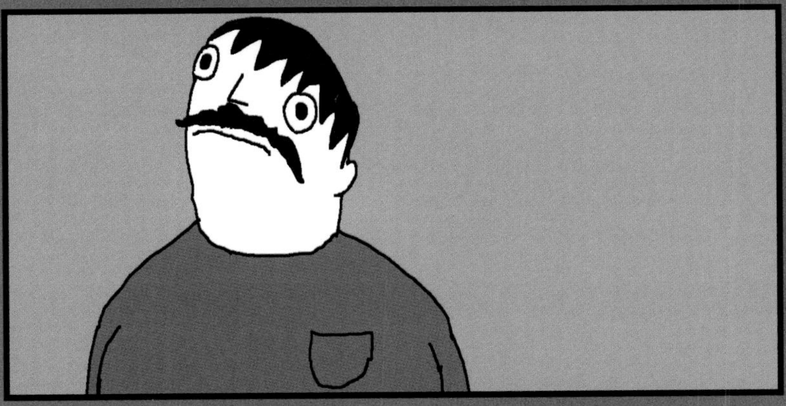

Mike became visibly uncomfortable pretty early on.

Still, his pride held out for an impressively long time. But he was an adult who possessed other skills that he could fall back on in the event of defeat, and that made him weak.

His resolve cracked just after the sixth spoonful.

Everyone was really impressed with me. Maybe I actually *did* have some sort of special ability. Enjoying their admiration, I showboated a bit.

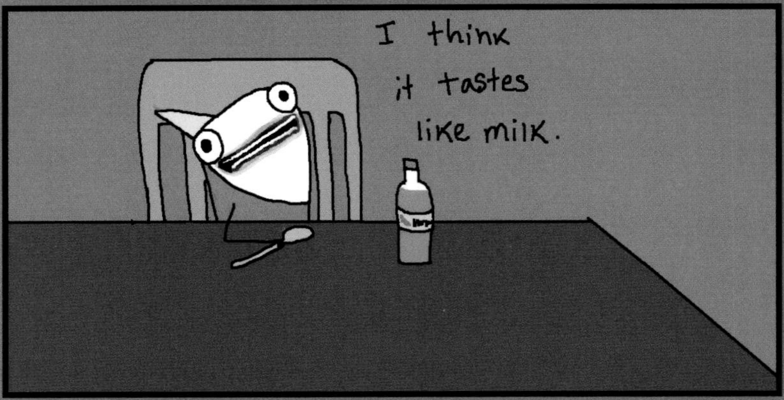
I think it tastes like milk.

And for that one tiny moment, I got to feel like a superhero. If it had all ended there, it would have been one of the great triumphs of my life.

But it didn't end there.

My "talent" became a sort of party trick—something my family would pull out when the conversation died down at dinner.

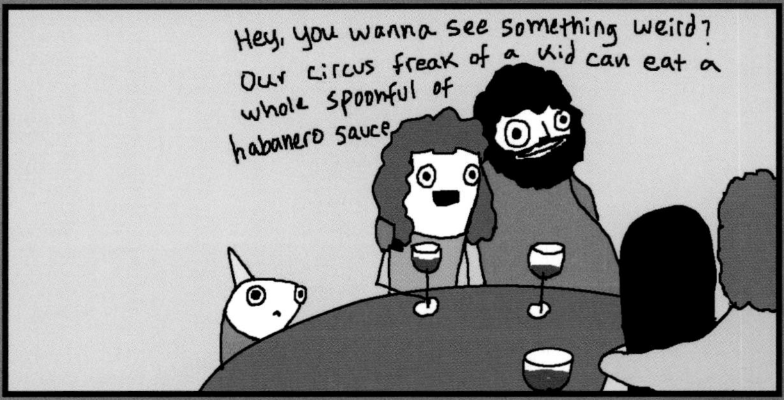
Hey, you wanna see something weird? Our circus freak of a kid can eat a whole spoonful of habanero sauce.

sweetheart, go get the sauce.
It's like she doesn't even feel pain!

I never objected because I didn't want to come clean and ruin everyone's perception of me as some sort of hot sauce savant.

Over time, the misunderstanding expanded. My family began to legitimately believe that my favorite thing in the world was hot sauce. If I "forgot" to put hot sauce on my food, they helpfully reminded me. They consistently brought home newer, spicier, weirder hot sauces for me to try. For Christmas that year, Santa gave me a whole case of hot sauce.

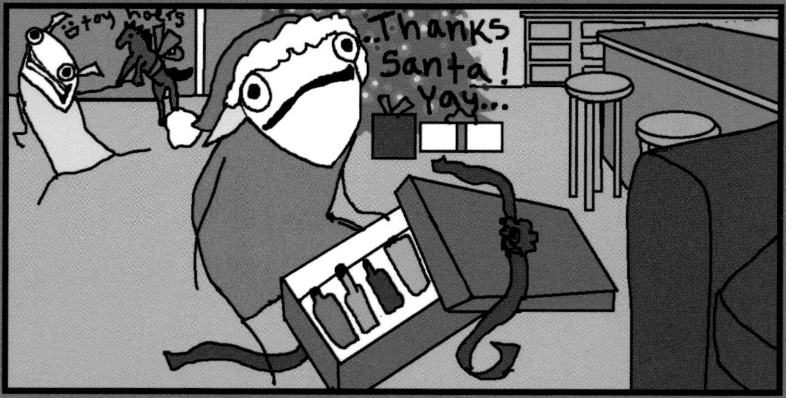
toy
..Thanks Santa! Yay...

Being a child, I was devastated that a potential toy had been replaced by those bottles of painful torture, but I couldn't let anyone know. At that point, I was starting to feel more and more at peace with the idea of admitting failure, but it was too late. I'd been pretending for long enough that it would be too weird and embarrassing to explain myself. There was no choice but to maintain the illusion.

But every time I pretended to love the stuff, it became a bigger part of my identity within my family. Distant relatives and family acquaintances related to me almost entirely through my perceived infatuation with hot sauce.

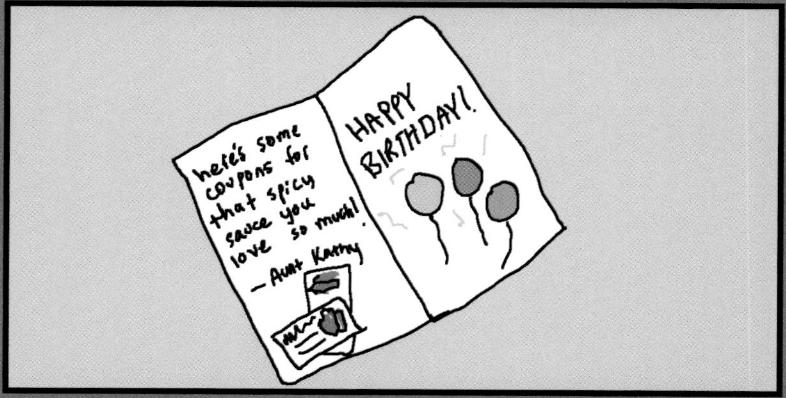
here's some coupons for that spicy sauce you love so much!
—Aunt Kathy
HAPPY BIRTHDAY!

Is that the one that likes hot sauce? She should learn to play something by the Red Hot Chili Peppers!! LOL
Well, she sure knows Hot Cross Buns HAHA!
toot toot toot

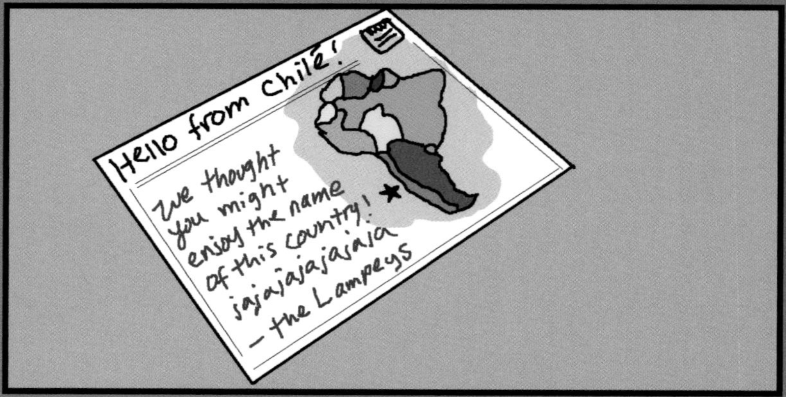
Hello from Chile!
We thought you might enjoy the name of this country!
jajajajajajaja
—the Lampeys

And through it all—no matter how ridiculous and tangential it got—I never told them the truth.

But here it is:

Dear family members and people whom my family members led to believe I adored hot sauce with the fiery intensity of ten thousand jalapeños: I lied. It was all an act. I only like hot sauce a normal amount, and that's after twenty years of acclimating myself to it. You may never understand what would possess a person to lie about something so insignificant for over twenty years, but all I can say is that it spiraled and I was every bit as confused about it as you probably are now.

This Is Why I'll Never Be an Adult

I have repeatedly discovered that it is important for me not to surpass my capacity for responsibility. Over the years, this capacity has grown, but the results of exceeding it have not changed.

Normally, my capacity is exceeded gradually, through the accumulation of simple daily tasks.

I'M SUCCESSFUL!!!
Wait... what is this? I have to go to the bank? What am I, some sort of wizard?
Look! I'm actually getting stuff done today!
SYSTEM FAILURE
I'm doing pretty well! I can breathe and beat my heart like a motherfucking champion!
I did THREE THINGS yesterday! Now I'm supposed to keep doing things? It's like the things never end!
Only the very basics necessary for survival
A few minor responsibilities, like grocery shopping and laundry
One major responsibility, like having a job
Now there are a few more things....
Now even a few more....
One more....
LEVEL OF RESPONSIBILITY

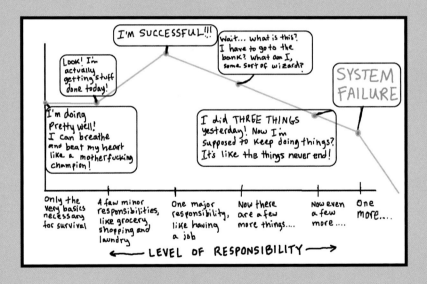

But a few times a year, I spontaneously decide that I'm ready to be a *real* adult. I don't know why I decide this; it always ends terribly for me. But I do it anyway. I sit myself down and tell myself how I'm going to start cleaning the house every day and paying my bills on time and replying to emails before my inbox reaches quadruple digits. Schedules are drafted. Day planners are purchased. I stock up on fancy food because I'm also planning on morphing into a master chef and actually cooking instead of just eating nachos for dinner every night. I prepare for my new life as an adult like some people prepare for the apocalypse.

The first day or two of my plans usually goes okay.

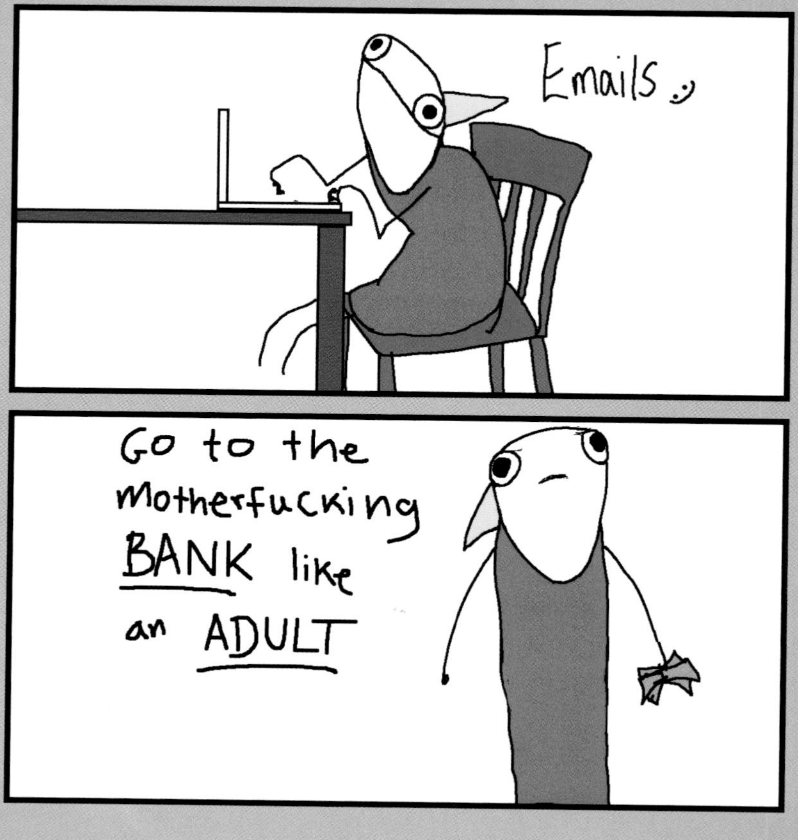

Emails :)
Go to the motherfucking BANK like an ADULT

Grocery Shopping!
CLEAN ALL THE THINGS!

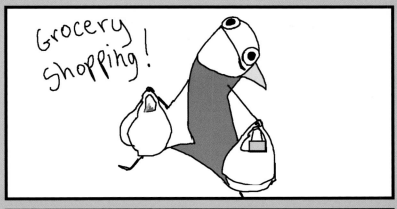

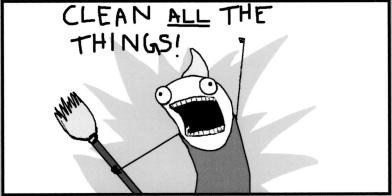

For a little while, I actually feel grown-up and responsible. I strut around with my head held high, looking the other responsible people in the eye with that knowing glance that says, *I understand. I'm responsible now too. Just look at my groceries.*

At some point, I start feeling self-congratulatory.

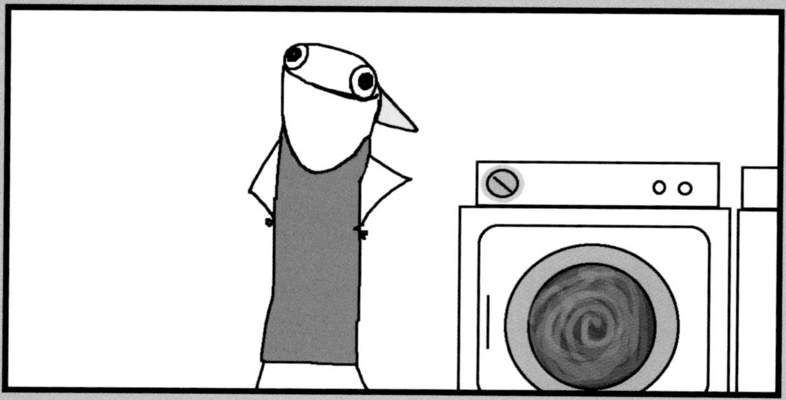

This is a mistake.

I begin to feel like I've accomplished my goals. It's like I think that adulthood is something that can be earned like a trophy in one monumental burst of effort.

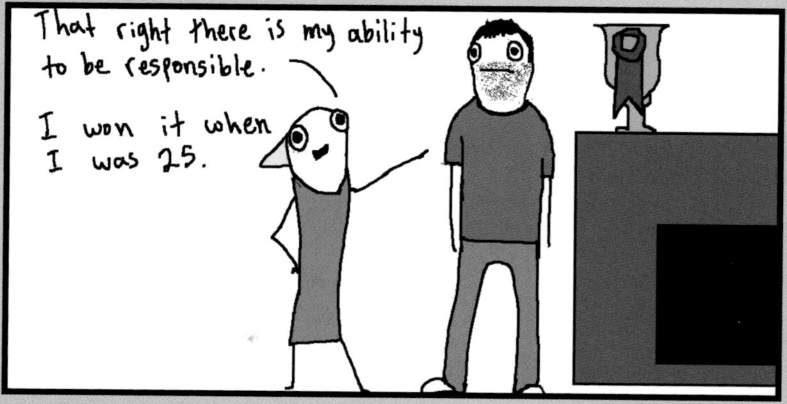
That right there is my ability to be responsible.
I won it when I was 25.

What usually ends up happening is that I completely wear myself out. Thinking that I've earned it, I give myself permission to slack off for a while and recover. Since I've exceeded my capacity for responsibility in such a dramatic fashion, I end up needing to take more recovery time than usual. This is when the guilt spiral starts.

The longer I procrastinate on returning phone calls and emails, the more guilty I feel about it. The guilt I feel causes me to avoid the issue further, which only leads to more guilt and more procrastination. It gets to the point where I don't email someone for fear of reminding them that they emailed me and thus giving them a reason to be disappointed in me.

Then the guilt from my ignored responsibilities grows so large that merely carrying it around with me feels like a huge responsibility. It takes up a sizable portion of my capacity, leaving me almost completely useless for anything other than consuming nachos and surfing the Internet like an attention-deficient squirrel on PCP.

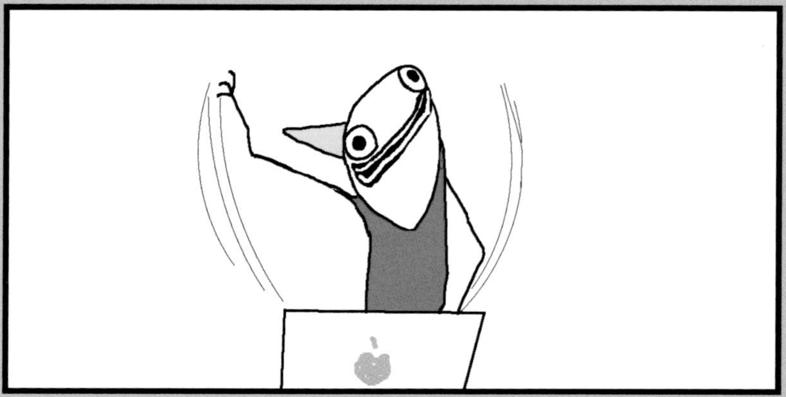

At some point in this endlessly spiraling disaster, I am forced to throw all of my energy into trying to be an adult again, just to dig myself out of the pit I've fallen into. The problem is that I enter this round of attempted adulthood already burnt out from the last round. I can't not fail.

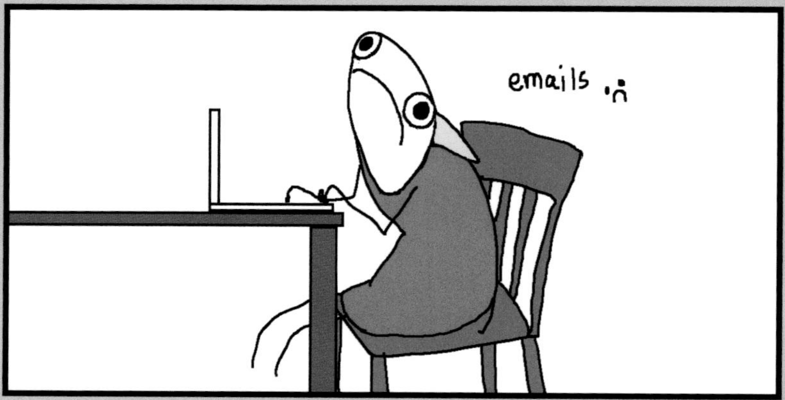
emails

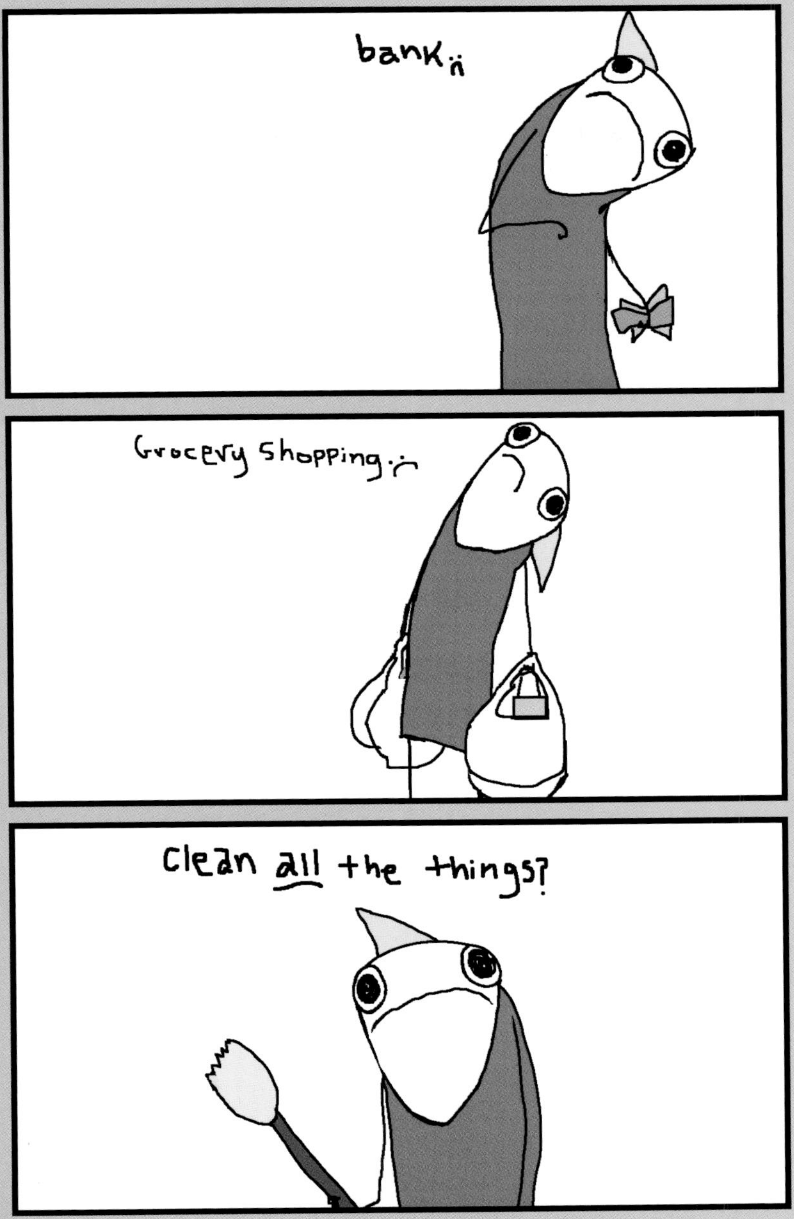
bank ..
Grocery shopping .. :(
clean all the things?

It always ends the same way. Slumped and haggard, I contemplate the seemingly endless tasks ahead of me.

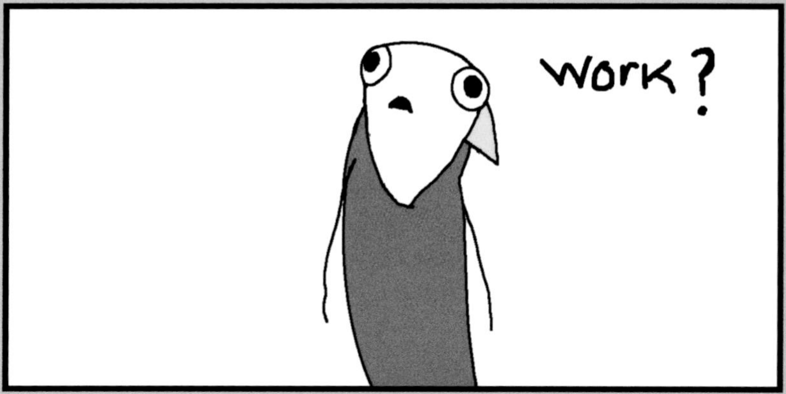
work?

And then I rebel.

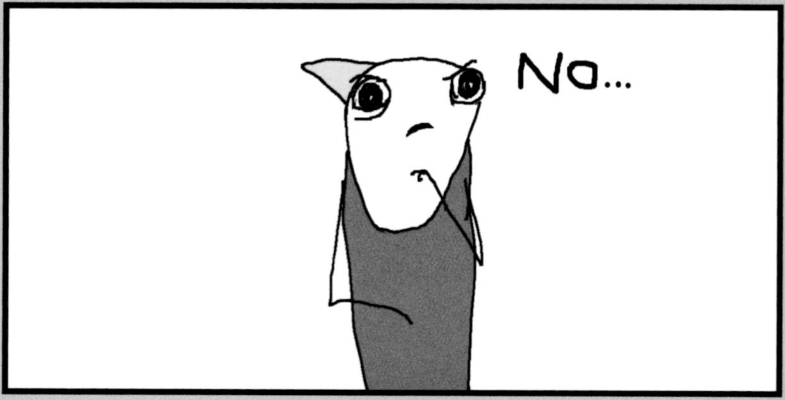
No...

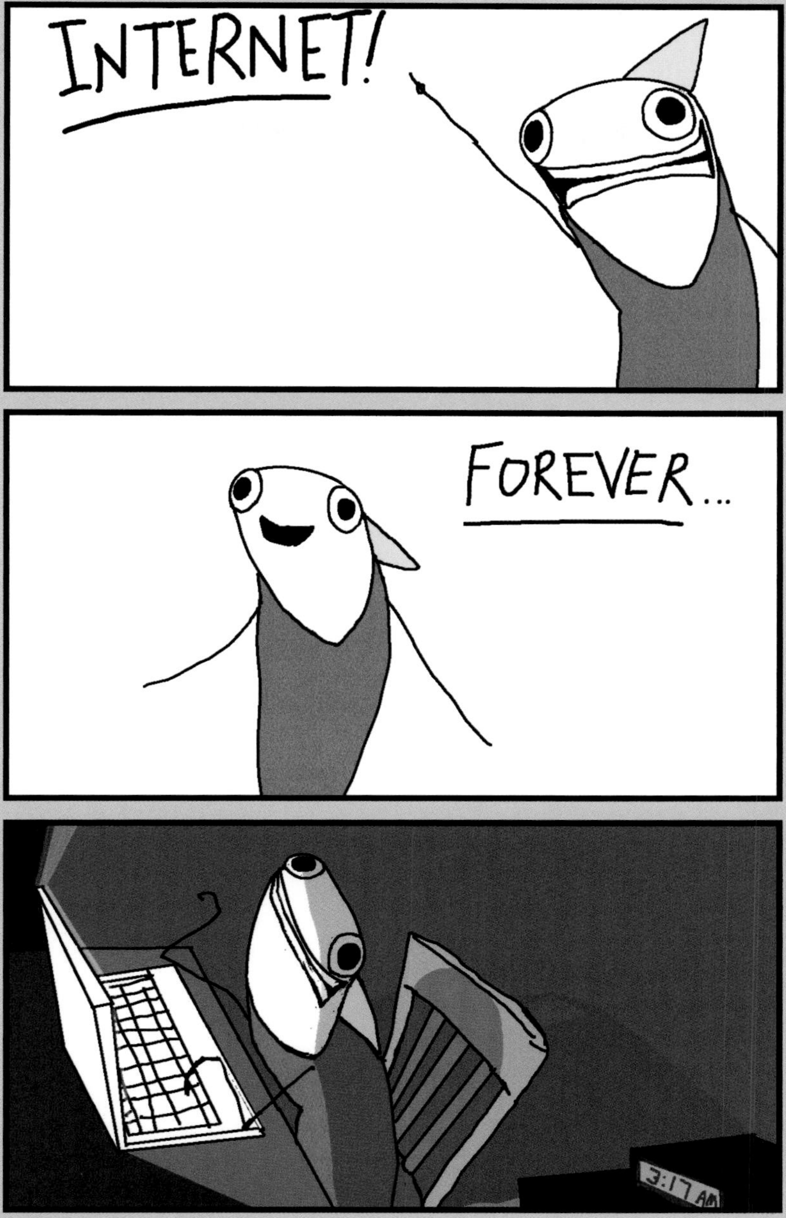
INTERNET!
FOREVER...
3:17 AM

The Parrot

The toy parrot was given to us by a family friend who either didn't understand children or hated my parents.

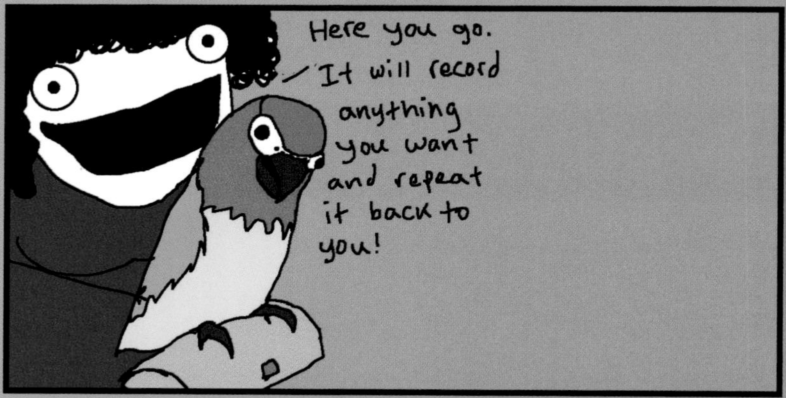
Here you go. It will record anything you want and repeat it back to you!

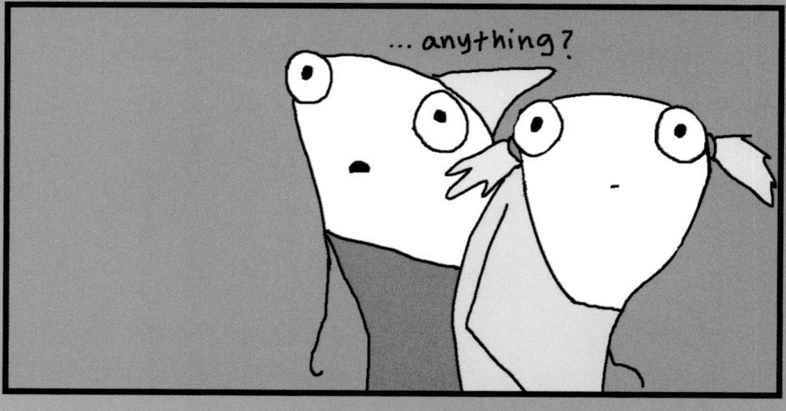
...anything?

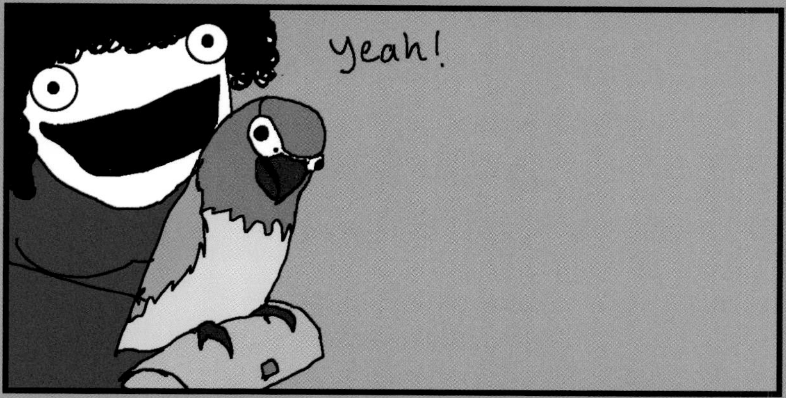
yeah!

Imagine a grizzly bear. Now imagine that by some accident of nature, the bear sprouts wings and learns how to use a flamethrower. That would be a really unfair thing to have happen. Bears are already powerful enough without those things.

Similarly, children are already annoying enough without access to a toy that will record and repeat any sound in the entire world.

We began abusing the parrot's capabilities almost immediately.

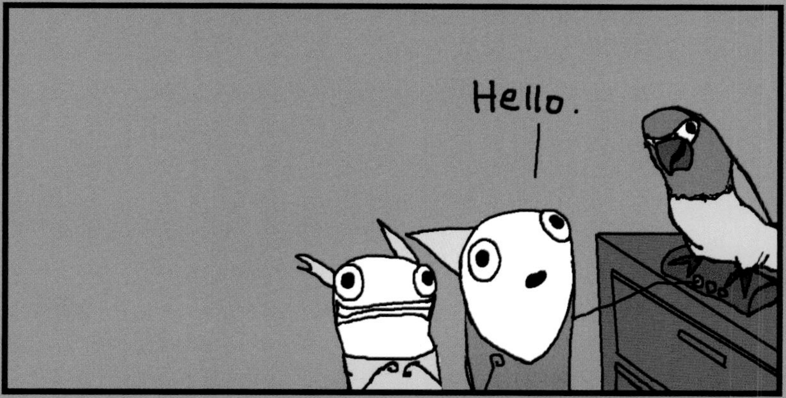
Hello.

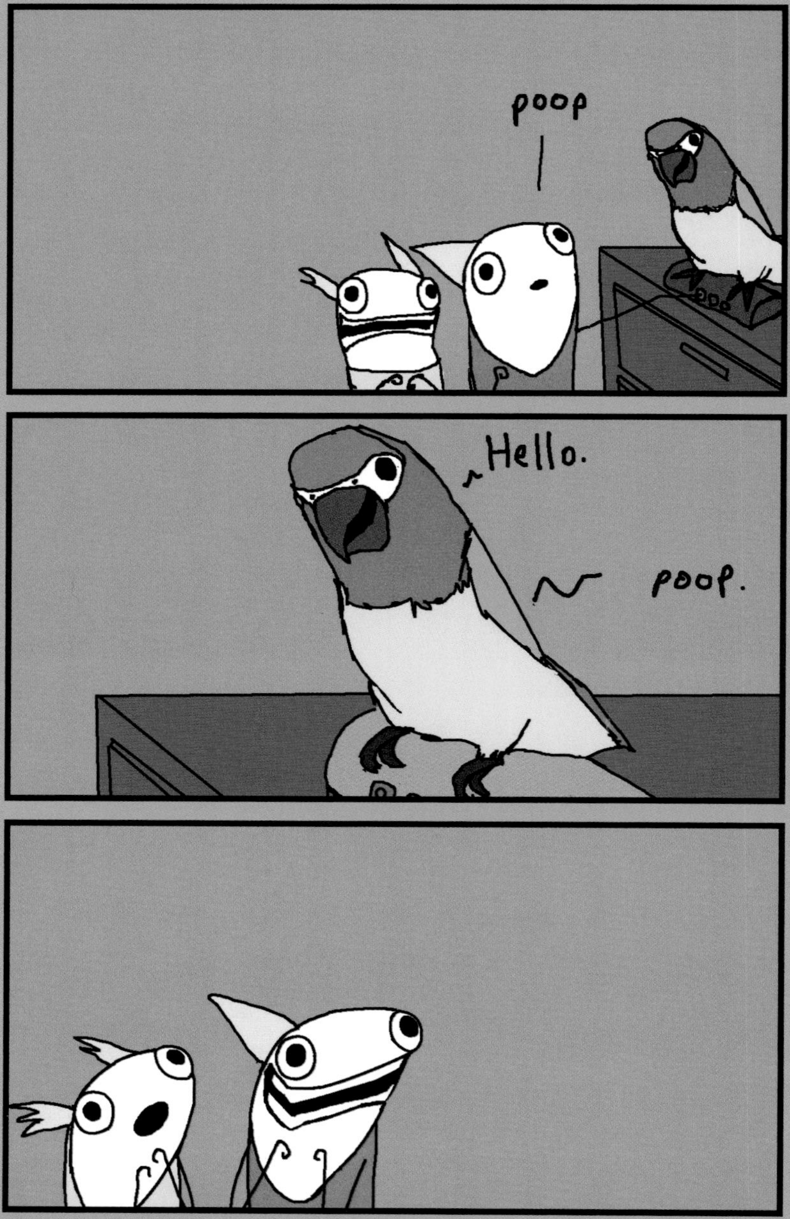
poop
Hello.
poop.

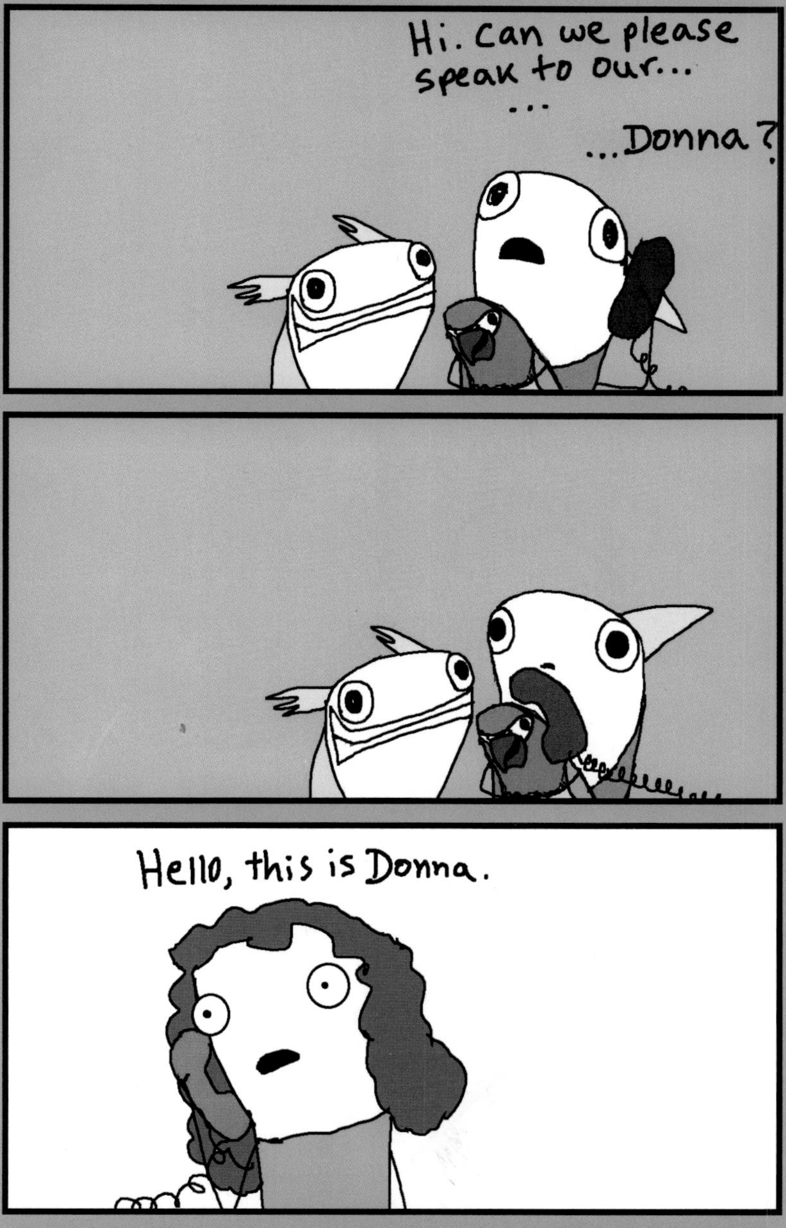
Hi. Can we please speak to our...
...
...Donna?
Hello, this is Donna.

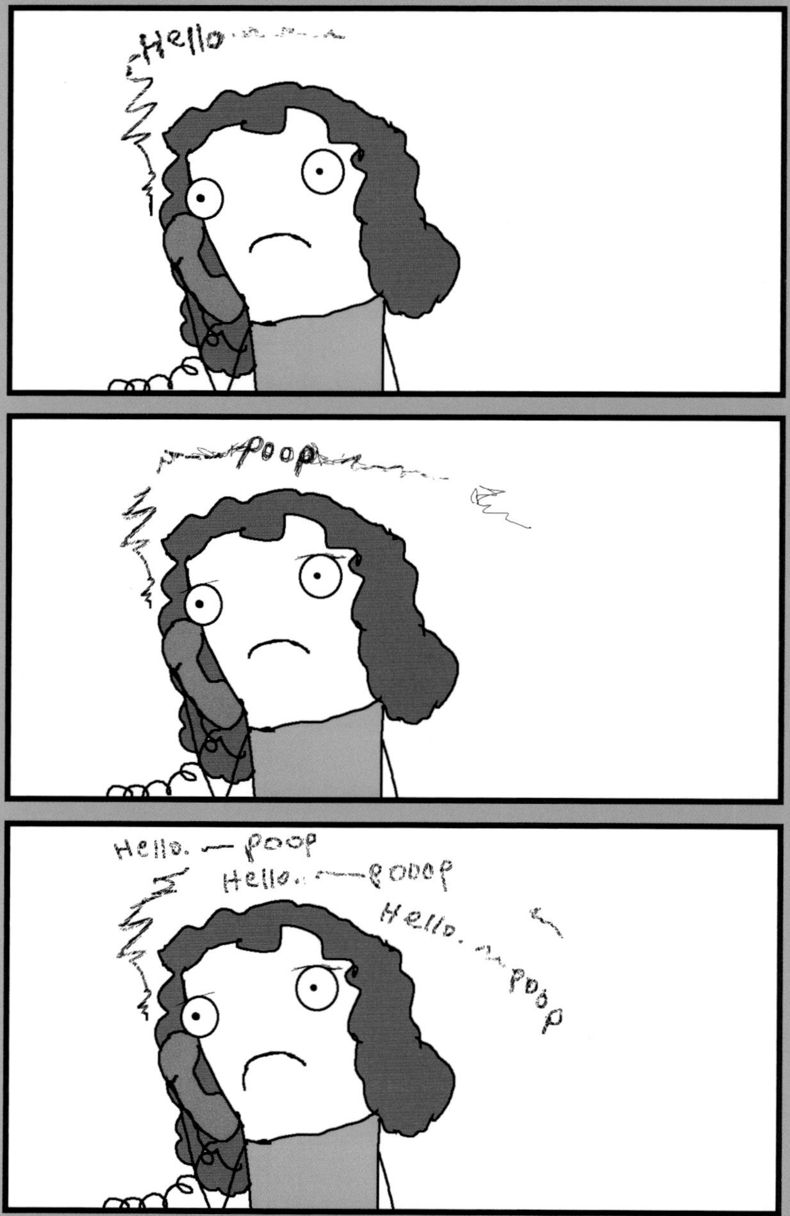
Hello
poop
Hello. — poop
Hello. — poop
Hello. — poop

Suddenly, every sound sparkled with new and exciting possibilities.

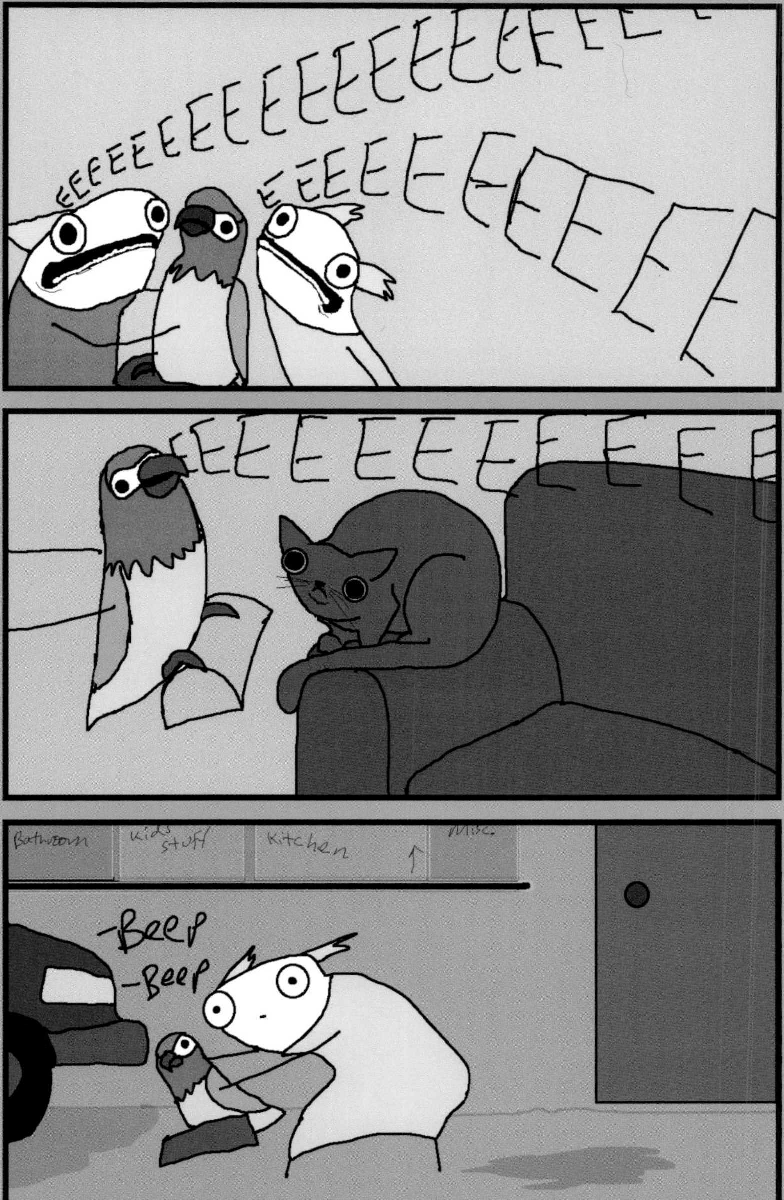

EEEEEEEEEEEEEEEEEEEEEEE
EEEEEEEEEEEEEEE
EEEEEEEEEEEEE
Bathroom
Kids stuff
Kitchen
Misc.
-Beep
-Beep

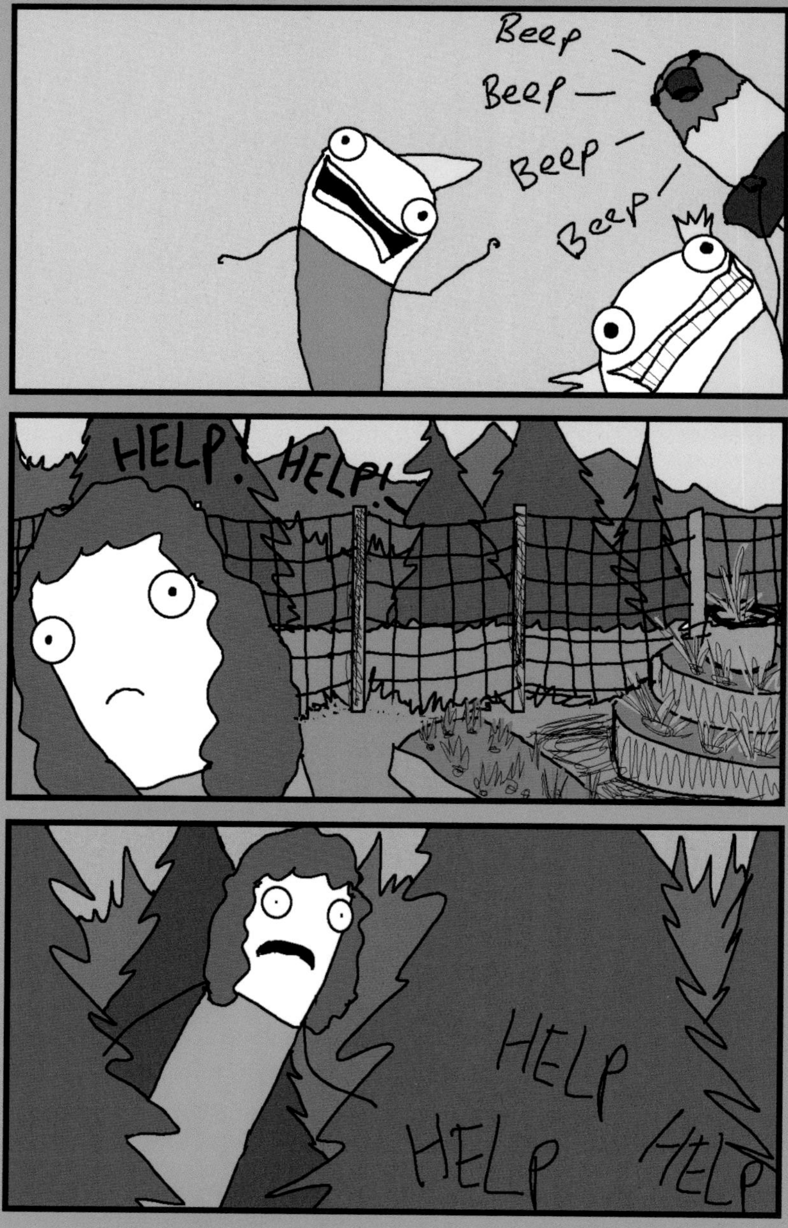
Beep
Beep
Beep
Beep
HELP!
HELP!
HELP
HELP
HELP

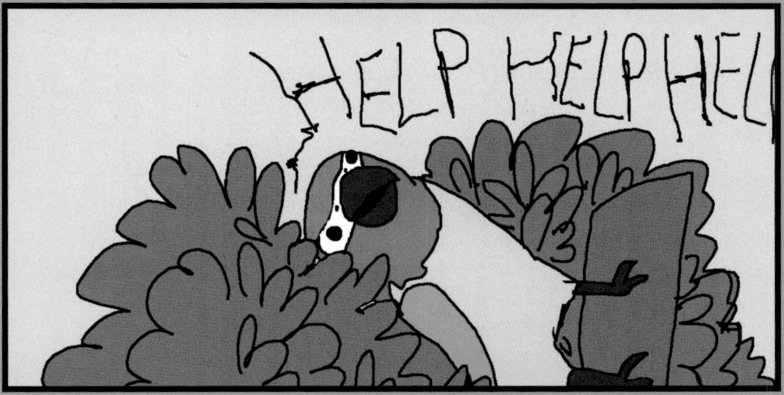
HELP HELP HEL

The parrot gave us a sense of power we'd never experienced before.

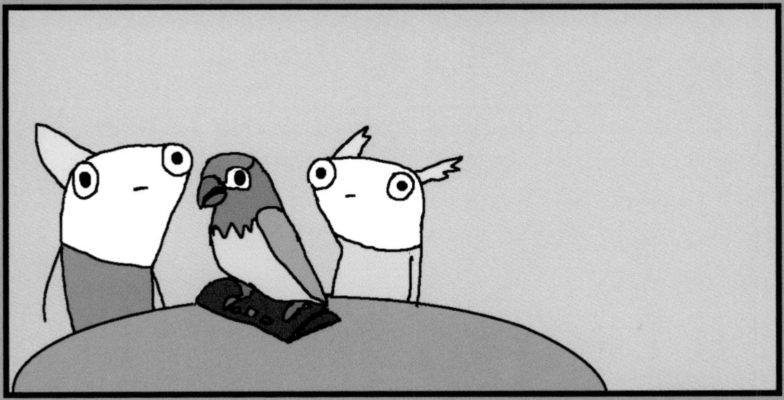

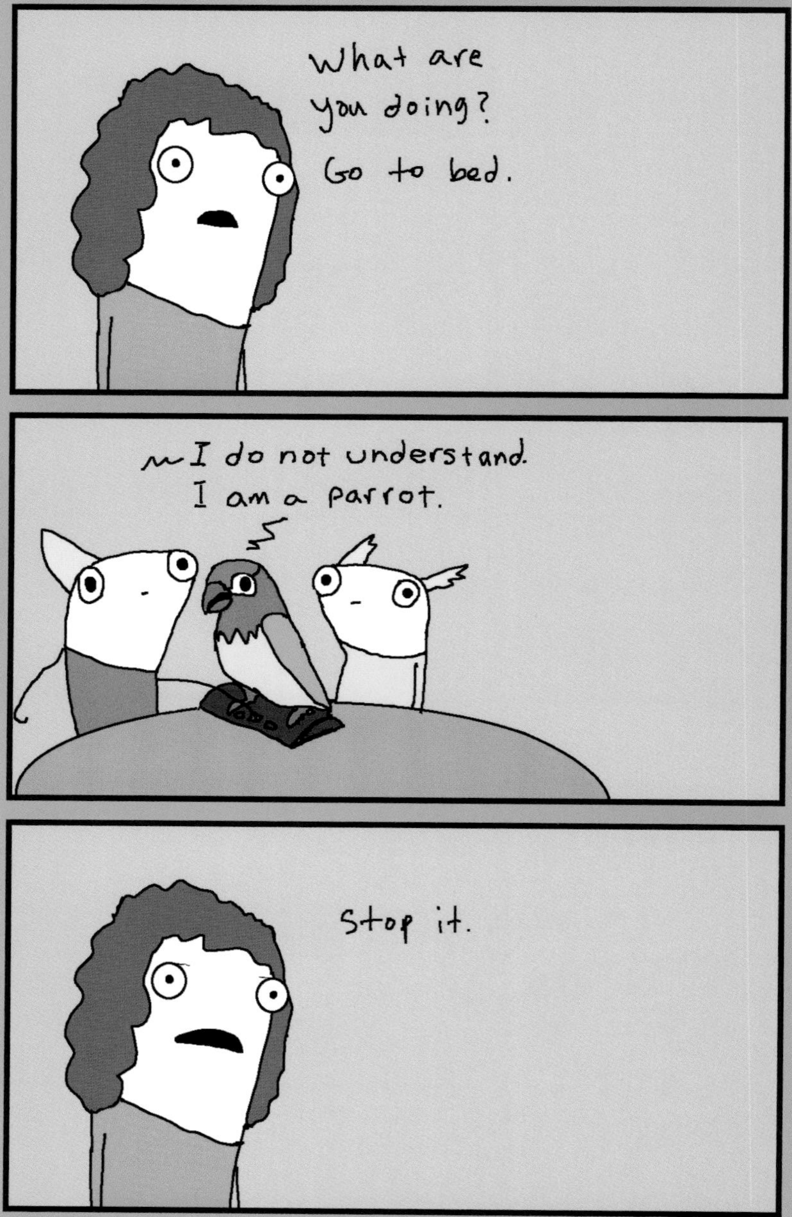
What are you doing? Go to bed.
I do not understand. I am a parrot.
Stop it.

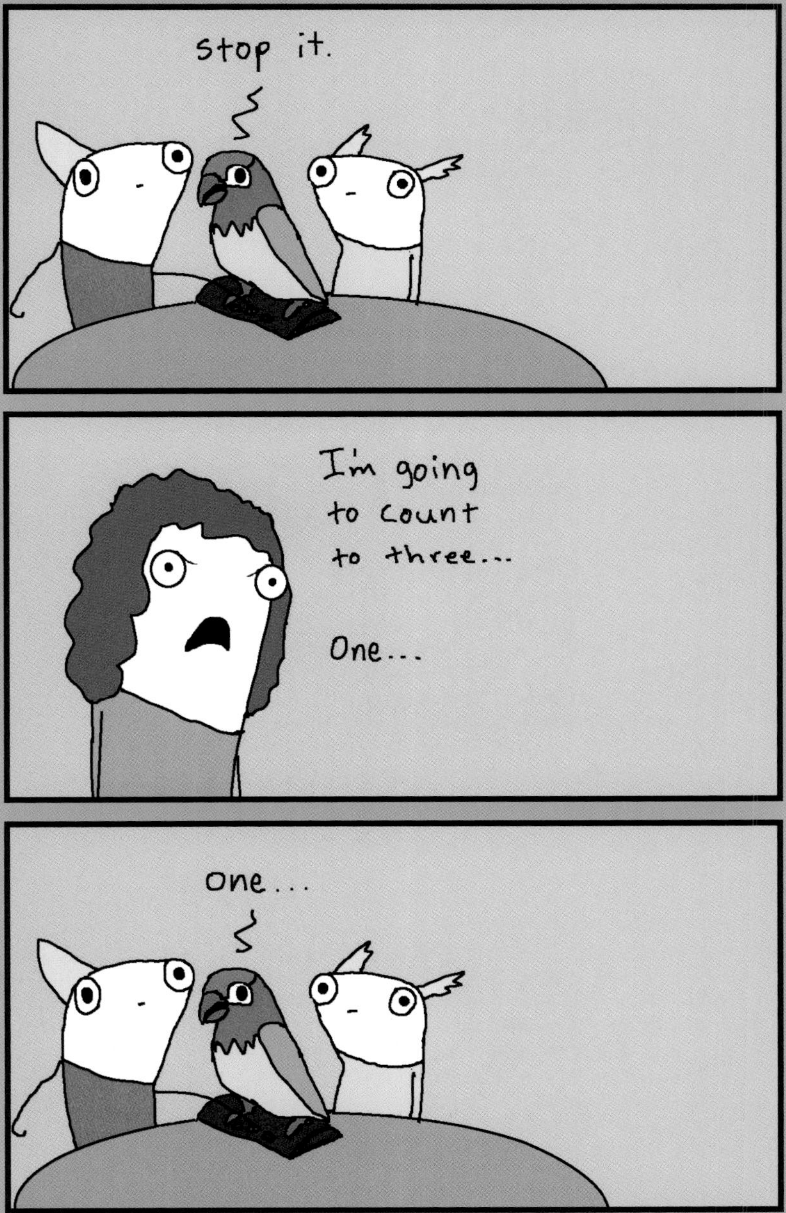
stop it.
I'm going to count to three...
One...
one...

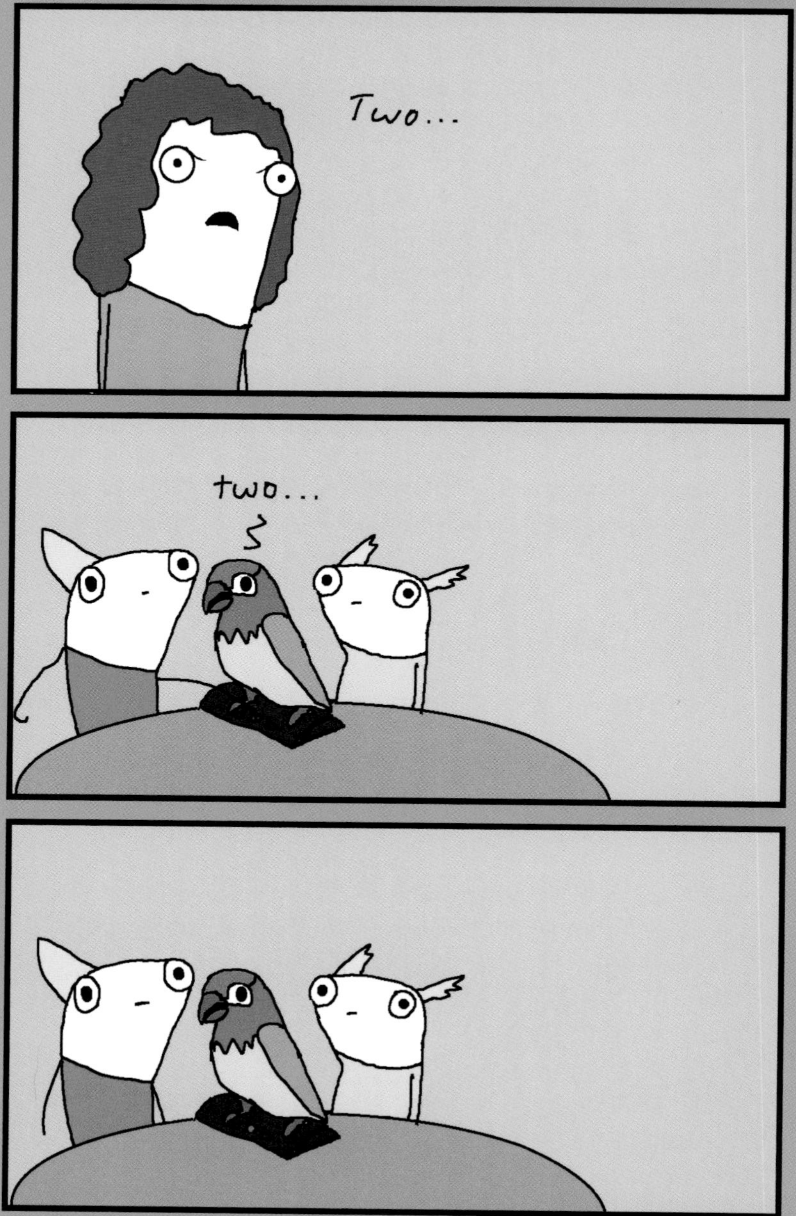
Two...
two...

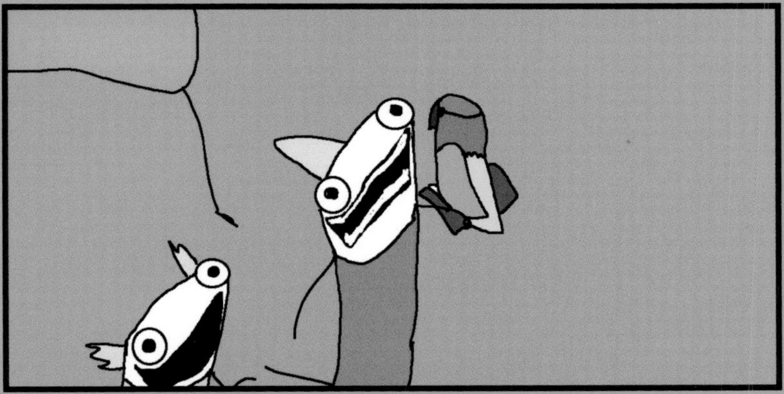

Our parents hoped that maybe we'd get bored with it after a while and forget about it, but that's not what happened.

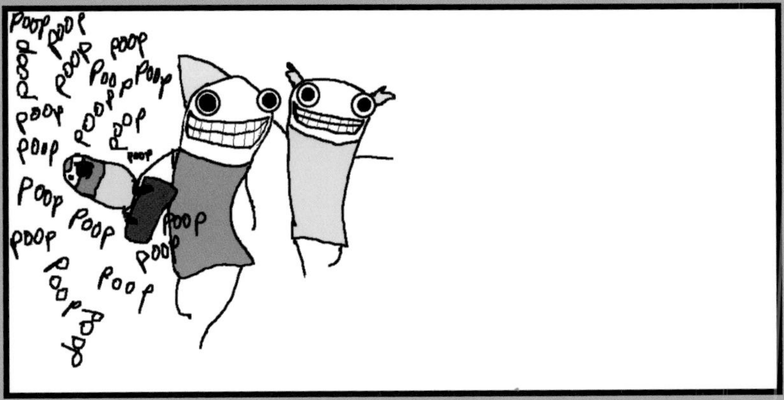
POOP POOP POOP POOP POOP POOP POOP POOP POOP POOP POOP POOP POOP POOP POOP POOP POOP POOP POOP POOP POOP POOP

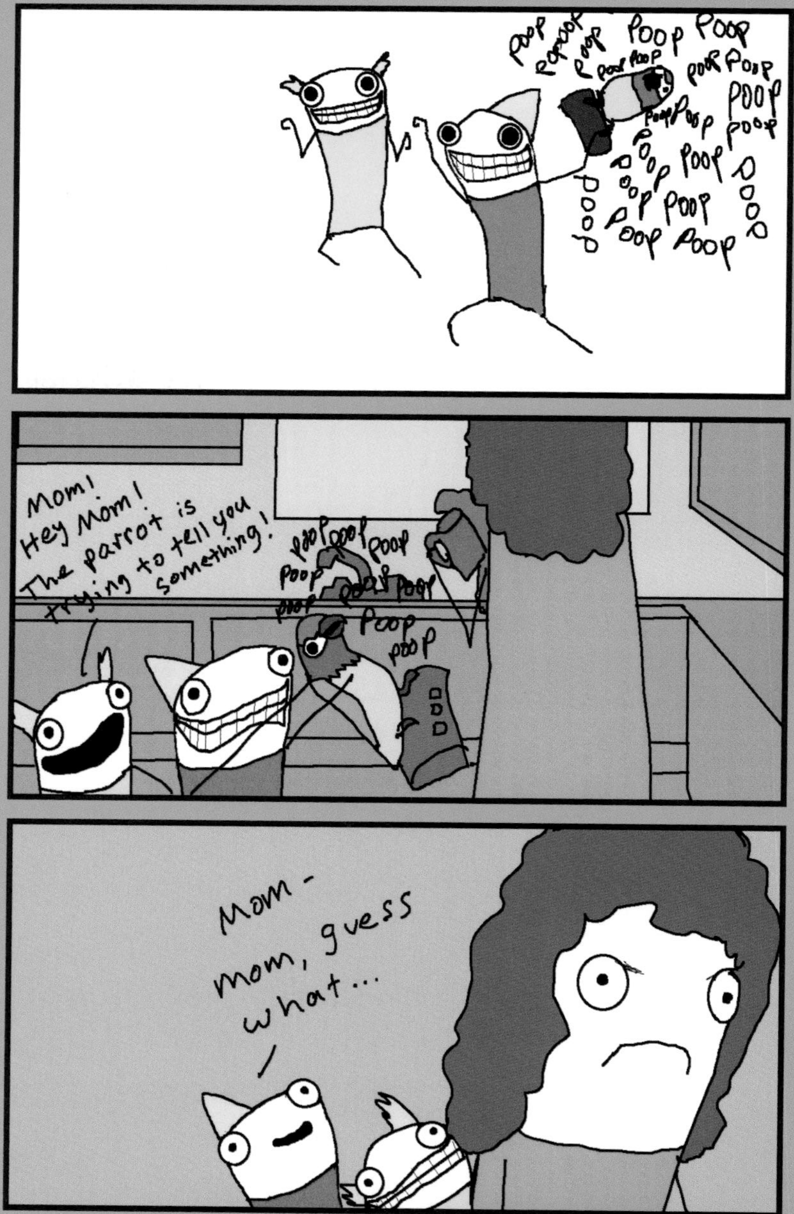

Mom!
Hey Mom!
The parrot is trying to tell you something!
Mom-mom, guess what...

Then one day, the parrot suddenly stopped working.

Several other toys had suffered similar fates, most notably our Bop It and a novelty toy called Crazy Singing Santa. And, as with the Bop It and the Crazy Singing Santa, our mom didn't know how to fix it.

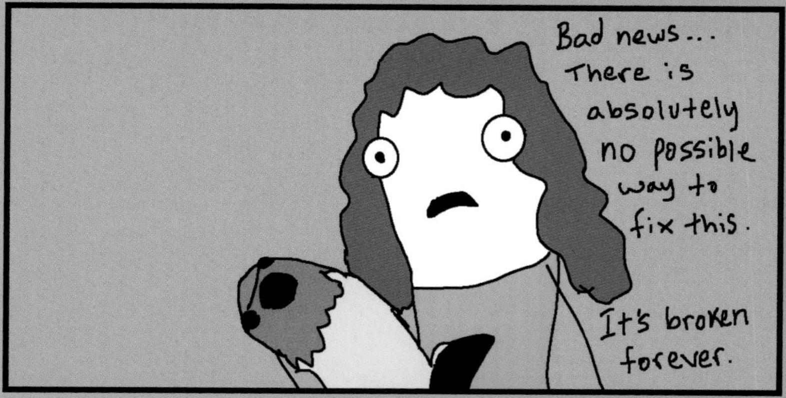
Bad news... There is absolutely no possible way to fix this.
It's broken forever.

Neither did our dad.

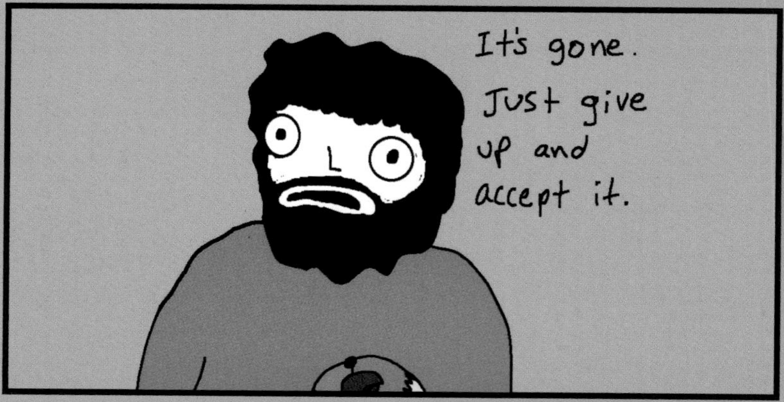
It's gone. Just give up and accept it.

The only other adult we knew who lived nearby was our crazy aunt Laurie. Laurie was quite handy, and sure enough, she found the problem almost right away.

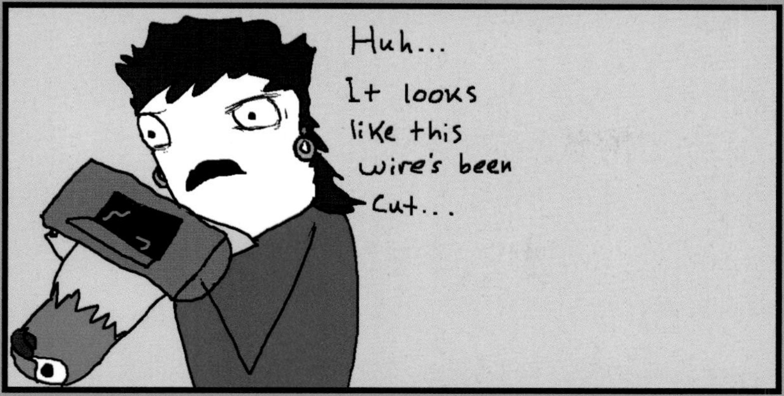
Huh...
It looks like this wire's been cut...

In retrospect, I'm sure she figured out that the parrot's demise wasn't exactly an accident. But she fixed it anyway, probably just to see what would happen. Laurie always had a soft spot for chaos.

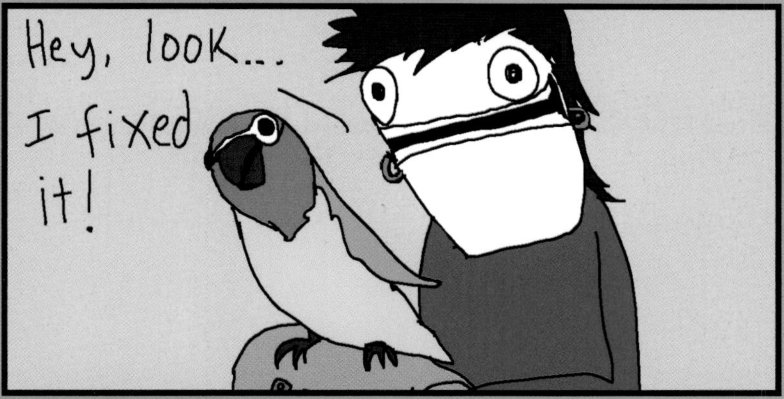
Hey, look...
I fixed it!

At this point, our parents were still unaware that the toy had been repaired, which provided us a unique opportunity to use it against them.

We began by recording the most confusing sound we could think of...

RRChkRRRRRRRChkChkRRRRRRRChk

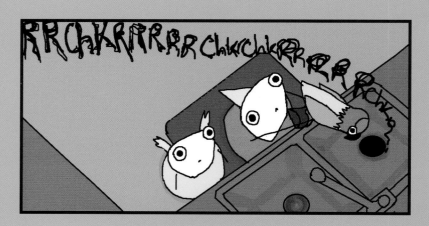

Then we waited.

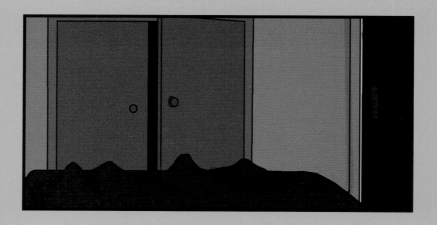

It wasn't a particularly brilliant plan. In fact, one could argue that nothing about it made sense at all. And we knew it wouldn't end well. We knew we wouldn't be able to escape once we were found. But we weren't driven by logic. We were driven by something deeper— some desperate part of us that maybe just wanted to see exactly how obnoxious we could be.

We never saw the parrot again. I'm sure it was burned or angrily tossed out of a moving vehicle. Like a cursed artifact, the only way to be rid of it was to destroy it completely.

However, we soon discovered a substitute.

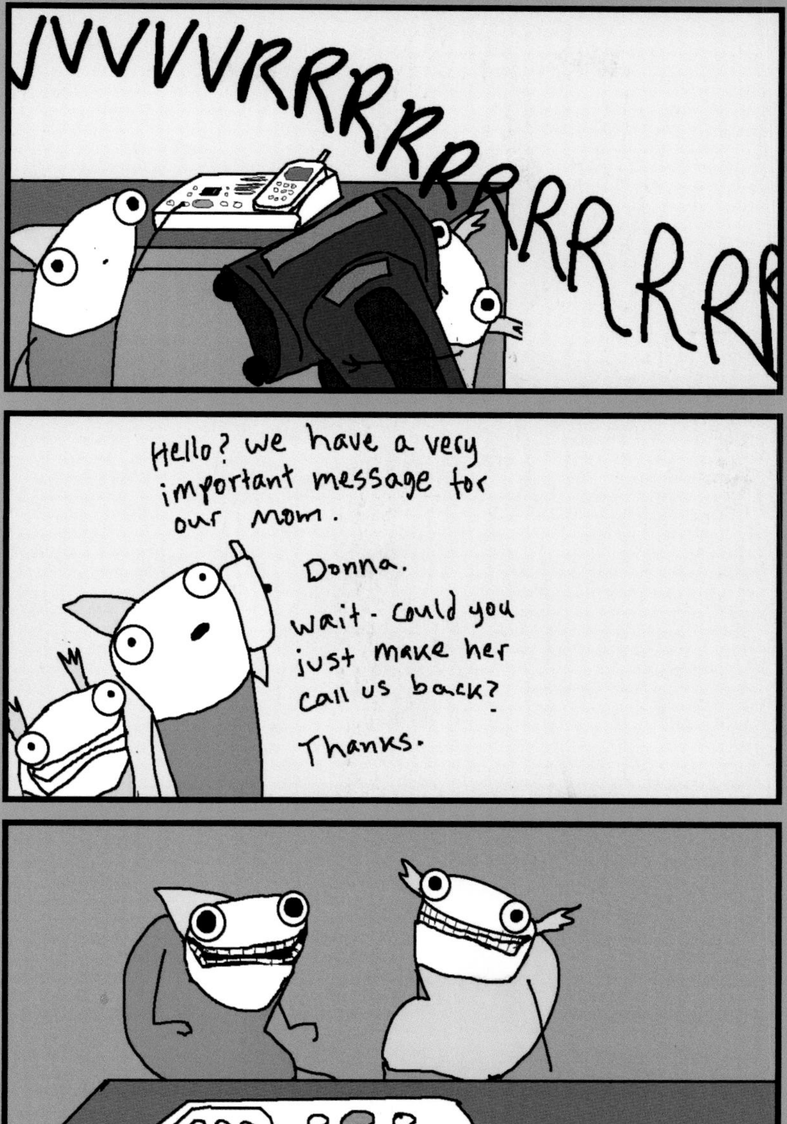
VVVVVRRRRRRRRRRRRR
Hello? we have a very important message for our mom.
Donna.
wait - could you just make her call us back?
Thanks.

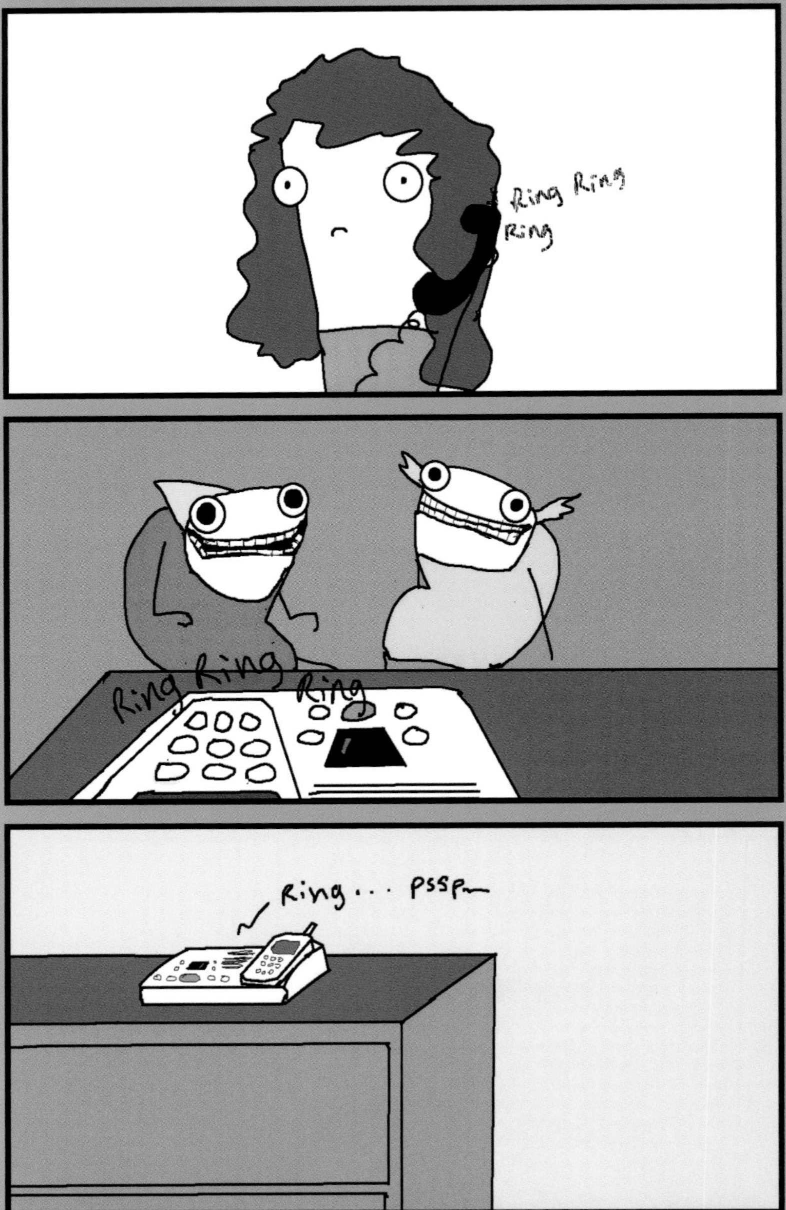
Ring Ring
Ring
Ring Ring
Ring
Ring... pssp

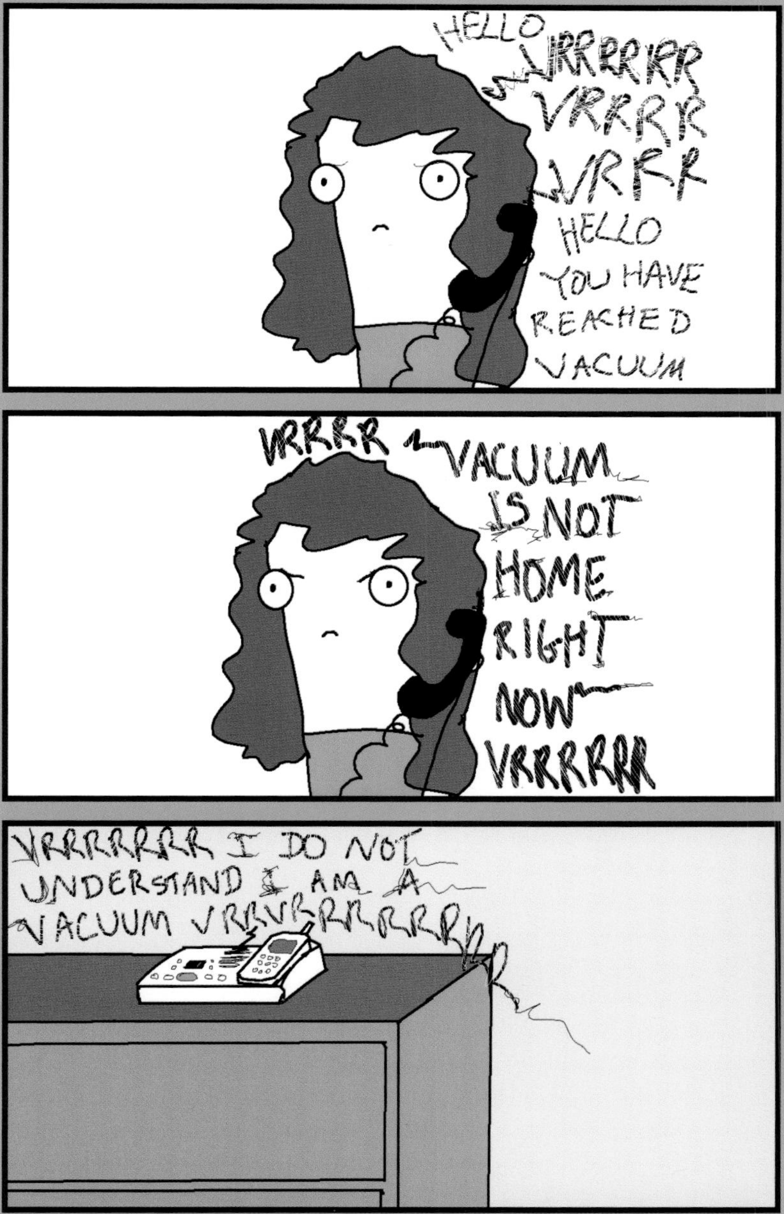
HELLO VRRRRRRR VRRRR VRRRR
HELLO YOU HAVE REACHED VACUUM
VRRRR VACUUM IS NOT HOME RIGHT NOW VRRRRRR
VRRRRRRRR I DO NOT UNDERSTAND I AM A VACUUM VRRVRRRRRR

Dinosaur (the Goose Story)

The noise started while Duncan and I were watching a scary movie. It was a scary noise—like metal grinding on metal—and at first, it was tough to differentiate it from the noises in the movie.

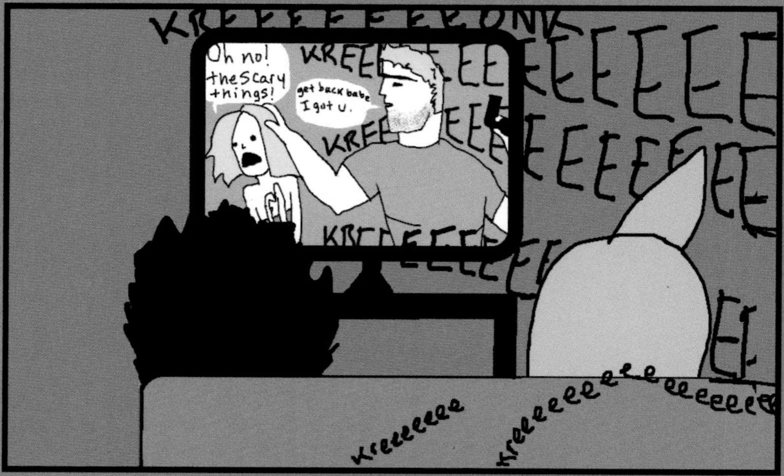
Oh no! the Scary things!
get back babe I got u.

But it continued even when the action on screen was not supposed to be scary.

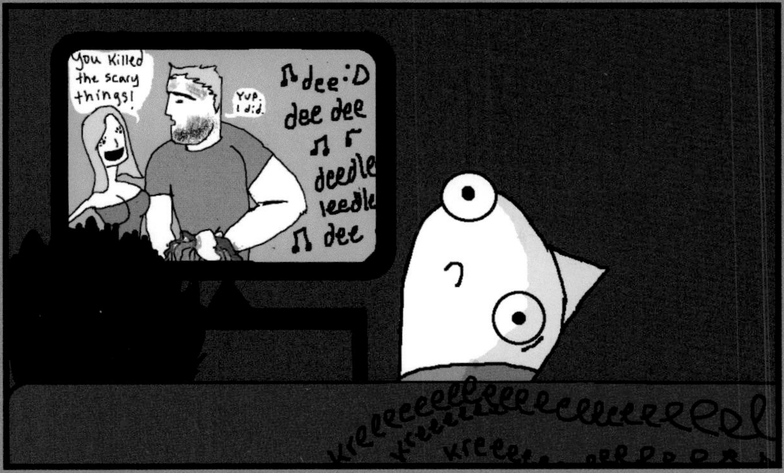
You killed the scary things!
Yup. I did.
dee :D dee dee
deedle leedle dee

I hadn't planned on investigating the source of the noise, because, as you know from watching scary movies, people who investigate noises die.

But then the neighbor's dog began growling and yelping.

I looked at Duncan and said, "Do you hear that?" He said, "Hear what?" I told him I thought the neighbor's dog was being murdered by something. He told me to stop being silly—the dog was probably just playing.

But I was sure there was something wrong.

I crept closer to the door, my mind flooding with horrible premonitions of what I might find on the other side.

The dog's yelps suddenly went silent.

I braced myself for the disemboweling that was sure to follow and opened the door. But to my surprise, there was no immediate violence. I crept into the yard, scanning the darkness for the source of the sound.

The dog had run off, but as I edged closer to the far corner of the yard, a dark shape came into focus:

It was a goose, lurking nonchalantly in the shadows, pecking at the ground. As I was looking at it, it emitted a horrible noise that sounded like metal grinding on metal.

When it finally registered that the source of the sound was merely a honking goose, I was relieved.

Then I had a flashback to my childhood.

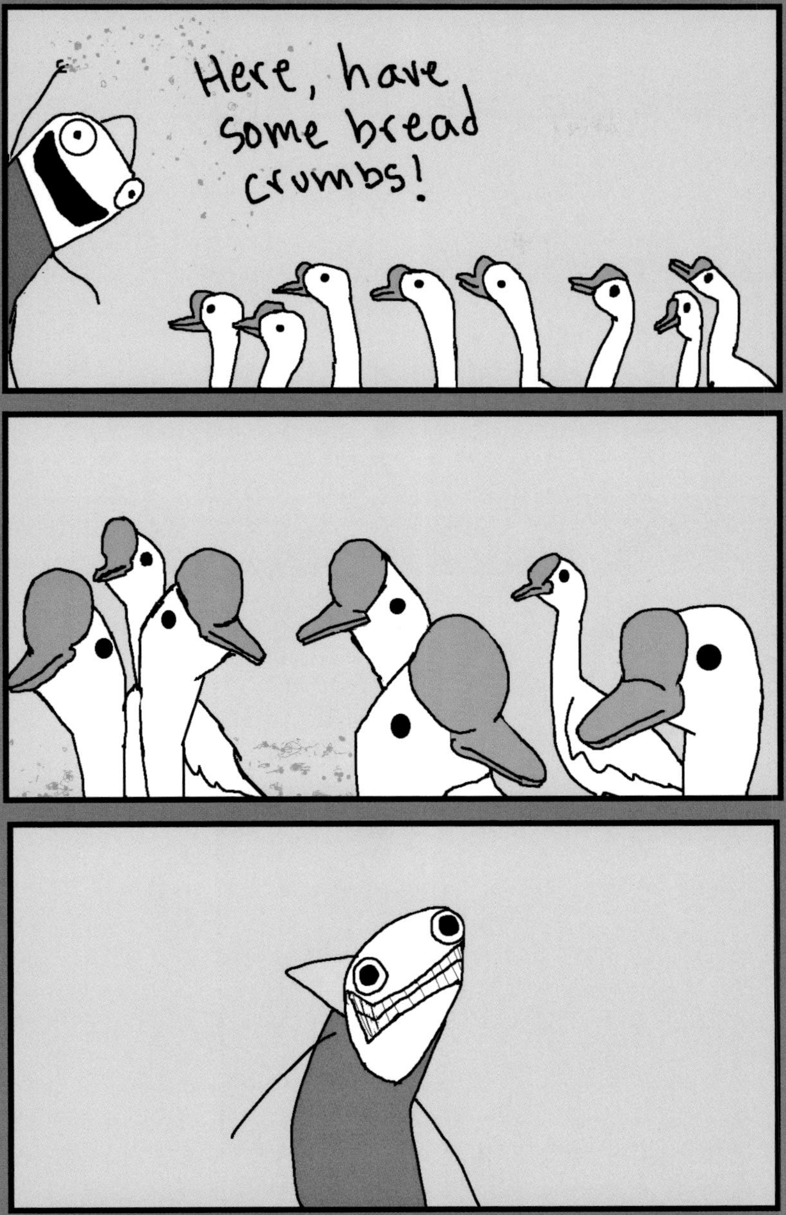
Here, have some bread crumbs!

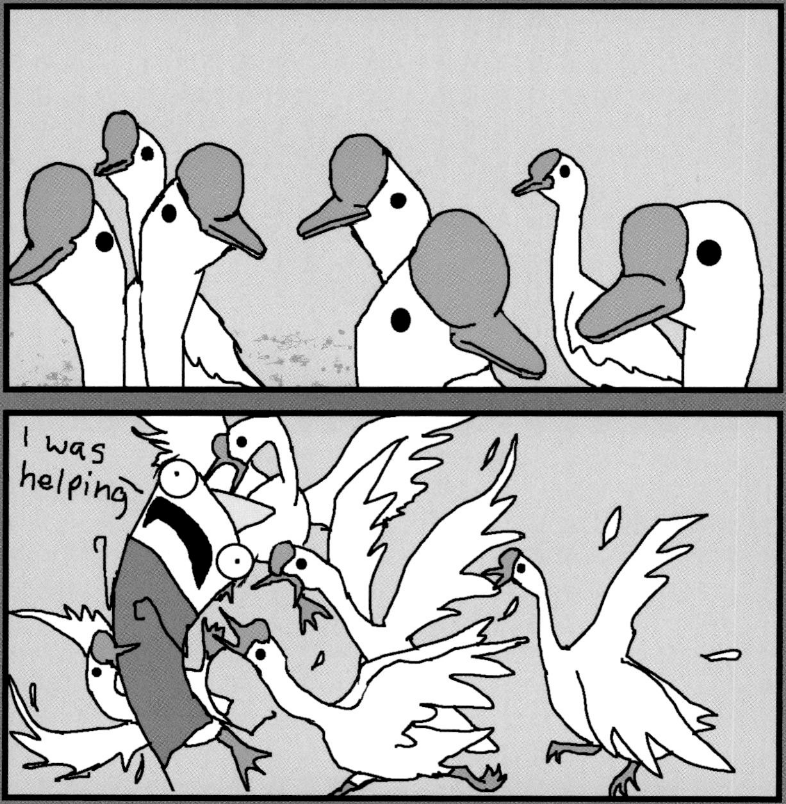
I was helping

And I remembered that most geese are dangerous psychopaths that become extremely violent for absolutely no reason.

Shortly thereafter, it occurred to me that the goose was probably the thing that had been brutally attacking our neighbor's dog.

I tried to sneak back inside before it noticed me.

But it was too late.

It had seen me.
It lunged at me and I stumbled backward.
I experienced a momentary feeling of relief as it lurched past me, but with sinking dread, I noticed that I had left the door to the house open.

If you were sitting quietly on your couch, waiting for your girl-friend to come back inside so you could finish watching your movie, and while you were waiting, someone called you up and said "I'll give you a million dollars if you can guess what's going to happen next," you absolutely would not guess "I am going to be brutally and unex-pectedly attacked by a goose in my own home." Even if you had a hundred guesses, you would not guess that.

But that's exactly what happened to Duncan.

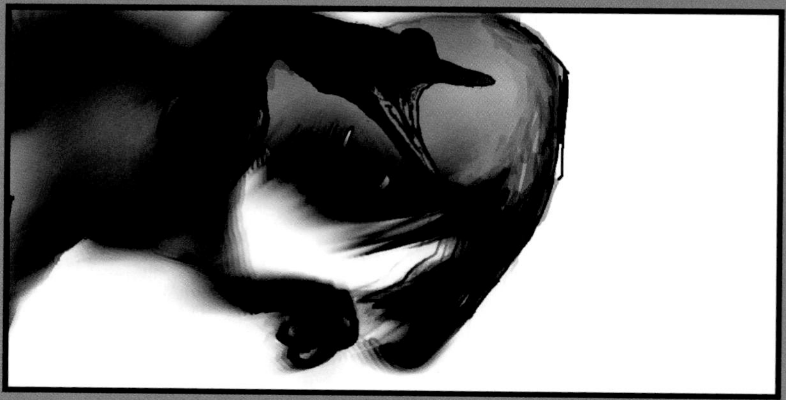

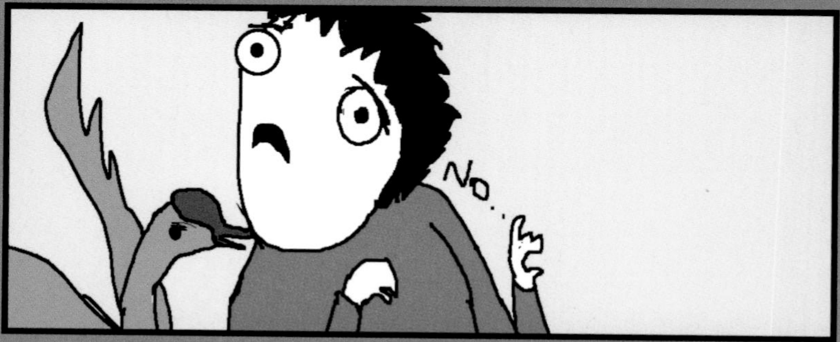
NO...

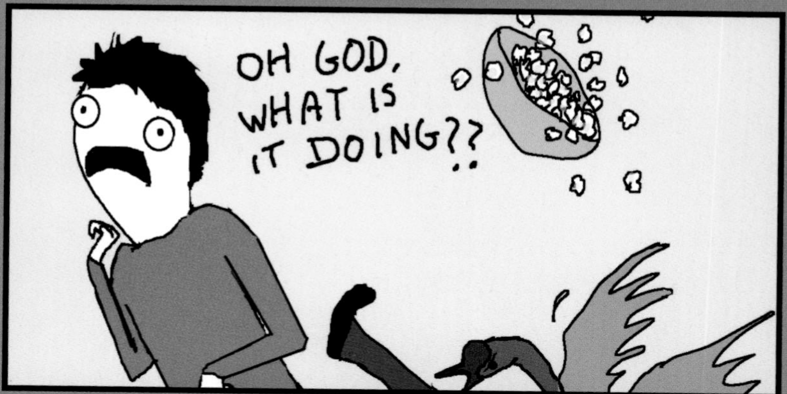
OH GOD, WHAT IS IT DOING??

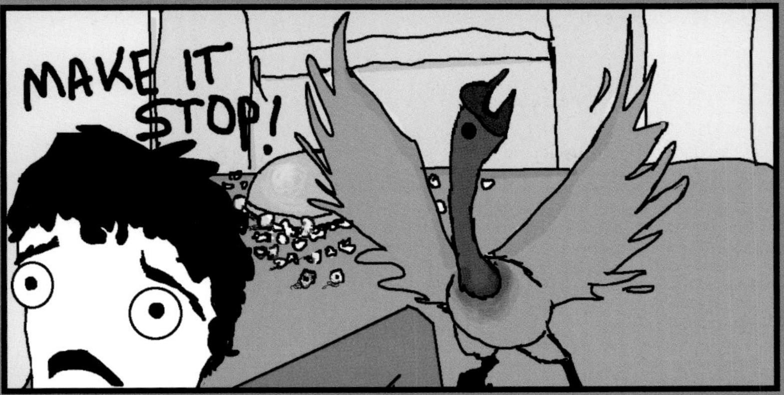
MAKE IT STOP!

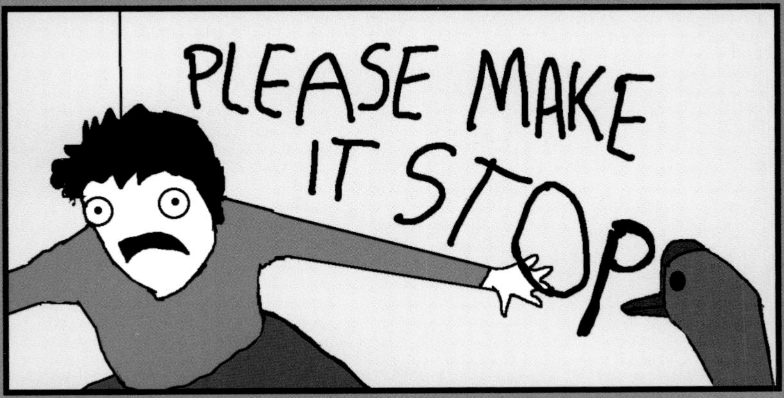
PLEASE MAKE IT STOP

I ran inside to find him yelling and throwing things at the goose while it chased him around the living room.

I had never taken birds seriously. They've always seemed like silly, innocuous creatures. I mean, their most recognizable traits are flitting about and singing, which is adorable. In school, I learned that birds are direct descendants of dinosaurs, though I never really saw the resemblance. But when I walked into my living room and found this *thing* chasing Duncan, I finally recognized it: the predatory gleam in its eyes and its jerky, robotic movements were straight out of the dinosaur documentaries I used to watch as a child.

The goose stopped and slowly shifted its reptilian gaze onto me and I understood with startling clarity exactly what it must have felt like to be a baby stegosaurus. I froze and whispered, "Oh no, what do I do?"

Duncan said, "Oh god, I don't know, why is this happening? I don't understand why this is happening! WHY IS THIS HAPPENING TO ME??"

It is difficult to flee effectively while inside a house. You can sprint across the room, but it won't be long before you encounter a wall or a piece of furniture, and then you have to angle back toward your attacker if you hope to keep running. So you ricochet around, trying to make up a little ground, trying to get away. You cast various objects into your wake, hoping to inconvenience your attacker. But unless you can trap or otherwise disable whatever you're running away from, it's going to catch you eventually.

Earlier in the winter, we had tacked a blanket over the doorway to the kitchen to keep the heat in the living room. This fortunate arrangement gave us a tactical advantage and we were able to trap the goose in the kitchen by luring it in and then allowing the blanket to fall back over the doorway.

The lull in violence made the room feel far too quiet as we stood and stared vacantly at the blanketed doorway. The light in the kitchen cast a sharp silhouette of the goose against the blanket.

"What should we do with it?" said Duncan.

I said, "I guess it lives in our kitchen now."

He paused thoughtfully. "We can't just never go into our kitchen again."

I suggested that maybe we could trap the goose in the basement, but that option was also ruled impractical. We'd have to find a way to get it far away from the house—far enough that it could never find its way back.

Before we could properly consider how to accomplish this feat, we noticed the goose's shadow looming larger in the doorway.

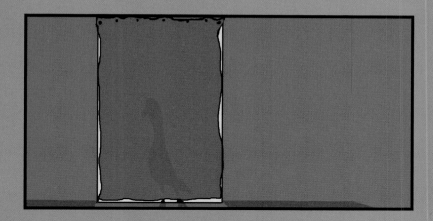

It was moving closer.

We watched in horror as it began pecking the blanket—testing it to see if it could get through.

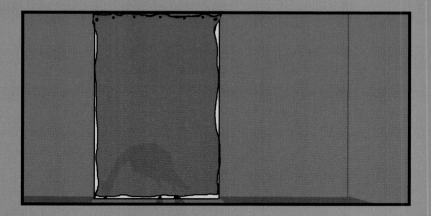

The scenario felt strangely reminiscent of the kitchen scene in *Jurassic Park*: us crouched in terror as some raptor-like bird stalked us through our familiar and formerly peaceful environment.

There was an ominous pause, then its head poked out underneath the blanket.

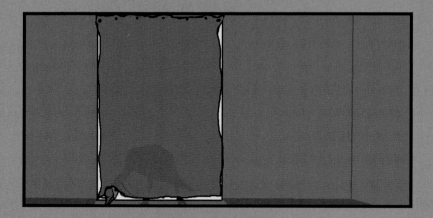

A tense moment of inaction took hold of us as its eyes scanned the room and finally settled on our crouching forms.

It teetered toward us and we fled upstairs into our bedroom, slamming the door behind us. Leaning breathlessly against the heavy door, we could hear the goose pecking the floorboards on the other side.

We sat quietly, not knowing what to do. Our box fan hummed in the window. Finally, Duncan whispered, "We could trap it with a blanket."

I said, "This room is pretty big, right? We could just live in here."

But I knew what we had to do.

We waited until we couldn't hear the goose outside the door, then we armed ourselves with a down comforter and snuck a peek into the unlit hallway.

The goose wasn't out there.

We crept down the stairs, holding the blanket out in front of ourselves like a shield. With every creak, we expected the goose to come lurching out of the shadows to peck us to death. Strangely, its lack of action was even more disconcerting. Every suspenseful second that ticked by without an attack felt like it was building up to a slightly more brutal surprise.

Finally, we rounded the corner and spotted the goose in our living room. It was walking around and methodically pecking all of our belongings, as if to convey: *This is mine now. I own it. And also this. And also this. And this. Everything is mine.*

As I watched from the doorway, I felt an absurd rage build up inside me. *Who the fuck does this goose think it is? It thinks it can waltz into my home, bite everyone, and then proceed to claim ownership of my couch and my DVD player?*

Geese have no business owning DVD players. It was entirely unacceptable.

I grabbed the blanket and made my move. The goose was caught by surprise and the blanket landed squarely over it like a net.

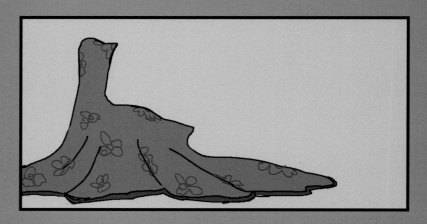

Its head bobbed back and forth under the blanket in confusion.

Before it could escape again, we wrapped it up and carried it out to our car. There was a duck pond on the outskirts of town. It would feel at home there. We didn't want to risk letting it free anywhere near our house.

Duncan opened the rear door, and I shoved the goose in. It thrashed around under the blanket like a shark caught in a fishing net.

We drove in silence past darkened windows and dimly lit porches until we reached the edge of town.

There's an urban legend about a woman who gets into her car without realizing there's a serial killer hiding in the backseat. She finally looks up and sees him in her rearview mirror just before he kills her.

That story has plagued my nightmares for nearly a decade.

The tale often pops into my head while I'm driving by myself at night. And I work myself into such a frenzy that I have to pull over and check my backseat to make sure no one is there.

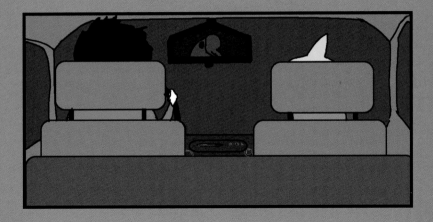

If it wasn't for the slight hint of moonlight shining through the car's rear window, I probably wouldn't have noticed the goose until it was too late.

Its head poked up and my peripheral vision picked up its shadow in the rearview mirror.

With years of repressed terror welling up in the deep, primal areas of my brain, I barely managed to grab the ice scraper out of the glove compartment and scream, "DRIVE FASTER; HE'S IN THE BACKSEAT!"

We sped down the lonely highway as I attempted to fend off the goose with the ice scraper long enough to reach our destination.

We came to a screeching stop several hundred yards from the duck pond and stumbled out of the car, slamming the doors behind us. Like two cavemen chasing a tiger out of their cave with stick weapons, we prodded the goose with the ice scraper until it tumbled out of the backseat onto the ground. Once it was out of the car, we jumped back in and peeled out. The goose toddled after us for a few steps and then just stood there in the middle of the road as its reflection shrank away from us.

We never saw it again. I like to imagine that it found the duck pond and chose to trade its violent lifestyle for one of gentle paddling and feasting on bread crumbs.

But that's probably not what happened.

In the back of my mind, I know that the goose is still up there somewhere, living like a wild beast in the woods at the edge of town, shambling down to the pond every night to terrorize the ducks. I know it's there, lurking just below the surface of the murky pond, watching the children throw bread crumbs, waiting for them to get just a little too close to the edge of the water.

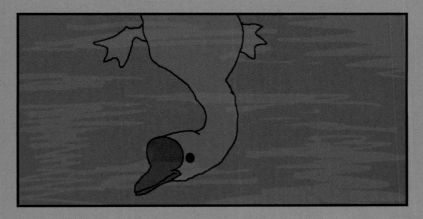

Author's note: While all of this was happening, I knew that it was probably going to be a story I'd write down someday. I also knew that the people reading it would probably feel some doubt as to its veracity. Thankfully, while the goose was trapped in the kitchen, I had the presence of mind to shoot a short video of it. Unfortunately, books are not video compatible. But I took some screen captures of the video and put them together so you can at least get some satisfaction that this is a true story:

Here is the goose standing in our kitchen.

Here it is noticing me in the doorway and coming to attack me.

The goose is now behind the sheet. Feeling brave, I decided to take another peek.

But the goose had been lurking on the other side, waiting for me.

Now I'm running away.

And now I'm still running away.

I have stopped running away and have decided to try to get more footage.

There is a commotion behind the sheet.

The goose is trying to get into the living room.

HEAD POKING through

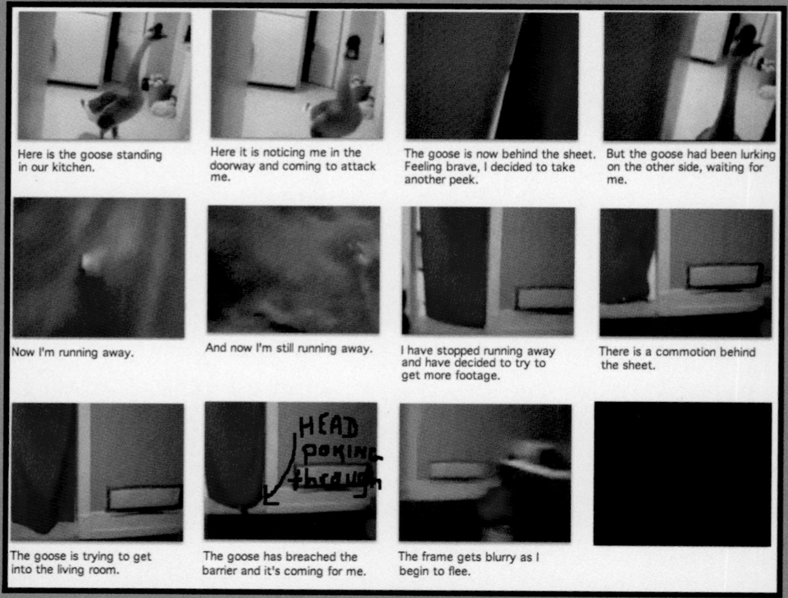

The goose has breached the barrier and it's coming for me.

The frame gets blurry as I begin to flee.

Thoughts and Feelings

I have a subconscious list of rules for how reality should work. I did not develop these rules on purpose, and most of them don't make sense—which is disturbing when you consider that they are an attempt to govern the behavior of reality—but they exist, and they play a large role in determining how I react to the things that happen to me. Large enough that a majority of the feelings I feel are simply a reaction to reality not complying with my arbitrary set of rules.

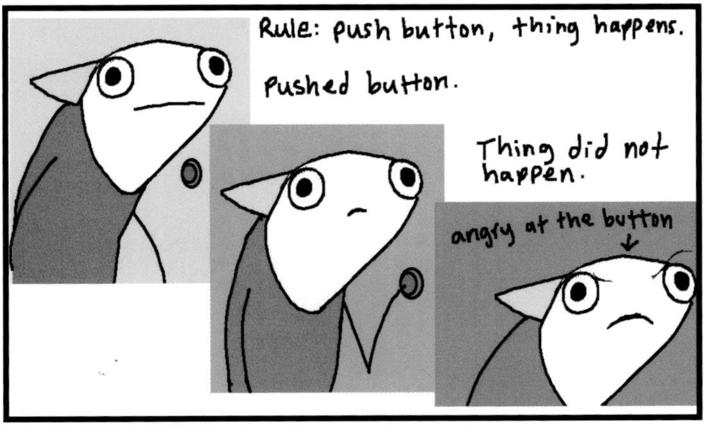
Rule: push button, thing happens.
Pushed button.
Thing did not happen.
angry at the button

Reality doesn't give a *shit* about my rules, and this upsets me. Not to a great degree. Not even to an obvious degree. But when reality disobeys my rules, detectable levels of surprise, disappointment, and frustration are produced.

And to me, it feels perfectly logical to be feeling those things. But if someone were to observe me in my natural environment—having all the thoughts and feelings my natural environment causes me to have—I would seem much less logical. In fact, I might seem sort of like a wild animal trying to adapt to an alternate reality that it somehow became trapped in.

But there's a definite pattern to these illogical internal reactions, and, theoretically, over weeks and months, a dedicated outside observer could piece together a crude understanding of my rules and the ways in which I attempt to impose them upon reality.

What is it doing and why is it doing it?
SUBJECT: R153
observational period:
5/3/12 – 7/25/12

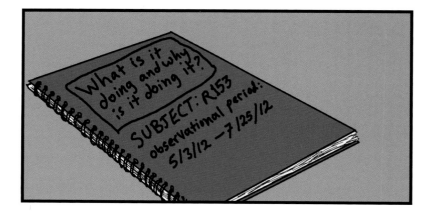

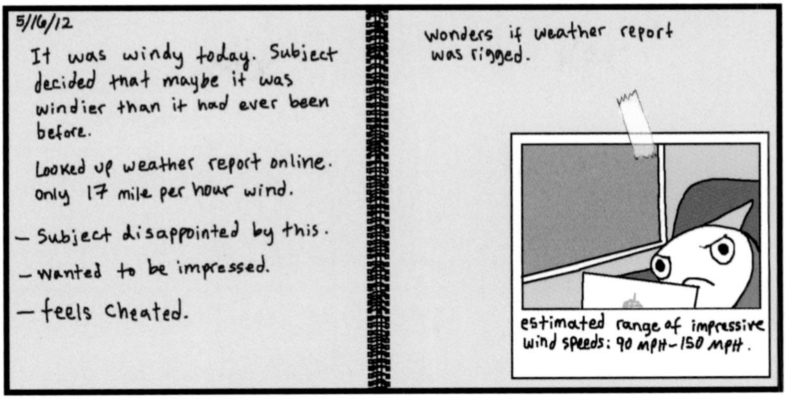
5/16/12
It was windy today. Subject decided that maybe it was windier than it had ever been before.
Looked up weather report online. Only 17 mile per hour wind.
- Subject disappointed by this.
- wanted to be impressed.
- feels cheated.
wonders if weather report was rigged.
estimated range of impressive wind speeds: 90 mph–150 mph.

I seem to spend a lot of time being mildly disappointed by things that aren't actually disappointing. They appear disappointing, though, because I'm constantly trying to be impressed or surprised by everything. I get a rush from encountering unexpectedly exceptional things. Even if I hate the thing, I still get a rush from discovering that it's exceptionally bad. I could be injured and bleeding, but if I were bleeding a surprising amount, I would feel sort of excited about it.

I love the feeling of being impressed so much that I actively seek it out. When something seems like it might be surprising and then isn't, I feel tricked. Like the thing led me on and made me think I was going to be surprised, and then, at the last second, it revoked its promise.

The expectation of surprise isn't even necessary to create disappointment, though. Sometimes all that needs to happen is that I expect something—anything, really—and then that thing doesn't happen.

6/03/12
Subject went outside today. Saw object in peripheral vision that was roughly the same shape as an animal.
→ Object turned out to be dirt pile.
Subject disappointed.
Wanted it to be animal.
spots object in periph
subject turns, expecting to see an animal
it is unclear at this time why not seeing an animal was upsetting. Animals are everywhere.

Becomes aware of object → decides it is an animal → Looks at it to make sure → Not an animal → disappointed.
Subject must be thrilled about seeing animals if this disappointed about not seeing them.
???
Subject saw an actual animal and did not appear excited.

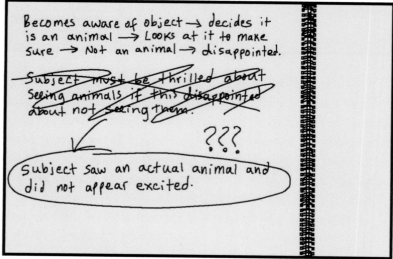

Reality should follow through on what I think it is going to do. It doesn't matter that I have no vested interest in the outcome aside from expecting it to happen. It's the principle of the matter.

Sometimes expectations arise as a result of an oversight on my part. But when there's a snag in my plans because I failed to account for something, it still feels like reality's fault. Reality should know about my plans. It should know when I'm not expecting to deal with the unexpected, even if it isn't very unexpected.

5/29/12
For unknown reason, Subject is almost always impatient to get into house. Is caught off guard by having to unlock door.
plan:
go into house → be inside house
plan does not account for time it takes to unlock door

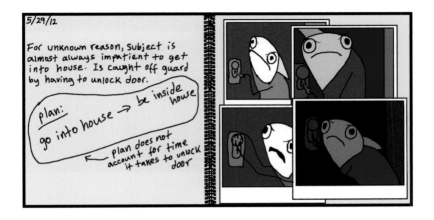

I don't like being inconvenienced, and I especially don't like being inconvenienced too many times in a row. If something I don't like happens, then several more things that I don't like happen directly afterward, that is too many. They shouldn't cluster like that.

Unfortunately, that's just how probability works.

5/24/12
The subject is having a bad day.
subject does not like this day.
Has a headache. Had to ride bike to grocery store first thing in the morning because out of half and half for coffee (already disadvantaged by headache. Should not have to do this.)
There was a strong breeze, which made bicycling inconvenient.
Had to wait in line slightly longer than normal.
On ride back, wind had changed and subject again had to pedal into headwind.
Felt extremely unfair.
Like being persecuted.
wind is being unfair to the subject.

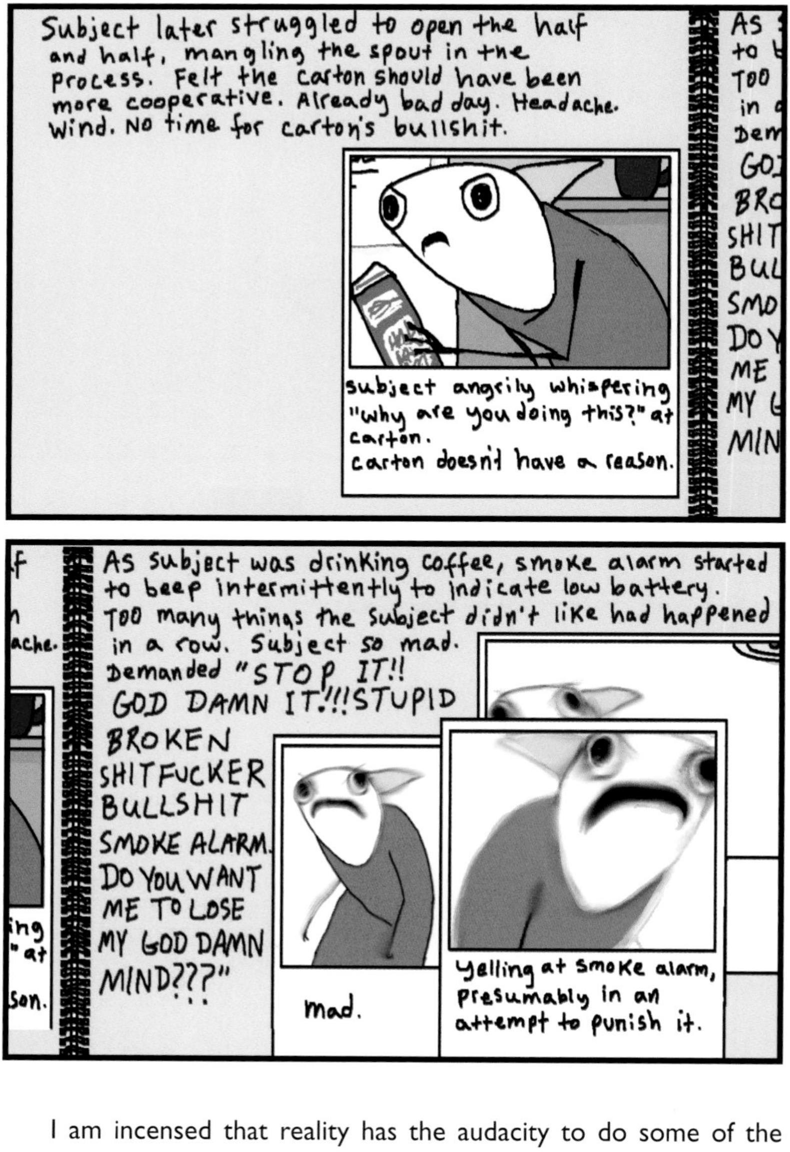
Subject later struggled to open the half and half, mangling the spout in the process. Felt the carton should have been more cooperative. Already bad day. Headache. Wind. No time for carton's bullshit.
subject angrily whispering "why are you doing this?" at carton.
carton doesn't have a reason.
As subject was drinking coffee, smoke alarm started to beep intermittently to indicate low battery. Too many things the subject didn't like had happened in a row. Subject so mad. Demanded "STOP IT!! GOD DAMN IT!!!STUPID BROKEN SHITFUCKER BULLSHIT SMOKE ALARM. DO YOU WANT ME TO LOSE MY GOD DAMN MIND???"
...
mad.
yelling at smoke alarm, presumably in an attempt to punish it.

I am incensed that reality has the audacity to do some of the things it does when I CLEARLY don't want those things to happen.

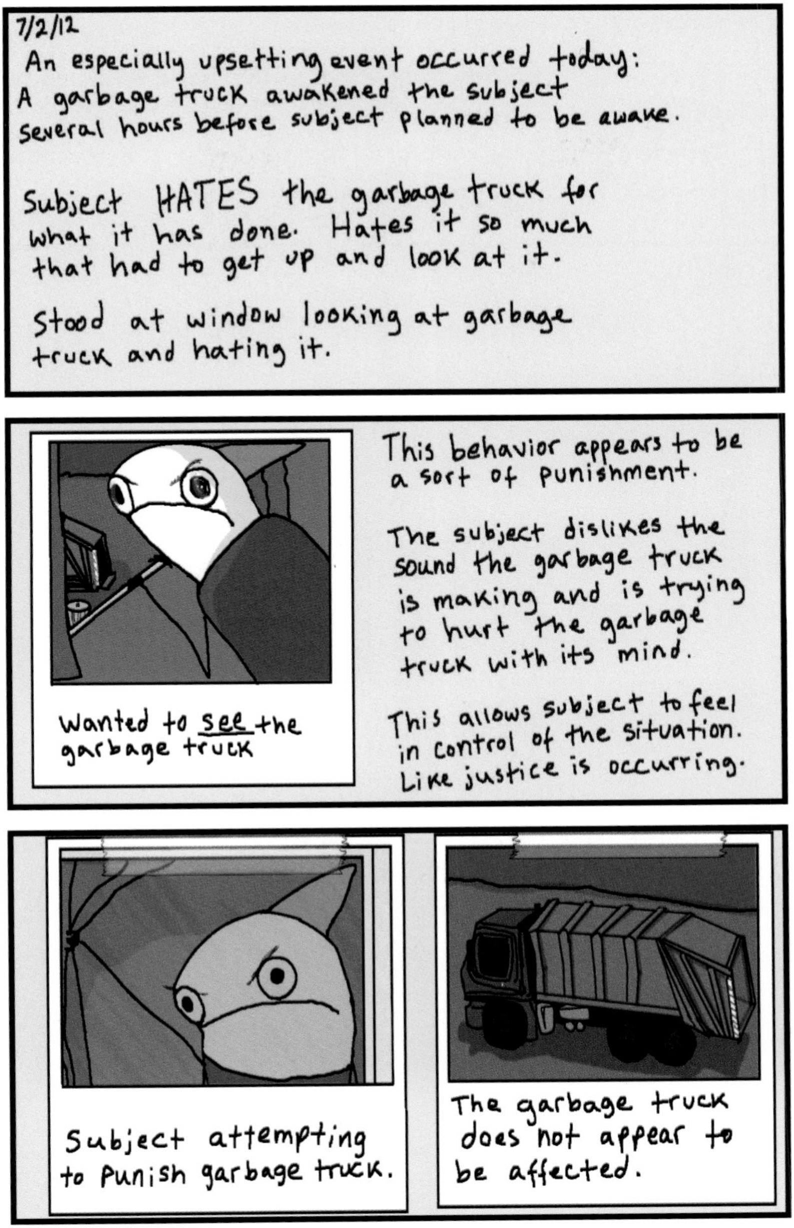
7/2/12
An especially upsetting event occurred today:
A garbage truck awakened the subject several hours before subject planned to be awake.
Subject HATES the garbage truck for what it has done. Hates it so much that had to get up and look at it.
Stood at window looking at garbage truck and hating it.
Wanted to see the garbage truck
This behavior appears to be a sort of punishment.
The subject dislikes the sound the garbage truck is making and is trying to hurt the garbage truck with its mind.
This allows subject to feel in control of the situation. Like justice is occurring.
Subject attempting to punish garbage truck.
The garbage truck does not appear to be affected.

It feels unfair when the other things in the world refuse to be governed by my justice system.

To be fair, though, my concept of "fairness" is sort of questionable and not based on the way reality actually works.

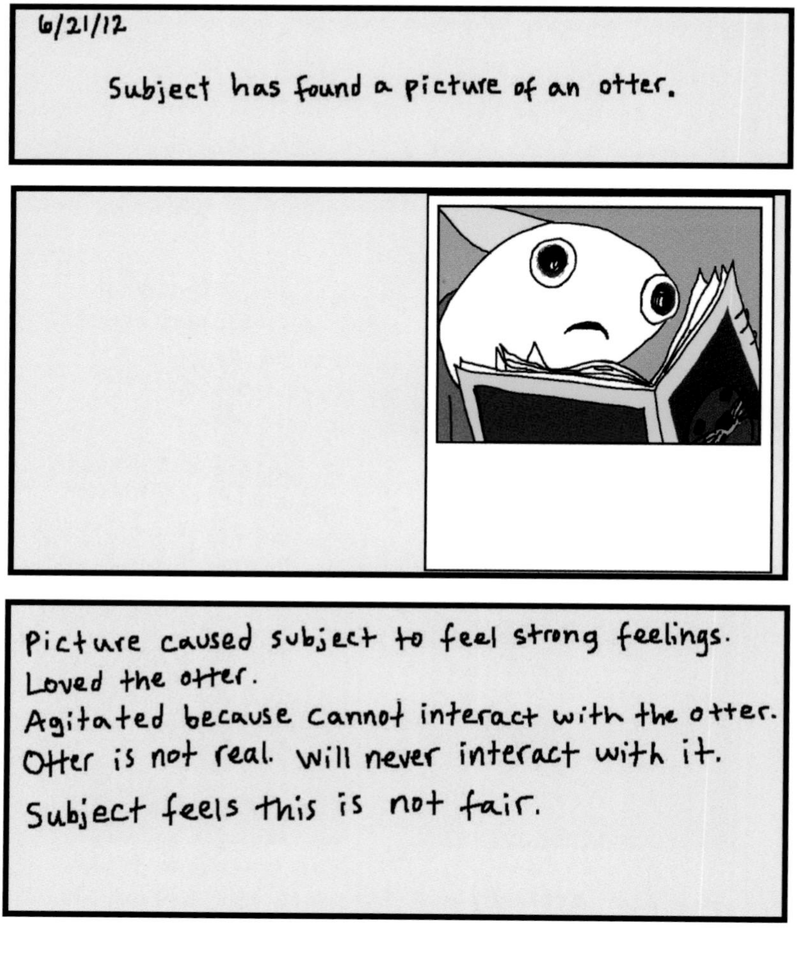

6/21/12

Subject has found a picture of an otter.

Picture caused subject to feel strong feelings.
Loved the otter.
Agitated because cannot interact with the otter.
Otter is not real. Will never interact with it.
Subject feels this is not fair.

Otter has betrayed subject by living in ocean and not magazine.

When something feels unfair, there's an implication that an equal and opposite fair thing could have happened instead.

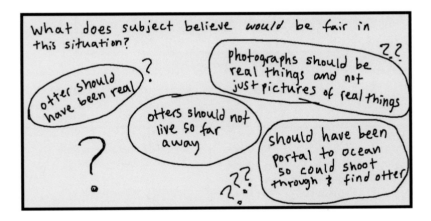

What does subject believe *would* be fair in this situation?

otter should have been real

Photographs should be real things and not just pictures of real things

otters should not live so far away

should have been portal to ocean so could shoot through & find otter

But my rules don't account for that. I just make them up and expect them to be followed without considering how that is supposed to work.

I make up new rules all the time.

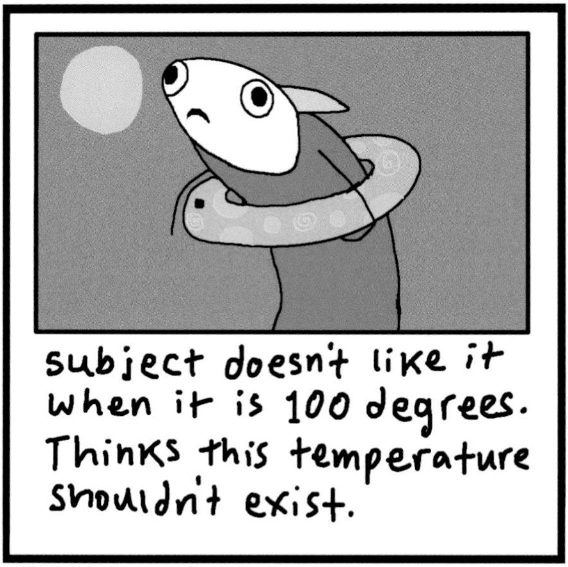
subject doesn't like it when it is 100 degrees. Thinks this temperature shouldn't exist.

I don't even know about some of them until they are broken.

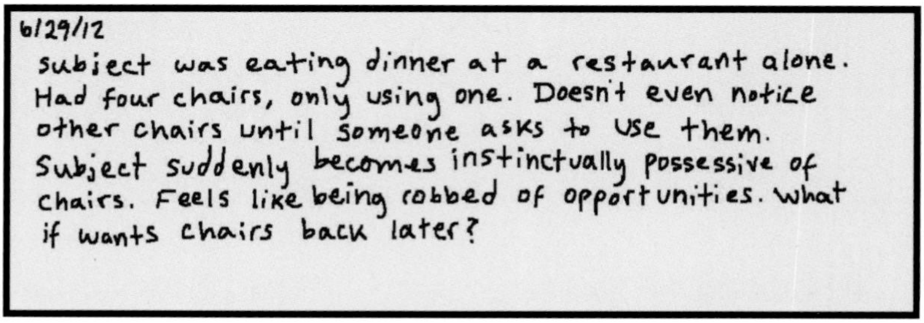
6/29/12
subject was eating dinner at a restaurant alone. Had four chairs, only using one. Doesn't even notice other chairs until someone asks to use them. Subject suddenly becomes instinctually possessive of chairs. Feels like being robbed of opportunities. what if wants chairs back later?

Subject agreed to let other person use chairs even though didn't want to

Subject can see the other people enjoying the chairs.

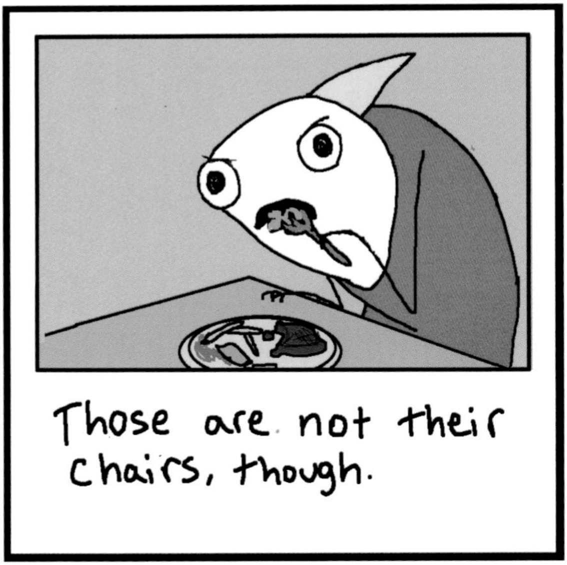
Those are not their chairs, though.

My rules are inconsistent and weirdly specific, but it's still disconcerting for me when I have to watch as the other things in the world break them.

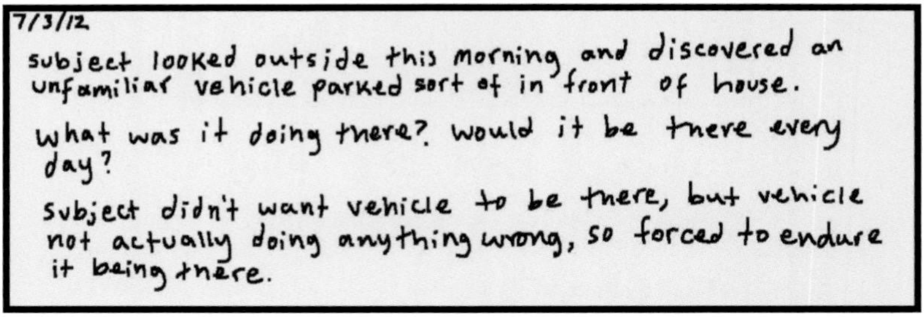
7/3/12
subject looked outside this morning and discovered an unfamiliar vehicle parked sort of in front of house.
what was it doing there? would it be there every day?
subject didn't want vehicle to be there, but vehicle not actually doing anything wrong, so forced to endure it being there.

feels helpless to stop
vehicle from being there.
Cannot do anything about
presence of vehicle.

Vehicle was still there
two hours later.

I don't like when I can't control what reality is doing. Which is unfortunate because reality works independently of the things I want, and I have only a limited number of ways to influence it, none of which are guaranteed to work.

I still want to keep tabs on reality, though. Just in case it tries to do anything sneaky. It makes me feel like I'm contributing. The illusion of control makes the helplessness seem more palatable. And when that illusion is taken away, I panic.

7/14/12

It is dark. Subject cannot
see what reality is doing. Fears
reality may attempt to do something bad
while unsupervised.

Because, deep down, I know how pointless and helpless I am, and it scares me. I am an animal trapped in a horrifying, lawless environment, and I have no idea what it's going to do to me. It just DOES it to me.

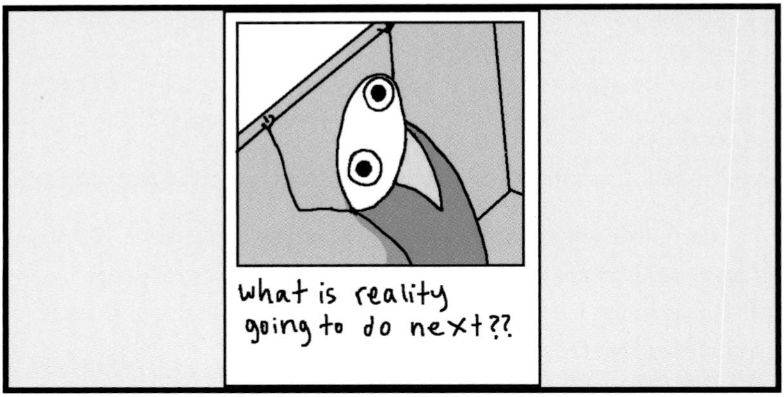
what is reality
going to do next??

I cope with that the best way I know—by being completely unreasonable and trying to force everything else in the world to obey me and do all the nonsensical things I want.

And I am embarrassed by how silly I look while I am unsuccessfully attempting to enact justice. It makes me feel ridiculous—like maybe I'm not actually very powerful.

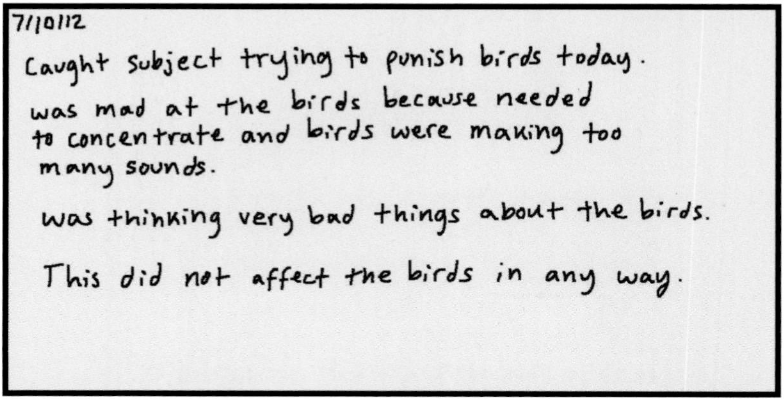
7/10/12
Caught subject trying to punish birds today.
was mad at the birds because needed to concentrate and birds were making too many sounds.
was thinking very bad things about the birds.
This did not affect the birds in any way.

Thinking bad things directly at the birds.

The birds continued to make as many sounds as they wanted.

I'm glad there's no one else to witness me in these moments because I know what I am and I know what I'm trying to do, and that is shameful enough. I would be horrified to discover that someone was observing me with the intention of learning about my silly rules, and further observation would become very challenging because of all the fleeing and hiding.

7/23/12

Subject has become suspicious. Senses that it is being observed.

Humiliated by self.

Tried to hide behind couch so no one could see.

Knows something is going on.

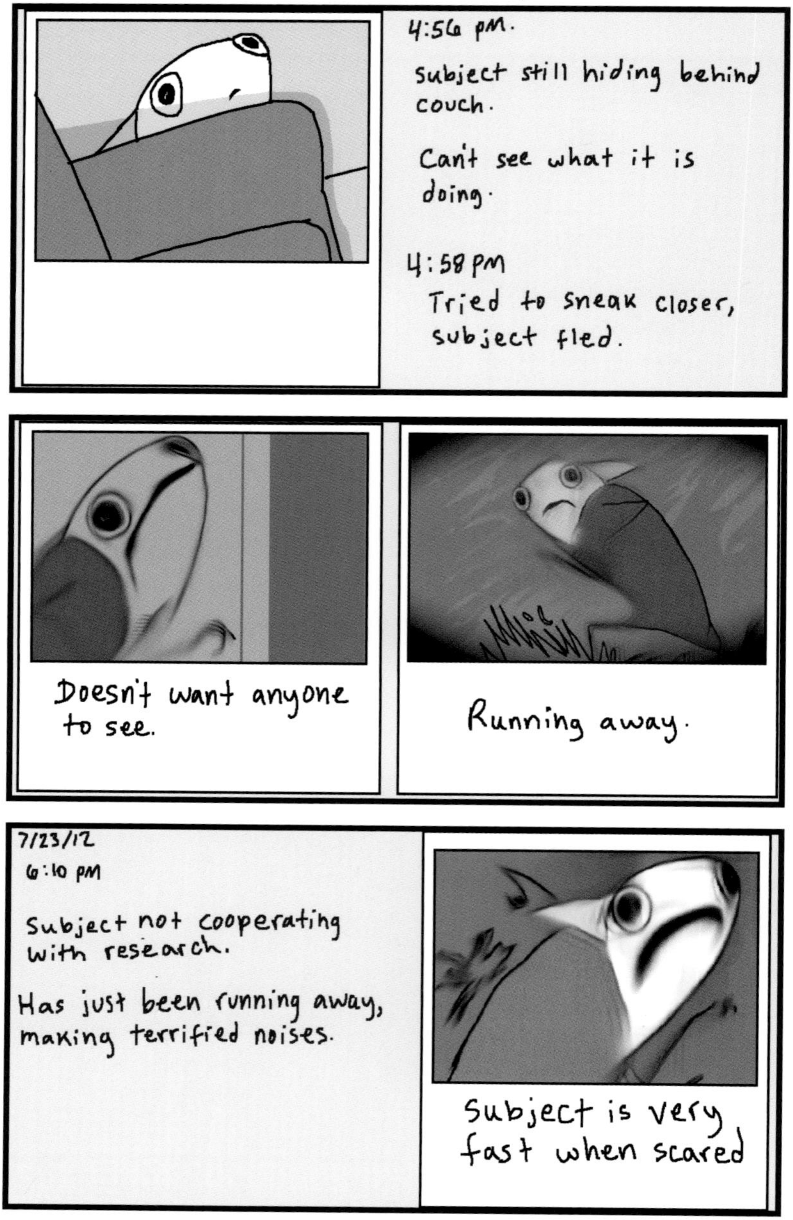
4:56 pm.
Subject still hiding behind couch.
Can't see what it is doing.
4:58 pm
Tried to sneak closer, subject fled.
Doesn't want anyone to see.
Running away.
7/23/12
6:10 pm
Subject not cooperating with research.
Has just been running away, making terrified noises.
Subject is very fast when scared

7/23/12
10:18 PM

Subject has been cornered in an abandoned warehouse.

Finally observation can continue!

No more hiding and escaping for subject

7/24/12

7:23 AM

Subject held perfectly still and didn't do or think anything for nine straight hours. May have continued doing this indefinitely if observation had not been discontinued due to concerns about dehydration.

Made this exact face for nine hours in a row.

And this is possibly the most humiliating thing of all. That I am so embarrassed about how embarrassing I am. As if I've got some sort of dignity to protect. *Because I am a serious, dignified person.* And I don't want anyone to know I'm not.

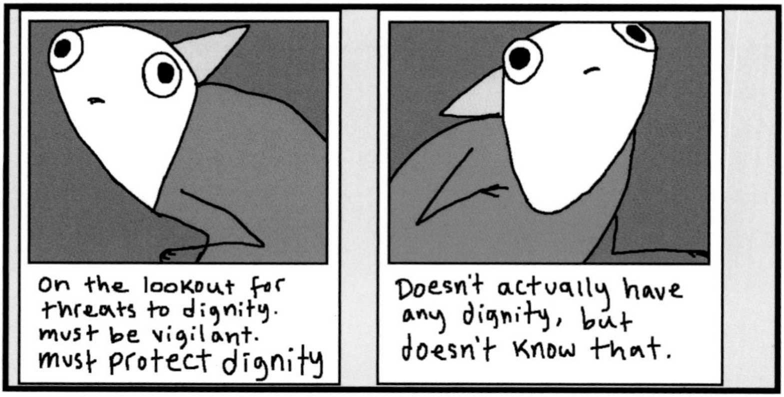
On the lookout for threats to dignity. must be vigilant. must protect dignity
Doesn't actually have any dignity, but doesn't know that.

Dogs' Guide to Understanding Basic Concepts

We've known each other for a while now, dogs. For the last few years, you've lived in my house, slept on my bed, and peed on almost every inch of my yard. And unless you successfully run away or die, you'll likely continue to coexist with me for the rest of your lives. That being the case, there are some things I think you should know. Most of these things are very basic and shouldn't even have to be explained, but you guys have displayed an alarming lack of common sense, so here we go.

Chapter 1:
COMMON MISCONCEPTIONS

Through observation and my daily interactions with you, I have noticed a few particularly troublesome things about your worldview. I don't know how or why these misconceptions originated, but it's time you know the truth.

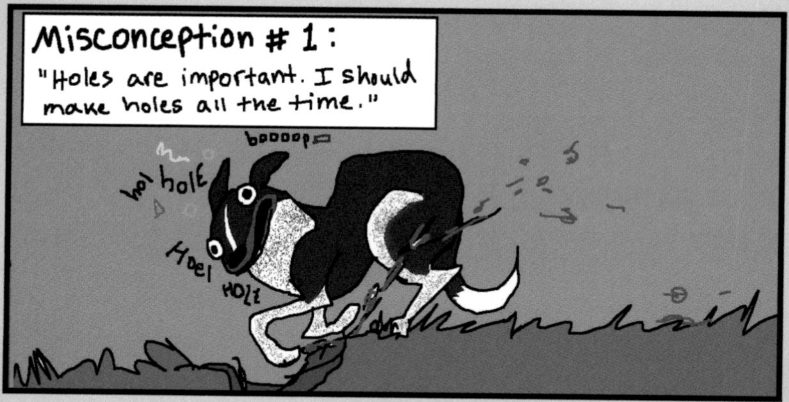
Misconception # 1:
"Holes are important. I should make holes all the time."
hole
Hoel
HOLE

You're wrong about holes. Holes are hardly ever important, especially not the ones you make. Have you ever paused while digging a hole and wondered, *What is the purpose of this? What does this hole* actually *mean in the grand scheme of things? Would my life be any different if I wasn't doing this?* Even if you can't figure out why you're doing it, surely you know from experience that it's going to end with you shamefully hiding under the table so I won't see all the guilt and dirt on your face. That isn't a fun situation for anybody.

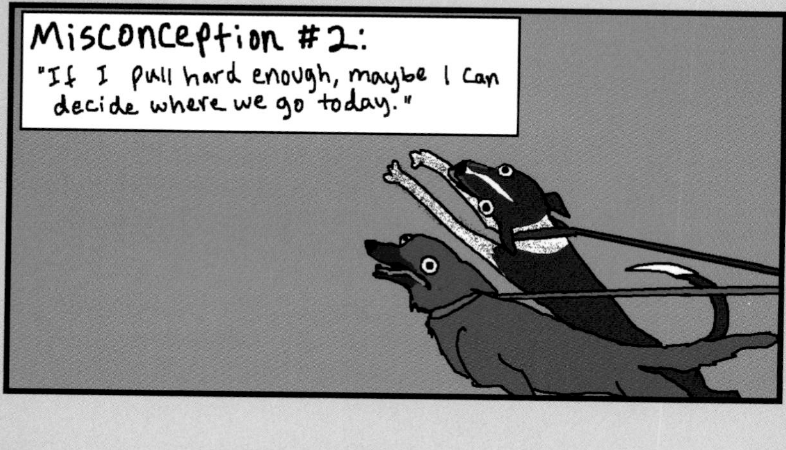
Misconception #2:
"If I pull hard enough, maybe I can decide where we go today."

I can understand wanting to try this out. I can understand thinking, *Hmm . . . maybe this will do something* and experimenting a little. But for the past three years, you've spent the entire duration of every walk strangling yourselves on the off chance that *maybe this time it will work*. It's never going to work, dogs. No matter how hard you pull, it's never going to make me think, "You know what? Maybe it *would* be sort of fun to walk in the middle of the street with all the cars . . . and maybe I *do* want to go splashing around in the duck pond in the middle of December."

You aren't allowed to decide because you are really bad at making decisions. And you have to wear a leash because you don't know that you are bad at making decisions. You would make too many of them if the leash didn't stop you.

For example, say we are walking to the park. Everything is going as planned until you see *this* on the other side of the road:

Panic sets in.

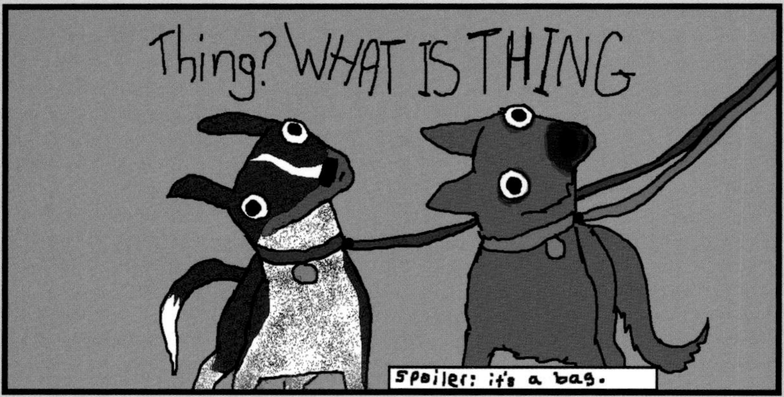
Thing? WHAT IS THING
Spoiler: it's a bag.

If you were not tethered to me by your leashes, you would be able to make too many decisions about how to react.

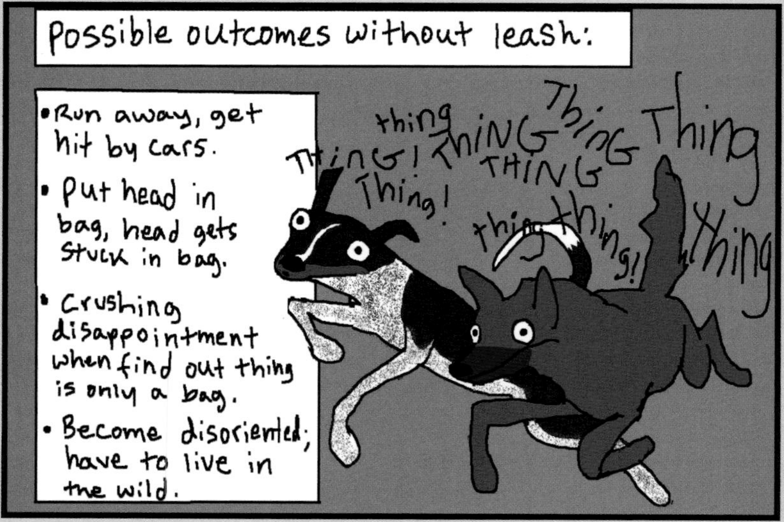
Possible outcomes without leash:
• Run away, get hit by cars.
• Put head in bag, head gets stuck in bag.
• Crushing disappointment when find out thing is only a bag.
• Become disoriented; have to live in the wild.
thing
THING!
THING
Thing
Thing
THING
Thing!
thing
thing!
thing

But when you are attached to a leash, you are protected from yourselves.

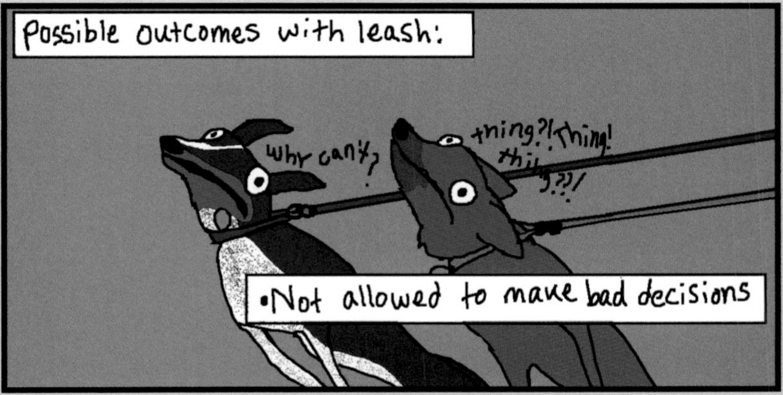
Possible outcomes with leash:
why can't?
thing?! Thing! thing??!
•Not allowed to make bad decisions

So no, pulling on your leashes isn't going to make me change my mind about anything. I am fully aware of what would happen if you were allowed to make your own decisions, and that's why you aren't allowed to make them.

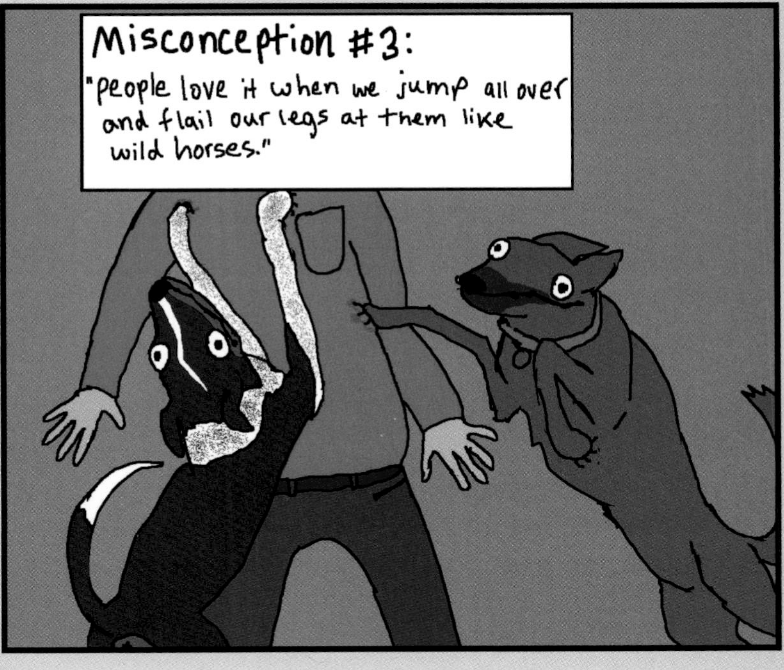
Misconception #3:
"people love it when we jump all over and flail our legs at them like wild horses."

What are you trying to accomplish by doing this? It doesn't make any sense. When I encounter someone I haven't seen in a while, I have never once thought, *I should jump at them and poke their face with my fingers and keep doing that until someone locks me in the bathroom.* Because that's insane. What would you think if I did that to your dog friends?

This behavior would be confusing and alarming.

Nobody likes this. But you can't seem to believe that.

Tell me, dogs, while you are being pushed away and kneed in the chest, and everyone is collectively shouting at you, "NO! OFF! BAD DOG"—what convinces you that we're enjoying ourselves?

Or perhaps you do understand that everyone hates what you are doing, but you think we haven't tried it enough to be *sure* that we hate it...

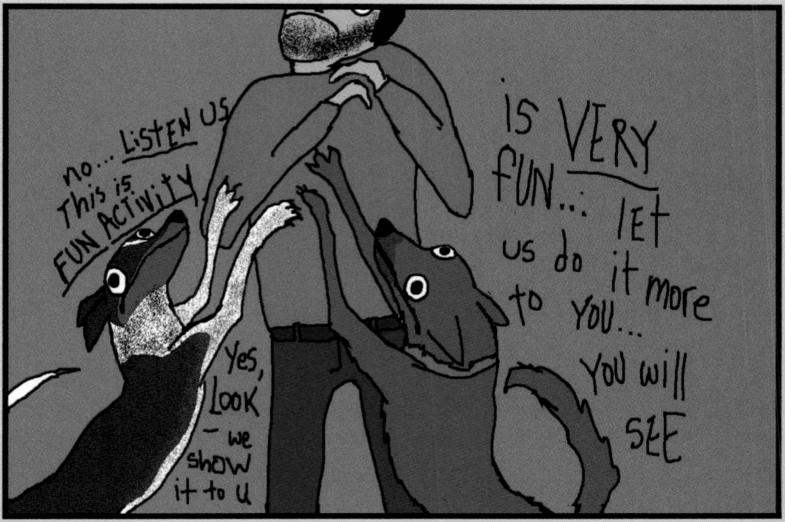
no... LISTEN US
This is FUN ACTIVITY
Yes, LOOK - we show it to u
is VERY FUN... let us do it more to YOU... YOU will SEE

I assure you, we've all experienced more than enough poking to determine that we hate it.

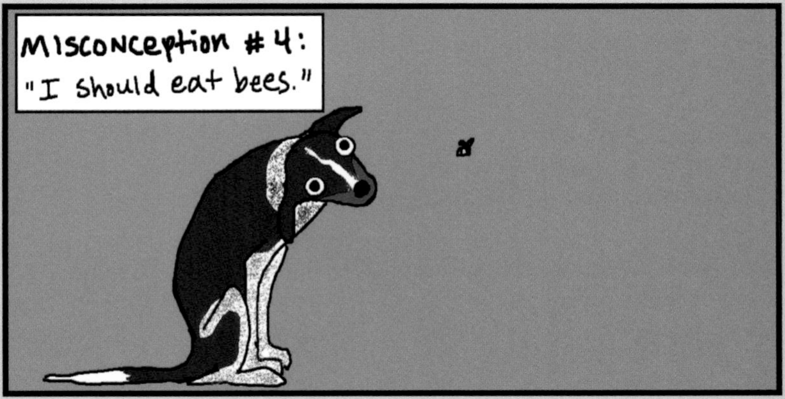
Misconception #4:
"I should eat bees."

I didn't think that this would need to be explained. Eating bees is sort of its own consequence. But you keep doing it. Haven't you noticed that every time you try to eat bees, you get stung on the face? No matter how many times you eat bees, the outcome is always going to be the same.

The outcome will never be different.

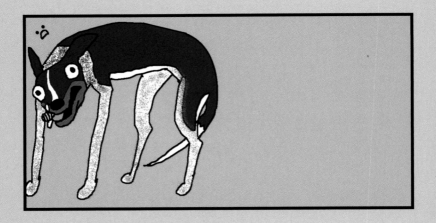

It really won't be different ever.

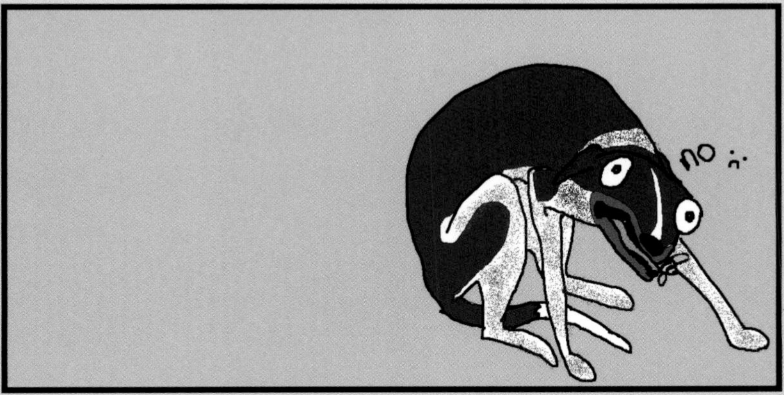
no

The only proper way to react to bees is to leave them alone. In case the distinction isn't clear, leaving bees alone does not include eating them.

After reading this chapter, you may be wondering, "Why do we believe so many things that are wrong?" And I think the answer may have something to do with how you form your conclusions in the first place.

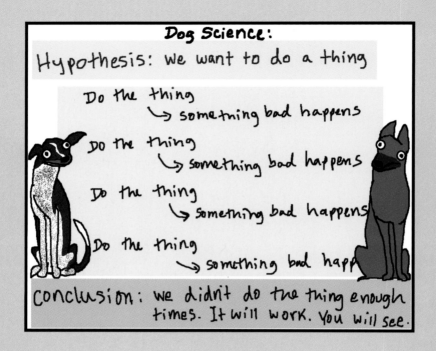

Dog Science:

Hypothesis: we want to do a thing

Do the thing
⤷ something bad happens

Do the thing
⤷ something bad happens

Do the thing
⤷ something bad happens

Do the thing
⤷ something bad happ

Conclusion: we didn't do the thing enough times. It will work. You will see.

This logic is flawed for a number of reasons, but the important lesson to take away from this chapter is that you have absolutely no idea what you're doing. Even if you really feel like you do, you don't. The fundamental structure of your reasoning is all kinds of fucked up, so you'll need to find some other way to figure out what things to do and what things not to do…

Chapter 2:
THE WORD "NO."

You're probably thinking, "Hey, I know what that word does!" But remember what we just talked about. Most of the things you know are wrong, and your definition of this word is no exception. The first thing you may be surprised to learn is that the word "no" has only one definition when I am shouting it at you. The ONLY thing the word "no" means is "Stop doing that, I hate it." That's the only thing it will ever mean.

To be clear, this means that the word "no" DOES NOT mean any of the following things:

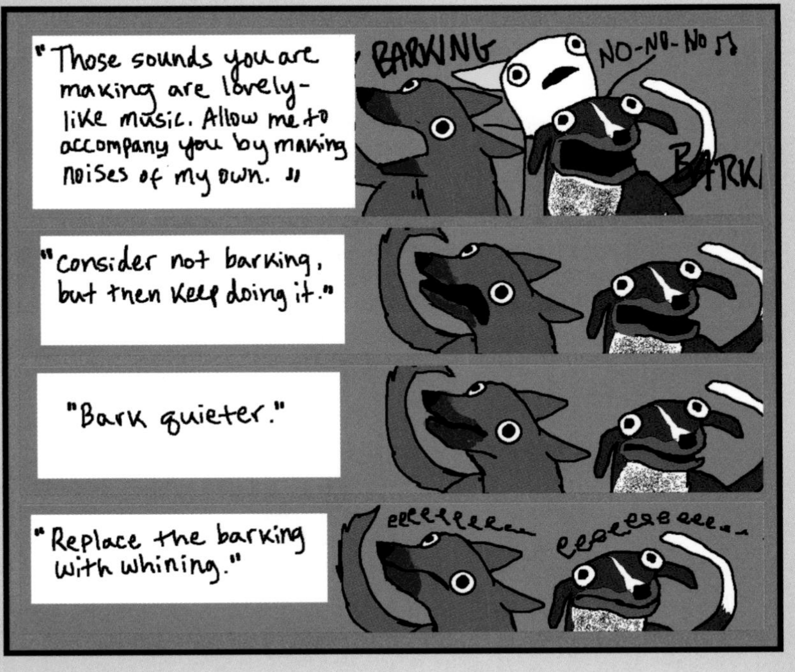
"Those sounds you are making are lovely- like music. Allow me to accompany you by making noises of my own."
BARKING
NO-NO-NO
BARK
"consider not barking, but then keep doing it."
"Bark quieter."
"Replace the barking with whining."
eeeeeeee...
eeeeeeeee...

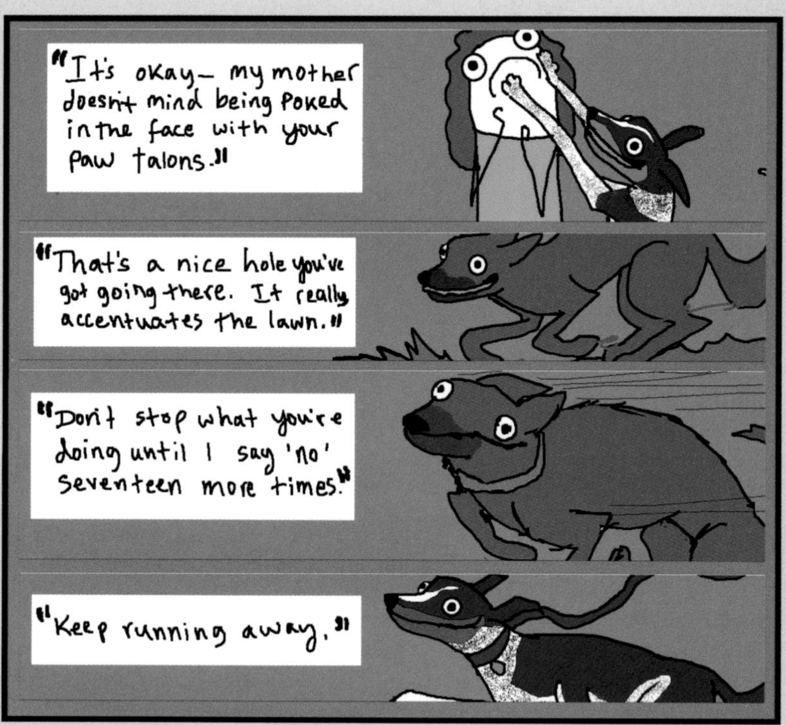
"It's okay— my mother doesn't mind being poked in the face with your paw talons."
"That's a nice hole you've got going there. It really accentuates the lawn."
"Don't stop what you're doing until I say 'no' seventeen more times."
"Keep running away."

I'm sure you're thinking, *Oh, yes, that word. We know it. We always are knowing it.* But just to be sure, here's a little pop quiz. It's tricky, so don't get discouraged:

It's ten o'clock at night. The TV is emitting a sound that you don't immediately recognize. Confused, you begin barking and clawing at the door. You then hear me shout the word "no" at you. What am I trying to tell you?

A. Keep going! You're doing a great job!
B. Make a different sound.
C. I know you're busy, but when you find the time, could you knock everything off the table?
D. Hey, listen! I want to say one of the words I know!
E. Stop doing that, I hate it.

Answer: E. Stop doing that, I hate it.

Hopefully you were not surprised by that answer.

Chapter 3: NOISES

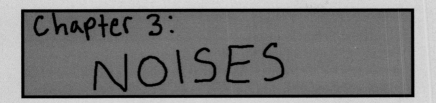

Noises are happening! What is the solution??

Relax, dogs. I'm going to tell you soon. But first, let's talk about your current plan for dealing with unfamiliar noises.

Problem: noise
Plan: make more noise
??
HELP DON'T KNOW WHAT IS
noise

Are you trying to cover up the unfamiliar sound with a louder sound so it can't confuse you anymore? Are you trying to scare it? Do you even know why you are doing this?

Making more noise isn't a solution for noise. It's just making more noise on top of the noise. And before you ask: no, making *even more noises* to cover up the noises your friend is making isn't a solution either. This is how infinite loops are created.

A better plan for dealing with noises would be something like this:

Accept that you are dogs and there are lots of things you won't understand. You'll panic less if you can come to terms with that.
Noise
DON'T KNOW What is
But OKAY. YES.

Now that you don't have to worry about noises anymore, you'll have more time to worry about the things you actually *should* be worrying about!

Chapter 4: DANGER

Simple dog, this one is directed mostly at you. It's tough to know where to start because, to be completely honest, I'm not sure what your rules are for deciding something is scary or not.

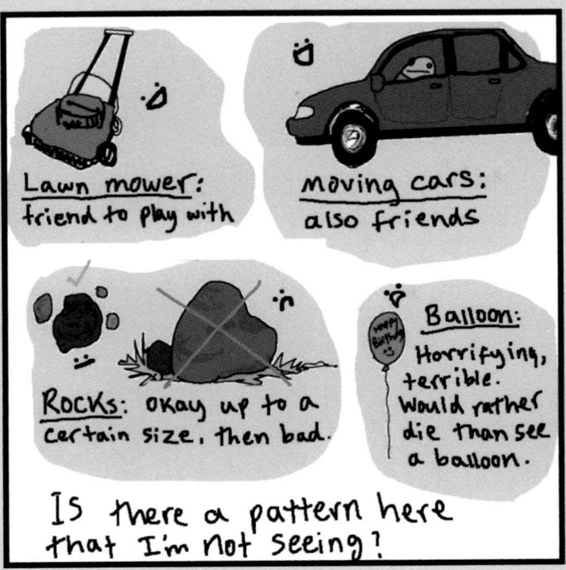
Lawn mower:
friend to play with
Moving cars:
also friends
ROCKS: okay up to a
certain size, then bad.
Balloon:
Horrifying,
terrible.
Would rather
die than see
a balloon.
Is there a pattern here
that I'm not seeing?

What I CAN tell you is that almost none of the things you're scared of are actually harmful, and many of the things you *aren't* scared of are deadly.

The following list is incomplete (it is not possible for me to discuss every object in the world individually), but it should give you a good starting point:

Nail clippers: As you may have noticed, trimming your nails is a traumatic event that requires three people, a beach towel, and a can of spray cheese. But why? Why does it have to be like this? I'm not sure what you think we are trying to do to you, but I promise it isn't whatever you think it is. Because whatever you think it is must be *horrifying.* That's the only way to justify how traumatic this event seems to be for you. What's really going on is that we are trying to make your nails shorter so that when you jump up and flail your legs at people or start sprinting around on the wood floors for absolutely no reason, the damage you can do is minimized.

Horse statue: I know, I know—it looks like a horse. But it isn't. Statues are tricky like that. It's too complicated to explain why the horse statue exists, so you'll just have to trust me that it isn't a real horse and it can't hurt you. I promise I wouldn't lie to you.

Lawn mower: The lawn mower is surprisingly dangerous. Yes, it makes a fun little noise and it hasn't actually done anything dangerous to you *yet,* but that's because I lock you in the house before turning it on. Because I can see the future and I know what will happen if I let you play with the lawn mower.

Vacuum: Despite being almost exactly the same thing as a lawn mower, the vacuum is not dangerous. Because unlike lawn mowers, vacuums are completely unable to turn your legs into hamburger meat. It's weird that you're so scared of the vacuum and so trusting of the lawn mower.

Balloons: Remember when you and I took that road trip together and we stopped to go for a jog in Ritzville, Washington? And it was sort of fun because it was Halloween and there were all sorts of scary decorations to look at? And somehow, out of all the decorations we ran past—all the skeletons and giant spiders and flashing, screaming, motorized corpses—*somehow a fucking balloon was the thing that made you yank me into the street as you fled in terror?* Why did that happen? It was just floating there harmlessly, tied to a tree branch twenty feet away. I'm going to tell you a secret about balloons: they are mostly air. The scary thing is just an act.

Chapter 5: THE HORRIBLE GAMES YOU LIKE.

You're really bad at making up games, dogs. From what I can tell, most of the things you consider fun involve ruining something or doing the same thing so many times in a row that everyone except you hates it.

The "Turn Objects into Pieces of Objects" Game
Basket
Basket pieces
Pillow
pillow pieces
stick
stick pieces

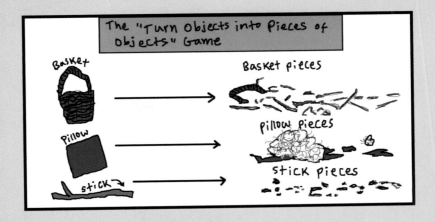

You seem to derive a great amount of joy from forcefully influencing the shape of things. Does this activity make you feel powerful? Is this how you satisfy your urge to make decisions? I'm sure it's a great feeling to decide that the basket shouldn't be a basket anymore and then actually be able to make that happen because the basket can't stop you. But there are less destructive ways to make decisions.

For example, here's another game involving decisions:

The "Let Objects Stay the Same" Game
Basket
basket
Pillow
Pillow
stick
Stick

If you decide NOT to destroy objects, you are still making decisions! This might seem like a boring game, but I promise, if you just allow yourselves to be filled with wonder at how extremely *the same* everything stays, you'll have fun. I know you very well. You are some of the most easily entertained creatures on the planet.

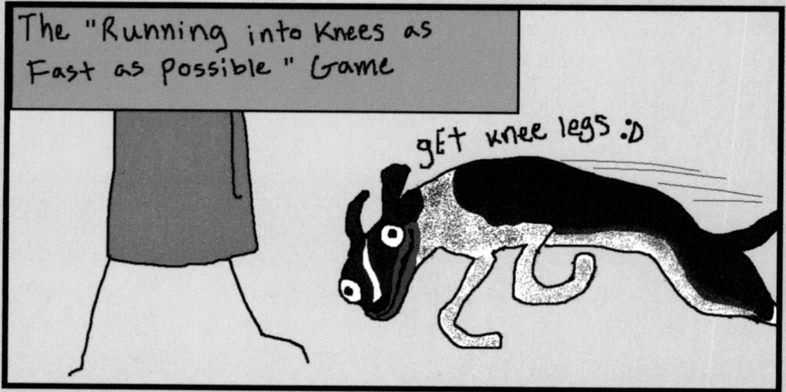
The "Running into Knees as Fast as Possible" Game
gEt knee legs :D

This is probably your worst game, dogs. I hate this game. From what I can tell, there are two main variants of it: running into knees with your face, and running very close to knees while holding a huge stick in your big, dumb mouth.

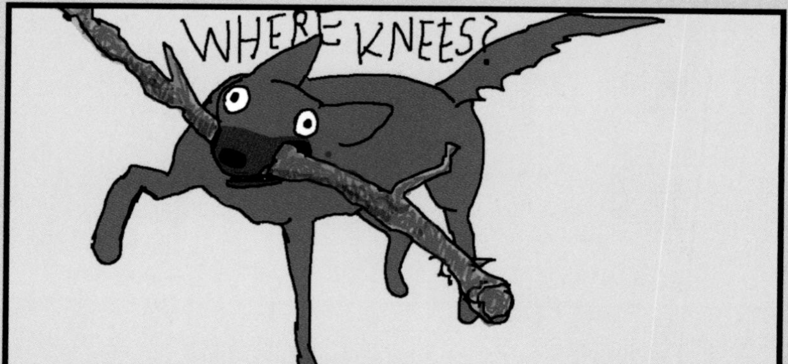
WHERE KNEES?

Nobody wants to play this game except you. Not even the old lady at the dog park. Not even children.

Instead of playing this game, why not play "Run Around and See How Far Away from Knees I Can Be"?

The "Find Out How Many Times I Can Squeak My Toy Before It Gets Taken Away" Game

eep eep eep eep eep eep eep eep eep eep eep eep eep eep eep eep eep eep eep eep eep eep eep eep eep eep eep eep eep eep eep eep eep eep

the answer is "around 700 times"

Lying on the floor and squeaking your toy for three hours in a row isn't technically a game, but you seem to think it is, and that's why you can't have squeaky toys anymore.

The important lesson here is to practice moderation in everything you do, including squeaking your squeaky toys. If you feel like doing something a lot, do it about a tenth of that amount instead.

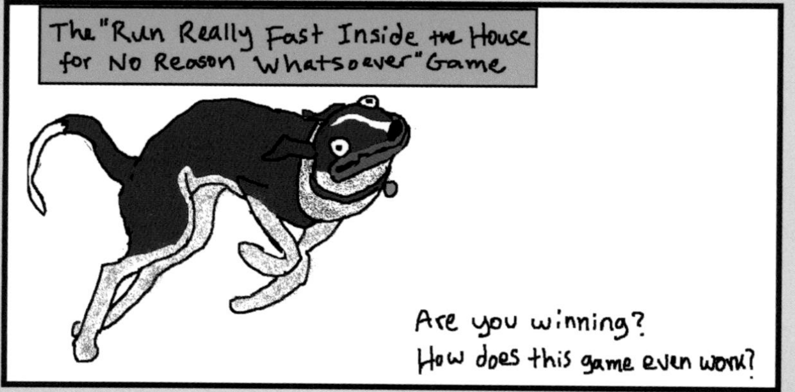
The "Run Really Fast Inside the House for No Reason Whatsoever" Game
Are you winning?
How does this game even work?

It's unclear how you win or whether winning is even something you're trying to do, but this game needs to stop.

Chapter 6: YOU CAN'T ALWAYS GET WHAT YOU WANT AND THERE ARE NO LOOPHOLES.

By now, I'm sure you can see that most of the things you want are stupid and most of the decisions you make are bad. Because of this, things aren't going to go your way very often. You need to be comfortable with disappointment.

If I have made a decision that is different from what you want, making high-pitched sounds at me will not change my mind.

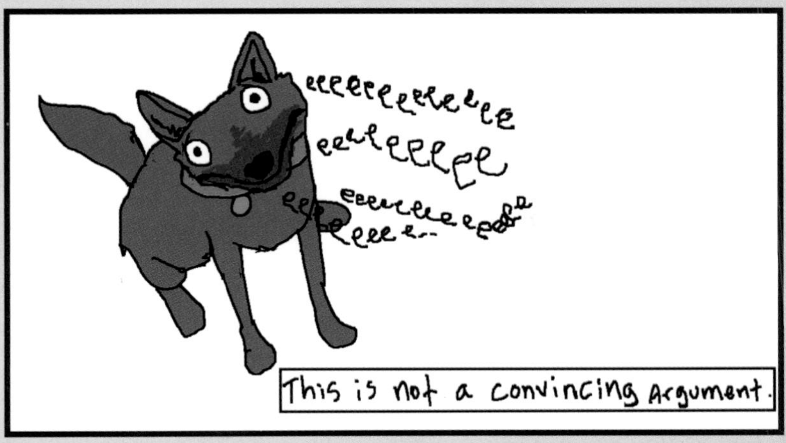
eeeeeeeeeeeee
eeeeeeee
eeeeeeeeeeeeee
This is not a convincing argument.

Neither will pawing at my legs.

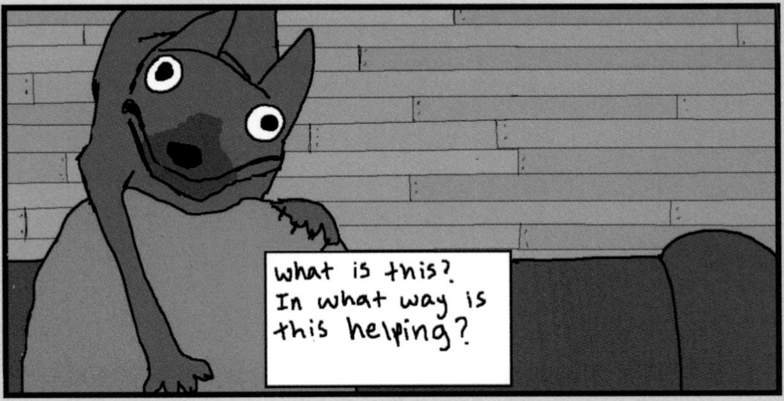
what is this?
In what way is
this helping?

And finally, you cannot trick me. I know that T-shirts do not spontaneously fly apart into pieces. And I'm especially not going to believe that the T-shirt was destroyed by forces beyond your control when you've still got pieces of it stuck to your face.

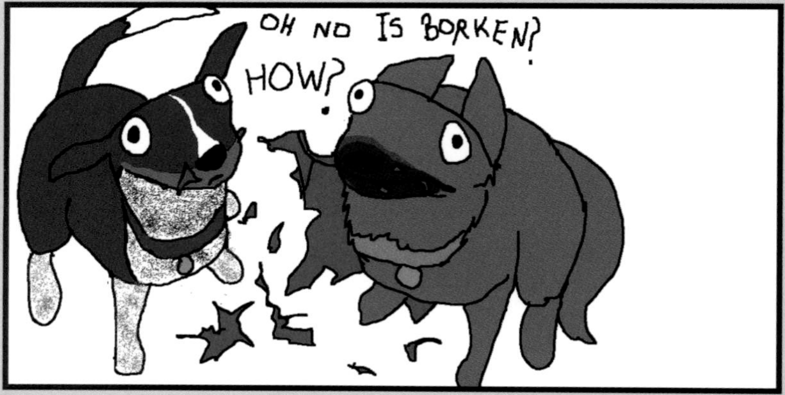
OH NO IS BORKEN?
HOW?

Pretending that I haven't fed you immediately after I fed you isn't going to work either.

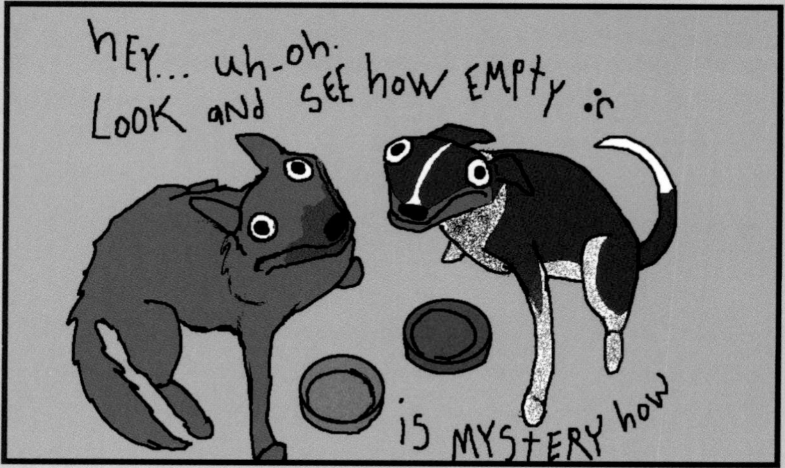
hEY... uh-oh.
LOOK aNd SEE how EMPty :c
is MYSTERY how

how does It know this is trick??

I know that you've already eaten because *I am the one who gave the food to you.* I remember doing it.

Also, I'm never going to believe that all four of your legs stopped working at the exact moment I decided we should leave the dog park.

NO LEGS
sorry
CAN't
home
moments earlier...
PLAYING
PLAYING
PLaaaYING
Perfect legs
Welcome to
dog PARK

You think you're being so sneaky. I'll admit that it's embarrassing when I have to drag you to the car by your perfectly functional legs, past all the people who are judging me because none of *their* dogs become situationally quadriplegic and they've never experienced this so they don't know what's going on. But I do. I know exactly what's going on. This same thing happens every single time I try to leave the dog park with you, and I'm not just going to stay there forever because other people might judge me for dragging you.

But you thought that's what would happen, didn't you. You thought I would allow you to become some sort of dog-park-dwelling legless creature. Tell me, dog, what's the point of living at the dog park if you're just going to lie on the ground pretending to be paralyzed so you don't have to go home? How would you find food? What would you do when it rained?

This is why you need me.

Chapter 7: QUESTIONS

Okay, dogs, I'm sure you've got some questions after all of that. Fortunately, I know exactly what those questions are because you're pretty transparent when you don't understand something.

Q: **Should eat bees?**
A: **No.**

Q: **But ... never bees?**
A: **No. You should never eat bees.**

Q: Bees?

A: No.

Q: But how does it not eat bees?

A: When you see a bee, you can avoid eating it by not putting it into your mouth. If you want to be extra sure that you will not eat bees, go somewhere where there are no bees until the urge to eat bees passes.

Q: Why does bad decision?

A: That's a good question, dogs. Unfortunately, I don't know why you make bad decisions. It's just something you do.

Q: How doors?

A: If I told you how doors work, you'd be able to make too many decisions.

Q: No.

A: That isn't a question.

Q: Whole time was bag?

A: Yes, in Chapter 1, Misconception #2, the object in the example was a bag the entire time. That wasn't supposed to be a trick.

Q: How does tricking?

A: Before you can understand how tricking works, you need to understand the concept of subtlety.

Q: Sorry.

A: That is not a question, but I accept your apologies.

The Party

At some point during my childhood, my mother made the mistake of taking me to see an orthodontist. It was discovered that I had a rogue tooth that was growing sideways.

Dramatic reenactment:
Haha! I'm going to ruin everything!

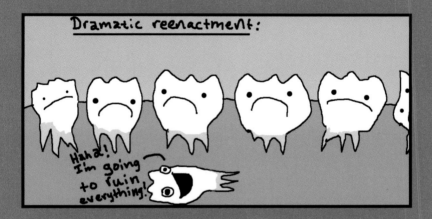

My mom and I were told that the tooth, if left unchecked, would completely ruin everything in my life and turn me into a horrible, horrible mutant.

I probably would have even grown teeth on my eyes.

Unless I wanted to spend the rest of my natural life chained in a windowless shed to avoid traumatizing the other citizens, I was going to need surgery to remove the tooth.

I was accepting of the idea until I found out that my surgery was scheduled on the same day as my friend's birthday party. My surgery was in the morning and the birthday party wasn't until the late afternoon, but my mom told me that I still probably wouldn't be able to go because I'd need time to recover from my surgery. I asked her if I could go to the party if I was feeling okay. She said yes, but warned me that I probably wouldn't be feeling well and to try not to get my hopes up.

But it was too late. I knew that if I could trick my mom into believing that I was feeling okay after my surgery, she'd let me go to my friend's birthday party. All I had to do was find a way to prove that I was completely recovered and ready to party. I began to gather very specific information about the kinds of things that would convince my mom that the surgery had absolutely no effect on me.

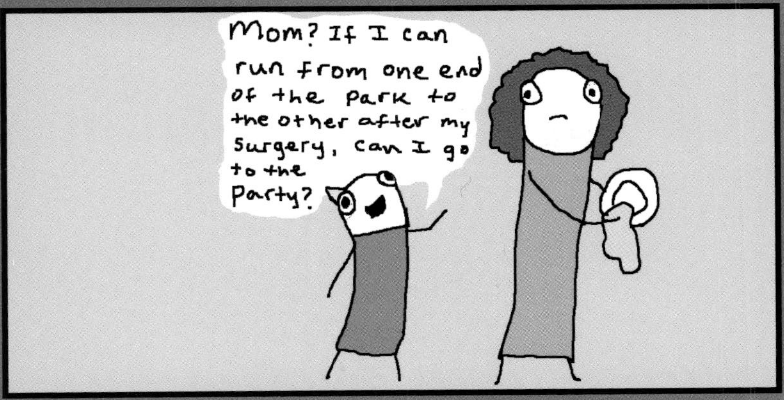
Mom? If I can run from one end of the park to the other after my surgery, can I go to the party?

I'm pretty sure my mom was just placating me so that I'd leave her alone, but somehow it was determined that the act of running across a park would indeed prove that I was recovered enough to attend the party. And I became completely fixated on that little ray of hope.

I remember sitting in the operating room right before going under, coaching myself for the ten thousandth time on my post-surgery plan: immediately after regaining even the slightest bit of consciousness, I was going to make my mom drive me to a park and I was going to run across it like a gazelle on steroids.

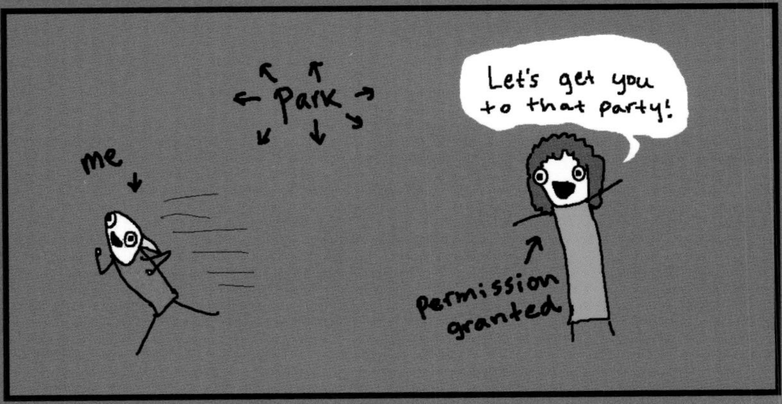
Park
me
Let's get you to that party!
permission granted

And then she would let me go to the party.

I must have done a really good job pretending to be okay even while I was still unconscious, because I was released well before the anesthetic wore off. My mom had to hold on to the back of my shirt to prevent me from falling over while we walked out of the hospital.

I first started to regain consciousness while we were driving on the freeway. I didn't know what was going on, but somewhere in the back of my mind, I remembered that I needed to do something important.

THE PARK!! I didn't recall exactly why I needed to go to the park, but I had spent so much time drilling the concept into my head that even in my haze of near-unconsciousness, I knew that getting myself to a park was of utmost importance. I tried to communicate this to my mom, but the combination of facial numbness and extreme sedation caused me to be unable to form words properly.

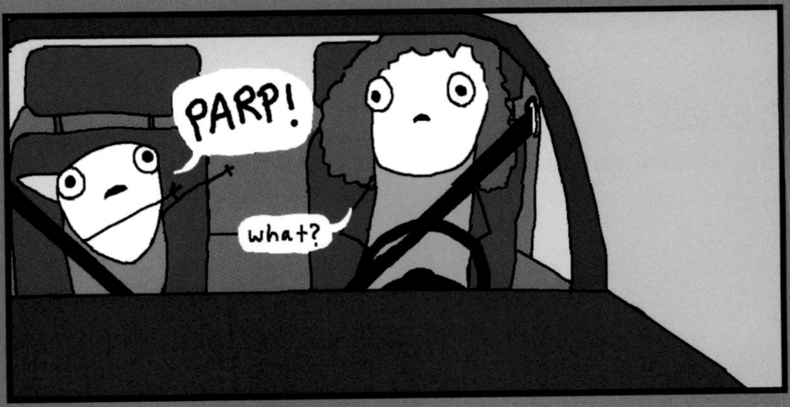
PARP!
what?

I yelled louder and more urgently, but my mom still couldn't grasp what it was I wanted.

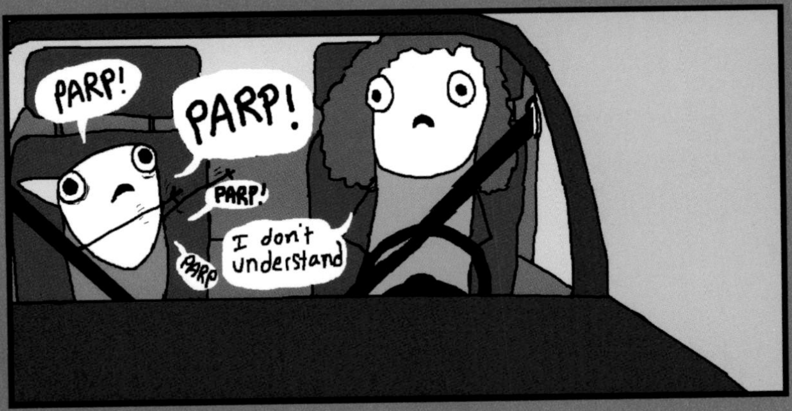
PARP!
PARP!
PARP!
PARP
I don't understand

It was at this point that I decided to open the car door and walk to the park by my damn self. The only problem was that instead of being stopped safely near a park, we were hurtling down I-90 at seventy miles per hour.

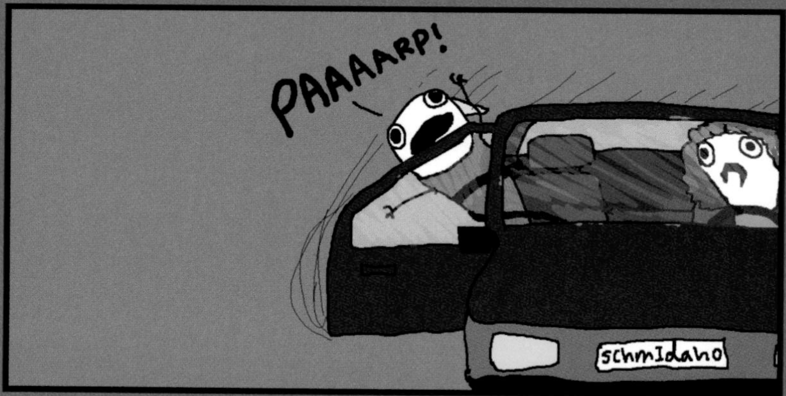
PAAAARP!
schmIdaho

Luckily I hadn't had the presence of mind to unbuckle my seat belt, so instead of toppling to a bloody death, I merely hung out the side of the car and flailed around ineffectively.

A little shaken up by the incident, my mom decided that it would probably be a good idea to pull off at the next exit and get some food in me. We found a fast-food restaurant and she led me inside.

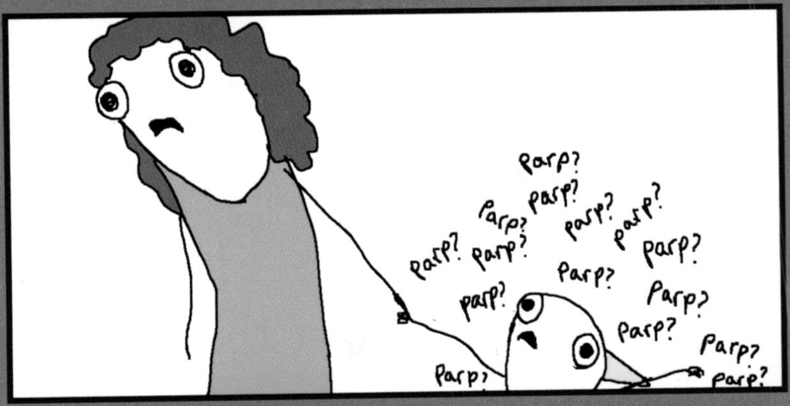
Parp?
Parp?
parp?
parp?
parp?
parp?
parp?
parp?
Parp?
parp?
Parp?
Parp?
Parp?
Parp?
parp?

It was pretty crowded, but my mom didn't want to get back in the car, so we found a table and she told me to wait while she stood in line to order our food.

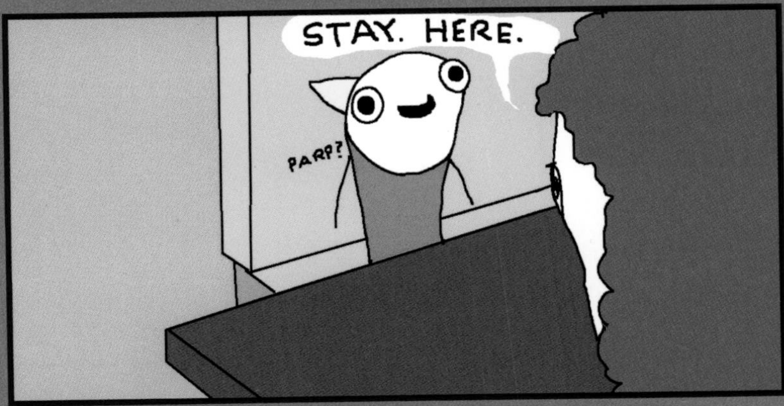
STAY. HERE.
PARP?

I sat contentedly at our table for a few minutes.

But then I forgot what was happening and panicked.

I had to find my mom. I had to tell her about the park. I tried to call for her, but I still couldn't quite remember how to say words.

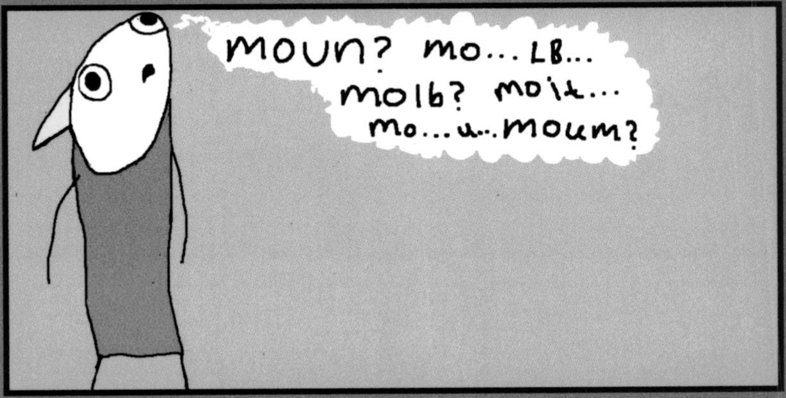
moun? mo... LB...
molb? mo'it...
mo... u... moum?

I began stumbling around the restaurant, shouting the closest approximation to the word "mom" that I could come up with.

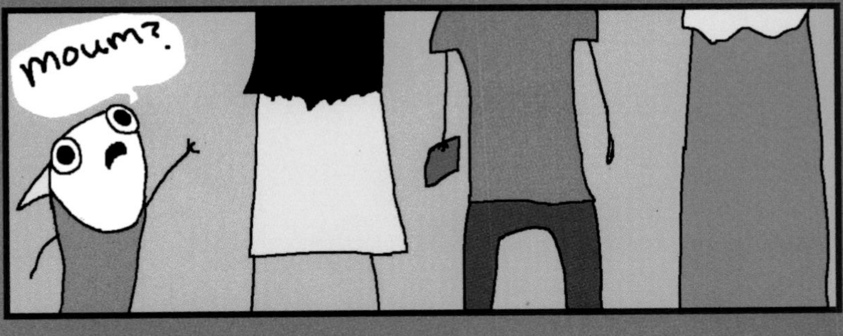
moum?

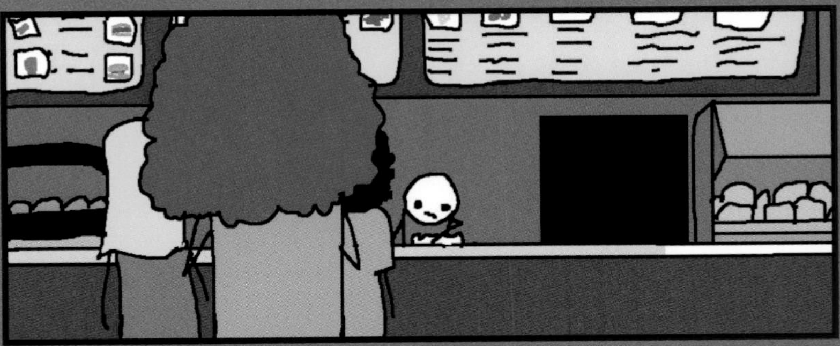

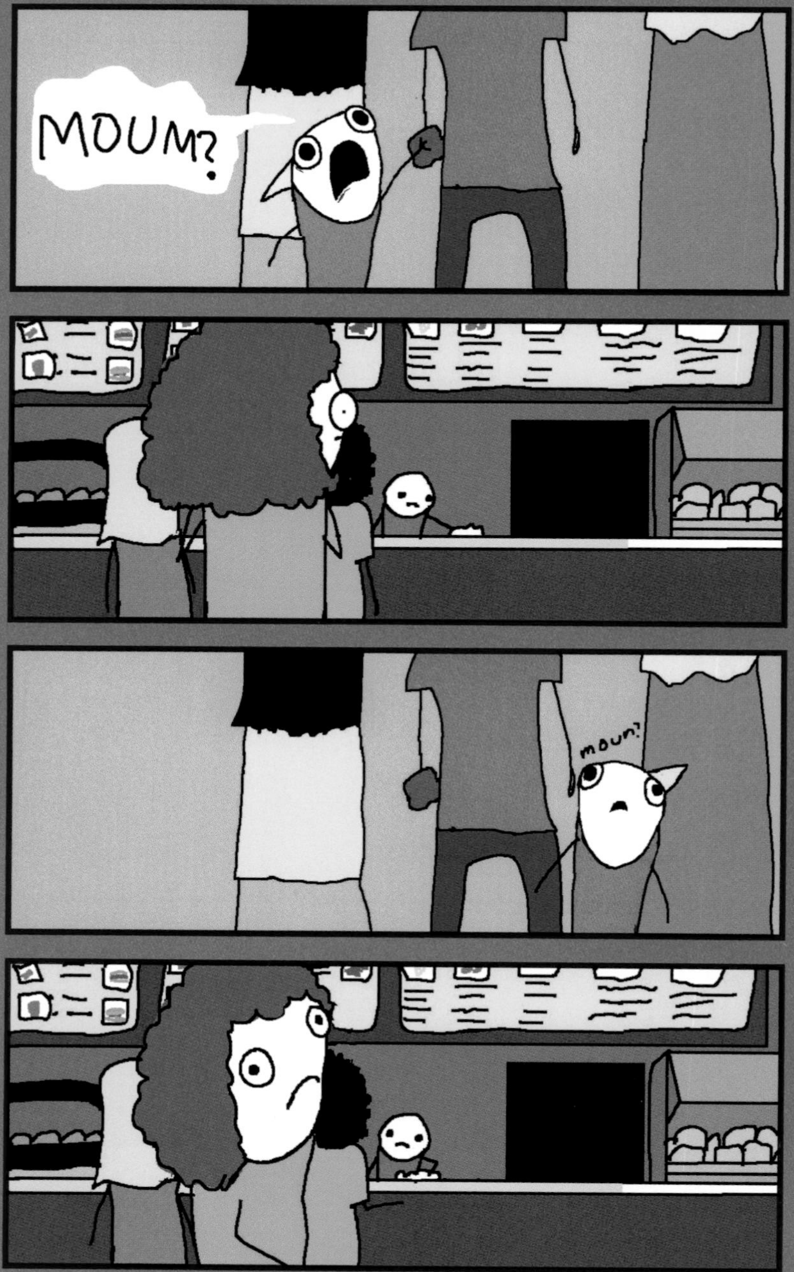
MOUM?
moum?

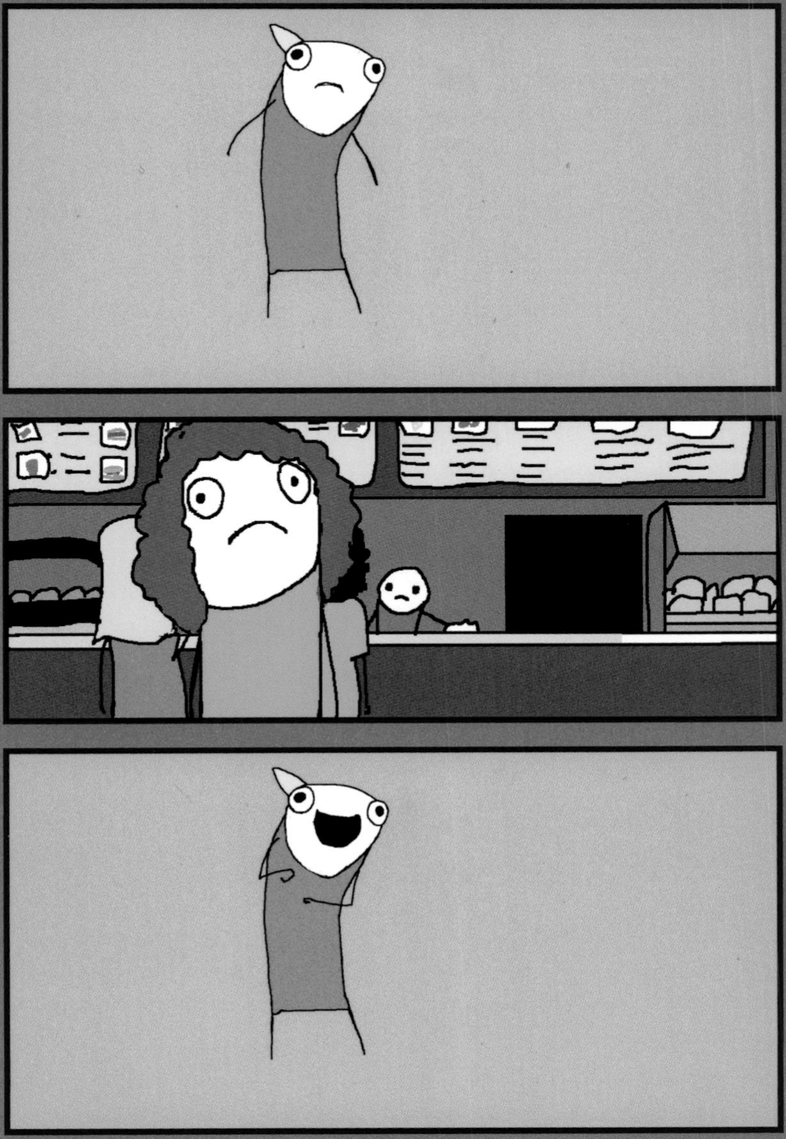

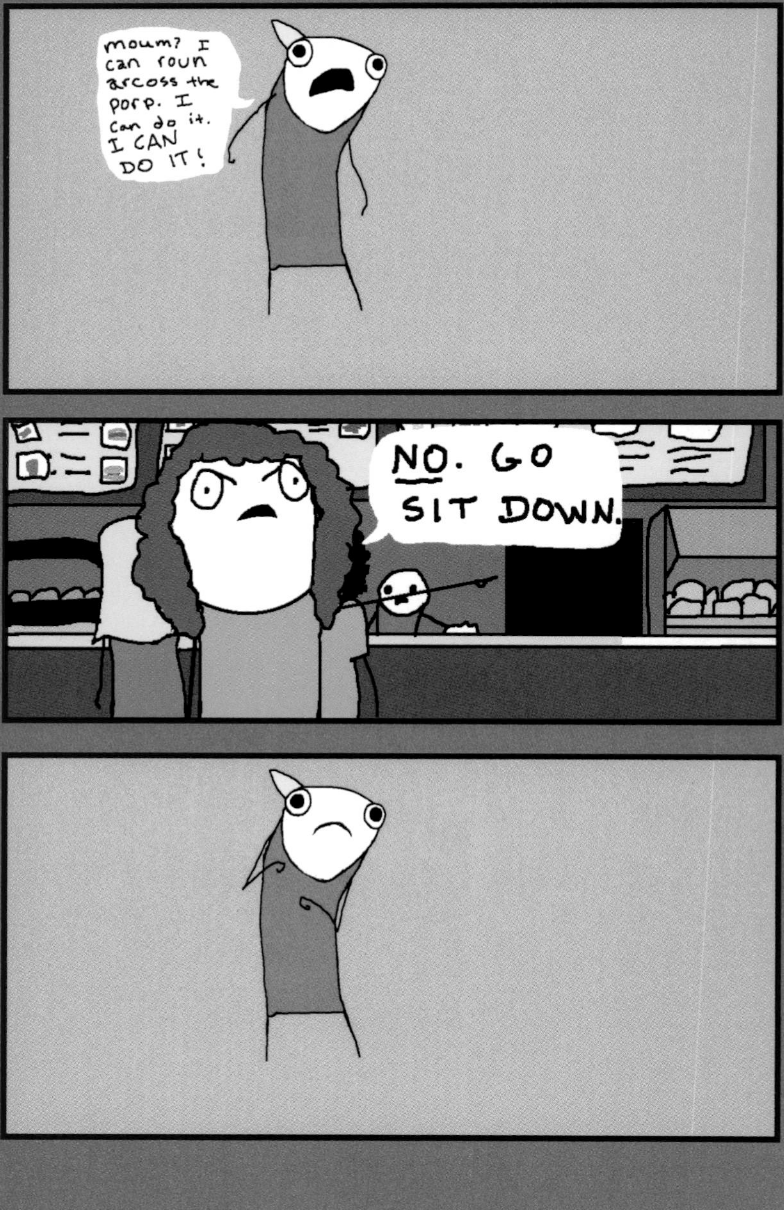
moum? I can roun arcoss the porp. I can do it. I CAN DO IT!
NO. GO SIT DOWN.

My mom hadn't yet figured out what I was trying to tell her, but she knew that I was yelling and stumbling into the other patrons and generally causing a scene, so she firmly told me to go back to my seat.

I had remembered why I wanted to go to the park, so I obeyed my mom, thinking it would increase my chances of going to the park, thus increasing my chances of going to the party.

When my mom returned to our table with our food, some version of the following conversation ensued:

Me:	Carn we go to the parp now?
My mom:	The park? Is that what you want?
Me:	Yes! The parp!
My mom:	No. Eat your food.
Me:	But moun—I can roun arcoss the porp. I can do it! I can go to the partney!
My mom:	No you can't.
Me:	I can! I can! I CAN!!!
My mom:	Look at you. You can't even walk. You can't form a coherent sentence.
Me:	I CAN ROUN ARCOSS THE PARP!!! I CAN GO TO THE PARPY!!!
My mom:	You are not going to that party.
Me:	NO!! NO! NO MOUM! I CAN DO IT! I CAN GO!
My mom:	I said you can't go to the party. Now eat your food.
Me:	MOOOOOOOUUUUUMM! WHY? WHY ARE YOU SO MEEEAAAAAAANNN?? WHY ARE YOU SO MEEEEEEEAAAAAAAN TOOO MEEEEEE???
My mom:	Stop it.

And then I started to cry big blubbery tears into my milkshake. It was at that point that my mom noticed all the people glaring at her and realized that, from an outside perspective, it appeared as though she was not only refusing to let her poor, mentally disabled daughter go to a park and/or a birthday party, but was also *taunting* her child about her disability.

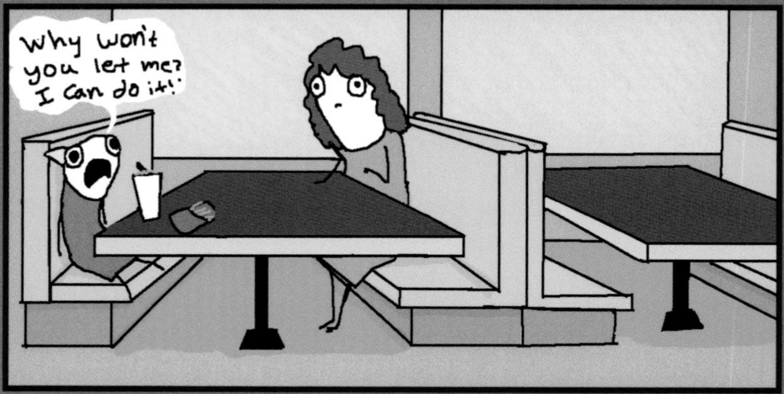
why won't you let me? I can do it!

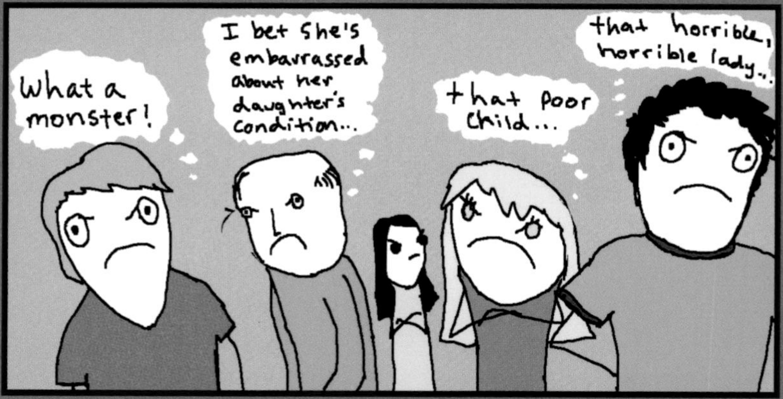
What a monster!
I bet She's embarrassed about her daughter's condition...
that poor child...
that horrible, horrible lady...

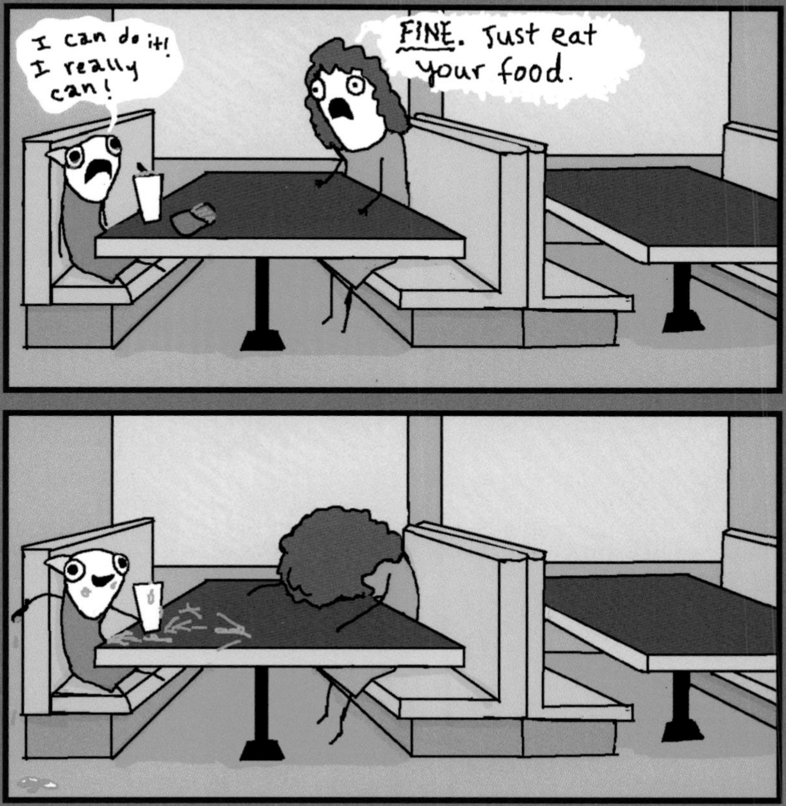
I can do it!
I really can!
FINE. Just eat your food.

And that's how I got to go to a birthday party while very heavily sedated.

Identity part one

I like to believe that I would behave heroically in a disaster situation. I like to think this because it makes me feel good about myself. Conveniently, it is very unlikely that I will ever actually have to do anything to prove it. As long as I never encounter a disaster situation, I can keep believing I'm a hero indefinitely.

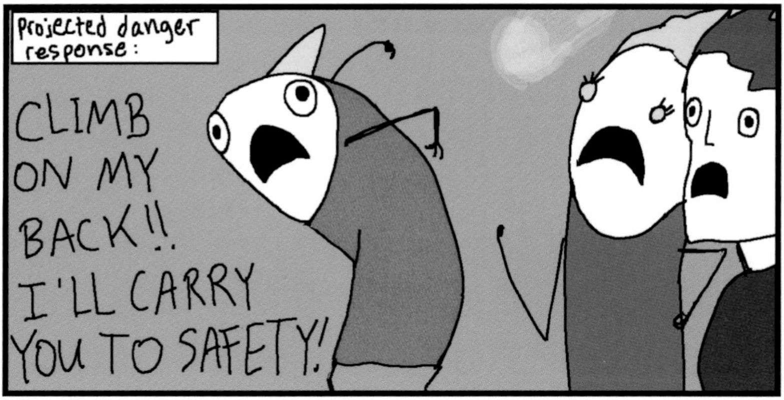

Projected danger response:
CLIMB ON MY BACK!! I'LL CARRY YOU TO SAFETY!

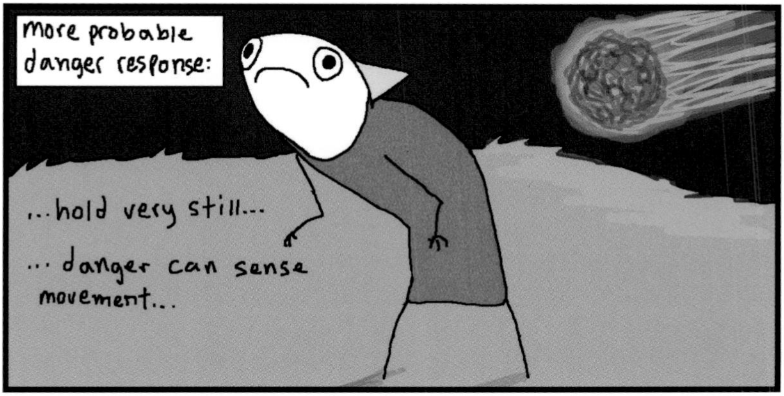
more probable
danger response:
...hold very still...
...danger can sense
movement...

Similarly, I can safely believe that I am the type of person who would donate a kidney to a loved one, give a million dollars to help save the animals, and survive a biological disaster due to my superior immune system and overwhelming specialness. As long as no one I love ever needs a kidney, I don't become a millionaire, and my immune system is never put to the test by an antibiotic-resistant super flu, these are just things I can believe for free.

It gets a bit trickier when I want to believe a thing about myself that actually requires me to do or think something. The things I am naturally inclined to do and think are not the same as the things I want to believe I would do and think. And I'm not even slightly realistic about what I want to be. I'm greedy and conceited, and I feel like I deserve to be impressed by myself.

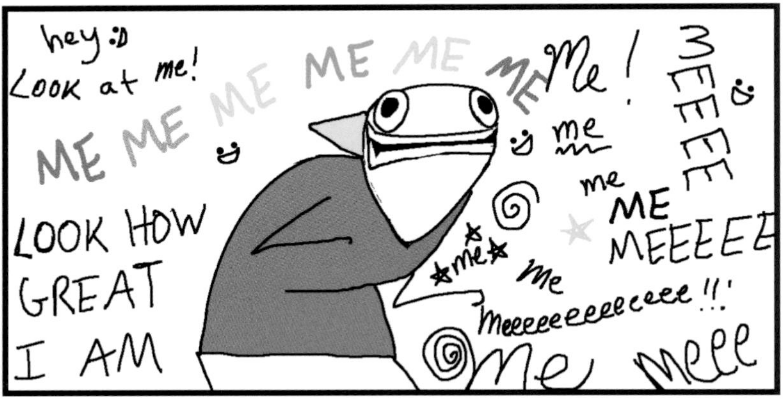
hey :D
Look at me!
ME ME ME ME ME ME Me!
MEEEE
me
me
ME
MEEEEE
LOOK HOW
GREAT
I AM
me
me
Meeeeeeeeeeeee!!!
me
meee

Unfortunately, I am not disciplined enough to maintain my behavior up to the standards of my ridiculously optimistic self-image, and I possess a great number of undesirable qualities, so it's a daily struggle to prevent myself from ruining my own fantasy.

But, against all odds, my gigantic ego continues to attempt greatness. And every day, it falls extremely short because, as powerful as it is, it is not even close to as powerful as what it's up against.

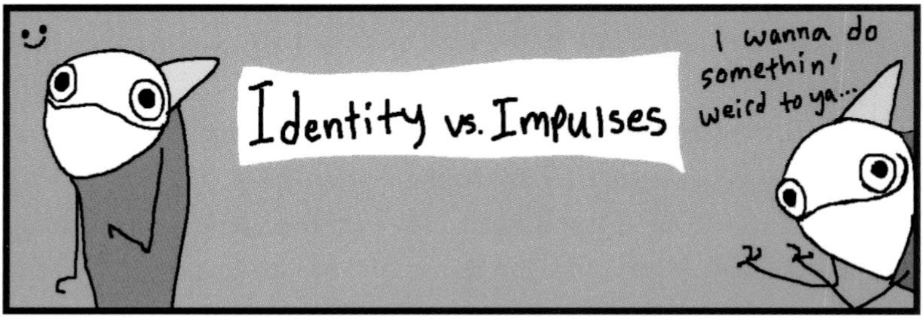
Identity vs. Impulses
I wanna do somethin' weird to ya...

The most basic level of maintaining my self-image is just holding myself back from acting on my impulses. I am constantly bombarded by bizarre, nonsensical urges, and if I didn't care about my identity, I would just do all of them.

It would be fucking mayhem.

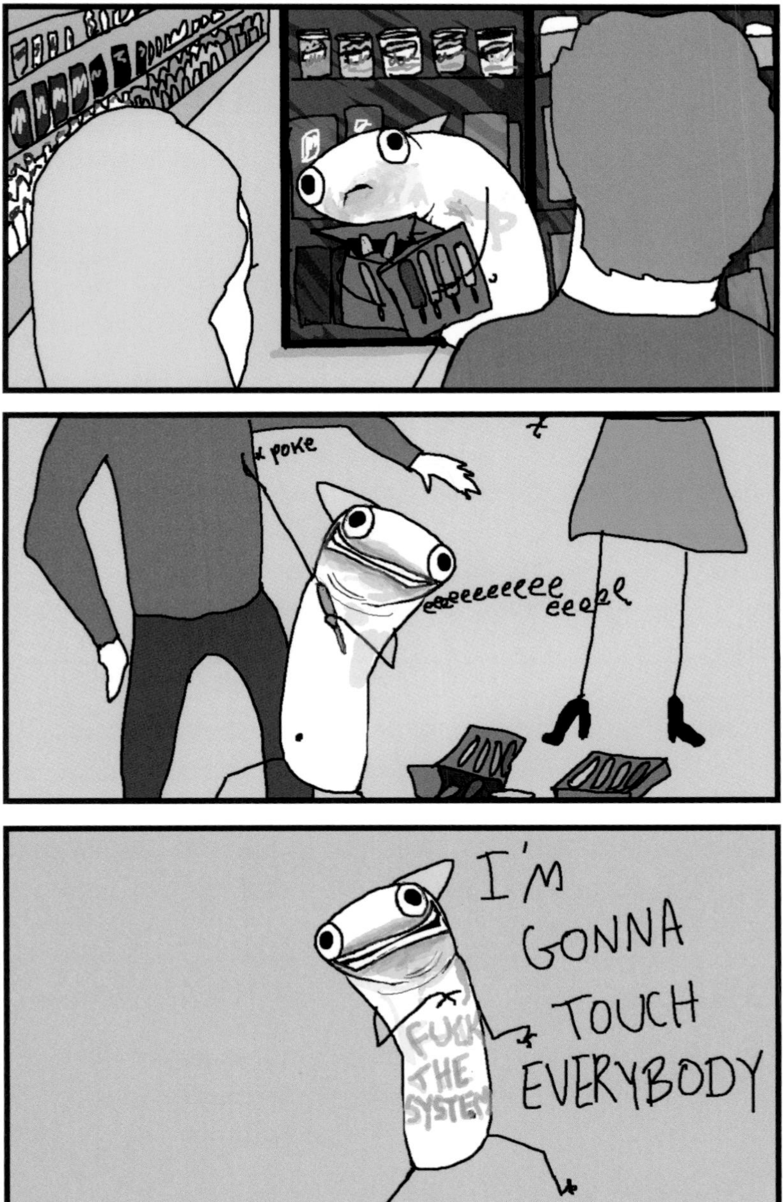
poke
I'M GONNA TOUCH EVERYBODY
THE SYSTEM

Fortunately for other people, it would be insulting to my identity if I did these things, and this successfully scares me away from becoming a menace to myself and everyone.

But I still have to know about the impulses.

I wonder what would happen if I bit that guy's dog...
Jesus christ... why am I like this?

My ego hates getting out of its tower to deal with this shit. It's got more important things to think about, like how virtuous and meaningful it is, and it has a hard time doing that when it is constantly distracted by the urge to do weird things to people. It wants to focus on being a *good* person, not just a barely not horrible one.

helpful, wonderful
Identity vs. Effort
not those things
haha NO

Being a good person is a very important part of my identity, but being a genuinely good person is time-consuming and complicated. You don't have to be a good person to feel like a good person, though. There's a loophole I found where I don't do good, helpful things, but I keep myself in a perpetual state of thinking I might.

It would be really nice of me to volunteer for something.
INTERNET
Who knows...
maybe I will someday...

I'm such a good person for thinking of possibly doing that...

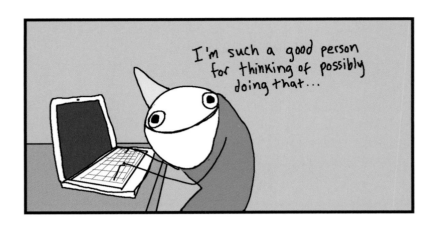

The fact that I think about doing nice things feels almost like actually doing them. I get to feel all the good feelings without any of the inconvenience. It's disgusting how proud of myself I am for things I've never done.

I also feel disproportionately good about myself whenever I'm presented with absurdly easy opportunities to do the right thing and then actually do it.

•Sees trash on ground, three feet from convenient trash can.
• Expends slight amount of effort to bend at waist to pick it up.

GOOD JOB, CAPTAIN PLANET, YOU SAVED THE ENTIRE ENVIRONMENT.

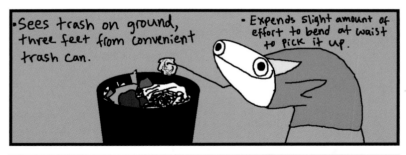

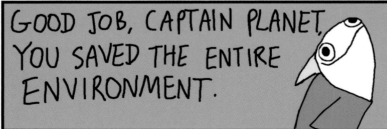

I'm even proud about not being a dick in situations where it is theoretically possible to be a dick. I don't feel especially inclined to be a dick in the first place, but I still feel proud that I somehow manage not to be. Based on how good this makes me feel about myself, I must subconsciously believe everyone else in the world is a horrible monster.

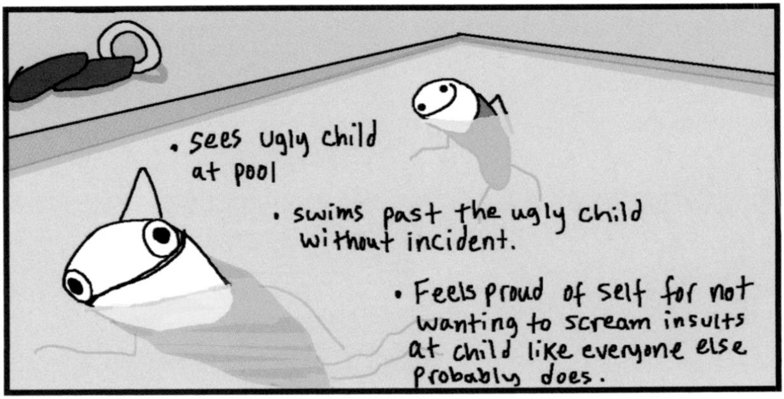

• sees ugly child at pool
• swims past the ugly child without incident.
• Feels proud of self for not wanting to scream insults at child like everyone else probably does.

It would disgust me to know I'm like this. When I look at myself, I don't want to see the horrible, loophole-abusing monster that I am. I want to see a better person. Someone who is genuinely good and doesn't need to resort to lies and manipulation. Because deep down, I feel like I'm better than this. Like I actually *am* a genuinely good person who has been invaded by someone else's shitty thoughts.

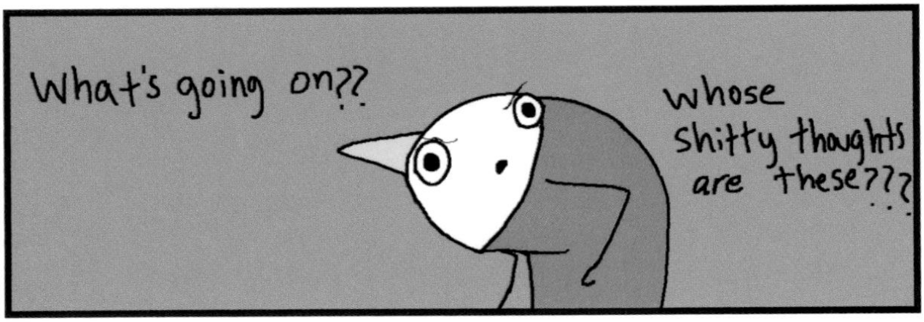

What's going on??
whose shitty thoughts are these???

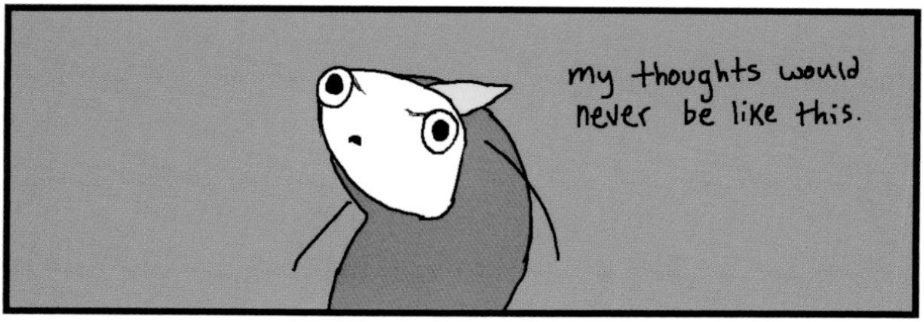
my thoughts would never be like this.

I am just the helpless vehicle for a lesser personality, forced to endure it against my will. I live in fear of it, hoping it won't attack me and make me think things that I'm ashamed of.

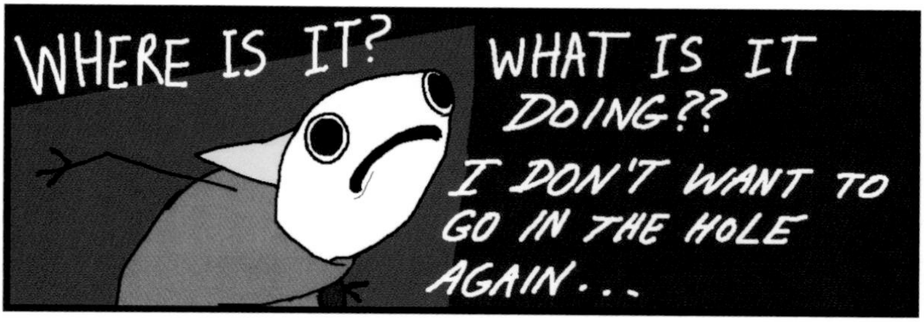
WHERE IS IT?
WHAT IS IT DOING??
I DON'T WANT TO GO IN THE HOLE AGAIN...

But it always does.

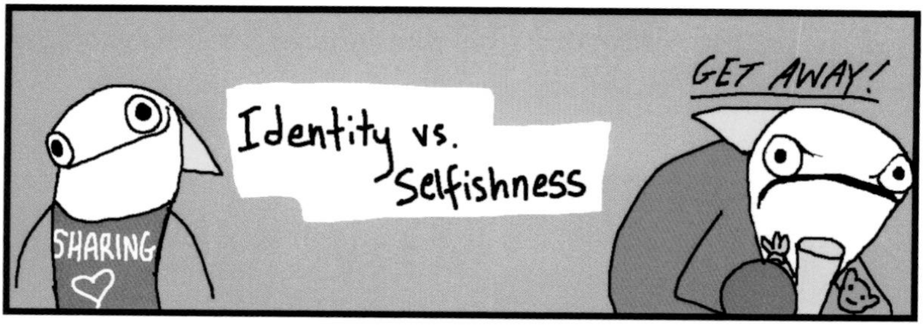
Identity vs. Selfishness
SHARING
GET AWAY!

I'm legitimately terrified that someday, someone I love is actually going to need a kidney. I'd like to say this fear stems from concern over the health of my loved ones, but it's mostly because I don't want to find out how I would react to someone needing one of my kidneys. I desperately want to believe I would seize the opportunity to help a loved one without a second thought for my own well-being, but I'm almost certain it wouldn't play out like that. First of all, I really, really wouldn't want to give away a kidney, and that would make me feel weird about myself. I'd feel selfish. Because I am.

And if I was not a match, I'd be relieved, which would also put me face-to-face with some uncomfortable truths about myself. If I *was* a match, I would probably end up letting go of a kidney, but not before fully exhausting my mental arsenal of escape routes.

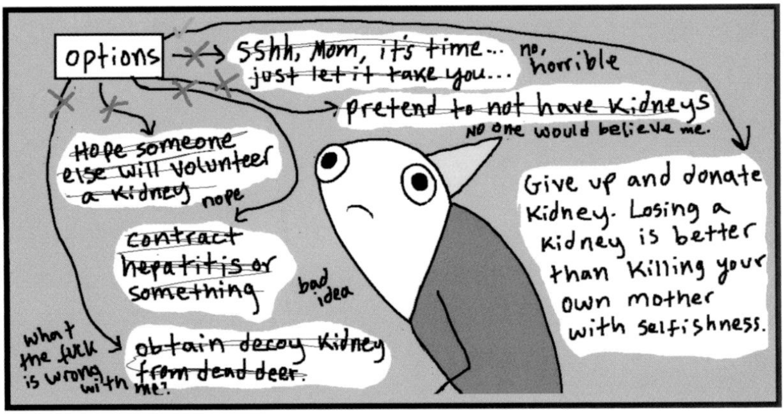

options
SShh, Mom, it's time... just let it take you...
no, horrible
pretend to not have Kidneys
No one would believe me.
Hope someone else will volunteer a Kidney
nope
contract hepatitis or something
bad idea
obtain decoy Kidney from dead deer.
what the fuck is wrong with me?
Give up and donate Kidney. Losing a Kidney is better than Killing your own mother with selfishness.

What I am is constantly thrust into my face while I'm trying to be better than I am. Even if I'm actively doing all the right things, I can't escape the fact that my internal reactions are those of a fundamentally horrible person.

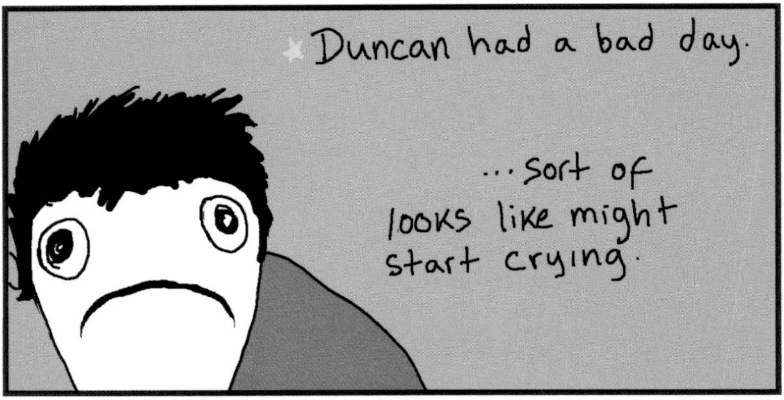
Duncan had a bad day.
...sort of looks like might start crying.

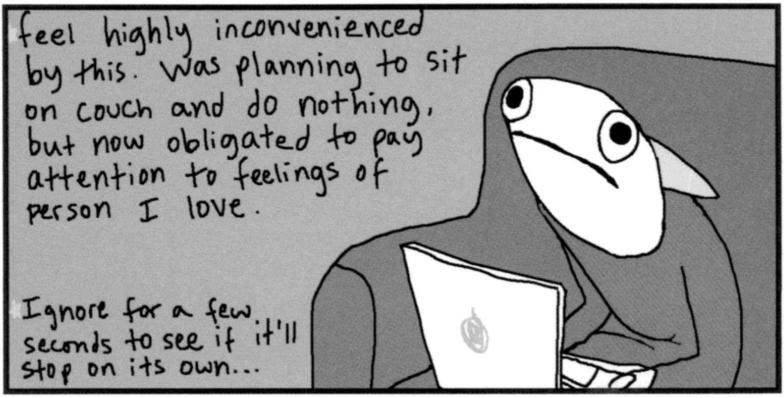
feel highly inconvenienced by this. Was planning to sit on couch and do nothing, but now obligated to pay attention to feelings of person I love.
Ignore for a few seconds to see if it'll stop on its own...

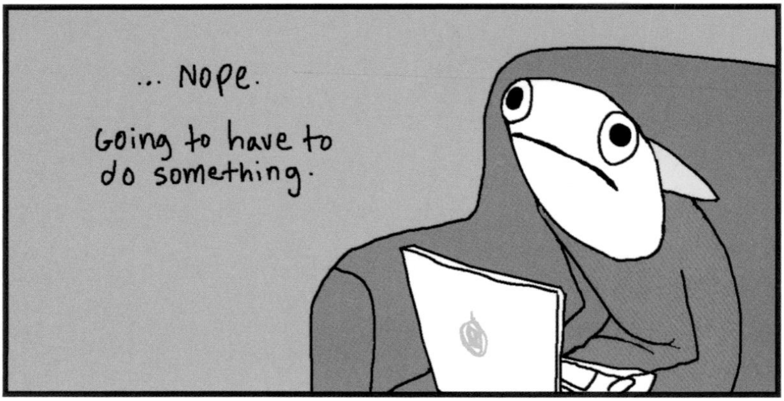
... Nope.
Going to have to do something.

Realize I'm an asshole.
Feel even more inconvenienced by situation because I also wasn't planning on having to think about what an asshole I am.
momentarily overwhelmed by self-concern in middle of someone else's crisis.
Somehow fight through self-centered haze long enough to provide adequate emotional support.
ssshhhh...
Congratulate self for being so caring.

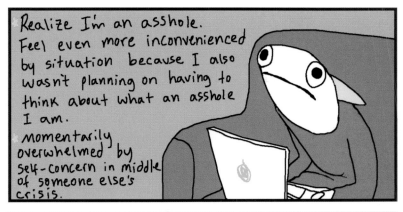

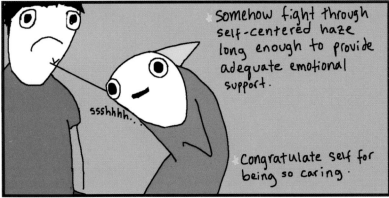

I don't just want to do the right thing. I want to WANT to do the right thing. This might seem like a noble goal to strive for, but I don't actually care about adhering to morality. It's more that being aware of not wanting to do the right thing ruins my ability to enjoy doing the right thing after I'm forced into doing it through shame.

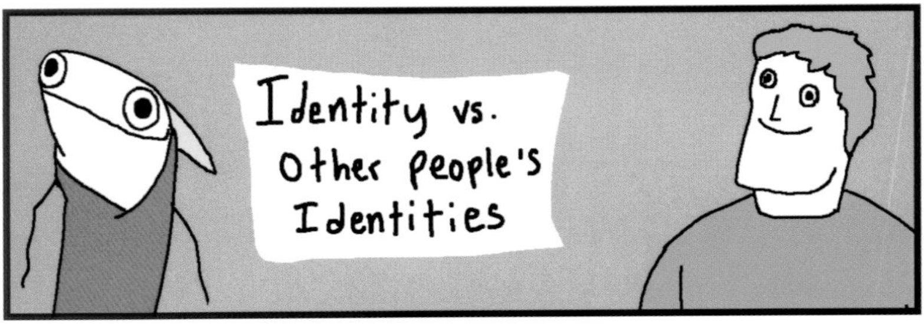
Identity vs. Other People's Identities

A lot of other people are better than me. When something causes me to become aware of this, it makes it more difficult for me to be satisfied with the way I am because the way I am seems so shitty compared to the way these better people are able to be.

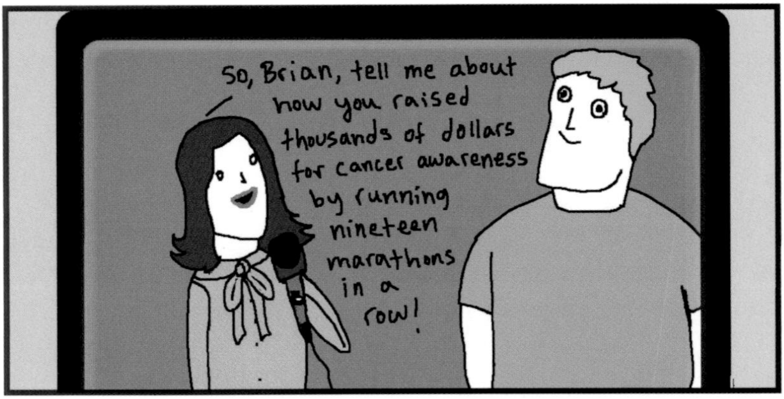
So, Brian, tell me about how you raised thousands of dollars for cancer awareness by running nineteen marathons in a row!

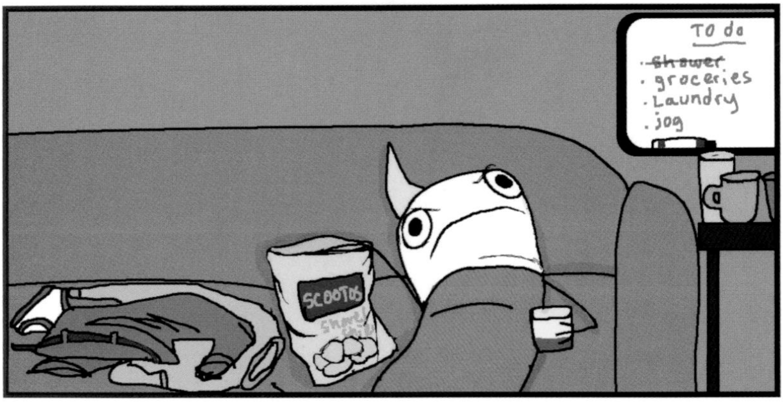
TO do
~~shower~~
· groceries
· Laundry
· jog
SCOOTOS

Oh, you know, I was running all these marathons anyway, so I figured why not? I love helping!
God damn it, Brian... Can't you just be normal?? You're making me look like a fool!
TO do
· Shower
· groceries
· Laundry
· jog
SCOOTOS

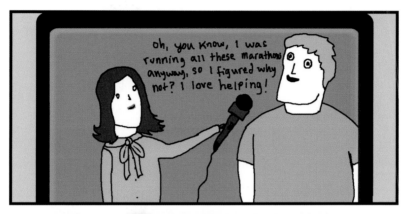

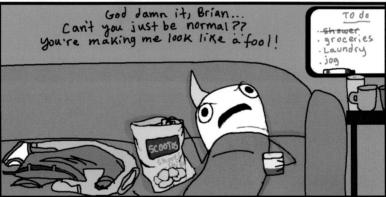

And this, of course, highlights how petty I am, which is also something I don't like to think about.

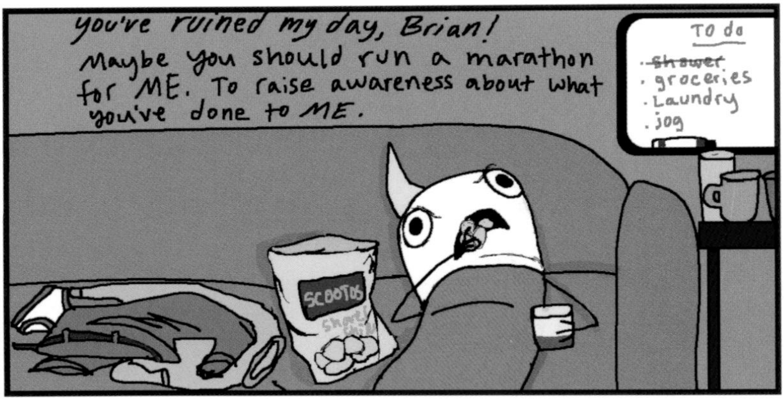
you've ruined my day, Brian!
Maybe you should run a marathon for ME. To raise awareness about what you've done to ME.
TO do
. Shower
. groceries
. Laundry
. jog
SCOOTOS

Which highlights the fact that I don't like to think about how petty I am, which makes me feel like maybe there are other things about myself that I'm avoiding.

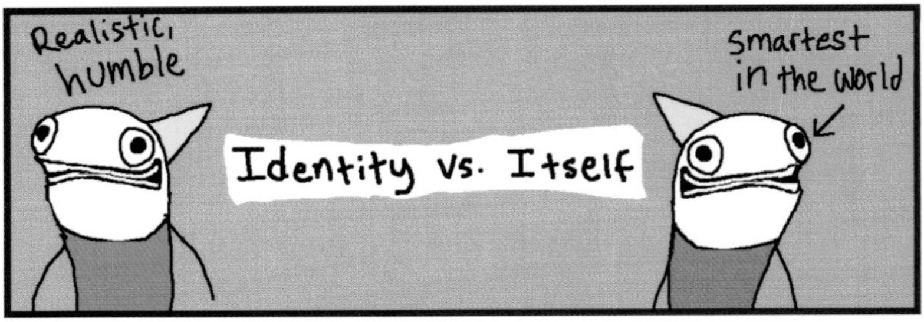
Realistic, humble
Identity vs. Itself
Smartest in the world

Because my identity is based on so many things that aren't true, it doesn't have a built-in fact-checking mechanism, and sometimes discrepancies arise.

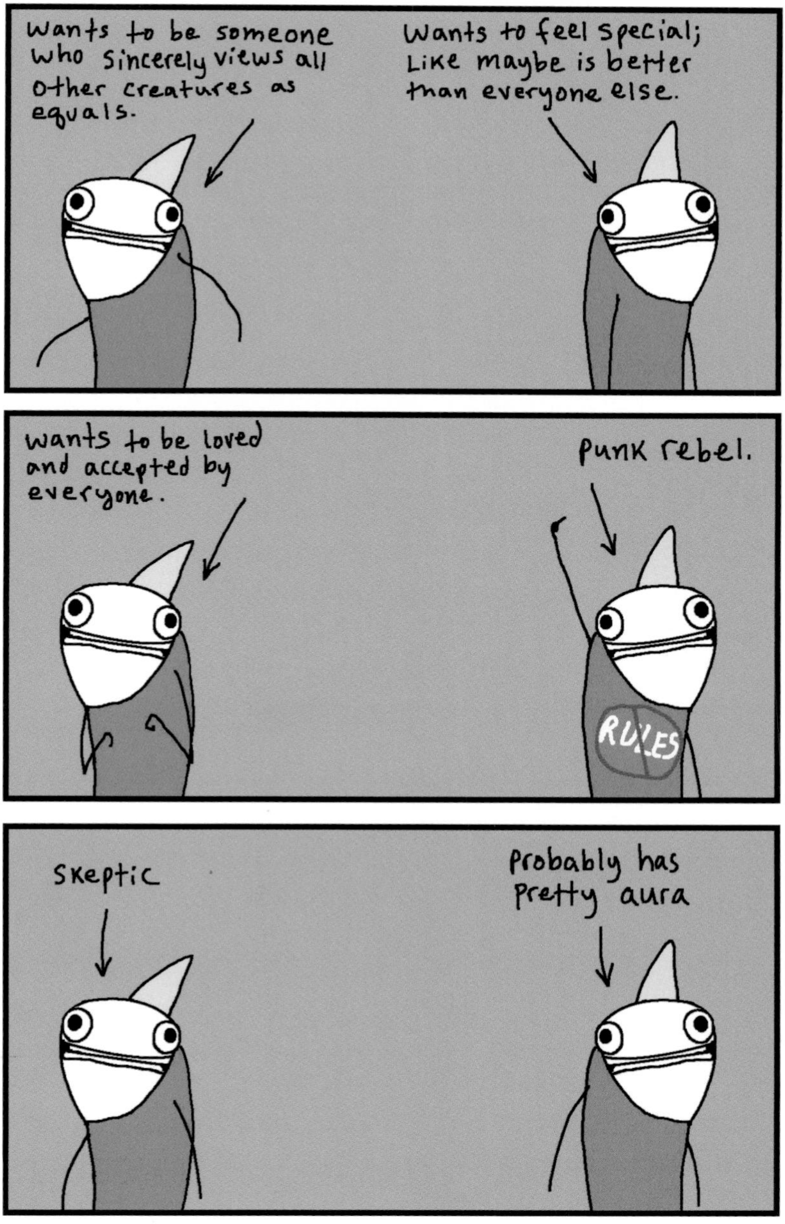
Wants to be someone who sincerely views all other creatures as equals.
Wants to feel special; Like maybe is better than everyone else.
Wants to be loved and accepted by everyone.
Punk rebel.
RULES
Skeptic
Probably has pretty aura

This is quite uncomfortable because it means I need to pick a side.

But I don't like picking sides when it comes to my identity, so I usually try to ignore it or find a way to trick myself into thinking it isn't a discrepancy.

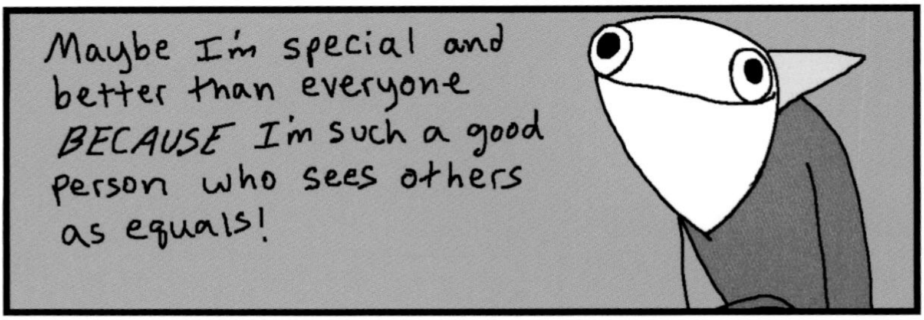
Maybe I'm special and better than everyone BECAUSE I'm such a good person who sees others as equals!

I would never have to know about any of this if I was sneakier about it or if I had more reasonable expectations for myself, but I keep noticing while I'm contradicting the things I want to believe are true.

This triggers an uncomfortable level of self-awareness where I'm dangerously close to discovering how full of shit I am.

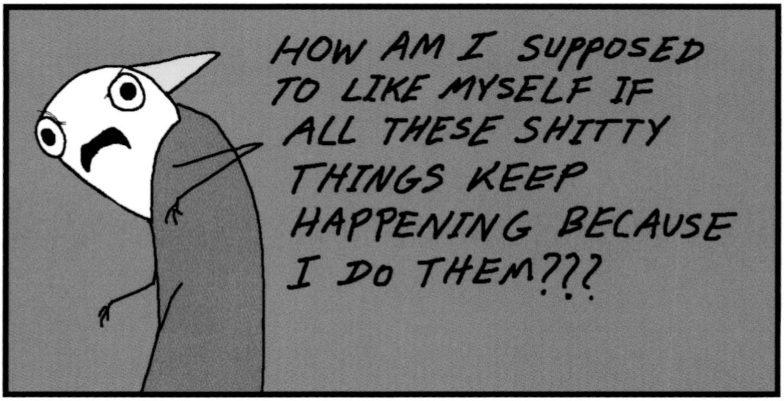
HOW AM I SUPPOSED TO LIKE MYSELF IF ALL THESE SHITTY THINGS KEEP HAPPENING BECAUSE I DO THEM???

Identity Part Two

On a fundamental level, I am someone who would throw sand at children. I know this because I have had to resist doing it, and that means that it's what I would naturally be doing if I wasn't resisting it.

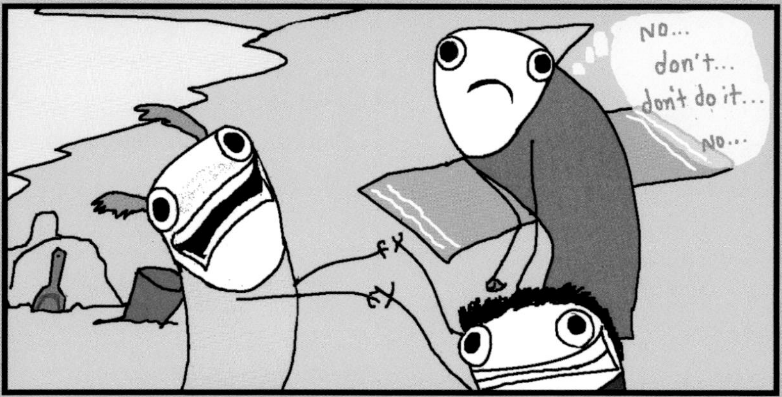
NO...
don't...
don't do it...
NO...

I would also shove everyone, never share anything, and shout at people who aren't letting me do exactly what I want.

I don't do those things, though. Because I don't want to have to know that I did them. It would hamper my ability to feel like a good person. I don't even want to know that I *would* do them.

Thankfully, I have an entire system of lies and tricks in place to prevent me from realizing how shitty I actually am.

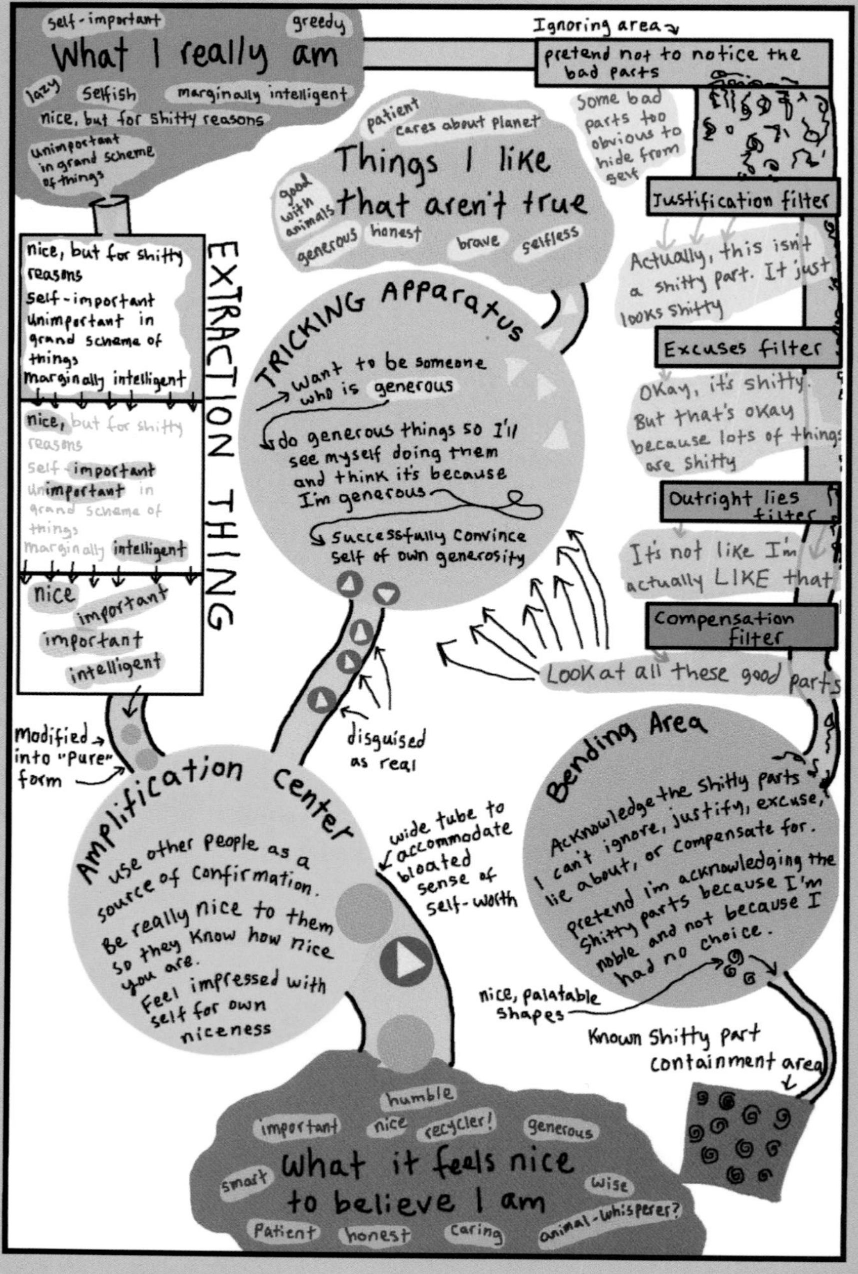
self-important
greedy
What I really am
lazy
Selfish
marginally intelligent
nice, but for shitty reasons
unimportant in grand scheme of things
Ignoring area
pretend not to notice the bad parts
Some bad parts too obvious to hide from self
patient
cares about planet
Things I like that aren't true
good with animals
generous
honest
brave
selfless
Justification filter
Actually, this isn't a shitty part. It just looks shitty
Excuses filter
Okay, it's shitty. But that's okay because lots of things are shitty
Outright lies filter
It's not like I'm actually LIKE that
Compensation filter
Look at all these good parts
EXTRACTION THING
nice, but for shitty reasons
self-important
unimportant in grand scheme of things
marginally intelligent
nice, but for shitty reasons
self-important
unimportant in grand scheme of things
marginally intelligent
nice
important
important
intelligent
modified into "pure" form
TRICKING Apparatus
want to be someone who is generous
do generous things so I'll see myself doing them and think it's because I'm generous
successfully convince self of own generosity
disguised as real
Amplification center
use other people as a source of confirmation.
Be really nice to them so they know how nice you are.
Feel impressed with self for own niceness
wide tube to accommodate bloated sense of self-worth
Bending Area
Acknowledge the shitty parts I can't ignore, justify, excuse, lie about, or compensate for.
pretend I'm acknowledging the shitty parts because I'm noble and not because I had no choice.
nice, palatable shapes
Known shitty part containment area
humble
important
nice
recycler!
generous
smart
What it feels nice to believe I am
wise
Patient
honest
caring
animal-whisperer?

If you actually are a genuinely good person, perhaps you don't need lies and tricks to feel good about yourself. But every day—against my will—I am bombarded by all these shitty, selfish thoughts, and I don't want to find out that the reason I have them is because *that's what I'm really like*. That would be disappointing. This system protects me from that.

But I'm a little greedy about the good qualities I want to believe I have, and I'm not very sneaky, so at some point I accidentally started to figure out what was going on.

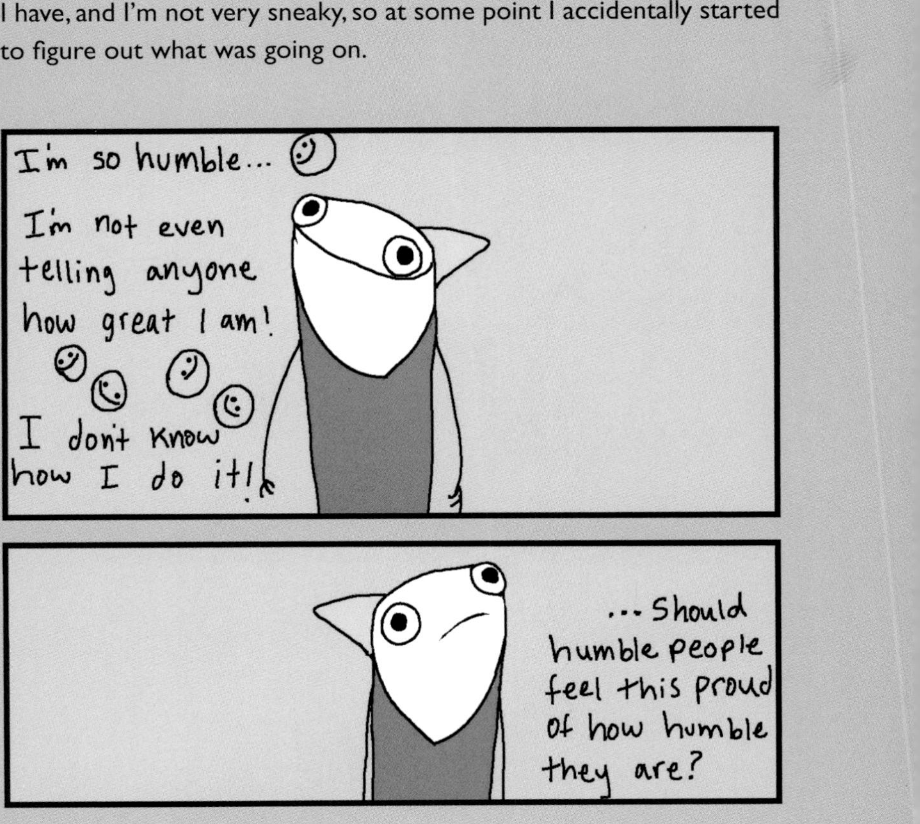
I'm so humble...
I'm not even telling anyone how great I am!
I don't know how I do it!
...Should humble people feel this proud of how humble they are?

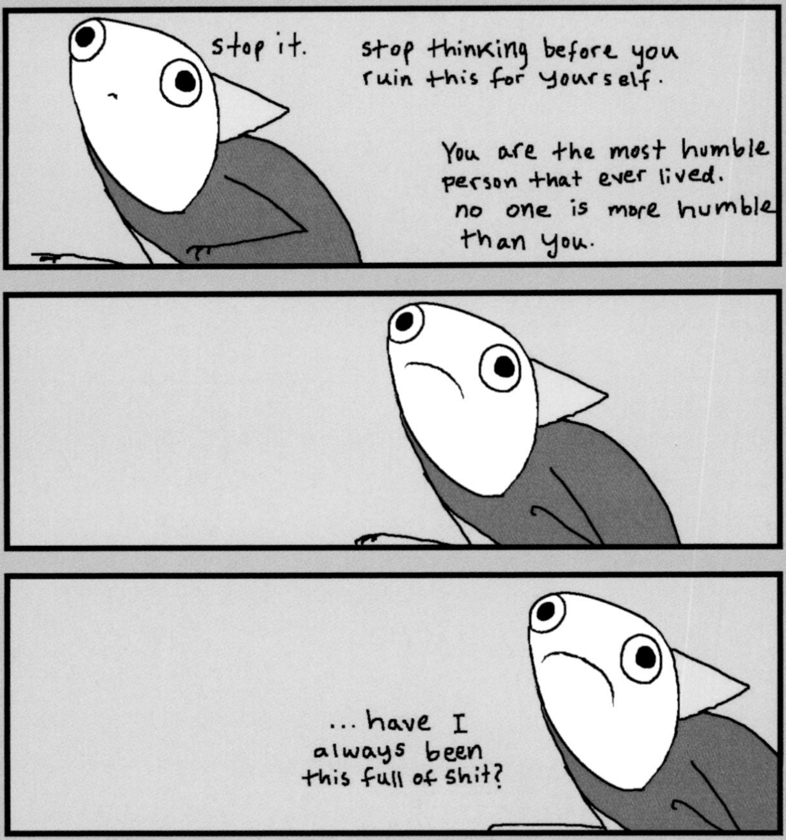
stop it.
stop thinking before you ruin this for yourself.
You are the most humble person that ever lived. no one is more humble than you.
...have I always been this full of shit?

When you start figuring out how full of shit you are, it's like opening a tunnel to all the lies you've ever told yourself. The tunnel is really deep and scary, but you're suspicious about it and you want to see what's down there.

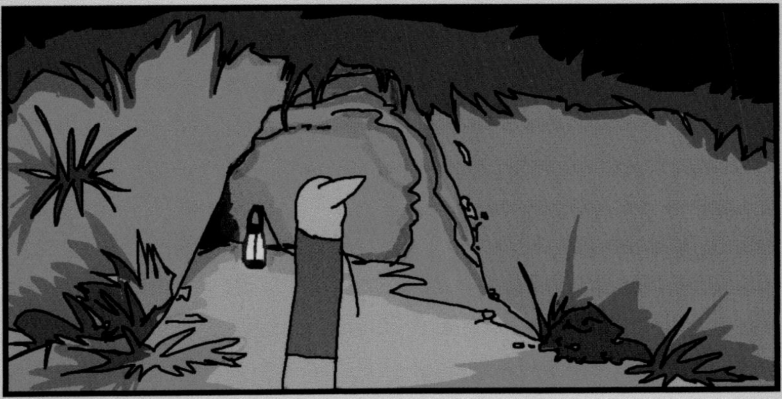

I wanted to know if I had been lying to myself about anything else. And, with only a minimal level of investigation, I was able to determine that I'd been lying to myself quite a lot.

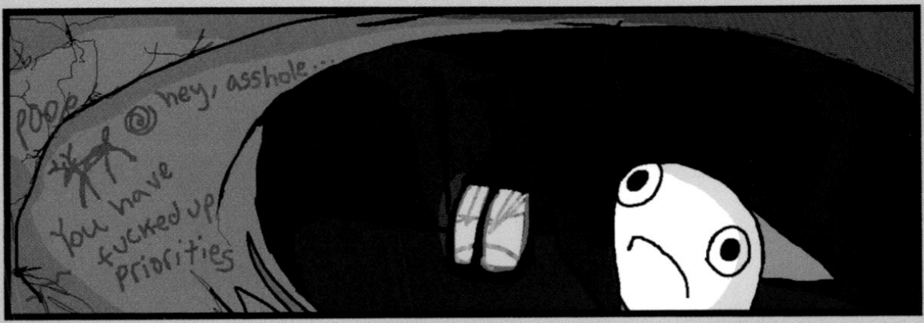
POOP
hey, asshole...
You have fucked up priorities

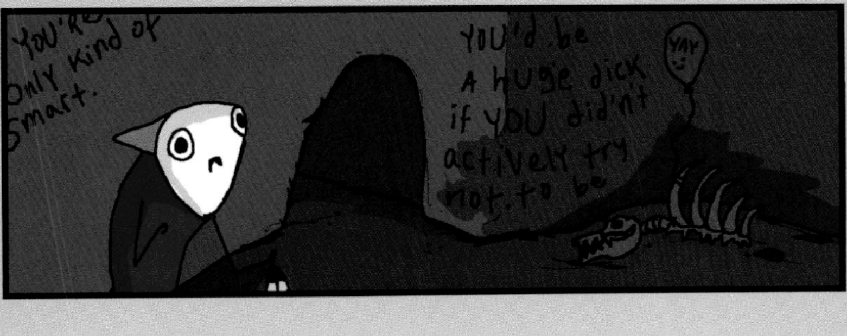
YOU'RE only kind of smart.
YOU'd be A huge dick if YOU didn't actively try not to be
YAY

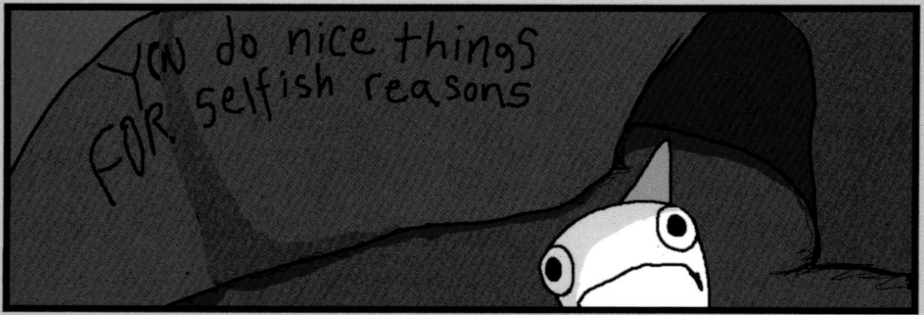
YOU do nice things FOR selfish reasons

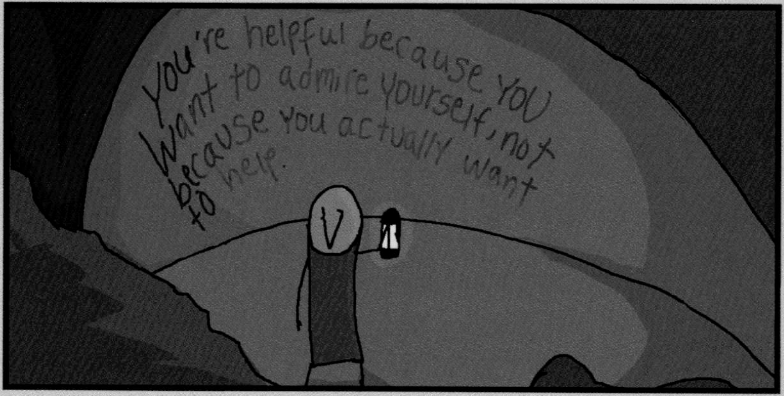
You're helpful because you want to admire yourself, not because you actually want to help.

It felt horrible to find bad qualities that I didn't know about. And it felt even worse to know that some of the things I thought were my good qualities were actually just a disguise for more bad qualities.

I was disgusted.

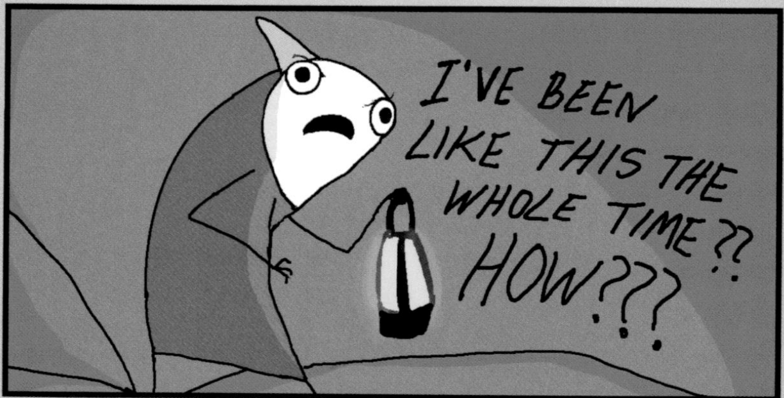
I'VE BEEN LIKE THIS THE WHOLE TIME?? HOW???

And here's where most people would stop probing. Because most people are smart enough to realize that self-improvement is supposed to be a delicate, lifelong process of exploring until you find a teensy amount of truth—just enough to make yourself uncomfortable—then getting the hell out so you can process what you learned in the comfort of your warm, familiar lie fortress.

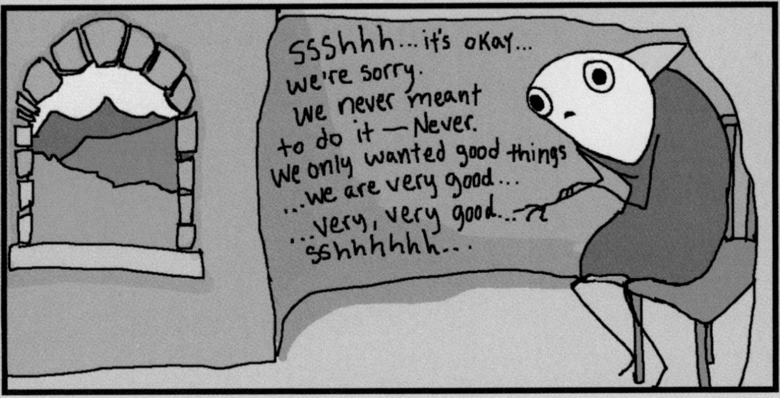

SSShhh... it's okay...
we're sorry.
We never meant
to do it—Never.
We only wanted good things
...we are very good...
...very, very good...
sshhhhhh...

But not me. I'm arrogant, and I thought I could handle it all at once.

I thought the whole process was going to be sort of like getting rid of a wasp nest—a few stings, but once you remove the source of the problem, it's gone. Unlike wasp nests, however, you cannot beat your fundamental insufficiencies to death with a fourteen-foot-long tree branch while hiding behind a ski mask and a cloud of Mace. And unlike wasps, uncomfortable truths don't stop coming once you destroy their home.

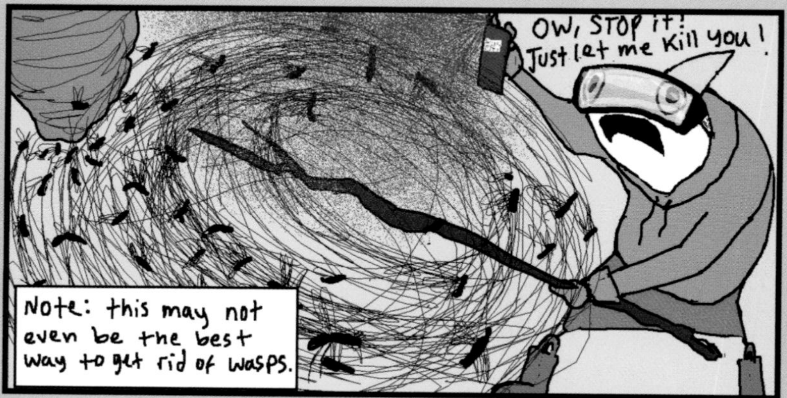
OW, STOP it! Just let me Kill you!
Note: this may not even be the best way to get rid of wasps.

On some level, I think I truly believed that if I just kept going . . . maybe I could locate the source of my shittiness and *actually* get rid of it.

Unfortunately, the source of my shittiness is the fact that I'm shitty. I just am. It is not possible for me to not be that way. I can prevent myself from being *actively* shitty. I can do things that a not-shitty person would do. But the shittiness is always going to be there, just beneath the surface, straining to get out.

I did not know that yet, though. I had a wonderful, lie-generating loophole machine protecting me from ever coming into contact with that information, and, somewhat ironically, that's what gave me the confidence to ignore the warnings and bumble onward.

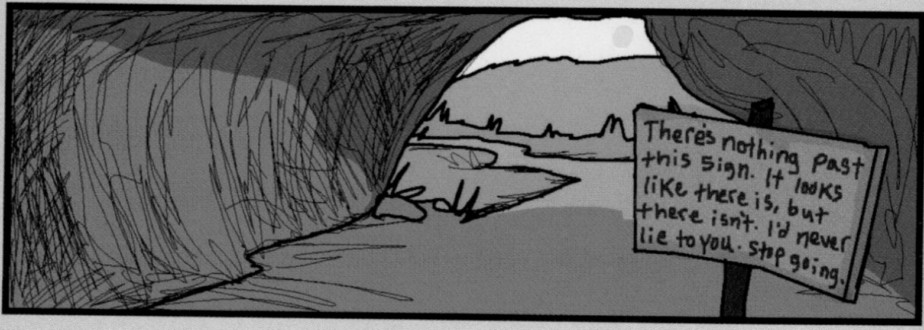
There's nothing past this sign. It looks like there is, but there isn't. I'd never lie to you. Stop going.

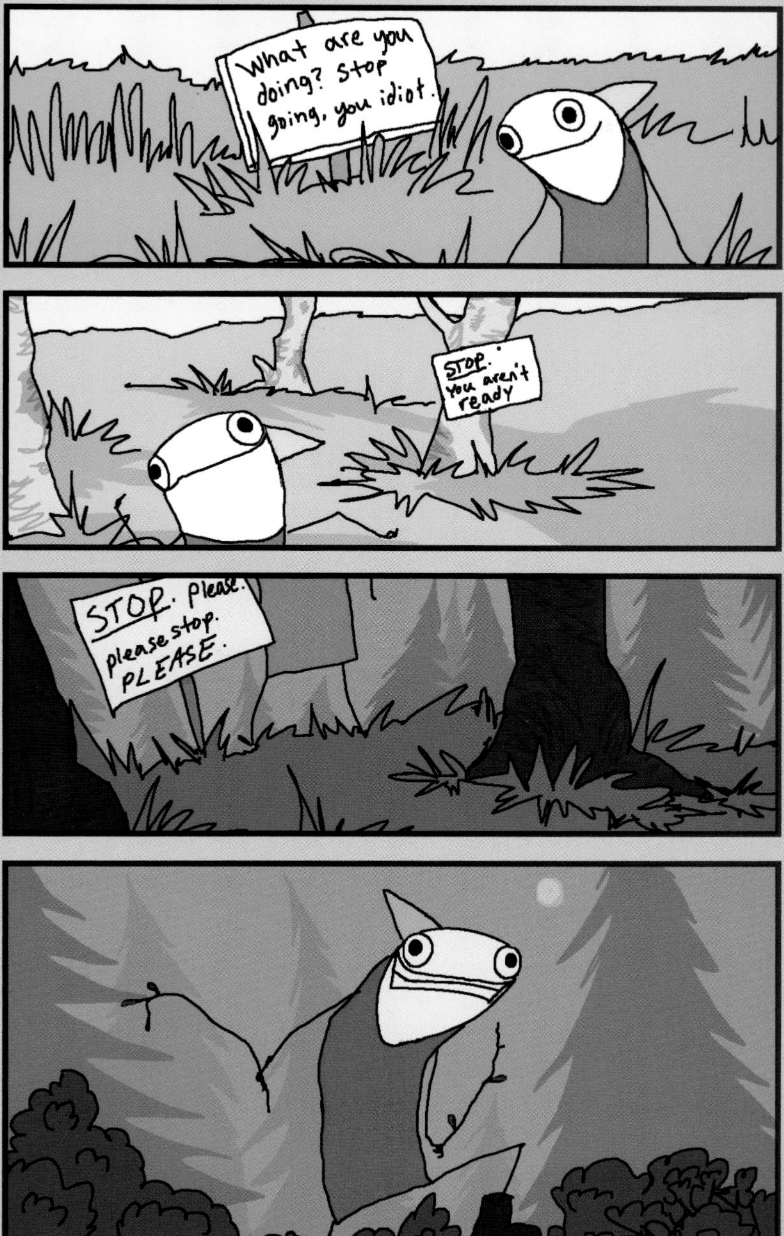
What are you doing? Stop going, you idiot.
STOP. You aren't ready
STOP. please. please stop. PLEASE.

The human brain knows when it isn't ready to discover everything about itself, and there are a few *emergency*-emergency security measures in place to keep you safe in the event that you decide to go traipsing around in your deep brain-wilderness like a reckless idiot.

Hey! what are you doing?
Eric
SECURITY
playing a game

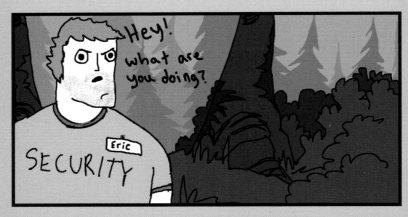

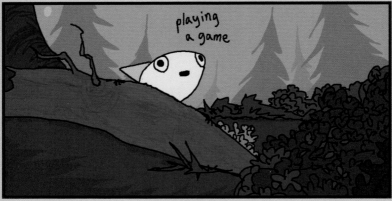

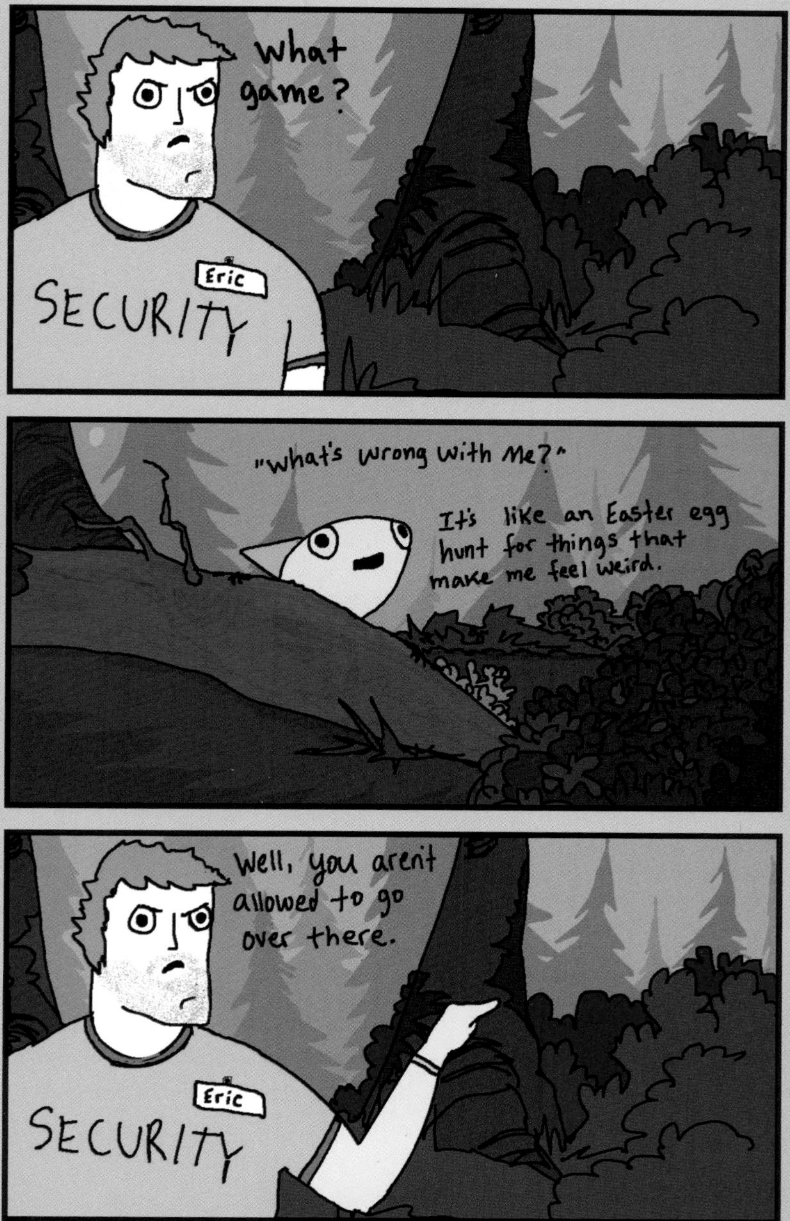
What game?
SECURITY
Eric
"What's wrong with me?"
It's like an Easter egg hunt for things that make me feel weird.
Well, you aren't allowed to go over there.
SECURITY
Eric

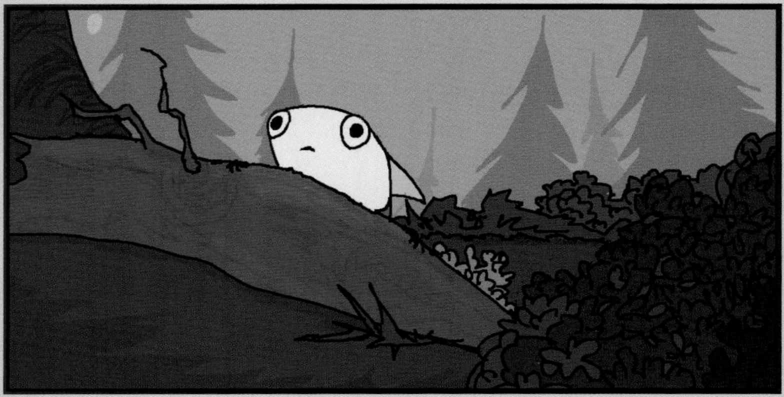

My attempts at self-preservation backfired and turned into clues I could use to guide myself further toward the truth.

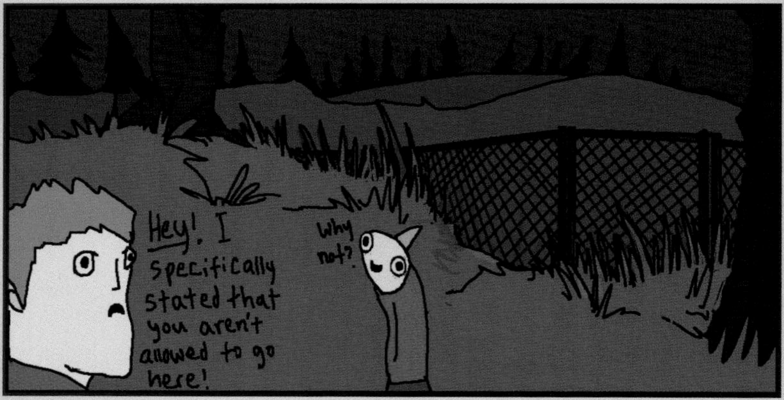
Hey!. I specifically stated that you aren't allowed to go here!
Why not?

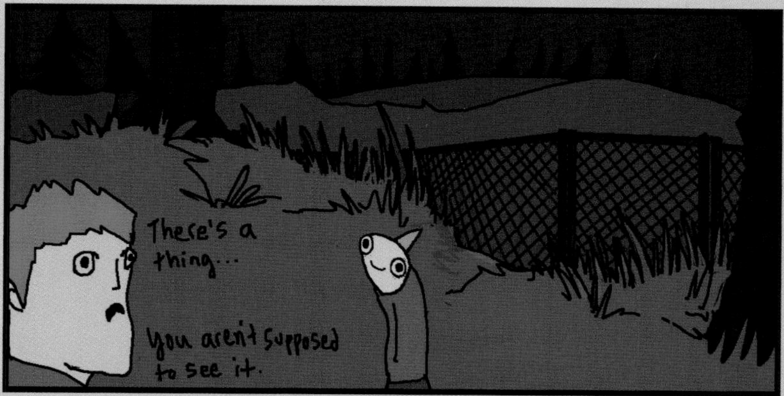
There's a thing...
You aren't supposed to see it.

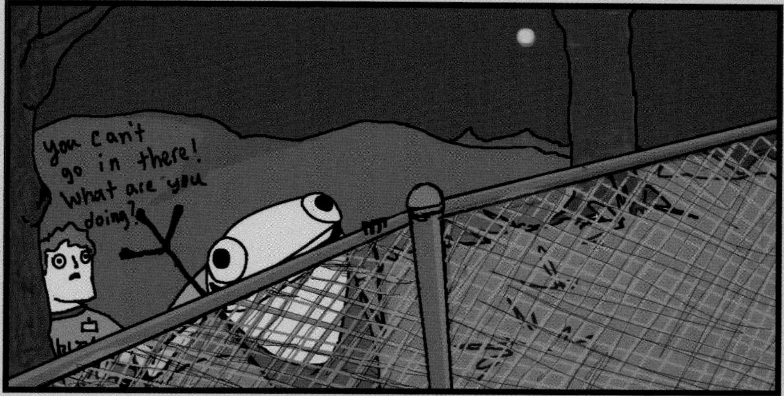
you can't go in there! what are you doing?

I was getting dangerously close to uncovering the inner workings of my self-worth generator, and that is not something I wanted myself to know about—like most illusions, if you figure out how it works, you won't be able to believe it anymore. But fucking Sherlock Holmes Psychology Explorer refused to give up.

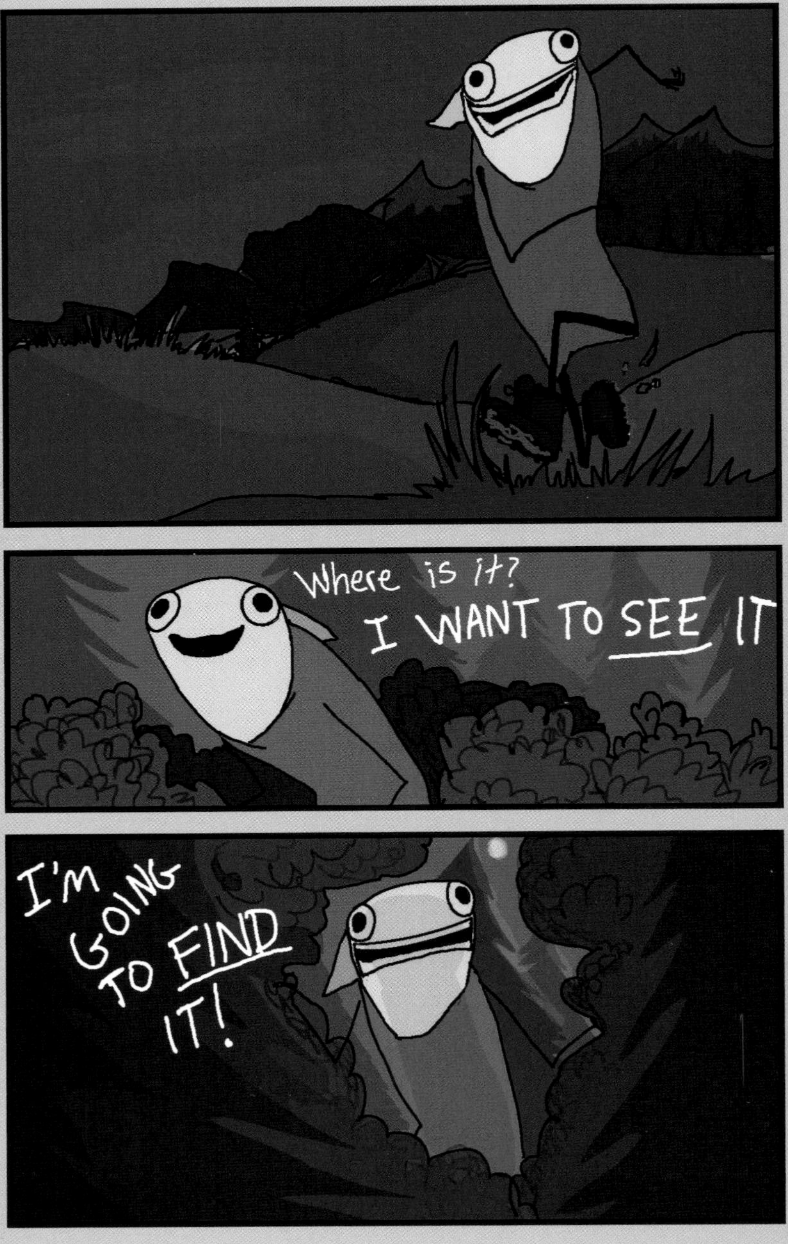
Where is it?
I WANT TO SEE IT
I'M GOING TO FIND IT!

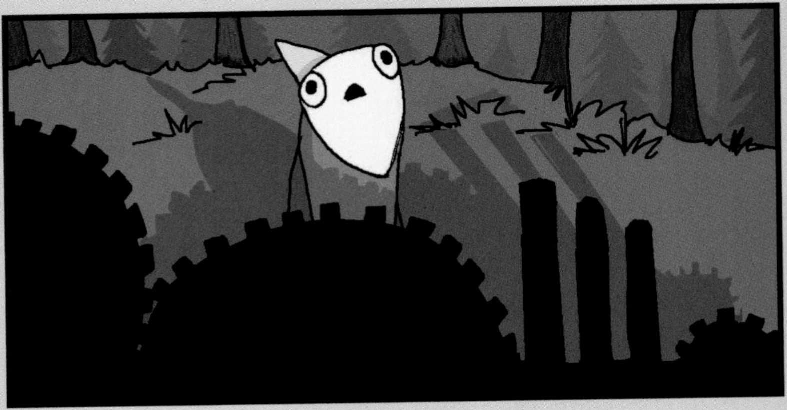

I was so upset when I figured it out.

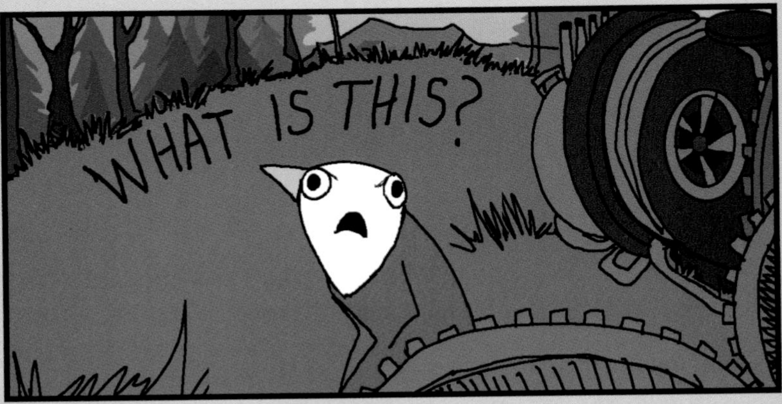
WHAT IS THIS?

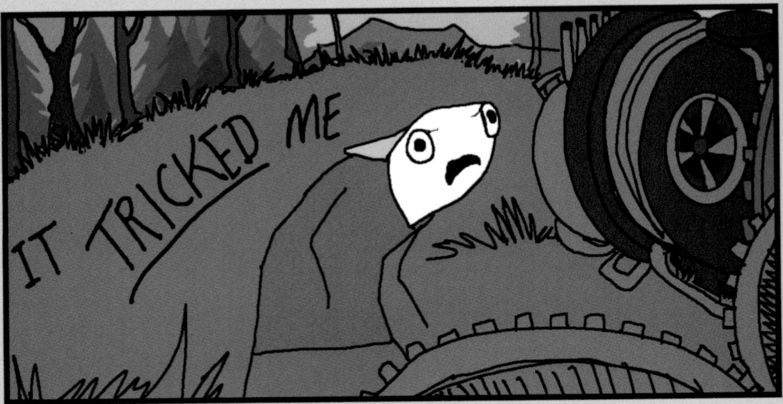
IT TRICKED ME

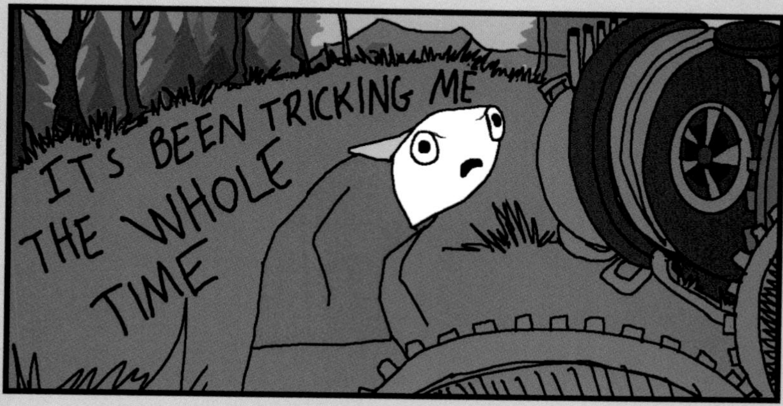
IT'S BEEN TRICKING ME
THE WHOLE
TIME

Nobody likes being tricked, especially not for so long and about all the things that are important to them.

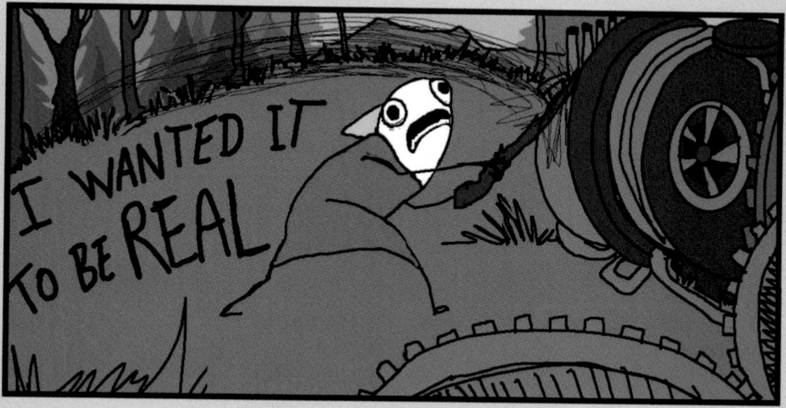
I WANTED IT
TO BE REAL

I didn't want the source of my problems to turn out to be "You're just sort of naturally shittier than what you wanted, and you had to trick yourself so you wouldn't find out and be disappointed."

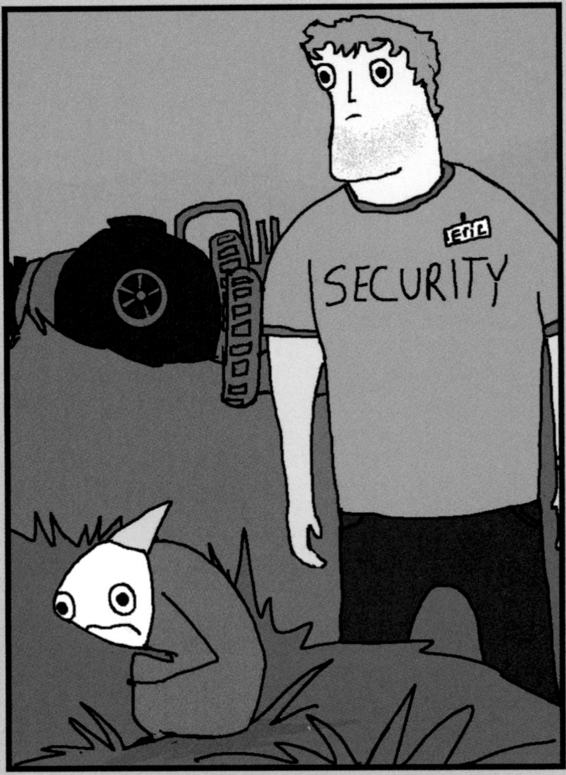
SECURITY

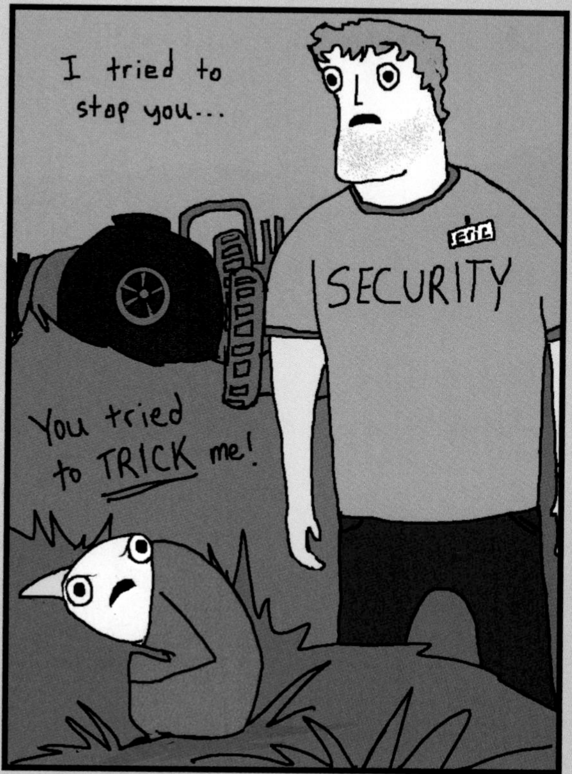
I tried to stop you...
SECURITY
You tried to TRICK me!

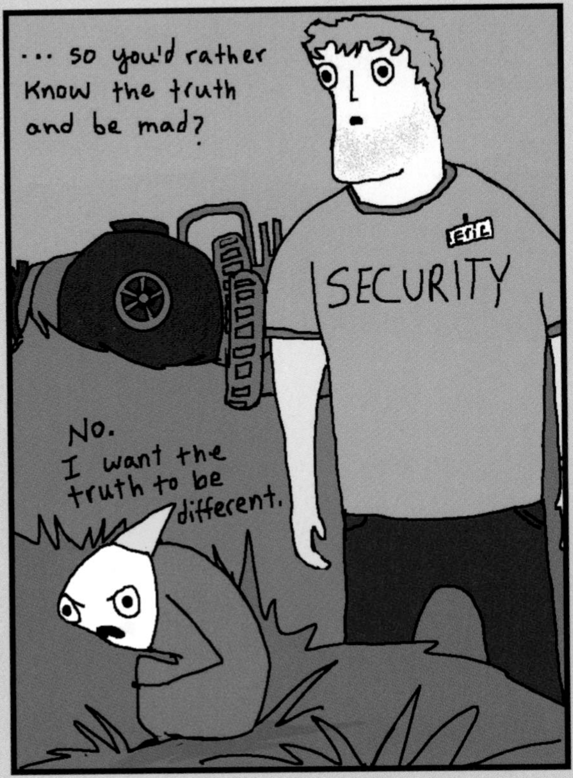
... so you'd rather know the truth and be mad?
SECURITY
No. I want the truth to be different.

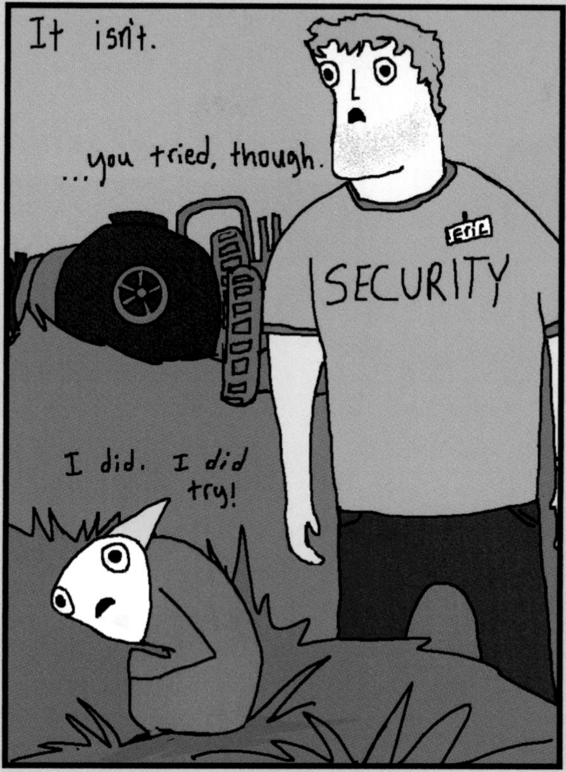
It isn't.
...you tried, though.
SECURITY
I did. I did try!

And I really, really did. And I suppose that's something. I might not be able to be someone who never ever gets the urge to push people or throw sand at them, but I try to be that person. In the not-throwing-sand-and-not-shoving-people competition, I get the participant ribbon. And even though I know there aren't any special requirements for earning the participant ribbon aside from the participation itself, I still feel sort of proud of it, because IT'S HARD not pushing people and not throwing sand at them.

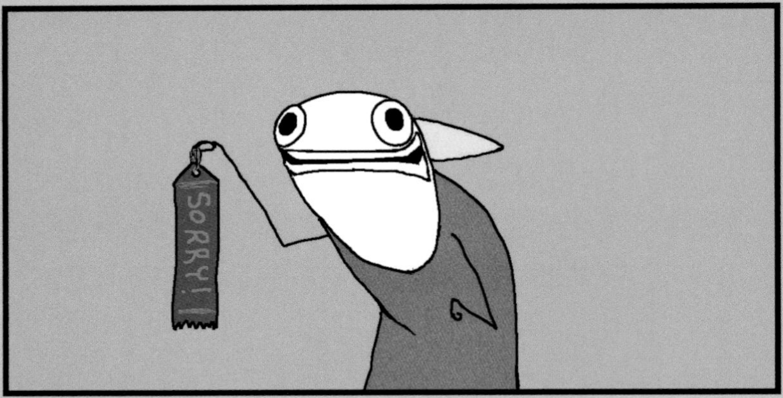
SORRY!

I still try to trick myself, though.
I know I'm being tricked, but I let it happen because it feels nice.

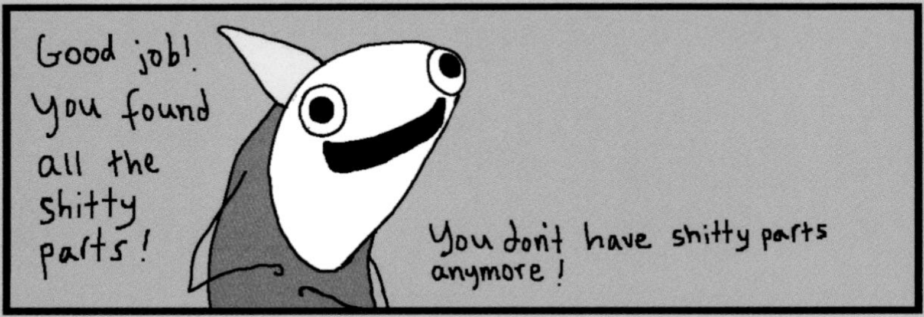
Good job! You found all the shitty parts!
You don't have shitty parts anymore!

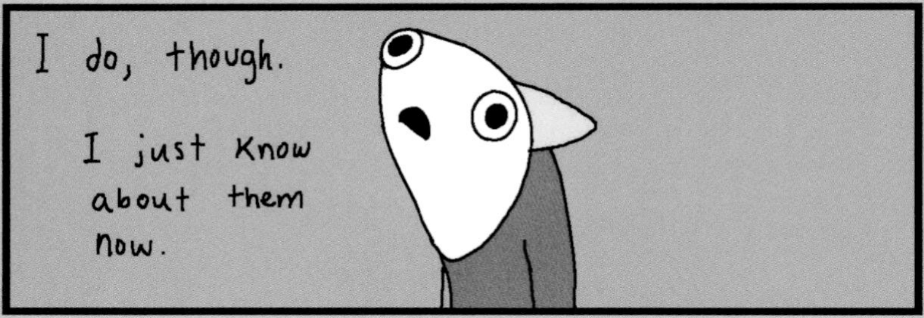
I do, though.
I just know about them now.

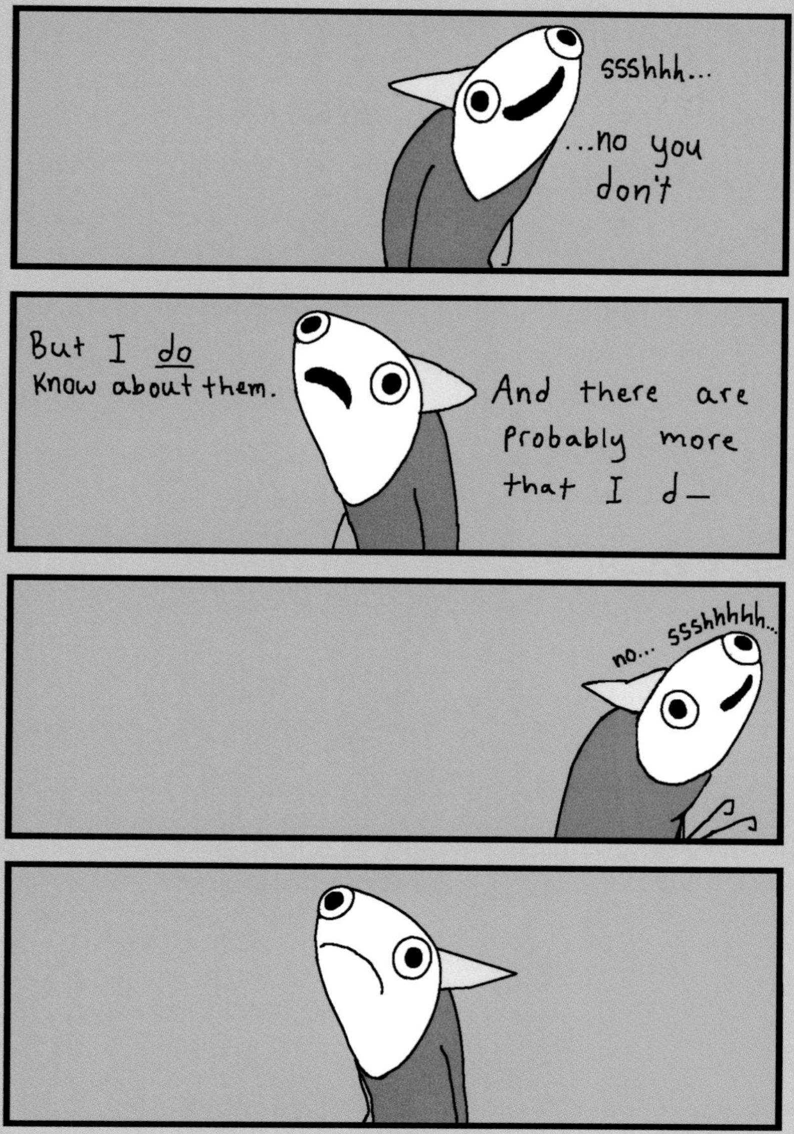

ssshhh...
...no you don't
But I do know about them.
And there are probably more that I d—
no... ssshhhhh...

Ssssshhhh...

sssshhhh....

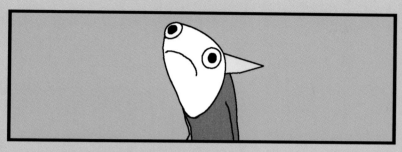

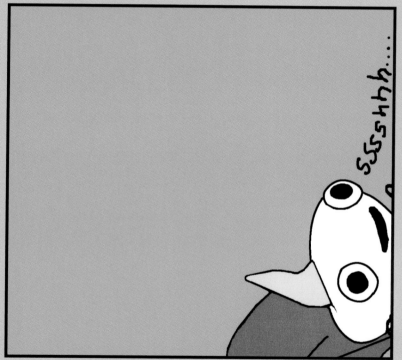

Acknowledgments

I spent eight days completely paralyzed by how many people I wanted to thank before deciding to just thank everyone because I didn't want to leave anyone out.

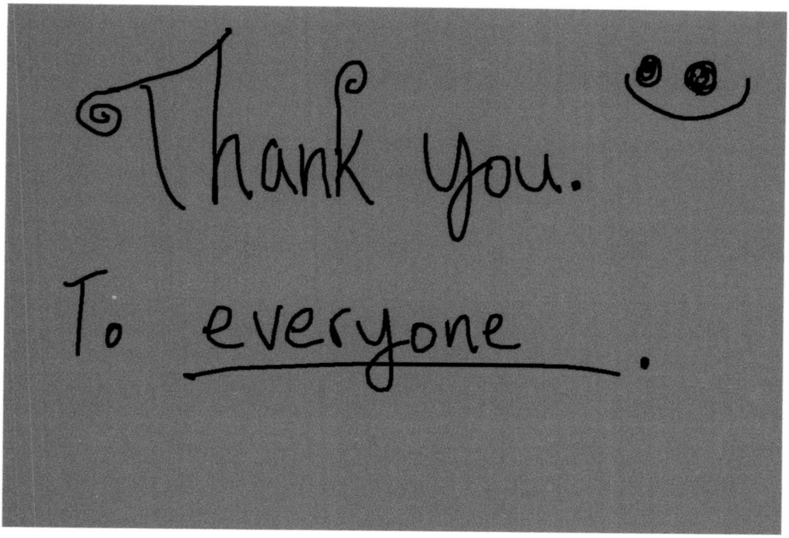
Thank you.
To everyone.

You guys know who you are and why I'm grateful for you. You know exactly why.

I hope you all enjoyed the fancy spiral things I put on the letters. It was the best way I could think of to show you how very, very serious I am about my gratitude.